Assessing Mul
Children

COMMUNICATION DISORDERS ACROSS LANGUAGES

Series Editors: Dr Nicole Müller and Dr Martin Ball, *Linköping University, Sweden*

While the majority of work in communication disorders has focused on English, there has been a growing trend in recent years for the publication of information on languages other than English. However, much of this is scattered through a large number of journals in the field of speech pathology/ communication disorders, and therefore, not always readily available to the practitioner, researcher and student. It is the aim of this series to bring together into book form surveys of existing studies on specific languages, together with new materials for the language(s) in question. We also have launched a series of companion volumes dedicated to issues related to the cross-linguistic study of communication disorders. The series does not include English (as so much work is readily available), but covers a wide number of other languages (usually separately, though sometimes two or more similar languages may be grouped together where warranted by the amount of published work currently available). We have been able to publish volumes on Finnish, Spanish, Chinese and Turkish, and books on multilingual aspects of stuttering, aphasia, and speech disorders, with several others in preparation.

Full details of all the books in this series and of all our other publications can be found on http://www.multilingual-matters.com, or by writing to Multilingual Matters, St Nicholas House, 31-34 High Street, Bristol BS1 2AW, UK.

COMMUNICATION DISORDERS ACROSS LANGUAGES: 13

Assessing Multilingual Children

Disentangling Bilingualism from Language Impairment

Edited by
Sharon Armon-Lotem, Jan de Jong and Natalia Meir

MULTILINGUAL MATTERS
Bristol • Buffalo • Toronto

Library of Congress Cataloging in Publication Data
A catalog record for this book is available from the Library of Congress.
Assessing Multilingual Children: Disentangling Bilingualism from Language
Impairment/Edited by Sharon Armon-Lotem, Jan de Jong and Natalia Meir.
Communication Disorders Across Languages
Includes bibliographical references and index.
I. Armon-Lotem, Sharon, editor. II. Jong, Jan de (Assistant professor of language and
communication), editor. III. Meir, Natalia, editor. IV. Series: Communication disorders
across languages.
[DNLM: 1. Language Development Disorders--diagnosis. 2. Child. 3. Language
Development. 4. Multilingualism. WL 340.2]
RJ496.L35
618.92'855–dc23 2014044710

British Library Cataloguing in Publication Data
A catalogue entry for this book is available from the British Library.

ISBN-13: 978-1-78309-312-0 (hbk)
ISBN-13: 978-1-78309-311-3 (pbk)

Multilingual Matters
UK: S: Nicholas House, 31-34 High Street, Bristol BS1 2AW, UK.
USA: UTP, 2250 Military Road, Tonawanda, NY 14150, USA.
Canada: UTP, 5201 Dufferin Street, North York, Ontario M3H 5T8, Canada.

Website: www.multilingual-matters.com
Twitter: Multi_Ling_Mat
Facebook: https://www.facebook.com/multilingualmatters
Blog: www.channelviewpublications.wordpress.com

The policy of Multilingual Matters/Channel View Publications is to use papers that
are natural, renewable and recyclable products, made from wood grown in sustainable
forests. In the manufacturing process of our books, and to further support our policy,
preference is given to printers that have FSC and PEFC Chain of Custody certification.
The FSC and/or PEFC logos will appear on those books where full certification has been
granted to the printer concerned.

Typeset by Deanta Global Publishing Services Limited.
Printed and bound in Great Britain by the CPI Group (UK Ltd), Croydon, CR0 4YY.

Contents

Contributors

Sharon Armon-Lotem, associate professor, Department of English Literature and Linguistics and The Gonda Multidisciplinary Brain Research Center, Bar-Ilan University, Israel. Her research interests are in language acquisition by monolingual and bilingual children with and without specific language impairment (SLI). She is particularly interested in linguistic features which can disentangle bilingualism and SLI, with a focus on syntax and its interfaces with morphology and semantics, and in the impact of internal and external variables on success in child second language acquisition.

Anne E. Baker, emeritus professor, Linguistics Department of Language and Literature, University of Amsterdam, Amsterdam, The Netherlands. She is particularly interested in the relationship between language and cognition, specifically in language development, multilingualism and disorders. Most of her recent work considers children who are multilingual with one of their languages being Dutch.

Ingrida Balčiūnienė is a lecturer in Lithuanian philolology at the Department of Lithuanian Language at Vytautas Magnus University, Kaunas, Lithuania. Her research interests are in the area of first language acquisition, with a special interest in conversation and discourse analysis.

Ute Bohnacker, professor of linguistics, Department of Linguistics and Philology, Uppsala University, Uppsala, Sweden. Her research expertise is mainly in first and second language acquisition, bilingualism, grammar and discourse, with a special interest in the Germanic languages. She is particularly interested in children growing up in Sweden with one or several languages. Her recent work has expanded towards impaired populations and examines typical and atypical multilingual child language development in a European context.

Shula Chiat, professor of child language, Language & Communication Science, City University London, UK. Her interests lie in typical and atypical language development. Her research focuses on the psycholinguistic processes involved in language acquisition – how children process the input they receive to establish the connections between forms and meanings in their language – and how these processes are affected in children with disorders of language and social communication.

Jan de Jong, assistant professor, University of Amsterdam, Amsterdam Center for Language and Communication, Amsterdam, The Netherlands. His primary interest is in the grammatical profile of children with specific language impairment (SLI), also in a bilingual context. He was the vice-chair of COST Action IS0804.

Elin Thordardottir, professor, ReykjavíkurAkademían, Reykjavik, Iceland, and professor, School of Communication Sciences and Disorders, McGill University, Montreal, Canada. Her research focuses on the typical language development and language disorders of monolingual and bilingual children, in particular those speaking Icelandic, Quebec French and English. A main interest of her work is how cross-linguistic results help clarify the nature of language impairment. She has developed language assessment tools for various language groups and conducted research on intervention efficacy with bilingual children.

Natalia Gagarina coordinates research on multilingual language acquisition at the Center for General Linguistics (ZAS) and directs the Berliner Association for Multilingualism. Her research concentrates on monolingual and bilingual (a)typical language acquisition in the following domains: lexicon, morphosyntax and discourse/narratives. Her research on Russian and German has resulted in the development and implementation of assessment tools and language support programs for bilingual children.

Daniela Gatt, lecturer, Department of Communication Therapy, Faculty of Health Sciences, University of Malta, Malta. Daniela Gatt is a speech-language pathologist who lectures on childhood communication disorders. Her current research interests are related to lexical development, early identification of language delay and impaired language development, particularly in bilingual contexts.

Ewa Haman, assistant professor, Psycholinguistics Unit, Faculty of Psychology, University of Warsaw, Poland. Ewa Haman is a developmental psycholinguist conducting research on lexical development in both monolingual and bilingual populations. Her main interests are related to accurate assessment of word knowledge in preschool children. She has designed several psychometric tools for Polish children and is the lead designer of Cross-Linguistic Lexical Tasks (CLTs) for bilingual and multilingual children.

Kristine Jensen de López, professor, Developmental Psychology, Clinic for Developmental Communication Disorders, Center for Developmental & Applied Psychological Science, Institute of Communication and Psychology, Aalborg University, Aalborg, Denmark. Her research interests are in the area of child language and language disorders. She is particularly interested in the interface of language, cognition and culture in lifelong development and in intervention.

Daleen Klop, senior lecturer, Division Speech-Language and Hearing Therapy, Department of Interdisciplinary Health Sciences, Stellenbosch University, Tygerberg, South Africa. Daleen Klop's research interests are in the area of early language and literacy development and disorders. Her special interest is the development of intervention programmes for children from disadvantaged communities who are at risk for scholastic failure.

Sari Kunnari, professor, Logopedics, Faculty of Humanities, Child Language Research Center, University of Oulu, Finland. Her research interests are in the area of child language acquisition with the aim to verify language-specific aspects through cross-linguistic comparisons. Besides typical speech and language acquisition, she is also interested in speech and language disorders in children with specific language impairment (both monolingual and bilingual) and in children with hearing impairment.

Magdalena Łuniewska, PhD student, Faculty of Psychology, University of Warsaw, Poland. Her research interests concern child language development, especially how children acquire words. She is also interested in psychometric aspects of language assessment.

Theo Marinis, professor, Multilingualism & Language Development, Department of Clinical Language Sciences, University of Reading, UK. His research focuses on language acquisition and processing across populations of typically and atypically developing children and adults. It aims to uncover how language processing develops over time in typical and atypical populations.

Natalia Meir, PhD student, Department of English Literature and Linguistics, Bar-Ilan University, Israel. Natalia Meir has an MA (*summa cum laude*) from Bar-Ilan University (Israel). Her thesis was on 'Discourse markers in narrative of bilingual Russian–Hebrew speaking pre-school children'. Currently, she is working on her PhD dissertation, which examines phonological processing and grammatical representations in monolingual and bilingual children with and without SLI speaking Russian and Hebrew. She was the Action Secretary of COST Action IS0804.

Ciara O'Toole, lecturer, Speech and Language Therapy, Department of Speech and Hearing Sciences, University College Cork, Ireland. Her research interests are in the area of paediatric speech and language delays and disorders. She currently has particular interest in children acquiring language in a bilingual context and has developed assessment tools to profile this development, helping to identify those at risk for language impairment.

Barbara Pomiechowska, PhD student, Centre for Brain and Cognitive Development, Department of Psychological Sciences, Birkbeck College, University of London, London, UK. She studies cognitive developmental neuroscience. She is particularly interested in linguistic, conceptual and communicative development of human infants. Her current research focuses on how label and concept knowledge influences object representations.

Philippe Prévost, professor of linguistics at François Rabelais University in Tours, France. His current research focuses on comparison of the acquisition of French morphosyntax in different contexts, such as autism, bilingualism, child second language acquisition and specific language impairment.

Esther Ruigendijk, professor of Dutch linguistics, Department of Dutch, The University of Oldenburg, Germany. Her research interests are in the area of psycholinguistics, specifically language disorders, first and second language acquisition and processing, with a special interest in syntax and the syntactic–discourse interface.

Petra Schulz, professor, German as a Second Language, Department of Psycholinguistics und Didactics of German, Goethe-University Frankfurt, Frankfurt/Main, Germany. Her research areas are first and second language acquisition and specific language impairment with a focus on the acquisition of semantics and syntax. Using experimental approaches to language acquisition, she addresses the question of the universality and robustness of developmental paths in different languages. She is also interested in applying research findings to language assessment and intervention.

Koula Tantele, clinical speech and language pathologist, employed by the Ministry of Education and Culture in public schools. Her special interest is narrative development in Greek-Cypriot children as well as narrative markers in specific language impairment in the same population.

Laurice Tuller, professor of linguistics, François-Rabelais University, Tours, France. Her current research focuses on comparison of different contexts of atypical acquisition of French: autism, child L2, hearing loss and SLI. She teaches linguistics, psycholinguistics and language pathology in the linguistics, cognitive science and speech-language pathology programmes at François Rabelais University.

Taina Välimaa, academy research fellow/adjunct professor, Logopedics, Faculty of Humanities, Child Language Research Center, University of Oulu, Finland. Her research interests are in the area of speech perception and speech and language development and its disorders in children with hearing impairment. She is also interested in bilingual speech and language acquisition and language impairments.

Joel Walters, professor, Bar-Ilan University, Israel. Joel Walters works on the interface of psycholinguistic and sociolinguistic aspects of bilingualism in early childhood and in mature adults with and without language impairments. His book *Bilingualism: The Sociopragmatic-Psycholinguistic Interface* was published by Erlbaum/Routledge in 2005. Other papers have appeared in *Language Learning, Bilingualism: Language and Cognition* and the *Journal of Multilingual and Multicultural Development*. His research has been funded by the Israel Science Foundation, GIF and BMBF. He is currently dean of the Faculty of Humanities at Bar-Ilan University.

Introduction

Sharon Armon-Lotem and Jan de Jong

The demographic changes in the Western world in the last three decades have led to a rapid growth in the number of bilingual children, and in many locations they represent a majority of the school population. The numbers of children who come to school with more than one language has increased over threefold since the year 2000 in Ireland, Italy and Spain and by 50% since 1997 in the UK, where one in six children does not speak English at home. In Europe, this situation is far from unique. With this increase in the number of bilingual children, researchers as well as educators and practitioners face a diagnostic dilemma. This dilemma arises from research that points at similarities in the linguistic manifestations of child second language (L2) acquisition and of specific language impairment (SLI). L2 learners often produce language forms resembling those of children with SLI. At present, medical, language and educational professionals have only limited diagnostic instruments to distinguish language-impaired migrant children from those who will eventually catch up with their monolingual peers. In the Netherlands, for example, bilinguals constitute 14% of the mainstream school population, but 24% of those in special schools for children with SLI (de Jong *et al.*, 2010). If there were no misdiagnoses, the percentage of bilingual children should be identical in mainstream and special schools, by definition.

The diagnostic dilemma has motivated a new field of research, the study of bilingual children with SLI, which aims at disentangling effects of bilingualism from those of SLI, making use of both models of bilingualism and models of language impairment. Bilingual children in Europe acquire a wide range of languages and language combinations. Only a minority of European languages have been studied in detail in terms of how language impairment manifests itself in children and which phenomena are clinical markers for SLI. There is even less research on how language impairment manifests itself in bilingual children, and on whether the severity of SLI is affected by the acquisition of more than one language. Finally, even tools for assessing the language development in monolingual children are available only for a small number of languages; existing tools are not comparable across languages, and they have not been normed for bilingual children, who generally do not conform to monolingual norms. This is problematic for differential diagnosis; it is very difficult to ascertain whether a bilingual

1

child, whose language development is delayed compared to monolingual children, has language impairment or whether the delay results from limited exposure.

The overlap among the features of bilingual and impaired language which leads to methodological and clinical confounds, led to the funding of the European Cooperation in Science and Technology (COST) Action IS0804 'Language Impairment in a Multilingual Society: Linguistic Patterns and the Road to Assessment' which aimed to resolve these confounds in order to improve assessment of language in minority children. The main objective of the COST Action was to profile bilingual SLI (henceforth Bi-SLI) by establishing a network to coordinate research on the linguistic and cognitive abilities of bilingual children with SLI across different migrant communities. The Action was motivated theoretically, (1) by how typological differences between the two languages of bilingual children with SLI impact on the manifestation of SLI in each language; and (2) by how bilingualism and language impairment, respectively, affect the performance of bilingual children with SLI; and practically, by challenges that multilingualism poses for the diagnosis and treatment of language-impaired bilingual children.

The purpose of the present book is to present Language Impairment Testing in Multilingual Settings (LITMUS)[1], a comprehensive set of tools designed and tested within the COST Action for assessing the linguistic abilities of bilingual children. These tools have all been piloted with monolingual children and with children who are speakers of a wide variety of language pairs and subsequently modified. In line with the motivation of the Action, the present book has three unifying themes:

(1) The linguistic aspects that are relevant for assessment of language impairment in a bilingual population – from syntax and its interfaces, to narratives as well as linguistic and non-linguistic processing.
(2) The practical concerns which arise when developing assessments for children with typologically different languages.
(3) The practical concerns which arise when developing assessments for bilingual children.

Following a short introduction about the COST Action, the targeted population and previous studies, the chapters of the book are organised by task and domain. Importantly, the tools are presented in this book in a way which makes it possible to extend them to other linguistic communities in which they can be adopted for disentangling bilingualism from SLI.

COST Action IS0804 – 'Language Impairment in a Multilingual Society: Linguistic Patterns and the Road to Assessment'

COST Action IS0804 'Language Impairment in a Multilingual Society: Linguistic Patterns and the Road to Assessment' started its networking under the auspices of COST in July 2009, bringing together in one research network researchers from most European countries as well as leading figures from the USA and Canada. The Action addressed the relatively new and less-researched problem of identifying bilingual children with SLI, a vulnerable group, which was an understudied population in Europe. The Action took a bilingual approach which drew from previous work on bilingualism and SLI. This new approach promoted:

(a) testing in both languages in tandem with tools that are sensitive to the nature of bilingual acquisition;
(b) testing which addresses several levels of linguistic and non-linguistic representation, also tapping into processing and memory skills which go beyond language use;
(c) testing which takes into consideration sociolinguistic factors beyond language and parental background, e.g. social identity, attitudes, preferences.

The main objective of this Action was to profile SLI by studying the linguistic and cognitive abilities of bilingual children with SLI across different migrant communities. This should make it possible to:

- disentangle bilingualism and SLI by establishing the relative contribution of each;
- show how Bi-SLI can be identified in both of a child's languages;
- explore the extent to which the manifestations of SLI are similar or different across languages in the same child;
- establish whether the nature and severity of SLI are affected by the acquisition of more than one language;
- establish whether linguistic shortcomings coincide with non-linguistic cognitive skills.

The joint focus on linguistic and cognitive abilities intends to overcome some of the difficulties caused by the similarities in the linguistic behaviour of monolingual SLI and typically developing bilingual (Bi-TD) children, as well as to address the extent to which language impairment can be described in terms of underlying processing phenomena rather than linguistic representations.

The Action focused on preschool children and children in their early school years because it is important to identify Bi-SLI before academic (literacy) requirements put an additional strain on them. Early identification in preschool years improves later intervention. Knowledge of the L2, which is necessary for bilingual testing, is often achieved only after two years of exposure. Since obligatory schooling starts in kindergarten at best and minority children are often raised in monolingual homes until they go to school, it was necessary to extend the scope of the Action to the early school years.

The second primary objective of the Action was to reconcile the methodologies of studies of language-impaired and Bi-TD children in order to improve comparability and to provide innovative techniques for assessing language impairment. To this end, the Action:

•   studied a broad range of skills, targeting a range of linguistic skills, using offline and online tasks, and cognitive skills involving executive functions;
•   tapped domains which were known to be vulnerable in monolingual children with SLI and bilingual children (e.g. verbal morphology, lexical knowledge), as well as domains which were not expected to be influenced by the bilingual setting (e.g. phonological processing in non-word repetition, narrative abilities);
•   developed bilingually oriented criteria and procedures to investigate typologically similar (e.g. Arabic/Hebrew, Dutch/German) and typologically different language pairs (Dutch/Turkish, Russian/German, Russian/Greek);
•   included not only major European languages, but also languages of non-European minority groups residing in Europe, such as Turkish, Arabic and South Asian languages (Hindi, Urdu, Gujaratti, Sylleti).

Due to the major overlap between diagnostic concerns and scientific research in the field of Bi-SLI, the Action aimed at both scientific and societal advances. Scientific advances included:

•   Identifying unique patterns in Bi-SLI whether qualitatively or quantitatively – in both of a child's languages.
•   Differentiating typical bilingual development from impaired development.
•   Evaluating whether symptoms of SLI are aggravated by the acquisition of more than one language.

The societal advances of the Action's work include the improvement of diagnosis and treatment of language impairments following progress in Bi-SLI studies. The present book is a first step to achieve these aims because it provides guidelines for developing instruments and test items to distinguish typically developing (TD) from SLI bilinguals.

Definitions

Definitional and methodological controversies in research on both bilingualism and SLI are major obstacles to addressing the questions outlined above and to ensuring comparability of international research (see Chapter 12 for a longer discussion).

For bilingualism, a functional definition is adopted, where bilingualism is defined as using two (or more) languages on a regular basis, and bilingual children are those who use two (or more) languages in their everyday life. Selection of homogeneous groups of *bilingual children* is complicated by a variety of background factors which influence acquisition of both the first language (L1) and L2. These include differences in socio-economic status (SES; e.g. immigrant, indigenous, privileged minorities); differences in age of first exposure to the L2 (early/late age of onset of acquisition of L2); birth order; family size; acquisition order (simultaneous/sequential); degree of exposure; acquisition contexts, e.g. one parent for each language at home vs L2 at kindergarten or school (Meisel, 2007); and prestige of languages. Of particular interest here is age of L2 onset as it distinguishes between simultaneous bilinguals who acquire both languages within their first year of life, early sequential bilinguals who acquire their L2 after their first year of life but before the age of 3, and sequential bilinguals who acquire their L2 after the age of 3 as they enter the schooling system. This latter group constitutes our main target group.

SLI is a primary deficit in linguistic abilities and language development (Bishop *et al.*, 2000). In England, the Bercow review (2008) reports that approximately 7% of 5-year-olds starting school in 2007 had significant difficulties with speech and/or language, and this situation is not unlike the situation elsewhere in Europe. SLI has been defined by exclusionary criteria as a language impairment which is unrelated to hearing loss, emotional and behavioural problems, intelligence and clear neurological problems (Bishop, 2006; Tallal & Stark, 1981). Inclusionary criteria make the SLI population very heterogeneous, with differing criteria and a controversy about which linguistic aspects are affected and to what extent (Bishop *et al.*, 2000; van der Lely, 1998). SLI is manifested at different linguistic levels (Leonard, 1998), but not all linguistic skills are equally impaired. A deficit in morphosyntax is often viewed as the key symptom (Crago & Gopnik, 1994; Rice & Wexler, 1996), but due to the heterogeneity of this population, children might show a more severe impairment at a different linguistic level. In addition to purely linguistic skills, auditory memory, working memory and executive function skills are also reported to be impaired among children with SLI

(Bishop & Norbury, 2005; Kohnert & Windsor, 2004). Controversies about what is affected by SLI notwithstanding, the chapters of this book together constitute our ideas of what is most important for the diagnosis of SLI in bilingual children. The different domains of language that may be affected by SLI, as well as co-occurring shortcomings in executive functioning, are thus reflected in the assessment tools outlined in this book.

For children with SLI and Bi-TD children, representation of linguistic knowledge may be incomplete or different. Processing of linguistic stimuli may also differ under the influence of duration, rate and salience, showing up as difficulties in memory, temporal integration or word-finding/lexical retrieval. Developing bilinguals, when compared to monolinguals, may also show evidence of different linguistic representations and/or difficulties in fluency related to their lexical knowledge or reduced exposure to each language. However, while bilingual children might resemble children with SLI in their linguistic behaviour, they may show advantages in the very executive function domains which are impaired in children with SLI, making this a potential domain in which the two populations can be distinguished. Of course, the situation is more complicated in children who are bilingual and language impaired (see Chapter 10).

Bilingual children with typical language development (TLD) and monolingual children with SLI, who may share surface characteristics in language, can also be distinguished using real-time research procedures. In such online processing tasks, bilingual children with TLD (even when they make production errors) are hypothesised to perform well (that is, like monolingual children with TLD), but children with SLI are hypothesised to perform poorly. While such research paradigms have been explored in more depth recently (cf. Chondrogianni & Marinis, 2012), also within the framework of the COST Action, they do not yet make diagnostic procedures available for clinical use.

In light of the confounds associated with language impairment and bilingualism, Bedore and Peña (2008), who offer a summary of the current situation in the USA, point to the necessity of further research for indicators of SLI in bilinguals. The present volume aims to offer some tested tools for doing exactly this.

Scientific Focus of This Book

Recent interest in children with Bi-SLI has often taken a bilingual approach examining both languages, while expanding the number of language pairs and linguistic domains addressed. Focus is not only on the syntax–morphology interface and on the morphosyntactic indicators within the verbal system (Jacobson & Schwartz, 2002; Paradis, 2010), but also on nominal morphology: gender agreement (Blom et al., 2008) and case marking (Rothweiler et al., 2010). The traditional focus on verbal morphology has led to the under-representation of languages in which noun morphology is more vulnerable.

Profiling the language abilities of bilingual children over time and how SLI manifests itself requires equivalent tasks and stimuli to be used in the child's two languages, and these need to address the specific linguistic and processing domains that are known to cause problems in monolingual children with SLI. To date, a very limited number of studies have investigated bilingual children with SLI where both languages are tested, and these have included only some of the vulnerable domains of children with SLI. This book takes the existing studies as a starting point and, in order to address the research questions above, investigates a larger set of SLI indicators than has been identified thus far. This may also be necessary because SLI studies thus far have not addressed the full typological range. In this book, we will define more precisely the bilingual contexts that can occur, and will present the designs to be used in cross-linguistic studies that address pairs of languages which are typologically similar (e.g. speakers of English in Germany, or speakers of Arabic in Israel), as well as pairs of languages which are typologically different (as is the case for speakers of Polish or Urdu in England, speakers of Turkish or Arabic in the Netherlands or speakers of Russian in Germany and Israel, for example). Importantly, the present book will not only target phenomena which are language dependent (syntax and interfaces with phonology, morphology, lexicon and semantics, narrative and discourse abilities), but it will also measure phenomena which are less language dependent (e.g. working memory and executive function skills).

The assessment tasks in this book are divided into four domains:

(1) Syntax and interfaces with morphology and semantics.
(2) Lexical and phonological processing.
(3) Narrative and discourse abilities.
(4) Executive functions.

The book further explores the use of parental questionnaires as an innovative means. They can isolate language delays/differences which are not necessarily due to Bi-SLI, but are related to background internal and external variables (e.g. age, length and amount of exposure, languages spoken at home, birth order, parental education and occupation) from those which are possible indicators of innate impairment (e.g. late onset of first words and word combination, family history of learning difficulty). Parental questionnaires, such as the Alberta Language and Development Questionnaire (ALDeQ; Paradis et al., 2010) were found to differentiate English learners who are TD from those with SLI. There were significant differences between children with bilingual typical language development (Bi-TLD) and Bi-SLI on early developmental milestones, which thus emerged as the strongest discriminator. The combination of information about different linguistic domains with background information is necessary to isolate language delays/differences which are not necessarily due to Bi-SLI and can make findings more useful for policymaking.

Many European and non-European languages were represented in COST Action IS0804, with researchers from 30 European countries. Consequently, this book offers a large typological diversity. Though it is impossible to provide exhaustive information on the structure of each of the different languages, the tasks presented in the book call for typological information on morphological and syntactic structures that is relevant to the assessments discussed. In several chapters, glossed examples of language-specific structures will be used to illustrate cross-linguistic differences and to show how tasks sometimes need to be adapted to account for them. This makes the book more useful to students and instructors of bilingualism and bilingual language impairment. Consequently, Chapters 1–5 all start with a brief overview of the target structures in which the cross-linguistic variation is shown. This is further supported by examples of the ways in which the different tasks are adapted for use in the different languages.

Syntax and Its Interfaces

Syntax and morphology are among the most established linguistic indicators of SLI, and are already a central focus of ongoing research on Bi-SLI (Armon-Lotem *et al.*, 2008; Chilla & Babur, 2008; de Jong *et al.*, 2007; Jacobson & Schwartz, 2002; Marinis, 2007; Papadopoulou *et al.*, 2009; Rothweiler *et al.*, 2007; among others). Studies on Bi-SLI often show that SLI in sequential bilinguals conforms to SLI characteristics of monolinguals. Processing studies in which reaction time to erroneous structures was measured have shown sensitivity to morphosyntactic errors among Bi-TD children but not among children with SLI (Chondrogianni & Marinis, 2012; Marinis & Saddy, 2013). Studies of Bi-SLI further examine question formation, passives, relatives and conditionals, as these structures challenge aspects of language which are difficult for children with SLI but are not more immune to bilingual input effects (Chiat *et al.*, 2013; Meir *et al.*, submitted; see Chapter 5 in this volume). Schulz and Roeper (2011) also suggest that exhaustivity, the ability to give multiple answers to complex questions, e.g. Who ate what?, may also lead to dissociation of bilingualism and SLI, as children with Bi-TLD demonstrate rapid progress in learning to respond accurately, while persistent deficits are reported for children with SLI.

This book presents the outcome of coordinated research on the development of syntax and its interface with morphology and semantics in bilingual children with SLI, aimed at identifying structures that are vulnerable for monolingual and bilingual children with SLI, but not for Bi-TD children. Sometimes, vulnerable structures are found not to be subject to cross-linguistic differences, while other times it is important to recognise the relevant cross-linguistic differences. Our underlying assumption was that structures that are more 'universal' could be indicative of SLI in bilingual children, while those, which may show evidence of cross-linguistic interference, are less likely so. The authors of the different chapters evaluated current research to select offline tasks which can reveal quantitative and qualitative differences between Bi-TD children and bilingual children with SLI.

For generating the LITMUS assessment battery, a set of morphosyntactic and syntactic phenomena in each language, which have been shown to be vulnerable in monolingual children with SLI, was targeted. In terms of morphosyntax, this included e.g. verbal inflections (third person -s in *He walks*), and auxiliaries (such as *is* in *He is walking*), plural marking on nouns and adjectives (such as the suffix *im* in *yeladim ktanim* 'little children' in Hebrew or *die kleinen Kinder* 'the little children' in German, determiners (such as *the* in *The boy walked*), prepositions (such as *at* in *He laughed at the girl* or *on* in *He turned on the light*), case marking (such as German *Sie schenkt dem Mann den Apfel*) and clitics (*la* in French as in *Le garcon la dessine* 'The boy is drawing her'). Omission and/or substitution of such morphemes is often taken to be an indicator of SLI, but in bilingual contexts such errors could reflect L2 characteristics and/or cross-linguistic influence. For example, Russian does not have definite articles, and Russian–Hebrew bilingual children often omit the definite article in Hebrew. The implication is that some grammatical morphemes, that are vulnerable in SLI as well as in typical bilingual development, are less suitable for assessment in bilinguals, or are crucially dependent on bilingual norms.

Morphosyntactic symptoms of SLI can occur in the verbal domain, the nominal domain or both. In a number of languages, one is affected, the other is not (or the phenomenon under observation is not a part of the language). For that reason, subject–verb agreement (the verbal domain) as well as case marking (the nominal domain) are included in the tasks presented below.

Chapter 1 (de Jong) presents a picture description task testing subject–verb agreement. *Subject–verb agreement* (e.g. third person –s in *He walks*) is affected by SLI in many languages, though certainly not all. In the languages affected, subject–verb agreement is seen as a prominent clinical marker of SLI. Errors may show as omissions or substitutions of inflectional morphemes. In English, omission is the dominant error type; in languages with a more elaborate verb paradigm, substitutions are also found. Explanations range from difficulties with specific cells of the agreement paradigm (Clahsen, 2008) to slow maturation of the ability to inflect verbs consistently (Rice *et al.*, 1995). In studies done on Dutch language production (e.g. Orgassa, 2009), shortcomings in verbal morphology were typical of both monolingual and bilingual children with SLI. This demonstrates that verbal morphology shows promise of being an index of SLI regardless of the child's status as a bilingual or monolingual speaker of the language.

Chapter 2 (Ruigendijk) looks into *case marking* with a picture description task with contrasting pictures. Case marking (e.g. *Sie schenkt **dem** Mann **den** Apfel*) is the morphological realisation of the syntactic relationship between a case assigner (i.e. the finite verb for subjects, the verb for objects and prepositional phrases) and specific semantic function. It is realised on the noun phrase, either on the determiner, the adjective and/or the noun itself. The production of case marking has been suggested to be vulnerable in SLI (Rice, 2000; Wexler *et al.*, 1998). Clahsen (1991), for instance, found an overuse of nominative for accusative and dative case contexts (and to a lesser extent also errors in the other direction). There is limited research on case marking in bilingual children with SLI, but first results on a study by Rothweiler *et al.* (2010) indicate that in Turkish–German Bi-SLI children, the realisation of accusative and dative case in their L1 Turkish is impaired as compared to TD children, in that the children often omit or substitute the case marking.

Chapter 3 (Prévost) presents an adaptation of an already available clitics test to the multilingual setting. Object clitics (e.g. *la* in French as in *Le garcon la dessine* 'The boy is drawing her') involve a certain degree of computational complexity as they usually appear in a (preverbal) position which is not the canonical object position of the languages in which they are found (see Jakubowicz & Nash, 2001; Zesiger *et al.*, 2010). Pronominal elements in general, and object clitics in particular, are used in order to refer to an element present in the discursive context. Monolingual children with SLI have been shown to have tremendous difficulties producing object clitics in obligatory contexts in various languages, specifically Romance ones, such as French (Chillier-Zesiger *et al.*, 2006; Hamann *et al.*, 2003; Jakubowicz *et al.*, 1998), Italian (Bortolini *et al.*, 2006; Bottari *et al.*, 2001) and Spanish (Bedore & Leonard, 2001; Bosch & Serra, 1997). Bilingual children have also been reported to struggle with object clitics, but these problems seem to be overcome faster than in monolinguals with SLI (Hamann & Belletti, 2006). Research on the production of object clitics by bilingual children with SLI is limited, but the few studies available so far point to vulnerability in this area as well (Jacobson & Schwartz, 2002; Paradis *et al.*, 2005/2006; Stavrakaki *et al.*, 2011).

Deficits at the *syntax–semantics interface* have been reported in monolingual children with SLI for verb meaning (e.g. Schulz *et al.*, 2001, 2006; Schulz & Kiese-Himmel, 2006; Schulz & Wittek, 2003), universal quantification (Penner, 1998) and the interpretation of *wh*-questions (de Villiers *et al.*, 2008). These phenomena have not yet been studied in bilingual children with SLI. Chapter 4 (Schulz) explores the interpretation of simple wh-questions such as Who is reading a book? and multiple wh-questions such as Who is eating what? or Who is giving what to whom?, as knowledge of exhaustivity is problematic in monolingual children with SLI (Roeper, 2004; German: Schulz & Penner, 2002; Schulz & Roeper, 2011). Recent results from SLI children acquiring German as their L2 (with different L1s) provide the first evidence that exhaustivity is problematic in Bi-SLI as well (Wojtecka & Schulz, 2011). The vulnerability of exhaustivity in SLI together with its cross-linguistically robust acquisition path makes this structure a very good candidate for disentangling typical from impaired bilingual acquisition.

In terms of syntactic structures, the book focuses on sentences with non-canonical word order, e.g. passives (The elephant was pushed by the giraffe), wh-questions (Who did the elephant push?) and relative clauses (The elephant who the giraffe pushed ran away), within a sentence repetition task as a measure of multiple structures. Chapter 5 (Marinis and Armon-Lotem) presents the principles of the sentence repetition task developed for over 20 language pairs. *Sentence repetition* tasks are increasingly recognised as a clinically sensitive tool for diagnosing language impairment in children. They are quick to administer, can be carefully targeted to elicit specific sentence structures and are particularly informative about children's lexical and morphosyntactic knowledge. A sentence repetition task including a wide range of phenomena has been developed for the action based on the School-Age Sentence Imitation test (SASIT) task (Marinis *et al.*, 2010) in order to investigate a range of phenomena within the same task.

Lexical and Phonological Processing

Apart from syntax and morphosyntax, phonological processing and auditory memory are often claimed to be impaired in children with SLI, but should be intact in Bi-TD children, offering a promising direction for disentangling the two. Previous research has revealed that monolingual and bilingual children with SLI perform poorly on non-word repetition tasks (Elin Thordardottir & Brandeker, 2013; Gathercole, 2006; Gathercole & Pickering, 2000; Girbau & Schwartz, 2007, 2008). These tasks require children to repeat non-existent words and tap primarily phonological memory, but can also address lexical processing when the words are designed to reflect syllable structure, stress patterns and phonotactic rules similar to words in the target language. Non-word repetition seems to discriminate well between bilinguals with and without SLI as it is less sensitive to the bilingual situation, when the range of consonants and vowels is familiar to the children. For example, Armon-Lotem and Chiat (2012) reported that Russian–Hebrew bilinguals show no significant differences from monolinguals in repeating non-words. Two follow-up studies show significant differences between children with Bi-TLD and children with Bi-SLI (Meir & Armon-Lotem, 2013). Finally, non-word repetition abilities have been claimed to depend on vocabulary development, and possibly correlate with the development of syntax.

Chapter 6 (Chiat) evaluates the potential of non-word repetition for identifying SLI in sequential bilingual (L2) children and distinguishing SLI from limited language due to limited language exposure. In order to identify the optimal test for detecting non-word repetition deficits and risk of SLI in L2 children, the proposed framework for non-word repetition includes a language-specific test and a relatively language-independent or 'quasi-universal' test, and specifies parameters to be systematically manipulated in each.

Achievements in lexical development are a potentially confounding factor for disentangling bilingualism and SLI. During early childhood (below age of 3 years), children with low vocabulary size (as measured e.g. by parental checklists like MacArthur–Bates Communicative Development Inventories [CDI]; Fenson et al., 2007) and children who are late talkers (who start to speak later than their peers) are potentially at risk to be diagnosed with SLI later in development (Zubrick et al., 2007). On the other hand, bilingual children can have a smaller vocabulary in one language when compared with their monolingual peers, which can be misinterpreted when the total vocabulary size (in both languages) is not taken into account as an early marker of SLI (Elin Thordardottir et al., 2006). However, some bilingual children below age 3 who are going to be diagnosed with SLI in the future can experience problems acquiring vocabulary and it is not yet established what level of vocabulary size in the early development of bilingual children can be treated as a threshold for being at risk for SLI. Thus, it is crucial to establish descriptive (not prescriptive) bilingual norms for assessment tools used for monolingual children or novel bilingual tools. In this way, a smaller vocabulary size in bilinguals will less often be misinterpreted as being below norm and at the same time the possibility of risk for SLI will not be rejected simply by the assumption that bilingual children are expected to have smaller vocabularies than their monolingual peers.

Chapter 7 (Gatt et al.) shows how using adaptations of CDIs for various languages in the language pairs of bilingual children can help in establishing such a threshold. CDIs are parental checklists most commonly used for the assessment of lexical development in monolingual populations. Using the CDI checklists for bilingual children enables an estimation of possible early gaps in vocabulary size between bilingual and monolingual populations. This can be done by comparing the results of bilingual children with monolingual norms (when available) or with a monolingual control group. Expecting that there will be approximately 7% of children with SLI (Tomblin et al., 1996) among bilinguals (as in monolingual populations), we can approximate the actual threshold of risk for SLI in bilinguals even if these children show generally lower vocabulary size than monolinguals. The chapter presents recommendations based on a study based on CDIs for

14 languages in which the vocabulary size of bilingual children aged 24–35 months is explored. The languages involved in the study are Polish, English, Maltese, Irish, Portuguese, French, German, Cypriot Greek, Turkish, Slovak, Italian, Greek, Hebrew and Russian. Cross-linguistic comparisons will enable conclusions about the generality of particular statistical effects of lower vocabulary in bilinguals.

Lexical deficits are among the earliest indicators of SLI (Leonard, 1998), partly because they appear early and partly because they are relatively easy to assess. Children's lexical knowledge can be estimated using checklist measures such as the MacArthur–Bates CDI and also by recording naturalistic data and elicitation (e.g. Barrière, 2007; De Houwer, 2009). Children with SLI show a delay in the onset of word production (e.g. first 50, 100, 200 words), in vocabulary size, and in terms of semantic categories. Bilingual children often exhibit smaller vocabularies in each of their languages (even though the number of words in the two languages put together may be larger than monolingual norms). Delayed lexical development is potentially an early sign of Bi-SLI (Gatt et al., 2008). Vocabulary tests can be used as a baseline for the assessment of children's language dominance/proficiency. Both vocabulary size and lexical processing can be studied in the same series of experimental tasks. The tasks presented in Chapter 8 (Haman et al.) involve assessing comprehension and production of nouns and verbs. Accuracy measured in these tasks may indicate the level of vocabulary size while reaction time measurement (comprehension and naming speed) can tap into the processing demands in both types of knowledge (passive and active) in two word classes (nouns vs verbs). Picture choice and picture naming were chosen as tasks least involving other types of linguistic knowledge except for accessing the meaning of separate words or relating referents to labels.

Narrative and Discourse Abilities

Telling a story, even from pictures, is difficult for children with SLI, since the ability to construct a narrative relies on a range of linguistic skills, including macrostructure discourse abilities and microstructure language abilities. Narrative abilities have been investigated widely in school-age children (e.g. Berman & Slobin, 1994; Peterson & McCabe, 1983), and there is now a rapidly growing literature on narratives elicited from bilingual children (Fiestas & Peña, 2004; Gutiérrez-Clellen, 2002; Lanza, 2001; Montanari, 2004; Pearson, 2001, 2002; Pearson & de Villiers, 2005; Ucelli & Páez, 2007) and from children with language impairment (e.g. Dodwell & Bavin, 2008), but research addressing the interface of bilingualism and language impairment in narrative production is still relatively limited (e.g. Cleave et al., 2010; Gutiérrez-Clellen et al., 2009; Iluz-Cohen & Walters, 2012; Simon-Cereijido & Gutiérrez-Clellen, 2009). These studies already show that while children with Bi-TLD can generate the basic structural elements of a story in both languages, children with Bi-SLI are more limited in microstructure features (e.g. vocabulary) and have difficulty generating stories which include a goal, attempt and outcome (Cleave *et al.*, 2010; Gutierrez-Clellen *et al.*, 2009; Simon-Cereijido & Gutiérrez-Clellen, 2009).

Narratives offer a number of advantages as an entry point to the study of bilingualism and language impairment. First, they allow a look at multiple linguistic levels in a single task, including lexis, morphosyntax, discourse structure and fluency. Second, the structure of children's narratives is relatively invariant across languages (Fiestas & Peña, 2004; Gutiérrez-Clellen, 2002; Pearson, 2002). Thus, narrative structure offers a baseline for looking at other more language-specific phenomena. In addition, narratives allow one to assess parallel measures across languages which allow within-subject, cross-language comparisons. Finally, in addition to macrostructure and microstructure features of narrative, narratives are capable of spontaneously eliciting phenomena that are unique to bilingual performance, i.e. code-switching.

Chapter 9 (Gagarina *et al.*) targets potentially diagnostic features manifested in narrative and discourse from six areas: (1) lexicon (lexical diversity, general all-purpose verbs, e.g. make/get, characteristic of children with SLI); (2) morphosyntax, especially tense and aspect markers appropriate to narrative discourse; (3) syntax, e.g. subordination or other means to distinguish main ideas from details; (4) narrative structure, e.g. story grammar categories, connectives, clause sequencing, cohesion; (5) discourse features, e.g. information density, elaborations, topic maintenance, explicitness; (6) fluency features including repetitions, false starts, pauses, discourse markers. The chapter presents two tasks (telling/retelling) which involve responses to picture stimuli and scripts constructed and designed to examine both *macrostructure* and *microstructure* information in narrative production.

Executive Functions

Of all cognitive skills, executive functions seem to offer a promising direction for disentangling bilingualism and SLI. Monolingual children with SLI perform worse than TD children on tasks tapping executive functions (e.g. Montgomery, 2002), such as the central executive in the model of Baddeley and Hitch (1974) and Baddeley (2007), and this suggests that they have a *deficit* in some executive functions. On the other hand, recent research on adult bilinguals has demonstrated that they have *enhanced* abilities in executive functions tapping inhibition and shifting (Bialystok, 2004), which relate to monitoring two languages at the same time and being able to switch between the two languages. Finally, studies of executive functions in children with Bi-SLI show a mixed picture

(Kohnert *et al.*, 2006). Engel de Abreu *et al.* (2012) found that bilingualism can benefit executive functions of children with Bi-SLI of low SES, while still distinguishing them from Bi-TLD. Iluz-Cohen and Armon-Lotem (2013) report enhanced inhibition and shifting abilities among children with Bi-TLD compared to children with Bi-SLI.

Cognitive (non-linguistic) tasks used in previous studies include the Embedded Figures Task (Pascual-Leone, 1989; Piaget & Inhelder, 1971) which tests inhibition, classification tasks (Ben-Zeev, 1977) which test shifting, or the more complex Tower of Hanoi which tests children's abilities to direct, organise, solve problems, monitor and plan behaviour, focus on targets and update working memory. Tasks of this type are also found in standardised tests such as the Cambridge Neuropsychological Test Automated Battery (CANTAB) or the Wisconsin Card Sorting test. Impairment in executive function could influence language abilities which have direct manifestations in bilinguals. A bilingual verbal fluency task (Luk & Bialystok, 2008) taps language control abilities, and can also serve as a measure of proficiency in both languages. A bilingual picture naming task (Festman *et al.*, 2007; Hernandez *et al.*, 2001) can be used to test language control, that is, interference of the non-target language.

Chapter 10 (Jensen de Lopez and Baker) presents four non-verbal domains of executive functions selected for further research with monolingual LI children, bilingual LI children and Bi-TD children: non-verbal executive-loaded working memory, non-verbal fluency, non-verbal inhibition and non-verbal planning/shifting. Although there are standardised computer-run batteries for executive function (e.g. CANTAB, DK-FS), these are costly and are often more difficult to run. Tasks were selected that are easy to administer and clinically friendly. A decision was made to favour tasks that are freeware.

The tasks which cover the four domains are complemented by an adaptation of the background questionnaires used by Paradis (2010, 2011) to the multilingual European context in Chapter 11 (Tuller). The chapter focuses on parental questionnaires designed for use with parents of children growing up in multilingual contexts, to collect information which could help determine whether a child experiencing language difficulties might have SLI. Background questionnaires are a valuable tool for identifying children who are at risk for SLI in bilingual populations. The parental questionnaires were tested with several teams for different bilingual populations. The pilots suggested that the questionnaires' results correlate with practitioners' assessment and led to guidelines for best practice in designing and using such tools across the European community and beyond. It is argued in the chapter that there is now growing support for the conclusion that parental questionnaires can be of considerable use as a tool with which it can be ascertained whether low language performance in a bilingual child is due to SLI.

The book ends with guidelines for assessment that revisit the tasks (Chapter 12, Elin Thordardottir). The chapter was prepared in order to promote consistency and comparability between studies carried out in different languages, and to encourage careful attention to methodological aspects involving the recruitment and selection of participants and the documentation of their characteristics. Given the large variability in clinical traditions, availability of tools and criteria in effect, there will necessarily be variability in the procedures used in the studies. The particular criteria recommended are based on current knowledge of bilingual acquisition and manifestation of SLI in bilingual children, and as such, are not meant to be final, but rather a reasonable approximation that can help increase the quality of work that is undertaken to set more firm criteria across languages. These guidelines outline some options that can help ensure comparability between studies and adequate documentation of the procedures used.

To conclude, the work presented in this book sheds light on four general traits:

- Bilingualism and SLI are not the same and can be disentangled.
- Bilingual children with SLI show error patterns of both bilingual children and monolingual children with SLI.
- Bilingualism and SLI seem not to show a cumulative effect, that is, the gap between bilingual children with and without SLI is not larger than the gap between monolingual children with and without SLI.
- Bilingualism might sometimes offer a partial compensatory mechanism for language and cognitive development in children with SLI. This, however, cannot replace therapy in any way.

While this book presents methods for testing children for SLI, the bilingual perspective offered in it is applicable to other conditions of language impairment in a bilingual population, as the tools are sensitive to the unique profile of bilingual children. While any of the presented tasks can be used for this purpose, the combination of, for example, the sentence repetition task with its reduced vocabulary, or the quasi-universal non-word repetition along with the narrative tasks is highly promising for evaluating the linguistic aptitude of bilingual children when language impairment is secondary as well.

Notes

(1)   The materials described in this book will be available free of charge on a companion website (www.bi-sli.org) upon request from the editors of the book.

References

Armon-Lotem, S., Danon, G. and Walters, J. (2008) The use of prepositions in bilingual SLI children: The relative contribution of representation and processing. In A. Gavarró and M. João Freitas (eds) *Language Acquisition and Development: Proceedings of GALA 2007* (pp. 41–46). Newcastle: Cambridge Scholars Publishing.

Armon-Lotem, S. and Chiat, S. (2012) How do sequential bilingual children perform on non-word repetition tasks? In A.K. Biller, E.Y. Chung and A.E. Kimball (eds) *Proceedings of the 36th Annual Boston University Conference on Language Development* (pp. 56–62). Somerville, MA: Cascadilla Press.

Baddeley, A.D. (2007) *Working Memory, Thought and Action.* Oxford: Oxford University Press.

Baddeley, A.D. and Hitch, G. (1974) The Psychology of Learning and Motivation: Advances in Research and Theory. Vol. VIII., pp. 47–90. New York: Academic Press.

Barrière, I. (2010) The vitality of Yiddish among Hasidic infants and toddlers in a low SES preschool in Brooklyn. In W. Moskovich (ed.) *Yiddish – A Jewish National Language at 100* (pp. 170–196) Jerusalem-Kyiv: Hebrew University of Jerusalem.

Bedore, L. and Leonard, L. (2001) Grammatical morphology deficits in Spanish-speaking children with specific language impairment. *Journal of Speech, Language, and Hearing Research* 44, 905–924.

Bedore, L.M. and Peña, E.D. (2008) Assessment of bilingual children for identification of language impairment: Current findings and implications for practice. *International Journal of Bilingual Education and Bilingualism* 11 (1), 1–29.

Ben-Zeev, S. (1977) The influence of bilingualism on cognitive strategy and cognitive development. *Child Development* 48 (3), 1009–1018.

Bercow, J. (2008) Review of Services for Children and Young People (0–19) with Speech, Language and Communication Needs. Report. See http://dera.ioe.ac.uk/8405/1/7771-dcsf-bercow.pdf (accessed 11 December 2014).

Berman, R.A. and Slobin, D.I. (1994) Narrative structure. In R.A. Berman and D.I. Slobin (eds) *Relating Events in Narrative: A Cross-Linguistic Developmental Study* (pp. 39–84). New York/London: Psychology Press.

Bialystok, E. and Martin, M. (2004). Attention and inhibition in bilingual children: evidence from the dimensional change card sort task. *Developmental Science*, 7 (3), 325–339.

Bishop, D.V.M. (2006) What causes specific language impairment in children? *Current Directions in Psychological Science* 15 (5), 217–221.

Bishop, D.V.M., Bright, P., James, C., Bishop, S.J. and van der Lely, H.K.J. (2000) Grammatical SLI: A distinct subtype of developmental language impairment? *Applied Psycholinguistics* 21 (2), 159–181.

Bishop, D.V.M. and Norbury, C.F. (2005) Executive functions in children with communication impairments, in relation to autistic symptomatology: I. Generativity. *Autism* 9 (1), 7–27.

Blom, E., Polišenská, D. and Unsworth, S. (2008) The acquisition of grammatical gender in Dutch. *Special issue of Second Language Research* 24 (3), 259–265.

Bortolini, U., Arfé, B., Caselli, M.C., Degasperi, L., Deevy, P. and Leonard, L. (2006) Clinical markers for specific language impairment in Italian: The contribution of clitics and non-word repetition. *International Journal of Language and Communication Disorders* 41 (6), 695–712.

Bosch, L. and Serra, M. (1997) Grammatical morphology deficits of Spanish-speaking children with specific language impairment. In A. Baker, M. Beers, G. Bol, J. de Jong and G. Leemans (eds) *Child Language Disorders in a Cross-Linguistic Perspective: Proceedings of the Fourth Symposium of the European Group on Child Language Disorders* (pp. 33–45). Amsterdam: Amsterdam Series in Child Language Development, University of Amsterdam.

Bottari, P., Cipriani, P. Chilosi, A.-M. and Pfanner, L. (2001) The Italian determiner system in normal acquisition, specific language impairment, and childhood aphasia. *Brain and Language,* 77 (3), 283–293.

Chiat, S., Armon-Lotem, S., Marinis, T., Polisenska, K., Roy, P. and Seeff-Gabriel, B. (2013) Assessment of language abilities in sequential bilingual children: The potential of sentence imitation tasks. In V.C. Mueller Gathercole (ed.) *Issues in the Assessment of Bilinguals* (pp. 56–89). Bristol: Multilingual Matters.

Chilla, S. and Babur, E. (2008) Specific language impairment in Turkish-German bilingual children: Aspects of assessment and outcome. In S. Topbaş and M. Yavaş (eds) *Communication Disorders in Turkish* (pp. 352–368). Bristol: Multilingual Matters.

Chillier-Zesiger, L., Arabatzi, M., Baranzini, L., Cronel-Ohayon, S. and Thierry, D. (2006) The acquisition of French pronouns in normal children and in children with specific language impairment (SLI). Unpublished manuscript, Université de Genève, Geneva.

Chondrogianni, V. and Marinis, T. (2012) Production and processing asymmetries of tense morphemes by English sequential bilingual children. *Bilingualism: Language and Cognition* 12 (1), 1–25.

Clahsen, H. (1991) *Child Language and Developmental Dysphasia. Linguistic Studies of the Acquisition of German.* Amsterdam: Benjamins.

Clahsen, H. (2008) Chomskyan syntactic theory and language disorders. In M.J. Ball, M. Perkins, N. Mueller and S. Howard (eds) *The Handbook of Clinical Linguistics* (pp. 165–183). Oxford: Blackwell.

Cleave, P.L., Girolametto, L.E., Chen, X. and Johnson, C.J. (2010) Narrative abilities in monolingual and dual language learning children with specific language impairment. *Journal of Communication Disorders* 43 (6), 511–522.

Crago, M. and Gopnik, M. (1994) From families to phenotypes: Theoretical and clinical implications of research into the genetic basis of specific language impairment. In R. Watkins and M. Rice (eds) *Specific Language Impairments in Children* (pp. 35–51). Baltimore, MD: Paul H. Brookes.

De Houwer, A. (2009) *Bilingual First Language Acquisition.* Bristol: Multilingual Matters.

de Jong, J. Orgassa, A., Çavuş, N., Baker, A. and Weerman, F. (2007) Verb Agreement in Turkish-Dutch Bilingual Children with SLI. Paper presented at ISB6, Hamburg.

de Jong, J., Çavuş, N. and Baker, A. (2010) Language impairment in Turkish-Dutch bilingual children. In S. Topbaş and M. Yavaş (eds) *Communication Disorders in Turkish* (pp. 288–300). Bristol: Multilingual Matters.

de Villiers, J., Roeper, T., Bland-Stewart, L. and Pearson, B.Z. (2008) Answering hard questions: Wh-movement across dialects and disorder. *Applied Psycholinguistics* 29 (1), 67–103.

Dodwell, K. and Bavin, E.L. (2008) Children with specific language impairment: An investigation of their narratives and memory. *International Journal of Language and Communication Disorders* 43 (2), 201–218.

Elin Thordardottir, Rothenberg, A., Rivard, M. and Naves, R. (2006) Bilingual assessment: Can overall proficiency be estimated from separate measurement of two languages? *Journal of Multilingual Communication Disorders* 4, 1–21.

Elin Thordardottir, and Brandeker, M. (2013) The effect of bilingual exposure versus language impairment on nonword repetition and sentence imitation scores. *Journal of Communication Disorders* 46, 1–16.

Engel de Abreu, P., Cruz-Santos, A., Tourinho, C.J., Martin, R. and Bialystok, E. (2012) Bilingualism enriches the poor: Enhanced cognitive control in low-income minority children. *Psychological Science: A Journal of the American Psychological Society* 23 (11), 1364–1371.

Fenson, L., Marchman, V.A., Thal, D.J., Dale, P.S., Reznick, J.S. and Bates, E. (2007) *MacArthur–Bates Communicative Development Inventories: User's Guide and Technical Manual* (2nd edn). Baltimore, MA: Brookes Publishing.

Festman, J., Rodriguez-Fornells, A. and Muente, T. (2007) Performance accuracy affected by control over bilingual language production: A study of balanced L2 users In S. Van Daele, A. Housen, F. Kuiken, M. Pierrard and I. Vedder (eds) *Complexity, Accuracy and Fluency in Second Language Use, Learning & Teaching* (pp. 65–76). Wetteren: Universa Press.

Fiestas, C.E. and Peña, E.D. (2004) Narrative discourse in bilingual children. *Language, Speech, and Hearing Services in Schools* 35, 155–168.

Gathercole, S.E. (2006) Nonword repetition and word learning: The nature of the relationship. *Applied Psycholinguistics* 27 (4), 513–544.

Gathercole, S.E. and Pickering, S.J. (2000) Assessment of working memory in six- and seven-year old children. *Journal of Educational Psychology* 92, 377–390.

Gatt, D., Letts, C. and Klee, T. (2008) Lexical mixing in the early productive vocabularies of Maltese children: Implications for intervention. *Clinical Linguistics and Phonetics* 22 (4–5), 267–274.

Girbau, D. and Schwartz, R.G. (2007) Non-word repetition in Spanish-speaking children with specific language impairment (SLI). *International Journal of Language and Communication Disorders* 42 (1), 59–75.

Girbau, D. and Schwartz, R.G. (2008) Phonological working memory in Spanish-English bilingual children with and without specific language impairment. *Journal of Communication Disorders* 41 (2), 124–145.

Gutiérrez-Clellen, V.F. (2002) Narratives in two languages: Assessing performance of bilingual children. *Linguistics and Education* 13 (2), 175–197.

Gutiérrez-Clellen, V.F., Simon-Cereijido, G. and Erickson Leone, A. (2009) Code-switching in bilingual children with specific language impairment. *International Journal of Bilingualism* 13 (1), 91–109.

Hamann, C., Ohayon, S., Dubé, S., Frauenfelder, U.H., Rizzi, L., Starke, M. and Zesiger, P. (2003) Aspects of grammatical development in young French children with SLI. *Developmental Science* 6 (2), 151–158.

Hamann, C. and Belletti, A. (2006) Developmental patterns in the acquisition of complement clitic pronouns: Comparing different acquisition modes with an emphasis on French. *Rivista di Grammatica Generativa* 31, 39–78.

Hernandez, A.E., Dapretto, M., Mazziotta, J. and Bookheimer, S. (2001) Language switching and language representation in Spanish-English bilinguals: An fMRI study. *NeuroImage* 14 (2), 510–520.

Iluz-Cohen, P. and Walters, J. (2012) Telling stories in two languages: Narratives of bilingual preschool children with typical and impaired language. *Bilingualism: Language and Cognition* 15 (1), 58–74.

Iluz-Cohen, P. and Armon-Lotem, S. (2013) Language proficiency and executive control in bilingual children. *Bilingualism: Language and Cognition* 16 (4), 884–899.

Jacobson, P. and Schwartz, R.G. (2002) Production of inflectional morphology in incipient Spanish-English bilingual children with SLI. *Applied Psycholinguistics* 23 (1), 23–41.

Jakubowicz, C., Nash, L., Rigaut, C. and Gerard, C.-L. (1998) Determiners and clitic pronouns in French-speaking children with SLI. *Language Acquisition* 7 (2–4), 113–160.

Jakubowicz, C. and Nash, L. (2001) Functional categories and syntactic operations in abnormal language acquisition. *Brain and Language* 77 (3), 321–339.

Kohnert, K. and Windsor, J. (2004) The search for common ground Part II. Nonlinguistic performance by linguistically diverse learners. *Journal of Speech, Language, and Hearing Research* 47 (4), 891–903.

Kohnert, K., Windsor, J. and Yim, D. (2006) Do language-based processing tasks separate children with language impairment from typical bilinguals? *Learning Disabilities Research & Practice* 21 (1), 19–29.

Lanza, E. (2001) Temporality and language contact in narratives by children bilingual in Norwegian and English. In L. Verhoeven and S. Stromqvist (eds) *Narrative Development in a Multilingual Context* (pp. 15–50). Amsterdam: John Benjamins.

Leonard, L. (1998) *Children with Specific Language Impairment*. Cambridge, MA: MIT Press.

Luk, G. and Bialystok, E. (2008) Common and distinct cognitive bases for reading in English Cantonese bilinguals. *Applied Psycholinguistics* 29 (2), 269–289.

Marinis, T. (2007) On-line processing of passives in L1 and L2 children. In A. Belikova, L. Meroni and M. Umeda (eds) *Proceedings of the 2nd Conference on Generative Approaches to Language Acquisition North America (GALANA)* (pp. 265–276). Somerville, MA: Cascadilla Proceedings Project.

Marinis, T., Chiat, S., Armon-Lotem, S., Gibbons, D. and Gipps, E. (2010) School-Age Sentence Imitation Test (SASIT). University of Reading, Reading.

Marinis, T. and Saddy, D. (2013) Parsing the passive: Comparing children with specific language impairment to sequential bilingual children. *Language Acquisition* 20 (2), 155–179.

Meir, N. and Amon-Lotem, S. (2013) Sensitivity and specificity of nonword repetition (NWR) and sentence repetition (SR) in discriminating bilingual children with and without specific language impairment (SLI). Paper presented at 29th World Congress of the International Association of Logopedics and Phoniatrics (IALP), Torino, Italy.

Meir, N., Walters, J. and Armon-Lotem, S. (under review) Disentangling SLI and bilingualism using Sentence Repetition Tasks: the impact of L1 and TL properties. *International Journal of Bilingualism*.

Meisel, J. (2007) The weaker language in early child bilingualism: Acquiring a first language as a second language? *Applied Psycholinguistics* 28 (3), 495–514.

Montanari, S. (2004) The development of narrative competence in the L1 and L2 of Spanish-English bilingual children. *International Journal of Bilingualism* 8 (4), 449–497.

Montgomery, J.W. (2002) Examining the nature of lexical processing in children with specific language impairment: Temporal processing or processing capacity deficit? *Applied Psycholinguistics* 23 (3), 447–470.

Orgassa, A. (2009) *Specific Language Impairment in a Bilingual Context: The Acquisition of Dutch Inflection by Turkish-Dutch Learners*. Utrecht: LOT Dissertation Series 220.

Papadopoulou, D., Rothweiler, M., Tsimpli, I.M., Chilla, S., Fox-Boyer, A., Katsika, K., Mastropavlou, M., Mylonaki, A. and Stahl, N. (2009) Motion Verbs in Greek and German: evidence from typically developing and SLI children In Tasos Tsangalidis (ed) Selected Papers from the 18th ISTAL (pp. 289–299). Thessaloniki, Greece: Monochromia Publishing.

Paradis, J. (2010) The interface between bilingual development and specific language impairment. *Applied Psycholinguistics* 31 (2), 227–252.

Paradis, J. (2011) Individual differences in child English second language acquisition: Comparing child-internal and child-external factors. *Linguistic Approaches to Bilingualism* 1 (3), 213–237.

Paradis, J., Genesee, F. and Crago, M. (2005/2006) Domain-general versus domain-specific accounts of specific language impairment: Evidence from bilingual children's acquisition of object pronouns. *Language Acquisition* 13 (1), 33–62.

Paradis, J., Emmerzael, K. and Sorenson Duncan, T. (2010) Assessment of English language learners: Using parent report on first language development. *Journal of Communication Disorders* 43, 474–497.

Pascual-Leone, J. (1989) An organismic process model of Witkin's field-dependence-independence. In T. Globerson and T. Zelniker (eds) *Cognitive Style and Cognitive Development* (pp. 36–70). Norwood, NJ: Ablex.

Pearson, B.Z. (2001) Language and mind in the stories of bilingual children. In L. Verhoeven and S. Strömqvist (eds) *Narrative Development in Multilingual Contexts* (pp. 373–398). Amsterdam: John Benjamins.

Pearson, B. (2002) Narrative competence among monolingual and bilingual school children in Miami. In K. Oller and R. Eilers (eds) *Language and Literacy in Bilingual Children* (pp. 135–174). Clevedon: Multilingual Matters.

Pearson, B.Z. and de Villiers, P.A. (eds) (2005) *Encyclopedia of Language and Linguistics* (2nd edn). Oxford: Elsevier.

Penner, Z. (1998) Sprachentwicklung und Sprachverstehen bei Ausländerkindern. Eine Pilotstudie bei Schulkindern in der deutschen Schweiz. In H. Wegener (ed.) *Eine zweite Sprache lernen* (pp. 241–261). Tübingen: Gunter Narr Verlag.

Peterson, C. and McCabe, A. (1983) *Developmental Psycholinguistics: Three Ways of Looking at a Child's Narrative*. New York: Plenum Press.

Piaget, J. and Inhelder, B. (1971) *Mental Imagery in the Child*. London: Routledge and Kegan Paul. (Original work published 1966.)

Rice, M. (2000) Grammatical symptoms of specific language impairment. In D.V.M. Bishop and L.B. Leonard (eds) *Speech and Language Impairments in Children: Causes, Characteristics, Intervention and Outcome* (pp. 17–34). Hove: Psychology Press.

Rice, M., Wexler, K. and Cleave, P. (1995) Specific language impairment as a period of extended optional infinitive. *Journal of Speech and Hearing Research* 38 (4), 850–863.

Rice, M.L. and Wexler, K. (1996) Toward tense as a clinical marker of specific language impairment in English-speaking children. *Journal of Speech and Hearing Research* 39 (6), 1239–1257.

Roeper, T. (2004) Diagnosing language variations: Underlying principles for syntactic assessment. *Seminars in Speech and Language* 25 (1), 41–56.

Rothweiler, M., Kroffke, S. and Babur, E. (2007) Verbal morphology in Turkish-German bilingual children with SLI. Paper presented at ISB6, Hamburg.

Rothweiler, M., Chilla, S. and Babur, E. (2010) Specific language impairment in Turkish: Evidence from case morphology in Turkish–German successive bilinguals. *Clinical Linguistics and Phonetics* 24 (7), 540–555.

Schulz, P., Wymann, K. and Penner, Z. (2001) The early acquisition of verb meaning in German by normally developing and language impaired children. *Brain and Language* 77 (3), 407–418.

Schulz, P. and Penner, Z. (2002) How you can eat the apple and have it too: Evidence from the acquisition of telicity in German. In J. Costa and M.J. Freitas (eds) *Proceedings of the GALA 2001 Conference on Language Acquisition* (pp. 239–246). Lisbon: Associação Portuguesa de Linguística.

Schulz, P. and Wittek, A. (2003) Opening doors and sweeping floors: What children with specific language impairment know about telic and atelic verbs. In B. Beachley, A. Brown and F. Colin (eds) *Proceedings of the 27th Annual Boston University Conference on Language Development* (Vol. 2; pp. 727–738). Somerville, MA: Cascadilla Press.

Schulz, P. and Kiese-Himmel, C. (2006) Verbverstehen und expressiver Wortschatzumfang bei sprech-/sprachentwicklungsgestörten Kindern. *L.O.G.O.S. Interdisziplinär* 14, 244–252.

Schulz, P. and Roeper, T. (2011) Acquisition of exhaustivity in wh-questions: A semantic dimension of SLI? *Lingua* 121 (3), 383–407.

Simon-Cereijido, G. and Gutiérrez-Clellen, V. (2009) A cross-linguistic and bilingual evaluation of the interdependence between lexical and grammatical domains. *Applied Psycholinguistics* 30 (2), 315–337.

Stavrakaki, S., Chrysomallis, M.A. and Petraki, E. (2011) Subject-verb agreement, object clitics, and wh-questions in bilingual French-Greek SLI: The case study of a French-Greek speaking child with SLI. *Clinical Linguistics and Phonetics* 25 (5), 339–367.

Tallal, P. and Stark, R. (1981) Speech acoustic-cue discrimination abilities of normally developing and language-impaired children. *Journal of the Acoustical Society of America* 69 (2), 568–574.

Tomblin, J.B., Records, N. and Zhang, X. (1996) A system for the diagnosis of specific language impairment in kindergarten children. *Journal of Speech and Hearing Research* 39 (6), 1284–1294.

Uccelli, P. and Paéz, M. (2007) Narrative and vocabulary development of bilingual children from kindergarten to first grade: Developmental changes and associations among English and Spanish skills. *Language, Speech, and Hearing Services in Schools* 38 (3), 225–236.

Van der Lely, H. (1998) SLI in children: Movement, economy, and deficits in the computational-syntactic system. *Language Acquisition* 7 (2–4), 161–192.

Wexler, K., Schütze, C. and Rice, M. (1998) Subject case in children with SLI and unaffected controls: Evidence for the Agr/Tns omission model. *Language Acquisition* 7 (2–4), 317–344.

Wojtecka, M. and Schulz, P. (2011) Exhaustive wh-questions in eL2 TD and SLI children. COST Action IS0804 Meeting, Language Impairment in a Multilingual Society, Eskişehir, Turkey.

Zesiger, P., Chillier-Zesiger, L., Arabatzi, M., Baranzini, L., Cronel-Ohayon, S., Franck, J., Frauenfelder, U.H., Hamann, C. and Rizzi, L. (2010) The acquisition of pronouns by French children: A parallel study of production and comprehension. *Applied Psycholinguistics* 31 (4), 571–603.

Zubrick, S., Taylor, C., Rice, M. and Slegers, D. (2007) Late language emergence at 24 months: An epidemiological study of prevalence, predictors and covariates. *Journal of Speech, Language, and Hearing Research* 50 (6), 1562–1592.

Part 1

Syntax and Its Interfaces

1 Elicitation Task for Subject– Verb Agreement

Jan de Jong

The marking of verbs for grammatical features of the subject of a sentence is called subject–verb agreement. Features that are marked this way are number, person and sometimes gender. Marking of agreement may be fused with tense. For instance, the third person singular –s in English verbs is used only for the present tense.[1] Importantly, agreement is an inflection that is determined by the syntactic context in which the verb is used (contextual inflection; Booij, 1994).

The agreement paradigm is different for each language where agreement occurs. Some languages (notably English) have very sparse paradigms, while other languages (e.g. Italian) have paradigmatic cells not only for singular and plural but also for first, second and third person. Slovene, for instance, has dual as well as plural marking. On the other hand, some languages (e.g. Swedish) do not have verb agreement morphology (although tense is marked in Swedish). There are also within-language differences between the marking for agreement of present and past.

Subject–Verb Agreement as a Vulnerable Area in Specific Language Impairment

Verb morphology is known to be a vulnerable domain in specific language impairment (SLI) in many languages, though certainly not in all: in some languages, noun morphology is more vulnerable than verb morphology (cf. Chapter 2 on case morphology). There are also cross-linguistic differences in the severity of verb agreement difficulties in SLI. Research by Leonard (1998) has revealed that inflection is better preserved if it is highly salient in the target language. The same is true for languages that have rich (or uniform) morphology. Together, these characteristics make agreement a strong cue in such languages. According to Leonard, this explains, for instance, why accuracy rates for inflection on verbs are much higher in the output of children with SLI in Italian than in English.

In the languages where verb inflection is affected, difficulties with verbal morphology are often seen as a reliable marker of SLI. Some

25

authors claim that this marker should be identified with tense rather than agreement (Rice *et al.*, 1995). However, the language for which the claim of tense as a clinical marker has most consistently been made, English, does not distinguish between overt marking of (present) tense and agreement, as in third person singular –s (the only overt affix in the present tense inflectional paradigm).

Other researchers, notably Clahsen (2008), claim that agreement problems outnumber tense problems and that the reverse pattern, i.e. impaired tense marking and intact subject–verb agreement marking, does not seem to exist in SLI (Clahsen, 2008: 176). In earlier work, Clahsen (1992) proposed that the contextual nature of verb agreement, captured in the Control Agreement Principle, is where the weakness of children with SLI should be located. This would explain why other features, such as plural marking on nouns, are better preserved in SLI: number marking on nouns is not contextual.

Tense and agreement errors may show as omissions or substitutions of inflectional morphemes. In English, a language with little overt marking in the first place, omission is the dominant error type. In languages with a more elaborate verb paradigm, substitutions are also found. Recently, Clahsen (2008) has suggested that problems in agreement may not show across the board, but rather in specific cells of the agreement paradigm. These affected cells may be language specific. This, again, may be explained alternatively by differential patterns of saliency (Bedore & Leonard, 1996). Another factor concerns the number and complexity of features to be marked. In Hebrew, past tense forms are marked for person, number and gender; in the present tense, person is not marked. Dromi *et al.* (1999) showed that this led to a discrepancy in performance for the present and past tense. They found that errors in second person past tense (masculine and feminine, singular and plural), as well as errors in present tense plural feminine, revealed differences between children with SLI and typically developing (TD) children. They characterised the errors as feature simplification/ reduction since they involved omission of the person marking in the past and the number or gender marking in the present.

When choosing a test domain for verb morphology that is valid across languages, however, agreement is a proper target, languages that lack agreement notwithstanding. The variation of inflectional paradigms makes it a fruitful area for research into the sources of linguistic disability in SLI. Studies on agreement morphology in monolingual children with SLI have addressed typologically different languages like German (Clahsen, 2008; Rothweiler *et al.*, 2012), Hebrew (Dromi *et al.*, 1999), Spanish (Bedore & Leonard, 2001), Italian (Leonard *et al.*, 1992), Finnish (Kunnari *et al.*, 2011), French (Franck *et al.*, 2004) and Greek (Stavrakaki *et al.*, 2008). These studies concern different linguistic contexts, test different hypotheses and sometimes propose different explanations for agreement difficulties in

SLI. Together, however, they demonstrate that agreement morphology is a domain that warrants investigation when assessing the linguistic profile of SLI.

Agreement morphology is also sometimes found to be weak in bilingual children without language impairment (e.g. Paradis & Crago, 2000, 2003). This observation leads to a diagnostic confound: are agreement difficulties in bilingual children with language delay due to their bilingualism or are they indicative of SLI?

In a study done on Dutch language production in Turkish–Dutch bilingual children (Orgassa, 2009), shortcomings in agreement morphology were shown to be typical of both monolingual and bilingual children with SLI. No differences were found between monolingual and bilingual TD children. Rothweiler *et al.* (2012) found similar patterns in Turkish–German children. In their study, Rothweiler *et al.* (2012: 42) found agreement problems in children with SLI who were grammatically quite advanced 'in that they consistently produced subordinate clauses and/or wh-questions from the first recording onwards'. Such findings suggest that verbal morphology shows promise of being an index of SLI regardless of the child's status as a bilingual or monolingual speaker of the language. In the context of this volume, dealing as it does with the assessment of SLI in a bilingual context, it provides another reason for including agreement morphology in the test repertoire.

Task Design: The General Format

Grammatical morphology is often tested by supplying sentences for the child to complete (a cloze procedure). However, this procedure has its drawbacks. An important one concerns the structure of the stimulus. Some exemplary items can show this.

In the Test of Early Grammatical Impairment (TEGI; Rice & Wexler, 2001), children are asked to complete sentence frames like:

(1) 'Here is a singer. Tell me what a singer does'.

Conti-Ramsden *et al.* (2001) uses another sentence frame to elicit a finite form:

(2) 'Sailors sail. This man is a sailor, so every day he (sails)'.

Stimuli may have different restrictions cross-linguistically. If applied to Dutch (or German), two problems arise here. Stimulus (1) can easily elicit an infinitive (zingen [Dutch] or singen [German], 'sing') instead of an inflected verb. Stimulus (2) cannot be translated into a similar frame in Dutch, since in Dutch a fronted temporal marker (like 'every day') leads to inversion of subject and verb. Whereas in English, one can supply the subject after which the child completes the sentence with a verb, in Dutch the verb, i.e. the very target of the task, is the first element after the temporal phrase so the verb cannot be elicited by prompting the subject. This is a language-specific problem, but similar phenomena are found in other languages, with similar or different word order patterns. Another problem with, for instance, the sentence frame (1) from the TEGI, is that it can only be used for the elicitation of third person verb forms. For English, this is sufficient, but it does not work for languages with richer agreement paradigms. The same is true for another useful device, contrastive stimuli, like the ones used in the Diagnostic Evaluation of Language Variation (DELV; Seymour *et al.*, 2003): 'The boys ride scooters, but not the girl. She...'.

In conclusion, the best way to create a task that is applicable across languages is to elicit a full sentence from the child.

Another requirement that derives from typological considerations is that the target verb be transitive. In some languages (again, Dutch, and to a lesser extent German) the presence of an object in the sentence can be used to establish whether the verb is in second or final position. Verb position, in these languages, correlates with verb form (the correlation is stronger in Dutch than in German; examples in Clahsen [1988] show that in German, more instances are found of finite forms in final position).

This can be illustrated by two utterances from a Dutch girl with SLI (aged 7;5) taken from a study by de Jong (1999):

(3)   toen papa en mama klap-en
      then papa and mama applaud.INF or .PRS-PL
(4)   mama kast open-doen
      mama cupboard open.do.INF

In early Dutch child language, children use infinitives rather than finite forms. They consistently use these infinitival forms in utterance-final position. Finite forms occur in second position. However, in (3), final position cannot be distinguished from second position. In (4), the second position is taken by the object and thus the verb is unambiguously final. Importantly, the infinitive form is homonymous: the plural form is identical. The implication then is that, given the form–position correlation, in (3) the verb could be inflected for number, in (4) it cannot.[2] The occurrence of utterances like (4) throughout the language sample supports the observation that this child manifests extended use of root infinitives (and also suggests that (3) should have an infinitival reading rather than a plural interpretation).

The decisions made about the design (eliciting full sentences, transitive verbs) allow for a procedure that can be carried out in as many languages as possible, so not many language-specific adaptations are necessary. Another decision that had to be made was that all cells of the paradigm (not just third, but also first and second person) should be included, given the variation across languages. This limited the use of stimuli like those in (1) and (2).

For the verbs included, the criterion was that they had an equivalent in each of the languages for which the task was created. Of course, this does not guarantee that stimuli are fully equivalent across languages. Additional criteria or considerations might hold for other languages and these may lead to deviations from the procedure, to ensure that no other variables interfere with the elicitation of agreement proper. For example, the use of pronouns in the task could affect performance in those languages in which the object pronoun takes the form of a clitic (see Chapter 3, this volume): clitics are known to be vulnerable in the language of children with SLI. Another variable is the influence of morphophonology on specific test items (see Pruitt & Oetting, 2009). It may be that the phonology of a particular verb stem makes it hard to identify the agreement marker as a separate morpheme, so that other verb stems are preferable. The verbs selected were 'wash' (as a practice item), 'push', 'pull', 'hug', 'pinch', 'tickle'. All resulting items are listed in Table 1.1. The next section will describe the way they are elicited.

Table 1.1 Target utterances for the subject–verb agreement task

I wash you
you wash me
he washes you
he washes her

I push you
I push him
you push me
you push him
he pushes me
he pushes you

I pull you
I pull him
you pull me
you pull him
he pull me
he pulls you

(Continued)

Table 1.1 (Continued)

I hug you
I hug him
you hug me
you hug him
he hugs me
he hugs you

I pinch you
I pinch him
you pinch me
you pinch him
he pinches me
he pinches you

I tickle you
I tickle him
you tickle me
you tickle him
he tickles me
he tickles you

Task Design: Procedure

The procedure is a picture description task. As Table 1.1 shows, third as well as first and second person are elicited. While elicitation of third person by picture description is a common and natural procedure, first and second person require a form of role play, by which the child is encouraged to take the perspective of one of the characters in the picture ('I') while the experimenter has a different role ('you'). The following procedure was designed to create that referential contrast.

The materials used are: two ring binders A5, with two holes, one with straps or a rubber band to enable setting it upright; stickers (insignia) in the form of a silver star, a red heart, a blue triangle; test pictures A5 landscape, holes at top, in a double set; an audio recording device; a form with all items; instruction text; and a see-through ziplock bag.

The setting is as follows: the child and the experimenter are sitting opposite each other. The booklet with the pictures and the practice items about washing are on the table and the loose experimental pictures are in a see-through zipped bag.

The experimenter starts by saying: 'This is a game about putting together a book with pictures. You have the book with the pictures in

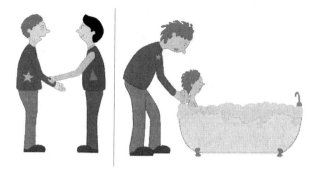

Figure 1.1 Items for 'pinching' and 'washing', with insignia

the right order, but look, my book has fallen apart. I want you to help me to put my book together. But let's have a look at the pictures first. Look, this person has a grey star, this one has a red heart. I will be one of them and you will be the other one. Which one would you like to be?' (see Figure 1.1).

The child then makes a choice, after which the experimenter introduces the practice items to familiarise the child with the procedure and, importantly, with the role that the child and the experimenter will take during the task:

'Great, here is the silver/red star/heart for you and I take the silver/red star/heart. So, the book is about us. Let's see what we are doing. In this picture I wash you, and in this picture you wash me. So, we need to be careful because there are many pictures about washing.

Oh, look, in this picture there is someone else and he has a blue triangle. Here he is washing you and here I am washing him'.

Note that besides the experimenter and the child ('you' and 'I') there is a third person involved ('someone else') to elicit third person singular ('he'). Now the experimenter takes the experimental pictures out of the bag and puts them on the table.

Experimenter: 'Now let's have a look at these pictures. These are about pushing and these are about pulling. These are about pinching and these are about tickling. We have hugging as well. So, we really need to be careful because there are different people doing different things.

Let's first sort them by what they are doing. Can you find pictures about hugging/tickling/pushing/pulling/pinching/washing?'.

The experimenter then takes the items with washing, which are the practice items and uses the following four as practice.

'Show me a picture with the boy. So, here "he washes you", and now you look at this one and you say: "He washes me". Now what happens in this picture? And what happens in this picture?'. Thus, the child is asked to describe two pictures as practice items: You wash him, I wash you.

The practice items are used to ensure that:

- The I/you contrast is working well.
- The verb used by the child is not progressive and is of the target tense.
- Both subject and object are overtly realised by the child.

If the child gets these three things right at least in the last practice trial, the experimenter moves to the experimental trials. If the child does not, the practice trials are repeated.

In the experimental trials, the experimenter guides the child as follows: 'To do this fast, you take the book and I take the cards. You tell me what is on the pictures and I put them in order to fix my book'.

'What happens on the first picture?'

'What happens next?'

Task Design: Simplified Procedure

The task as described above depends on the use of insignia (star, heart, triangle) to identify the persons in the picture. As the description of the task shows, the design requires that the child as well as the test administrator takes roles. The disadvantage of this procedure is that it demands some theory of mind skills; it is a pretend game. These skills are not always fully available to children with language impairment. Piloting has shown that the task can also be carried out with one sign per picture (only for I, you; he being by default the 'other person') or even without insignia.

In the pilot study, Bittner carried out the procedure without any insignia (Dagmar Bittner, p.c.) (Figure 1.2). The procedure started out with the child arranging the pictures in order to create a properly organised 'book' (see above). During this preparation, the actions were named (and thus the verbs were modelled in nominalised form). The three characters

Figure 1.2 Item for 'pinching', without insignia

were introduced. The larger person was the researcher; the smaller person was the child (as in the illustration for 'wash' in Figure 1.1). The third person (in Bittner's experiment this person was named by the child and thus was: papa, or the man, or the other one) was identified beforehand by different clothing. After dividing the roles in this way, the child was asked to identify the (practice) items productively, as in: 'This is the picture: I (verb) you, You (verb) me', etc. This exercise should prepare the child for the proper expression of the verb frame. For each item, the picture was named with the stimulus phrase: 'This is the picture:...'.

Language-specific addition

For languages that mark gender on the verb (as in Hebrew), pictures are included for female hairstyles so the experimenter can create pictures that represent the gender distinction, depending on the roles of experimenter and child. These can be applied to the characters pictured (Figure 1.3).

Although the task does not apply sentence completion, sentences used in the presentation of the task or with the practice items are influenced by language typology. For instance, a sequence like 'I wash you' is not common in pro-drop languages, which can have subject-less sentences. While it may be decided to use (emphatic) pronominal subjects anyway to clarify the task, in the child's productions pro-drop will occur naturally. The following example (from Croatian) illustrates this, also note that the object here is cliticised (Gordana Hrzica, p.c.).

(5) Perem   te
     pere-m   te
     V-pres-1st-sg pro-2nd-sg-clit
     'I wash you'

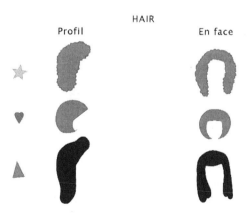

Figure 1.3 Hairstyles for indicating gender in test items

Problems with elicitation

For several reasons, children may fail to produce the target utterance. Below, some unwanted responses are listed, together with instructions for dealing with them and for encouraging children to produce the target utterance.

(1) The child drops the object: 'He pushes'. Say: 'I have two pictures with "he pushes". Can you say the whole thing?' If the child again omits the object then show the practice picture and say 'Remember? Here you said "He washes you"'.
(2) The child drops the subject: 'push him'. Say: 'I have two pictures that go with "push him". Can you say the whole thing? Can you say what's happening and who is doing it?' If the child again omits the subject then show the practice picture and say 'Remember? Here you said "He washes you"'.
(3) The child drops subject and object. See (1) and (2).
(4) The child uses incorrect inflection or omits inflection: 'He push me'. These are genuine errors, not failures in carrying out the task, so don't provide negative feedback and move to the next item.
(5) The child uses a different verb from the verb list push→pull, tickle→pinch. If there is such a picture, show the picture that would match and ask: 'Is this the right picture?'. If there is no such picture, say: 'I don't have such a picture. Do you mean tickling?'. If it doesn't work, move on. Since the task targets agreement marking, one might consider accepting the child's non-target response, provided it is analysable. More specifically, if the target form is a regular form, an irregular (non-target) form might be discarded but a different regular form could be accepted as an expression of the child's mastery of the inflectional paradigm, just as the target response would be accepted.
(6) The child uses a different verb, not from the verb list. Say: 'No, we only have pictures about pulling, pushing, etc.'.
     One might consider accepting the child's non-target response, provided it is analysable (and names the action correctly). See (5).
(7) The child does not use first and second person but uses only third person pronouns or full determiner phrases (DPs).[3] 'The boy tickles him'. Say: 'Look, this is not a boy, this is you'. Show the practice picture and say 'Remember?'. Quote the child's previous response. The same applies to third person instead of second person, etc. Find a matching practice picture.
(8) The child doesn't respond. Do the practice with modelling.

Coding and Analysis

Since languages have different verb inflection paradigms, coding and analysis cannot be uniform. Nevertheless, for each language it is important that the responses are divided into responses that can and cannot be analysed. Non-analysable utterances are, for instance, utterances that lack verbs. In languages that are non-pro-drop, the presence of the subject is required; without that, agreement with the subject cannot be verified. The situation is more complex in pro-drop languages.

A Pilot Study

Bittner (p.c.) carried out the task in German in the simplified version described above, with monolingual and bilingual TD children. The monolingual participants included four 3-year-olds (age range: 3;5.0–3;11.26); five 4-year-olds (4;3.1–4;11.22) and ten 5-year-olds (5;0.0–5;9.24). Also included were a Moroccan–German child (5;1.24) and a Mongolian–German child (4;9.29). A third child (Italian–German, 3;1) could not do the task.

For each child there were 30 data points (five verbs × six contexts; see Table 1.1). The 4-year-olds had 150 data points and scored 98% correct. The 5-year-olds (300 data points) also had 98% correct. The oldest 3-year-old (3;11.26) performed 28 out of 30 items correct. The other 3-year-olds either did not want to talk or did not understand the task (i.e. the I/you distinction).

These results must be treated with caution. Together, they suggest that the task can be used from around 4 years of age. Also, it seems that agreement is mastered by the TD children from the age of 4. It may be that the younger children also have acquired verb agreement, but do not fully understand the task. The task was also successfully completed by two of the bilingual children (the Moroccan–German child made one error).

The results of this pilot study show that the task can indeed be carried out in the simplified version (instead of the full procedure described above). However, more piloting is necessary, also given the ceiling effects found in the monolingual TD children.

Acknowledgements

The task was developed together with Esther Ruigendijk, Theo Marinis and Sonja Eisenbeiss. The pictures were created by Sofia Miliopoulos. Dagmar Bittner carried out a pilot task with the materials and suggested the simplified version of the task. The reviewers' comments were very helpful. Thanks to all, as well as to COST IS0804 members for their comments.

Notes

(1) 'Fusion' is used here as a descriptor. Theoretically, whether agreement and tense are fused is debatable. Wexler *et al.* (2004: 154), addressing a similar context within the Dutch inflectional paradigm, claim that for third person singular present tense in that language 'there is no particular reason to assume that Agr and Tense have fused into one projection for morphological purposes'.

(2) Of course, unlike in (3) the subject in (4) is singular. However, the same rationale is valid here. A verb ending in –en that precedes the object would be analysed as a substitution in a singular context.

(3) In several languages, pronouns are marked for case. Chapter 2 on case marking by Ruigendijk addresses case marking in DPs. If one wants to analyse case marking on pronouns, the agreement task can be used for that purpose as well.

References

Bedore, L. and Leonard, L. (2001) Grammatical morphology deficits in Spanish-speaking children with specific language impairment. *Journal of Speech, Language, and Hearing Research* 44, 905–924.

Booij, G. (1994) Against split morphology. In G. Booij and J. van Marle (eds) *Yearbook of Morphology 1993* (pp. 27–49). Dordrecht: Kluwer.

Clahsen, H. (1988) *Normale und gestörte Kindersprache: Linguistische Untersuchungen zum Erwerb von Syntax und Morphologie.* Amsterdam: John Benjamins.

Clahsen, H. (1992) Linguistic perspectives on specific language impairment. *Theorie des Lexikons. Arbeiten des Sonderforschungsbereichs 282.* Düsseldorf: Universität Düsseldorf.

Clahsen, H. (2008) Chomskyan syntactic theory and language disorders. In M.J. Ball, M. Perkins, N. Mueller and S. Howard (eds) *The Handbook of Clinical Linguistics* (pp. 165–183). Oxford: Blackwell.

Conti-Ramsden, G.M., Botting, N.F. and Faragher, B. (2001) Psycholinguistic markers for specific language impairment (SLI). *Journal of Child Psychology and Psychiatry* 42 (6), 741–748.

Dromi, E., Leonard, L.B., Adam, G. and Zadoneisky-Ehrlich, S. (1999) Verb agreement morphology in Hebrew speaking children with specific language impairment. *Journal of Speech, Language and Hearing Research* 42 (6), 1414–1431.

Franck, J., Cronel-Ohayon, S., Chillier, L., Frauenfelder, U.H., Hamann, C., Rizzi, L. and Zesiger, P. (2004) Normal and pathological development of subject–verb agreement in speech production: A study on French children. *Journal of Neurolinguistics* 17 (2-3), 147–180.

Jong, J. de (1999). *Specific language impairment in Dutch: inflectional morphology and argument structure.* Unpublished doctoral thesis. Rijksuniversiteit Groningen

Kunnari, S., Savinainen-Makkonen, T., Leonard, L., Mäkinen, L., Tolonen, A.-K., Luotonen, M. and Leinonen, E. (2011) Children with specific language impairment in Finnish: The use of tense and agreement inflections. *Journal of Child Language* 38 (5), 999–1027.

Leonard, L.B. (1998) *Children with Specific Language Impairment.* Cambridge, MA: MIT Press.

Leonard, L.B., Bortolini, U., Caselli, M.C., McGregor, K.K. and Sabbadini, L. (1992) Morphological deficits in children with specific language impairment: The status of features in the underlying grammar. *Language Acquisition* 2 (2), 151–180.

Orgassa, A. (2009) *Specific Language Impairment in a Bilingual Context: The Acquisition of Dutch Inflection by Turkish-Dutch Learners* (Dissertation Series 220). Utrecht: LOT.

Paradis, J. and Crago, M. (2000) Tense and temporality: Similarities and differences between language-impaired and second-language children. *Journal of Speech, Language and Hearing Research* 43 (4), 834–848.

Pruitt, S.L. and Oetting, J.B. (2009) Past tense marking by African American English-speaking children as a function of socioeconomic status. *Journal of Speech, Language, and Hearing Research* 52 (1), 2–15.

Rice, L. and Wexler, K. (2001) *Test for Early Grammatical Impairment*. San Antonio, TX: The Psychological Corporation.

Rice, M.L., Wexler, K. and Cleave, P. (1995) Specific language impairment as a period of extended optional infinitive. *Journal of Speech and Hearing Research* 38, 850–863.

Rothweiler, M., Chilla, S. and Clahsen, H. (2012) Subject verb agreement in specific language impairment: A study of monolingual and bilingual German-speaking children. *Bilingualism: Language and Cognition* 15 (1), 39–57.

Seymour, H.N., Roeper, T. and de Villiers, J.G. (2003) *Diagnostic Evaluation of Language Variation – Screening Test (DELV-ST)*. San Antonio, TX: The Psychological Corporation.

Stavrakaki, S., Vogindroukas, I., Chelas, E. and Goushi, S. (2008) Subject-verb agreement in SLI and child L2: A comparative approach to Greek SLI and (un)impaired child L2. In A. Gavarró and M.J. Freitas (eds) *Language Acquisition and Development: Proceedings of GALA 2007* (pp. 413–423). Newcastle: Cambridge Scholars Publishing.

Wexler, K., Schaeffer, J. and Bol, G. (2004) Verbal syntax and morphology in Dutch normal and SLI children: How developmental data can play an important role in morphological theory. *Syntax* 7 (2), 148–198.

2 Contrastive Elicitation Task for Testing Case Marking

Esther Ruigendijk

Introduction

Case marking is the morphological realisation of a syntactic relationship between a case assigner (i.e. the finite verb for subjects, the verb for objects or prepositions for objects) and a noun phrase. There are also languages (e.g. Russian and Turkish) in which case marking can be the morphological realisation of a specific semantic function, for instance a location, or an instrument (for example in Russian: 'devochka pishet pisjmo ruchk**oj**', girl-NOM writes letter-ACC pen-INS, 'the girl writes the letter with a pen'. The nominative form of 'pen' would be 'ruchk**a**'). Languages vary greatly with regard to their overt realisation of case, as well as the number and types of cases that are morphologically realised. Case is realised on the noun phrase. Depending on the language, it is either realised on the determiner, on the adjective and/or as a suffix on the noun itself. Roughly speaking, we can divide languages into two types with respect to the type of case realisation: languages with suffix case or synthetic case marking like Russian, Turkish or Finnish (see (1) and (2) for an example of Russian and Turkish, case morphology is in boldface), where case is mainly realised through inflectional suffixes and languages with a more periphrastic case system like German or Rumanian, (see (3) for an example of German, case-marked articles are in boldface. Note that there is no distinction between feminine nominative and accusative in German[1]), in which case is mainly realised through an auxiliary word, here the determiner.[2] Case is realized with suffixes in by far the most languages (Spencer, 2009).

Languages also vary with respect to the number of cases that are marked morphologically. German, for instance, only distinguishes four cases (nominative, accusative, dative and genitive), whereas Russian distinguishes six cases (the same, plus prepositional and instrumental; some authors would add vocative to this list) and Turkish distinguishes seven cases (the same as for German plus ablative, instrumental and locative). Hungarian has been claimed to have up to 18 cases (this is under debate: one could argue that some of these 'cases' are postpositions

38

instead of 'real cases' – a discussion of this would be beyond the aim of this chapter).

(1) Russian
   (a) korol' celuet korolev**u**
       king-NOM kisses queen-ACC[3]
   (b) korolev**a** celuet korol**ja**
       queen-NOM kisses king-ACC
(2) Turkish
   (a) **kral** kraliçe**yi** öptü
       king-NOM queen-ACC kisses
   (b) kraliçe kral**ı** öptü
       queen-NOM king-ACC kisses
(3) German
   (a) **der** König küsst **die** Königin
       the-NOM king kisses the-ACC queen
   (b) **die** Königin küsst **den** König
       the-NOM queen kisses the-ACC king
   (c) **die** Prinzessin hilft **dem** König
       the-NOM princes helps the-DAT king

In theoretical linguistics, a distinction is made between structural and lexical case assignment (see Chomsky, 1981). Structural case assignment is based on the structural position of a noun phrase. For instance, subject noun phrases are assigned nominative case by the finite verb of the sentence, and the object noun phrase of a transitive verb is assigned accusative case by the verb of the sentence. In example (3) this means that the finiteness of the verb 'küsst' (kisses) assigns nominative case to, e.g. 'der König' (the-NOM king) in (3a), and the verb 'küssen' (to kiss) assigns accusative case to the object 'den König' (the-ACC king) in (3b). Lexical case assignment (sometimes also called inherent case assignment[4]) on the other hand, depends on the lexical items themselves and is not predictable on the basis of the structural position of a noun phrase. For instance, in languages like German, Russian and Turkish, there are transitive verbs that assign dative case to their object noun phrases (instead of the structurally expected accusative). 'To help' can serve as an example of such a verb for all three languages, see also (3c), where 'hilft' assigns dative case to its object 'dem König' (the-DAT king) instead of the structurally expected accusative case. These lexical cases have to be learned item by item, and although there is overlap, there is also variation between languages with respect to which verb assigns which case. This means that verbs that assign accusative case in one language to the direct object ('to hug', 'umarmen' in German) assign dative case in another language ('to hug', 'sarılmakın' in Turkish). This information is assumed to be part of the lexical entry of these verbs, which overrules structural case assignment.

Case in Acquisition and in Children with Specific Language Impairment

When case is acquired depends on the type of language that is being acquired. Unfortunately, there is not all that much information on the time course of case acquisition. Generally, case is acquired earliest in agglutinative languages like Turkish and Hungarian, then in Slavic and Baltic languages and later in languages with a periphrastic case system, like German (for an overview, see Eissenbeiss *et al.* [2009]). Data from Turkish children show first case oppositions at age 1;3 (Aksu-Koç & Ketrez, 2007; and see Topbaş, 1997), and for two Finnish children even at age 1;0 and 1;1 (Laalo, 2002). In Turkish children, the case system seems to be more or less completely in place before the age of 3 (Aksu-Koç & Slobin, 1985; Batman-Ratyosyan & Stromswold, 2001). Gagarina and Voeikova (2002) showed first case oppositions for Russian around age 1;9–2;2 (with some variations between children). Babyonyshev's data (1993) point in the same direction. She found very few mistakes in structural case marking in two children between age 1;6–2;0 and 2;1–2;7. These children, however, still made errors in lexical case, and it has even been argued that acquisition of the full system may take until the age of 6 (Polinsky, 2006). For German, Klampfer and Korecky-Kröll (2002) found the first case oppositions at age 2;3, whereas data from Tracy (1986) showed an even later acquisition. She found systematic differentiation of nominative and accusative case around the beginning of the third year, whereas dative marking occurred later, around 3;6 or later. Tracy too mentioned that (productive) case marking generally appears earlier in languages with suffix case marking, such as Turkish and Slavic languages. To support this observation, she referred to studies by Slobin (1982), Zakharova (1973) and Popova (1973).

Studies on case marking in (early) second language (L2) acquisition show a somewhat mixed pattern, which is likely partly due to the fact that they all differ with respect to (a) the type of bilingualism that is investigated (bilingual first language [L1] acquisition vs successive bilingualism or early L2) and (b) the combination of languages that is studied (with or without overt case marking and different types of case-marking systems). This makes it difficult to draw any strong conclusions on how problematic case marking in general is in early L2. One of the first studies was done by Meisel (1986), who studied dative case marking in German/French bilingual children and concluded that they acquire the German dative only slightly later than the accusative and at the same time as monolingual children. Schmitz (2006) showed, however, that dative case marking is problematic and is not yet completely acquired at age 5;0 in bilingual German/Romance (French or Italian) children. Note for these studies that German does have overt case marking on noun phrases, whereas French and Italian only mark certain pronouns, but not lexical noun phrases.

Examining language combinations in which both language systems have overt case marking, Schönenberger *et al.* (2013) demonstrate that Turkish learners of German (early L2) pattern with monolingual learners of German with respect to their use of both structural and lexical case (nominative, accusative and dative) in spontaneous speech production (see Rothweiler *et al.*'s [2010] bilingual control group as well). Structural case marking, here nominative, accusative and dative in double object constructions, was at ceiling, whereas lexical case, here dative after specific verbs and prepositions, still caused some problems. Their experimental data showed, however, somewhat more errors with structural dative case realisation in double object sentences by bilingual children (2;5- to 5-year-old, L1 Turkish, Russian or Polish) than by monolingual German-speaking children, although the monolingual children made many case errors on dative case as well. Note that all these languages have overt case marking on the noun phrase, with one crucial difference: German uses articles with case marking, whereas Polish, Turkish and Russian do not have articles, but case suffixes instead. For yet another combination, namely Russian which has overt case marking via suffixes (see (1)) and American English which has no case marking on noun phrases, only on pronouns, it has been shown that children develop a kind of two-case system (nominative-accusative) instead of the full Russian system (Bar-Shalom & Zaretsky, 2008; Polinsky, 2006). This variant of Russian has been called American Russian, and from these studies it remains unclear how the L1 input of these children should be characterised. Is it Russian, is it Russian from L1 Russian speakers with language attrition? In any case, this short summary makes it clear that it is difficult to draw any strong conclusions on case marking in early L2 acquisition. Case marking may be a vulnerable domain here, but more data are definitely needed from carefully controlled populations in order to use case marking as a clinical marker in bilingual SLI.

The production of case marking has been suggested to be vulnerable in SLI (Bishop, 1994; Clahsen, 1991; Loeb & Leonard, 1991; Rice, 2000; Wexler *et al.*, 1998). Most research on case production in SLI, however, has been done on English, a language with a relatively impoverished case system (English, like Dutch and Romance languages, only shows case distinctions on pronouns: nominative versus objective case: I vs me, he vs him, etc., hence the focus of this research was on the realisation of subject pronouns). In a study on German, Clahsen (1991) found an overuse of nominative in accusative and dative case contexts (and to a lesser extent also errors in the other direction), indicating that case may be a vulnerable domain in SLI (see, however, Eissenbeiss *et al.* [2006] for other results on

German). For languages with a richer morphology, it has been claimed that nominal inflection is affected in SLI, suggesting that case too may be problematic (on Italian, Hebrew, Hungarian, Serbo-Croatian and Greek, see Leonard [1998] for an overview).[5] For instance, Italian children with SLI very frequently omit articles and clitics compared to TD children with the same mean length of utterance (MLU) (Leonard et al., 1992; Sabbadini et al., 1987; and see Prévost [Chapter 3, this volume] on clitic production). Hebrew children with SLI more often omit the accusative case marker 'et' in obligatory contexts than TD children (see Dromi et al., 1993; Rom & Leonard, 1990). Also, Mastropavlou and Marinis (2002) showed that Greek children with SLI have more problems with case marking, specifically with genitive case marking on definite articles, than with gender and number marking. They argue that this performance corresponds to article use of a later stage of language in TD children, which suggests a delay in the acquisition of case.

There is even less research on case marking in bilingual children with SLI, but first results on a study by Rothweiler et al. (2010; see de Jong et al. [2010] for similar results) indicate that in Turkish–German bilingual children with SLI, the realisation of accusative and dative case in their L1 Turkish is impaired as compared to TD children, in that these children more often than TD children omit or substitute the case marking, which is remarkable considering the very early acquisition of case in Turkish TD children (see above).

This chapter describes a newly developed case elicitation task, which can be used with young children (approximately from age 3–4 onwards up to age 8–9) to examine the production of case morphology in typologically different languages such as German, Russian, Polish, Hebrew, Greek, Albanian, Turkish and Serbian. The main aim of the task is to elicit case-marked noun phrases with different cases in both transitive and double object constructions. This means that for a language like German case marking on the determiner is examined (see (3)), whereas for languages like Russian or Turkish (see (1) and (2)) the realisation of case suffixes directly attached to the noun is examined. The task focuses on nominative, accusative and dative case, and makes it possible to compare structural versus lexical case in languages in which this is relevant. Ablative is included for languages with a richer case morphology (e.g. Turkish). A slightly different variant of the task is included to enable testing of genitive possessive case marking.

Task Design

In order to get a good impression of children's ability to produce different types of case morphology, as well as different cases, a task was needed with which we could both control the target production of the child and enable language production that is as non-imitative as possible.

Sentence repetition was therefore not an option, although of course, during a sentence repetition task, error patterns can provide relevant insight into how problematic specific instances of case morphology are for a child (see Marinis & Armon-Lotem, this volume). However, for correctly repeated utterances, one can never be sure that the child can actually produce the structure himself/herself as well. For this, additional information from a relatively free production task is needed. A regular picture description task was not an option either, since this normally leaves too much room for fantasy, and this would lead to too many non-targeted descriptions (with different verbs, nouns, etc.). Hence, the types of case and case morphology we are interested in would not be optimally controlled for since these are either dependent on specific verbs and/or on specific gender and declination classes of nouns. For these reasons, case morphology is here elicited within a contrastive elicitation task using picture description with which we can control for specific types of cases and have the child realise (complete) sentences more or less on his/her own.

A description of the pictures used in this task elicits case marking on the subject, direct and indirect object in order to elicit nominative, accusative and dative/genitive case and some language-specific structures that exemplify other cases, e.g. genitive possessive and ablative. The task consist of two parts. The first part is designed to elicit transitive and ditransitive sentences with the aforementioned cases, and the second part is designed to elicit noun phrases with possessive (and hence genitive) case.

The task consists of two warm-up items for the first part and a maximum of 60 experimental items (depending on which conditions are relevant for the language). Language-specific adaptations so far have been made for Albanian, Croatian, German, Greek, Hebrew, Hindi, Palestinian Arabic, Polish, Russian, Serbian and Turkish. There are items for six different verbs[6] that can be used to elicit subjects and accusative direct objects (for which the five that work best are selected for an individual language) and five different ditransitive verbs to elicit accusative direct objects as well as dative indirect objects. Furthermore, for language-specific purposes, there are items with six different verbs that can be used to elicit dative objects with transitive verbs (relevant for instance for German, Russian, Turkish and Polish), and there are items with five different verbs that can elicit ablative case (relevant for instance for Turkish). Finally, six different items were created for examining genitive-possessive constructions; one of those can be used as a warm-up item for this part of the task. All subjects and direct objects in transitive sentences are animate, and half of the subjects and direct objects in the transitive sentences (this holds for accusative- and dative-assigning verbs) are feminine and the other half are masculine. Direct objects in double object constructions are inanimate (their gender depends on the language being tested, and has not been controlled for systematically), the indirect objects are all masculine persons. We tried to use noun phrases that are highly familiar to children. They are typical professions and figures from fairy tales (e.g. king, queen, princess, cook, doctor and police officer). The items are provided in (4) through (7).

(4) Warm-up items for the first part:
    (a) The grandfather washes the boy and the grandmother washes the girl.
    (b) The man writes the woman a letter and the boy writes the girl a postcard.

(5) Language-independent conditions:
Items for subject-verb-object (SVO) sentences with transitive verbs, a NOM subject and an ACC object.
    (a) The policeman pushes the witch and the princess pushes the knight.
    (b) The king pulls the woman and the witch pulls the policeman.
    (c) The magician hugs the fairy and the woman hugs the king.
    (d) The cook (masc) kisses the queen and the fairy kisses the magician.
    (e) The doctor (masc) tickles the nurse and the queen tickles the cook (masc).
    (f) The knight catches the princess and the nurse catches the doctor (masc).

Items for subject-verb-object-object (SVOO) sentences with ditransitive verbs, a NOM subject, a DAT/GEN indirect object and an ACC direct object.
    (a) The cook (masc) gives the king the spoon and the cook gives the knight the fork.
    (b) The captain shows the policeman the ring and the captain shows the fireman the watch.
    (c) The clown sends the magician the letter and the clown sends the hunter the booklet.
    (d) The king gives the cook the hat/the king gives the doctor the watch.
    (e) The footballer shows the referee the ball and the footballer shows the goalkeeper the prize cup.

(6) Language-specific conditions:
Items for SVO sentences with transitive verbs, a NOM subject and a DAT object (depending on the language: items (a)–(f) work for German for instance, but this has to be established per language).
    (a) The knight thanks the queen/the princess thanks the king.
    (b) The king congratulates the princess/the fairy congratulates the clown.
    (c) The clown waves at the fairy/the nurse waves at the policeman.
    (d) The policeman helps the nurse/the witch helps the cook.

(e) The cook (masc) follows the dancer (fem)/the queen follows the knight.

(f) The cook looks at the dancer and the queen looks at the soldier.

Items for SVO sentences with transitive verbs, a NOM subject and an ABL object (depending on the language; these items work for Turkish for instance, but this has to be established per language).

(a) The hunter escaped from the cook and the cook escaped from the police.

(b) The rabbit gets out from the hat and the hedgehog gets out from the box.

(c) The princess came from the castle and the captain came from the boat.

(d) The king ate from the fish and the queen ate from the dessert.

(e) The policeman looks down from the window and the clown looks down from the balcony.

(7) Language-specific conditions second part:
Items for noun phrases with a GEN possessor.

(a) This is John's mask and this is Mary's mask.

(b) This is John's hat and this is Mary's hat.

(c) This is John's bag and this is Mary's bag.

(d) This is John's watch and this is Mary's watch.

(e) These are John's glasses and these are Mary's glasses.

(f) This is John's T-shirt and this is Mary's T-shirt.

Description of the Task Procedure

First part

This is a picture description task that consists of contrasting pictures. For this task, a set of pictures is needed (either presented via PowerPoint on a notebook or printed out on DIN A4 pages), an audio recording device and a scoring form with all items and instructions. The task is administered on a one-to-one basis. The whole session has to be recorded for later transcription, scoring and data analysis. During testing, only notes are made of the procedure (regarding repetitions, use of priming). There are no restrictions to the order in which the two (or more) languages of a child are tested when a child acquires two case-marking languages. It is, however, suggested not to test both languages on the same day, but with a couple of days in between. Furthermore, in order to be able to compare acquisition in both languages within the same developmental stage, ideally there should not be more than two weeks in between testing the two languages.

In the task, two contrasting pictures are presented next to each other for each item. An example of the pictures can be seen in Figure 2.1. Ideally,

Figure 2.1 An example of the contrastive elicitation task for case morphology. Target: The cook is kissing the queen and the fairy is kissing the wizard

the children produce the sentences for both pictures themselves, in order to elicit most data points. The child is told that this is a little game in which he/she is asked to tell the experimenter what is happening exactly on the pictures ('can you tell me exactly who is doing what to whom?'). There are two practice items, one with the verb 'washing' and one with 'writing' (see above), which are used to familiarise the child with the task. These should be used to get the child to produce as much as possible of the sentence contents himself/herself. The practice items should be repeated if necessary. For all items, it is crucial that the verb is cued. The most important reason for this is that the pictures may be described with alternative verbs, which may elicit a different argument structure and/or different case morphology. The verb has to be cued in a consistent way. Also, cueing of the verb should not give away case morphology, so ideally, the verb is cued as a bare infinitive, or nominalised, or in any alternative form in the language that is being tested that does not provide information about the argument structure or the case morphology that the verb assigns. To avoid naming problems with the nouns, these can be cued as well, especially when they first occur. Preferably, the nouns are named together with the child in the indefinite nominative form, since this enhances the chance of descriptions with definite nouns. Moreover, this enables the child to get acquainted with the persons/objects on the pictures. Especially with L2 learners, not all relevant vocabulary may be acquired yet. Therefore, naming the nouns together before realising the full picture description makes this part of the task easier for the child.

The experimenter introduces each item with a language-specific version of the following: 'Look what we see here, this is about "nominalised V" (e.g. kissing), Can you tell me what that is? And that? (repeat to have the child name all nouns). Yes, this is a cook, that's a queen, that's a fairy and that's a wizard. Could you tell me what happens here exactly?'. The expected response on this item would be something like: the cook is kissing the queen and the fairy is kissing the wizard.

In case the children do not describe the first picture spontaneously themselves, the first option would be to provide the subject of the picture to the child, like this: 'here the cook....?', so that the child can complete the sentence (...is kissing the queen), and one can follow up with: 'yes, and here...?'. Ideally, this is done for the practice items only, and the regular items are tested without any help.

If this still does not make the child describe the sentence independently, the first sentence can be given as a prime. The way to do this would be to say: 'so here, the policeman is kissing the witch, and here...?'. If this is necessary, again first this should be tried with the practice items only and then one should move on to the test items without priming, if possible. If this does not work either, as a last resort, because data points will be lost this way and data becomes less comparable between children and languages, the whole task can be done with priming the first conjunct. This way for each condition only 5 sentences instead of 10 will be realised by the child himself/herself. This is of course preferred over no data at all and may especially be a useful alternative with younger children.

If one item doesn't work immediately, but the child does understand the task and produces other items, one can move on to the next item, and repeat the 'missed items' at the end. It is important to make notes of these changes, and also it should be marked on the score sheet whether an item was repeated and whether priming with the subject or of the complete first sentence part was necessary.

Second part: Possessives

Testing of possessives starts with one picture that includes John and Mary (who should obviously get language-specific easy and regular names consisting of one or two syllables which can be clearly marked for genitive, i.e. the genitive marking and the last consonant of the names should not assimilate). The picture shows a cupboard with their possessions (see Figure 2.2). This is to introduce the child to the two subjects, as well as to their possessions. It is important that the child pays enough attention to this picture. All possessions (shirt, watch, hat, mask, glasses, bag) on this introductory picture should be named together with the child. Preferably, the child names all the objects himself/herself. It should be ensured that the child knows which item belongs to whom without using the genitive yet. Instead one could say 'look here is the cupboard with stuff that belongs to John, look what he has: a t-shirt, a mask, a watch, etc... so these things belong to John'. Then the test starts with one of the six items as a practice item, in German the item 'maske' (mask) is used for this, but one can take

Figure 2.2 Introductory picture for the elicitation of genitive possessives and one example picture of 'this is Mary's shirt and this is John's shirt'

any item. The practice item can again be primed with the first possessor–possessed pair if necessary, but after that this should be avoided. The items can be cued with 'what have we got here…?' or 'look here, this is…? …and this is?'.

Coding the Results

After running the task, all utterances of the child should be transcribed carefully. What counts as a correct or an incorrect response partly depends on the language that is being tested; additionally, the types of errors that will and can be made will depend on the type of language(s) being acquired. For instance, in a periphrastic language like German it may be 'easier' for the child to simply omit the case marking, by leaving out the determiner, whereas in agglutinative languages the omission of the morphological marker might lead to non-words (e.g. omitting the case marking from the Russian word 'devocka', girl-NOM, would lead to *devock, a non-word[7]) and hence substitutions are more likely. For the following part, this has to be kept in mind. Language-specific error coding will be needed for every new language for which the task is adapted. The coding principles described here are developed on the basis of two smaller pilot studies with German monolingual and Russian–Dutch bilingual children and discussions with task developers from other languages.

Coding is done in four stages per item. The first step is to check whether an analysable utterance has been realised. In this stage, irrelevant utterances (not describing the picture in any relevant way) and null responses are filtered out. Of course, it is relevant to note how many of these responses occur per condition, since they might indicate problems with this specific condition. An example of a response from the German task (the response comes from a Russian–German bilingual child) that could be analysed as 'irrelevant' can be found in (8).

(8) Target: der Kapitän zeigt dem Feuerwehrmann die Uhr
the-NOM captain shows the-DAT fireman the-ACC watch
Response: Feuerwehr Feuerwehr zu Kapitän gehen
Fire brigade fire brigade to captain go-INF

In the second stage, it needs to be established whether the verb and the noun phrases that have been produced are similar enough to the target. Note that it is not the aim of the task to test lexical access; however, changes in the verb or noun phrase may affect the case morphology that was intended and hence affect comparability between items. For the verb being 'similar enough to the target' means: a verb with the same argument structure and the same case-assigning properties. For the nouns, this would mean a noun with the same gender, and depending on the language, a noun that is definite and/or in the same declination class as the noun that was elicited. For instance, if in German, instead of the dative-assigning verb 'danken' (to thank) the child realises 'grüßen' (to greet), the correct case assigned to the object should be accusative instead. Hence, this verb is not similar to the target verb with respect to the case it assigns. The verb of course would be a relatively adequate description of the picture, which shows how important cueing the verb is. Should a child in German use a verb like 'streicheln' (to pet/caress) instead of 'kitzeln' (to tickle), we can count this as similar enough to the target verb (even though technically it doesn't describe the picture perfectly), since the argument structure of the verb 'streicheln' is the same as for 'kitzeln' and both verbs assign structural accusative case. To give another example in Russian, should the child use a noun from a different declination class than the one intended, of course the case morphology changes, meaning that this too leads to a different noun than the target noun phrase.

However, if a noun is realised which is different from the target noun, but still in the same declination class, we can treat it as if it were a target noun. It is important to realise that the aim of the task is not to examine vocabulary, but case morphology; hence, any lexical errors that do not affect case morphology can be ignored. Finally, in German, if an indefinite noun is used for one of the animate noun phrases, it becomes very hard to distinguish nominative and accusative case marking. For feminine nouns, nominative and accusative would be the same, and for masculine nouns it would be 'ein' versus 'einen', whereas the latter in colloquial speech is often pronounced with a slightly prolonged 'n'. Since this is hard to distinguish, responses like these cannot be counted as (in)correct and should be treated separately from the definite nouns. In this second stage too, full noun phrases are separated from pronouns. Should a child realise pronouns, these need to be analysed separately.

The third step is to establish whether these non-target and target-like utterances are grammatically correct or not. This way, the total amount of correct forms for nominative, accusative and other cases can be established, which is the first important result from the task. Note that non-target utterances can still be analysed here; for instance, if as in the example mentioned before an accusative-assigning verb is used instead of a dative-assigning verb, and the noun phrase is case-marked accordingly, then it would count as a correct accusative case, just adding to the number of possible accusative 'items'. The same holds for the example given for Russian; if a noun from a different declination class was used, say 'mužina' (man-NOM) instead of 'kapitan' (captain-NOM), we can still analyse whether case was realised correctly or not, and add it to the score of – in this example – the number of nominative realised correctly. Pronouns (personal pronouns, demonstratives) should be treated separately in this step, since case marking on these words is different from case marking on nouns in many languages. Should case marking on pronouns be of specific interest, then this can be elicited using the subject–verb agreement task (de Jong, this volume).

The final step would be to analyse the types of errors that have been made on the ungrammatical utterances. This has to be done per syntactic function. This means, for all subjects, an analysis is made of which types of errors are made. The same has to be done for accusative and dative objects in single and double object constructions, for ablative objects as well as for genitive possessors. For each syntactic position, it is analysed whether (a) the argument is realised at all, (b) whether there is a case marker or not, (c) what case is realised and (d) whether other errors are made that are relevant to case marking (gender, number or declination class errors for instance). Examples of each error type are given in (9).

(9) (a) argument omission
        Target: der König schenkt dem Arzt die Uhr
        The-NOM king gives the-DAT doctor the-ACC watch
        Response: der König... schenkt der Arzt..dem Arzt
        The-NOM king... gives the-NOM doctor the-DAT doctor
        (self-correction)
     (b) case-marking omission
        Target: Der Koch folgt der Ballerina/Tänzerin
        The-NOM cook follows the-DAT dancer (fem)
        Response: Der Koch folgt Ballerina
        The-NOM cook follows dancer (fem)
     (c) case-marking substitution
        Target: Der Clown schickt dem Zauberer einen Brief
        The-NOM clown sends the-DAT magician a-ACC letter
        Response: Der Clown schickt den Zauberer einen Brief
        The-NOM clown sends the-ACC a-ACC letter
     (d) other error (here: gender marking)
        Target: der König zieht die Frau

The-NOM/MASC king pulls the-ACC woman
Response: das König zieht die Frau
The-NOM/NEU pulls the-ACC woman

This will result in the total number of argument omissions, as well as the number of case-marking omissions, case substitutions and other errors. Depending on the language, error categories may be added. As a consequence, the contents of the category 'other errors' may differ across languages as well.

First Pilot Data and Conclusion

First pilot data from eight monolingual German children (age 5;7–9;3) and 21 bilingual Russian–Dutch children (age 4;0–6;3, all without language impairment) living in the Netherlands indicated that the task can be performed with children from these different age groups and that it leads to interpretable results.

The German children performed very well on nominative subjects, and on accusative direct objects, independent of the sentence structure (almost at ceiling level). Dative objects, both in transitive and ditransitive sentences, caused some more problems, resulting from overuse of accusative objects in dative contexts, especially but not exclusively so for masculine noun phrases (realising, e.g. 'den König', the-ACC king, instead of 'dem König', the-DAT king). These results suggest that for testing bilingual children and children with SLI, more data are needed for conclusive group comparisons.

A first analysis of the data from the Russian–Dutch bilingual children showed that these children realised more non-target-like structures which were not necessarily ungrammatical. This again supports the procedure of coding the results in more stages, as suggested above. Many of these non-target-like structures resulted from vocabulary problems: the children did not know the exact word for the referent of a noun phrase in Russian (while this is their L1, since living in the Netherlands, Dutch was the dominant language for these children). When children show these naming problems, it is suggested that more time is spent naming the nouns on the pictures together, to avoid these issues. Also, instead of using the target nouns (like king, cook, knight, etc.), one could resort to using more generic nouns instead (like man, guy or something similar), as long as the same declination class/gender is used. The data of the Russian–Dutch children also showed some interesting effects. The children made mistakes in case morphology, both in accusative and in dative case. Lexical dative case seemed to be a bit more problematic though. The older the children were, the less errors they seemed to make and children with two Russian parents seemed to make fewer errors than children with only one Russian parent. These results of course have to be interpreted carefully. However, they show that the case elicitation task can indeed elicit case errors and furthermore they show how important awareness of the goal of the task is, that is, one should concentrate on the case morphology, and not on vocabulary issues.

Acknowledgements

I would like to thank the COST Action IS0804, and all collaborators who helped discuss and further develop and/or translate the case task into several different languages: Theo Marinis, Jan de Jong, Sonja Eissenbeiss, Seyhun Topbaş, Ozlem Cangokce Yasar, Bibi Janssen, Naama Friedmann and Alexandra Peroviç. The artist, Sofia Miliopoulos, for drawing the pictures and of course, the audience of several COST meetings for helpful suggestions and feedback.

Notes

(1) Note that this is a slight simplification, since both adjectives and nouns themselves can also have a case-marking suffix in German, e.g. der König umarmt **den** kleine**n** Junge**n** (the-NOM king hugs the-ACC small-ACC boy-ACC). The task we present here focuses on simple noun phrases without adjectives though, which (with one exception) have case marking on the determiner in German only. Of course, for a more thorough analysis of case-marking abilities in German (or any language for that matter), a more detailed task would be needed. Since the main purpose was to enable testing for case marking cross-linguistically, we kept the task as simple as possible to avoid too many language specifics.

(2) Note that there are more possible classifications here; we could also classify in, for instance, ergative vs accusative languages. The focus here is on the overt realisation though, since this is relevant for the purpose of the task described here. For more information on case types, variations, etc., see the Oxford Handbook of Case (Malchukov & Spencer, 2009).

(3) NOM refers to nominative, ACC to accusative, DAT to dative, GEN to genitive and ABL to ablative case in this chapter.

(4) Chomsky (1995) uses the term *inherent* case assignment; other authors, however, use the term *lexical* case assignment for the same phenomenon, since information about this type of case assignment is assumed to be specified in the lexical information of a verb. For the latter reason, I prefer this term; moreover, the term *inherent case* is also used for a third type of case assignment, namely for the case of adjuncts, which does not depend on a case-assigning category or on syntactic configuration (following Dürscheid, 1999).

(5) Note that these studies didn't necessarily focus on case morphology.

(6) The criteria for selecting these verbs were the following: the verbs needed to be depictable, morphologically simple, child-friendly (hence: no killing, hitting, shooting, etc.), culturally acceptable, translatable in many languages and most importantly they should assign the same case in different languages. For this reason, it was not possible to take other relevant factors like age of acquisition or frequency into account, since we would have ended up with not enough verbs.

(7) Note that this does not hold for all declension classes, since the nominative and accusative are the bare stem in some declension classes in Russian.

References

Aksu-Koç, A. and Slobin, I.D. (1985) The acquisition of Turkish. In I.D. Slobin (ed.) *The Cross-Linguistic Study of Child Language* (pp. 839–878). Mahwah, NJ: Erlbaum.

Babyonyshev, M. (1993) The acquisition of Russian case. In C. Philips (ed.) *Papers on Case and Agreement II* (MIT Working Papers in Linguistics 19) (pp. 1–44). Cambridge, MA: MIT Press.

Bar-Shalom, E.G. and Zaretsky, E. (2008) Selective attrition in Russian-English bilingual children: Preservation of grammatical aspect. *International Journal of Bilingualism* 12 (4), 281–302.

Batman-Ratyosyan, N. and Stromswold, K. (2001) Early bare stems in an agglutinative language. In H.-J. Do, L. Domínguez and A. Johansen (eds) *Proceedings of the 25th Annual Boston University Conference on Language Development* (pp. 102–113). Sommerville, MA: Cascadilla Press.

Bishop, D. (1994) Grammatical errors in specific language impairment: Competence or performance limitations? *Applied Psycholinguistics* 15 (4), 507–550.

Chomsky, N. (1981) *Lectures on Government and Binding.* Dordrecht: Foris Publications.

Chomsky, N. (1995) *The Minimalist Program.* Cambridge, MA: MIT Press.

Clahsen, H. (1991) *Child Language and Developmental Dysphasia. Linguistic Studies of the Acquisition of German.* Amsterdam: Benjamins.

de Jong, J., Çavus, N. and Baker, A. (2010) Language impairment in Turkish-Dutch bilingual children. In S. Topbaş and M. Yavas (eds) *Communication Disorders in Turkish* (pp. 288–300). Bristol: Multilingual Matters.

Dromi, E., Leonard, L.B. and Shteiman, M. (1993) The grammatical morphology of Hebrew-speaking children with specific language impairment: Some competing hypotheses. *Journal of Speech Language and Hearing Research* 36 (4), 760–771.

Dürscheid, C. (1999) *Die verbalen Kasus des Deutschen: Untersuchungen zur Syntax, Semantik und Perspektive.* Berlin: De Gruyter.

Eisenbeiss, S., Narasimhan, B. and Voeikova, M. (2009) The acquisition of case. In A. Malchukov and A. Spencer (eds) *The Oxford Handbook of Case* (pp. 369–383). Oxford: Oxford University Press.

Gagarina, N. and Voeikova, M. (2002) Acquisition of case and number in Russian. In U. Stephany and M.D. Voeikova (eds) *Development of Nominal Inflection in First Language Acquisition. A Cross-linguistic Perspective* (pp. 179–216). Den Haag: Mouton de Gruyter.

Klampfer, S. and Korecky-Kröll, K. (2002) Nouns and verbs at the transition from pre- to protomorphology: A longitudinal case study on Austrian German. In M.D. Voeikova and W.U. Dressler (eds) *Pre- and Protomorphology: Early Phases of Morphological Development in Nouns and Verbs* (pp. 61–74). Munich: Lincom.

Leonard, L.B. (1998) *Children with Specific Language Impairment.* Cambridge, MA: MIT Press.

Loeb, D.F. and Leonard, L.B. (1991) Subject case marking and verb morphology in normally developing and specifically language-impaired children. *Journal of Speech and Hearing Research* 34 (2), 340–346.

Malchukov, A. and Spencer, A. (2009) *The Oxford Handbook of Case.* Oxford: Oxford University Press.

Mastropavlou, M. and Marinis, T. (2002, June) Definite articles and case marking in the speech of Greek normally developing children and children with SLI. Poster session presented at the EuroConference on the Syntax of Normal and Impaired Language, Corinth, Greece.

Polinsky, M. (2006) Acquisition of Russian: Uninterrupted and incomplete scenarios. *Glossos* No. 8. See http://www.seelrc.org/glossos/ issues/8/polinsky.pdf (accessed 15 December 2014).

Popova, M.I. (1973) Grammatical elements in the speech of preschool children. In C.A. Ferguson and D.I. Slobin (eds) *Studies of Child Language Development* (pp. 269–280). New York: Holt, Rinehart and Winston.

Rice, M.L. (2000) Grammatical symptoms of specific language impairment. In D.V.M. Bishop and L.B. Leonard (eds) *Speech and Language Impairments in Children: Causes, Characteristics, Intervention and Outcome* (pp. 17–34). Hove: Psychology Press.

Rom, A. and Leonard, L.B. (1990) Interpreting deficits in grammatical morphology in specifically language impaired children: Preliminary evidence from Hebrew. *Clinical Linguistics and Phonetics* 4 (2), 93–105.

Rothweiler, M., Chilla, S. and Babur, E. (2010) Specific language impairment in Turkish: Evidence from case morphology in Turkish–German successive bilinguals. *Clinical Linguistics and Phonetics* 24 (7), 540–555.

Sabbadini, L., Volterra, V., Leonard, L.B. and Campagnoli, M.G. (1987) Bambini con disturb specific del linguaggio: aspetti morpfologici. *Giornale di Neuropsichiatria in Età Evolutiva* 7, 213–232.

Schmitz, K. (2006) Indirect objects and dative case in monolingual German and bilingual German/Romance language acquisition. In D. Hole, A. Meininger and W. Abraham (eds) *Datives and Other Cases* (pp. 239–268). Amsterdam: John Benjamins.

Schönenberger, M., Sterner, F. and Rothweiler, M. (2013) The acquisition of case in child L1 and child L2 German. In S. Stavrakaki, M. Lalioti and P. Konstantinopoulou (eds) *Advances in Language Acquisition* (pp. 191–199). Cambridge: Cambridge Scholars Publishing.

Slobin, D.I. (1982) Universal and particular in the acquisition of language. In E. Wanner and L. Gleitman (eds) *Language Acquisition: The State of the Art* (pp. 128–170). Cambridge: Cambridge University Press.

Spencer, A. (2009) Case as a morphological phenomenon. In A. Malchukov and A. Spencer (eds) *The Oxford Handbook of Case* (pp. 185–199). Oxford: Oxford University Press.

Topbaş, S. (1997) Phonological acquisition of Turkish children: Implications for phonological disorders. *European Journal of Disorders of Communication* 32 (4), 377–396.

Tracy, R. (1986) The acquisition of case morphology in German. *Linguistics* 24 (1), 47–78.

Wexler, K., Schaeffer, J. and Bol, G. (2004). Verbal syntax and morphology in Dutch normal and SLI children: How developmental data can play an important role in morphological theory. *Syntax* 7 (2), 148–198.

Wexler, K., Schütze, C. and Rice, M. (1998) Subject case in children with SLI and unaffected controls: Evidence for the Agr/Tns omission model. *Language Acquisition* 7 (2–4), 317–344.

Zakharova, A.V. (1973) Acquisition of forms of grammatical case by preschool children. In C.A. Ferguson and D.I. Slobin (eds) *Studies of Child Language Development* (pp. 281–292). New York: Holt, Rinehart and Winston.

3 Elicited Production of Object Clitics

Philippe Prévost

What are Object Clitics?

Object clitics are pronominal elements that stand for the object of a verb. They are found in a variety of languages such as Albanian, Greek (Standard Greek and Cypriot Greek), Romance languages (e.g. Catalan, French, Italian, European Portuguese, Romanian and Spanish), Slavic languages (e.g. Croatian, Polish and Serbian) and Creole languages (e.g. Cape Verdean), as can be seen in (1).[1]

(1)	(a)	Burri lyen **shtepine**.	→	Burri **e** lyen.	Albanian
	(b)	Omi pinta **kasa**.	→	Omi pinta-**l**.	Cape Verdean
	(c)	L'home pinta **la casa**.	→	L'home **la** pinta.	Catalan
	(d)	Čovjek boja **kuću**.	→	Čovjek **je** boja.	Croatian
	(e)	L'homme peint **la maison**.	→	L'homme **la** peint.	French
	(f)	O andras vafi **to spiti**.	→	O andras **to** vafi.	Standard Greek
	(g)	O andras vafi **to spiti**.	→	O andras vafi **to**.	Cypriot Greek
	(h)	L'uomo dipinge **la casa**.	→	L'uomo **la** dipinge.	Italian
	(i)	Mezczyzna maluje **dom**.	→	Mezczyzna maluje **go**.	Polish
	(j)	O homem pintou **a casa**.	→	O homem pintou-**a**.	Portuguese (Europ.)
	(k)	Omul vopseşte **casa**.	→	Omul **o** vopseşte.	Romanian
	(l)	Čovek boji **kuću**.	→	Čovek **je** boji.	Serbian
	(m)	El hombre pinta **la casa**.	→	El hombre **la** pinta.	Spanish

'The man is painting the house'→'The man is painting it'.

Pronominal elements in general, and object clitics in particular, are used in order to refer to an element present in the discursive context (e.g. Question: Where did you buy this book? Answer: I bought it at the store across the street) or in the immediate environment – in this case the referent of the pronoun is obvious, thus using a noun is not necessary (e.g. someone holding a dirty shirt and asking: Should I wash it?). Object clitics can be marked for person, gender, number and case. In this chapter, I will only deal with third person singular object clitics in accusative case. As shown in Table 3.1, the form of object clitics may vary, not only according to gender, but also according to the sounds with which they co-occur in the

Table 3.1 Examples of third person singular object clitics in various languages

Language	Gender distinction			No gender distinction
	Feminine	Masculine	Neuter	
Albanian	–	–	–	e
Catalan	la/l'	el/l'/lo	–	–
Cape Verdean	–	–	–	l
Croatian	je/ju	ga	ga	–
French	la/l'	le/l'	–	–
Cypriot Greek	ton	tin	to	–
Standard Greek	ton	tin	to	–
Italian	lo/l'	la/l'	–	–
Polish	ją	go	je	–
European Portuguese	o	a	–	–
Romanian	o	il, l	–	–
Serbian	je	ga	ga	–
Spanish	la/le	lo/le	lo	–

sentence. In particular, when the following word, typically the inflected verb, starts with a vowel sound, the object clitic may appear in an elided form, as in Catalan, French and Italian (see the example from French *La fille l'arrose* 'The girl is splashing him/her').

Object clitics have properties that distinguish them from other pronouns, in particular strong (or tonic) pronouns (see Kayne [1975] for an early discussion of clitic properties). Specifically, clitics cannot receive contrastive stress (see (2)), they cannot appear on their own, for example as the sole answer to a question (see (3)) and they cannot be coordinated (see (4)), in contrast to strong pronouns; instead, object clitics remain unstressed and they need to be attached to a host, for instance the inflected verb

(2)	(a)	*L'homme **LA**	peint.			French
		the man her+CL	paints			
	(b)	L'HOMME / LUI	peint	la	maison.	
		the man him+STR	paints	the	house.	
		'THE MAN / HE	is	painting	the house'.	
(3)	(a)	*L'homme peint	la	maison	et **le.**	French
		the man paints	the	house	and it+CL	
	(b)	L'homme et elle	peignent	la	maison.	
		the man and she+STR	paint		the house	
		'The man and she are painting the house'.				
(4)		Qui as- tu rencontré? ***Le** / Lui / Alexandre.				French
		whom have you met him+CL / him+STR / Alexandre				
		'Whom did you meet? Him / Alexander'.				

Another particularity of object clitics is that in many cases they do not appear in the position typically reserved for objects in the language. For instance, in many Romance languages, where the most common word order is subject–verb–object, object clitics appear in front of the verb (proclisis), rather than after it (enclisis). This is particularly true when the verb is inflected, as shown in the examples from Catalan, French, Italian, Romanian and Spanish in (1).[2] In other languages, such as Cypriot Greek and European Portuguese, object clitics may appear in different positions. Preverbal positioning is required in certain contexts, such as wh-questions and embedded clauses with an overt complementiser, as shown in the examples from European Portuguese in (5). In other cases, such as main declarative clauses, object clitics appear after the inflected verb, as in (1g) and (1j).

(5) (a) Quem a   pintou? / *Quem pintou-a?
        who it+CL   paint
        'Who paints it?'
    (b) Eu disse que o   homem a   pintou. / *Eu disse que o homem pintou-a.
        I said that the man   it+CL painted
        'I said that the man paints it'.

In Slavic languages, such as Croatian and Serbian, there is a strong second position effect for object clitics. In main clauses, the object clitic tends to appear in the second position, either literally, where the clitic may split a constituent, as in (6a), or right after the first constituent, as in (6b). Note that the examples in (6) are identical in Croatian and in Serbian.

(6) (a) Moja ga   mama kupa svaki dan.
        my   him+CL   mum bathes every day
    (b) Moja mama ga   kupa svaki dan.
        my   mum him+CL bathes every day
        'My mum bathes him every day'.

Finally, in Polish the object clitic can appear either preverbally or postverbally, although according to Tryzna (2009) there is a strong preference for postverbal placement, as in (1i). When the object clitic is preverbal, it cannot occupy the clause-initial position; rather, another element must occur before it, as in (7).

(7)   (a) Wczoraj go   widziałam.
            yesterday him+CL saw
            'I saw him yesterday'.
       (b) *Go widziałam wczoraj.   (from Tryzna, 2009: 15–16)

The Development of Object Clitics

Monolingual children

The development of object clitics has been observed to be delayed in typical language development (see Varlokosta *et al.* [submitted] for an extended review). Object clitics emerge later than subject and reflexive clitics, between the ages of 2;6 and 3;0, and object omission and use of a lexical noun phrase (NP) instead of the clitic are commonly found in contexts where pronominalisation is expected. For example, clitic omission up to at least 4 or 5 years of age has been reported for Catalan (Gavarró *et al.*, 2006; Wexler *et al.*, 2004), Cypriot Greek (Petinou & Terzi, 2002), European Portuguese (Costa & Lobo, 2006), French (Hamann *et al.*, 1996; Jakubowicz & Rigaut, 2000; Zesiger *et al.*, 2010), Italian (Schaeffer, 1997) and Spanish (Fujino & Sano, 2002).[3] In other languages, target-like use of object clitics is observed earlier, as in Standard Greek (Tsakali & Wexler, 2003), Romanian (Babyonyshev & Marin, 2006) and Serbo-Croatian (Ilic & Ud Deen, 2004). Another aspect of the development of object clitics is that although it is delayed, when object clitics are produced, they tend to appear in target-like positions. This is particularly the case for proclisis languages, such as most Romance languages, as seen above, and Standard Greek. In languages with enclisis, such as Portuguese and Cypriot Greek, overgeneralisation of the enclisis pattern is reported (Costa *et al.*, to appear; Duarte & Matos, 2000; Petinou & Terzi, 2002). Varlokosta *et al.* (submitted) have shown that by the age of 5 the production of object clitics is target-like in most of the 11 clitic languages that they looked at. The experimental protocol that was developed for that study was the starting point of the elicitation production task described in the final section of this chapter.

In children with specific language impairment (SLI), the developmental tendencies observed in typically developing (TD) children are exacerbated. Object clitics have been shown to be very slow to develop, and in many languages the avoidance of object clitics in oral production is considered a clinical marker of SLI. This has been argued for French (Chillier-Zesiger *et al.*, 2006; Grüter, 2005; Hamann, 2004; Hamann *et al.*, 2003; Jakubowicz *et al.*, 1998; Paradis, 2004; Tuller *et al.*, 2011), Italian (Bortolini *et al.*, 2006) and Spanish (Bedore & Leonard, 2001; Bosch & Serra, 1997; De la Mora *et al.*, 2004; Jacobson & Schwartz, 2002; but see Wexler *et al.*, 2004).

Bilingual children

Delay in the emergence of object clitics has been reported in bilingual development as well. This is the case in simultaneous bilingualism, as in Basque/Spanish (Ezeizabarrena, 1996; Larrañaga, 2000) and Swedish/French (Granfeldt & Schlyter, 2004), as well as in successive bilingualism, with an age of onset over 4 years, for instance second language (L2) French

(Haiden, 2011; White, 1996) and L2 Greek (Chondrogianni, 2008; Tsimpli & Mastropavlou, 2007). By and large, clitic placement is reported to be correct in L2 acquisition (but see Hulk [2000] on simultaneous Dutch/ French acquisition). It is also worth noting that in most of the studies on successive bilinguals, object clitics are absent in the children's first language (L1). An exception is Belletti and Hamann (2004), who reported on Italian/ French acquisition, and who argued that the presence of object clitics in the L1 may speed up their development in the L2 (see also Tsimpli [2010] on French/Greek bilinguals).

Several studies have also compared child L2 learners with children with SLI, reporting similar low production rates of object clitics when compared to age-matched monolinguals (Grüter, 2005; Paradis, 2004). However, the period during which object clitics are omitted by L2 children is of limited duration and is overcome faster than in children with SLI, as shown by Hamann and Belletti (2006) who reported data on L2 French (see also Chondrogianni [2008] where ceiling performances on object clitics are reported in L2 Greek).

Research on the production of object clitics by bilingual children with SLI is extremely limited, and the few studies available so far point to difficulties in this area as well (see Paradis et al. [2005/2006] and Stavrakaki et al. [2011] where low performance on object clitics in French are reported in English/French and Greek/French language combinations, respectively).

Developing a Task Eliciting the Production of Object Clitics

In order to further investigate the vulnerability of object clitics in bilingual SLI, an elicited production task was designed to be run in different languages with object clitics.

Design of the task

The protocol adopts the methodological framework commonly found in experimental studies examining the development of clitics via elicited production (following work by Jakubowicz et al. [1998]): each test item consists of a picture, as in (8), with either two characters or one character and an object, which the experimenter introduces to the child. The experimenter then asks the child a question about the action shown in the picture, making sure that the question contains (at least) an NP corresponding to the object of the verb. Such a stimulus question is meant to establish the object NP as a discourse topic. An object clitic referring back to this topic is thus expected in the answer provided by the child. In this context, use of the object NP mentioned in the lead-in question, while not ungrammatical, is infelicitous (see Avram, 1999; Babyonyshev

& Marin, 2004; Castilla, 2009; Costa & Lobo, 2006, 2007; Manika *et al.*, 2011; Pérez-Leroux *et al.*, 2008; Smith *et al.*, 2008; Tsakali & Wexler, 2004; Tuller *et al.*, 2011; Wexler *et al.*, 2004; Zesiger *et al.*, 2010).[4] This methodology is very straightforward, and children understand very easily that they are expected to describe the action shown in the picture.

(8)

Experimenter:	Regarde! Il y a une fille et il y a une girafe. Dis-moi: qu'est-ce que la fille fait avec la girafe?
	'Look! There is a girl and there is a giraffe. Tell me: what is the girl doing with the giraffe?'
Expected answer:	Elle la lave.
	she her+CL washes
	'She is washing it'.

The task contains 19 items: 2 warm-up items meant to familiarise the child with the task, 12 test items meant to elicit object clitics and 5 distractor items targeting reflexive clitics, as in (9). The test is therefore quite short and easy to administer. The pictures that are used are also particularly appealing to 5- and 6-year-old children, the targeted population. Finally, it is important to mention that all stimulus sentences are in the present tense, so as to limit the number of variables to be manipulated. The answers provided by the children are also expected to be in the present tense.

(9)

Experimenter:	Regarde! Voici une girafe. Dis-moi: Que fait la girafe?
	'Look! Here's a giraffe. Tell me: What is the giraffe doing?'
Expected answer:	Elle se lèche.
	she herself+CL licks
	'It's licking itself'.

The task was largely inspired by the object clitic elicitation probe that was developed within COST Action 33 (see Varlokosta *et al.*, submitted). In particular, most of the target verbs that had been decided upon and the pictures that had been drawn for that probe were maintained. The final list of verbs which was retained for the adaptation of the task in the different languages is in (10). These verbs are all transitive across these languages. Note that the distractor verbs formed a subgroup of the verbs targeted by the test items. For each verb, the test item version came before the distractor version in the actual task, so as not to influence the answers of the children. The test can be found in Appendix A.

(10) (a) Warm-up items: bite, throw
(b) Test items: comb, cut, draw, dry, eat, lick, paint, pull, push, wash, wake up, wet
(c) Distractor items: cut, hide, lick, wash, comb

Although the protocol was similar for all languages, adaptations were made in some cases in order to account for particular cross-linguistic differences. In particular, the verbs 'read' and 'tear' (along with accompanying pictures) were used in the Albanian version instead of the verbs 'comb' and 'draw'. Another version of the test was also developed in order to accommodate languages in which omission of an object clitic is grammatical in main clauses, such as European Portuguese. In this language, answering the question in (8) 'What is the girl doing with the giraffe?' with 'She is cleaning' (without the object) is perfectly fine. In this alternative version, the lead-in scenario differs from the stimulus described above in that it triggers the production of an object clitic in an (adverbial) embedded clause starting with 'because'. In European Portuguese, omission of the object clitic is ungrammatical in such constructions. The lead-in sentence follows the stimulus designed for the COST Action 33 object clitic elicitation task (based on Costa & Lobo, 2007), which was adapted to the pictures of the COST Action IS0804 task. An example of the stimulus leading to the because-clause and corresponding to the picture in (8) is given in (11). Note that in European Portuguese, the object clitic appears before the verb in the because-clause, similarly to what we saw in (5b).

(11) Experimenter: The girl is washing the giraffe, and the giraffe is clean. Why is the giraffe clean? The giraffe is clean because the girl...
Expected answer: ... is cleaning it.

Apart from using different stimuli, the two versions of the task also differ in two important ways. First, in the because-clause type stimulus, the experimenter names the action corresponding to the picture, in contrast to the other stimulus where the child is expected to guess what the verb is. Second, the referent corresponding to the targeted object clitic is named four times in the because-clause type stimulus (versus twice in the other stimulus) which makes its prominence in the discourse stronger, which in turn may increase the production of an object clitic.

Instructions on how to administer the task

The test comes as a PowerPoint presentation to be administered on an individual basis. The stimuli are not pre-recorded, so the experimenter must produce them orally (for the list of stimuli for each item, see Appendix A). It is recommended that each testing session be audio- or even video-recorded so as to facilitate future analysis. The test is very easy to run and children understand very quickly what is expected from them. There is also an answer sheet where the experimenter can write down the answer(s) given by the child for each item (see Appendix B).

For each item, the experimenter should first draw the child's attention to what is depicted. All characters and objects present in the picture must be named (e.g. Look! Here is a girl and here is a giraffe). Then the experimenter asks a question about the characters and/or objects (e.g. Tell me: What is the girl doing with the giraffe?). For the distractors, only one character is named in the question (e.g. Tell me: What is the cow doing?).

During the warm-up session, which contains two items following the protocol described above, the child becomes accustomed to producing object clitics. If the child uses an object clitic, the experimenter should move to the next item. If the child doesn't produce an object clitic, the expected answer should be provided by the experimenter. For instance, if the child says 'The boy is throwing the ball' for the first warm-up item (as an answer to 'What is the boy doing with the ball?'), the experimenter should react by giving the child the expected answer (e.g. OK, this is good. You could also say 'He's throwing it'. Alright?) The item should then be run again in order to make sure that the child would indeed use a clitic (e.g. So, again, what is the boy doing with the ball?). At the end of the warm-up session, the experimenter should pause and ask the child if he/she has understood the task and if he/she is ready to proceed.

During the test, it is very important that the child produces transitive verbs – preferably the target verbs – so that object clitics may be used. If a child doesn't answer with a transitive verb and a direct object, the target verb should be provided and the question asked again. For example, if a child answers 'She's working' to the question 'What is the girl doing with the giraffe?' (in (8)), the experimenter should react by saying 'Ok. Now, how would you say this with "wash"? What is the girl doing with the giraffe?'.

If the child doesn't respond or doesn't seem to understand the question, the experimenter should start again by naming the characters and objects in the picture and then ask the question again. If no answer is produced, the target verb should be given to the child and the question should be asked once more. If the child produces another verb or doesn't answer anything, the experimenter shouldn't insist and should move to the next item.

In some cases, the child uses an object NP that corresponds to a body part, as in (12).

(12)   Experimenter: What is the girl doing with the giraffe?
       Child: She's washing its neck.

While the child's answer is grammatical and felicitous, it does not provide a context in which an object clitic could be used. In these cases, the question should be rephrased and it should include the body part, e.g. 'What is the girl doing with the neck of the giraffe?'. This should yield the production of an object clitic (She's washing it).

Finally, it is important to point out that when the child uses the target verb but no clitic, no correction should be provided. It is also crucial for the experimenter to remain positive and to give encouragement to the child throughout the task, even when unexpected answers are given (e.g. Yes, that's good! Good job! etc.).

Dealing with the data

A pre-filled Excel sheet is provided for entering personal information on the child, the answers produced by the child and the errors. Automatic calculations are performed each time new data are entered, in particular the total number (and percentage) of target object clitics produced by the child.

Personal information

Personal information on the child includes the following: name, gender, mother tongue, date of birth and testing date, as in (13).

(13)	1	A	B	C	D	E	F	G	
	2	Child	Gender	L1	Date of birth	Date of testing	Age	Age	
	3	Name	M/F		day/month/year	day/month/year	(in months)	year	month
	4								

All dates (in columns D and E) should be entered as day/month/year. The age of the child will then be calculated automatically in months, as well as in years and months. Other variables, such as the age at which exposure to the target language started and the length of exposure to the target language, which can be obtained via the parental questionnaire (see Chapter 11, this volume), may be inserted in new columns.

Coding the answers

For each item of the task – warm-up, test item (targeting object clitics) and distractor (targeting reflexive clitics) – there are several possible answers already identified in the Excel sheet, as illustrated in (14). The coding procedures are similar to those developed in COST Action 33.

(14)

1	Test item 1 (comb)									
2	Target clitic	Other clitic (felicit)	Other acc clitic (infelicit)	Other clitic (infelicit)	Other clitic (ungram)	NP	Omission	Strong	Other	Error g/n/c/v/p/d/r
3										

Possible answers include the production of the target clitic, another clitic, an object NP or a strong pronoun, the omission of the object clitic, as well as other kinds of answers (such as 'I don't know' or the use of the verb 'be' or of an intransitive verb). Some examples of answers for warm-up and test items are provided in (15); examples for distractors appear in (16). The examples given in (15) are based on the following stimulus question in French: Que fait la petite fille avec la girafe? 'What is the little girl doing with the giraffe?', and those given in (16) are based on Que fait la girafe? 'What is the giraffe doing?'. The different types of answers may differ in terms of felicity and grammaticality. Some answers are felicitous (and grammatical), such as the use of a dative clitic and an object NP (typically corresponding to a body part), as in (15b). Others are infelicitous but grammatical, such as the use of an accusative clitic with the wrong gender (e.g. due to L1 influence) or number, as in (15c') and (15c''), use of a reflexive clitic, as in (15d) or use of an object NP, as in (15f). Yet other answers are ungrammatical, such as the use of a clitic with the wrong case, as in (15e), use of a strong pronoun, as in (15g) and omission of the clitic, as in (15h).[5] Other kinds of responses are listed in (15i).

(15)   Warm-up and test items (targeting object clitics)

(a)   Target clitic   Elle la   lave.[6]
                        she her+CL   washes
                        'She's washing her'.

(b)   Other clitic   Elle lui   lave   le   cou.
      (felicitous)   she to+her+CL washes the neck
                        'She's washing her neck'.

(c)   Other acc clitic   (c')   Elle le   lave.
      (infelicitous)   she him+CL washes
                      'She's washing him'.
                (c'')   Elle les   lave.
                        she them+CL washes
                      'She's washing them'.

(d)   Other clitic   Elle se   lave.
      (infelicitous)   she herself+CL washes

(e)	Other clitic	Elle lui lave.
	(ungrammatical)	she to+him+CL washes
(f)	Object NP:	Elle lave la girafe.
		she washes the giraffe
(g)	Strong pronoun:	Elle lave elle.
		she washes her
(h)	Omission:	Elle lave.
		she washes
(i)	Other:	– no answer
		– the child doesn't know
		– use of the verb 'be': La girafe est toute mouillée.
		the giraffe is all wet
		– use of intransitive verb: La petite fille travaille.
		the little girl works

For distractors, production of an accusative or dative clitic instead of a reflexive clitic results in infelicity and ungrammaticality, respectively, as in (16b) and (16c).

(16) Distractors (targeting reflexive clitics)

(a)	Target clitic:	Elle se lèche.[7]
		she herself+CL licks
		'She licks herself'.
(b)	Other clitic:	Elle la lèche.
	(infelicitous)	she her+CL licks
(c)	Other clitic:	Elle lui lèche.
	(ungrammatical)	she to+her+CL licks
(d)	Omission:	Elle lèche.
		she licks
(e)	Other:	– no answer
		– the child doesn't know
		– use of the verb 'be': La girafe est propre.
		the giraffe is clean
		'The giraffe is clean'.
		– use of intransitive verb: La girafe joue.
		the giraffe plays

For each answer given by the child, the number '1' should be entered in the appropriate column. For example, if the child uses an object NP as an answer to a test item (e.g. She's washing the giraffe), '1' should be entered in the NP column for that item.

Coding the errors

Errors should be entered in the Error column. The following codes should be used:

'g':   Gender error on the object clitic (the child uses an accusative clitic, but with the wrong gender), as in (15c').

'n':   Number error on the object clitic (the child uses an accusative clitic, but with the wrong number), as in (15c").

'c':   Case error on the clitic (the child uses the target verb, or a transitive verb, and a non-accusative clitic – and the sentence is ungrammatical); this typically applies to the use of dative case, as in (15e).

'r':   Reflexive clitic error (the child uses the target verb, or a transitive verb, and a reflexive clitic instead of a non-reflexive accusative clitic), as in (15d).

'a':   Accusative clitic error (the child uses the target verb, and a non-reflexive accusative clitic instead of a reflexive clitic), as in (16b).

'v':   Use of a different verb (the child uses a transitive verb, but it differs from the target verb; e.g. 'clean' instead of 'wash' in the previous example).[8]

'p':   Placement error of the object clitic (the child uses an object clitic but the clitic does not appear in its target position; for example it appears after the verb instead of before the verb in French, as in elle lave la 'she washes her' instead of elle la lave).[9]

'd':   Use of clitic doubling is ungrammatical. In some languages, as in Standard Greek, there is a distinction between grammatical and ungrammatical clitic doubling. In the case where the clitic doubling used by the child is incorrect, the letter 'd' (for ungrammatical doubling) should be entered into the Error column. Recall that if clitic doubling is correct, as in the example given in Note 6, the number '1' should be entered in the Target clitic column. There is no specific coding for correct clitic doubling.

The appropriate letter should be entered in the Error column. Note that if the child produces a dative clitic which is correct (typically together with a body part, e.g. Elle lui lave le cou 'She's to+her washing the neck'), the number '1' should be entered in the Other clitics (felicitous) column and nothing should be entered in the Error column. If, on the other hand, the use of a dative clitic leads to an ungrammatical sentence, e.g. elle lui lave 'she to+her washes', the number '1' should be entered in the Other clitics (ungrammatical) column and the letter 'c' (for case error) should be entered in the Error column. Finally, if an accusative clitic bearing the wrong gender is produced (e.g. Elle le lave 'She's him washing' when referring to a giraffe, masculine in French), a '1' should be entered in the Other accusative clitics (infelicitous) column and the letter 'g' (for gender error) should be entered in the Error column.

Automatic calculations

All calculations are done automatically on the production of clitics (first on object clitics, then on reflexive clitics) and on errors. Calculations on clitics focus on the total production and percentages of:

- Target clitics.
- Other clitics (felicitous).
- Other accusative clitics (infelicitous).
- Other clitics (infelicitous).
- Other clitics (ungrammatical).
- Felicitous clitics (target clitics+other clitics [felicitous]).
- Accusative clitics (target clitics+other accusative clitics).
- Overall clitic production (felicitous clitics+other accusative clitics [infelicitous]+other clitics [infelicitous]+other clitics [ungrammatical]).

The results are given in raw numbers and in percentages (based on the number of answers given on either test items or distractor items). Calculations on errors provide the number of:

- Gender errors ('g').
- Number errors ('n').
- Case errors ('c').
- Reflexive clitic errors ('r').
- Accusative clitic errors ('a').
- Verb changes ('v').
- Placement errors ('p').
- Clitic doubling errors ('d').
- Overall number of errors.

Finally, some check columns are included in the Excel sheet in order to make sure that no mistake has been made when entering the data.

Acknowledgement

I would like to thank the following who helped out with the design of the task and with their comments on this chapter: Adriana Belletti, Solveig Chilla, Carla Contemori, Candice Coyer, Anna Gavarró, Kleanthes Grohmann, Gordana Hržica, Enkeleida Kapia, Martyna Kozlowska, Aude Laloi, Aneta Miekisz, Alexandra Perovic, Mihaela Pirvulescu, Fernanda Pratas, Ianthi Tsimpli, Laurie Tuller, Jasmina Vuksanovic and Spyridoula Varlokosta. Special thanks to João Costa and his drawer Gabriela Bruno, and to Naama Friedmann for her drawing talent.

Notes

(1) In many languages, in particular Romance languages and Standard Greek, the form of object clitics is similar to that of definite determiners, as can be seen in some examples in (1).

(2) When an auxiliary precedes the verb, the object clitic is placed in front of it, as in Spanish (see (i)). Furthermore, the object clitic of an infinitival verb may appear either in front of the main (inflected) verb or after the infinitival verb, as in Catalan, Italian and Spanish (see (ii)). In French, on the other hand, the object clitic always precedes the infinitival form, as in (iii).

(i)   El hombre la   está pintando.   Spanish
      the man   it+CL is   painting
      'The man is painting it'.

(ii) El hombre la   quiere pintar / El hombre quiere pintarla.   Spanish
      the man   it+CL wants paint   the man   wants paint it+CL
      'The man wants to paint it'.

(iii) L'homme veut   la   peindre.   French
      the man wants it+CL   paint
      'The man wants to paint it'.

(3) In contrast to Fujino and Sano (2002), Wexler et al. (2004) found few cases of object clitic omission after age 3 in monolingual children learning Spanish.

(4) Although these studies all follow a similar protocol whereby the referent of the object clitic is established in the discursive background, they differ in exactly how this is being established (see Varlokosta et al. [submitted], for more details).

(5) Note that ungrammatical answers may stem from properties of the L1. For example, French/European Portuguese bilingual children may omit the object clitic in French because object omission in European Portuguese is possible, as seen above.

(6) This includes cases of clitic doubling where the object clitic is used along with the object NP, as in La petite fille la lave, la girafe 'The little girl's washing it, the giraffe'.

(7) As seen in Note 6, clitic doubling also counts as production of a clitic, as in La girafe, elle se lave 'The giraffe, it washes herself'.

(8) In some instances, use of a different (transitive) verb doesn't technically correspond to an error, as in the example given here. Yet for the purpose of tracking the children's behaviour, any verb change with respect to what is expected should be treated as an error.

(9) Although the object clitic is misplaced, it is still being produced. For this reason, the number '1' should be entered in the Target clitic column.

References

Avram, L. (1999) Auxiliaries and the Structure of Language. Bucharest: Editura Universității din București.

Babyonyshev, M. and Marin, S. (2004) Object clitics in child Romanian. In A. Brugos, M.R. Clark-Cotton and S. Ha (eds) Proceedings of the 29th Annual Boston University Conference on Language Development (pp. 49–60). Cambridge, MA: Cascadilla Press.

Babyonyshev, M. and Marin, S. (2006) Acquisition of Romanian pronominal clitics. Catalan Journal of Linguistics 5, 17–44.

Bedore, L. and Leonard, L. (2001) Grammatical morphology deficits in Spanish-speaking children with specific language impairment. *Journal of Speech, Language, and Hearing Research* 44, 905–924.

Belletti, A. and Hamann, C. (2004) On the L2/bilingual acquisition of French by two young children with different source languages. In P. Prévost and J. Paradis (eds) *The Acquisition of French in Different Contexts: Focus on Functional Categories* (pp. 147–176). Amsterdam: John Benjamins.

Bortolini, U., Arfé, B., Caselli, M.C., Degasperi, L., Deevy, P. and Leonard, L. (2006) Clinical markers for specific language impairment in Italian: The contribution of clitics and non-word repetition. *International Journal of Language and Communication Disorders* 41 (6), 695–712.

Bosch, L. and Serra, M. (1997) Grammatical morphology deficits of Spanish-speaking children with specific language impairment. In A. Baker, M. Beers, G. Bol, J. de Jong and G. Leemans (eds) *Child Language Disorders in a Cross-linguistic Perspective: Proceedings of the Fourth Symposium of the European Group on Child Language Disorders* (pp. 33–45). Amsterdam: Amsterdam Series in Child Language Development, University of Amsterdam.

Castilla, A. (2009) Morphosyntactic acquisition in monolingual 3-, 4-, and 5-year-old Spanish-speaking children. In V. Marrero and I. Pinera (eds) *Linguistics: The Challenge of Clinical Application. Proceedings of the II International Conference on Clinical Linguistics.* Madrid: Euphonia Ediciones.

Chillier-Zesiger, L., Arabatzi, M., Baranzini, L., Cronel-Ohayon, S. and Thierry, D. (2006) The acquisition of French pronouns in normal children and in children with specific language impairment (SLI). Unpublished manuscript, Université de Genève.

Chondrogianni, V. (2008) The acquisition of determiners and clitic pronouns by child and adult L2 learners of Greek. Unpublished doctoral dissertation, University of Cambridge.

Costa, J. and Lobo, M. (2006) A aquisição de clíticos em PE: omissão de clíticos ou objecto nulo? In J. Barbosa and F. Oliveira (eds) *XXI Encontro Nacional da Associação Portuguesa de Linguística. Textos seleccionados* (pp. 285–293). Lisboa: APL.

Costa, J. and Lobo, M. (2007) Clitic omission, null objects or both in the acquisition of European Portuguese. In S. Baauw, F. Drijkoningen and M. Pinto (eds) *Romance Languages and Linguistic Theory 2005* (pp. 59–72). Amsterdam: John Benjamins.

Costa, J., Fiéis, A. and Lobo, M. (to appear) Input variability and late acquisition: Clitic misplacement in European Portuguese. *Lingua.* See http://www.sciencedirect.com/science/article/pii/S002438411400117X (accessed 8 December 2014).

De la Mora, J., Paradis, J., Grinstead, J., Flores, B. and Cantu, M. (2004) Object clitics in Spanish-speaking children with and without SLI. Poster presented at the 25th Annual Symposium on Research in Child Language Disorders, University of Wisconsin–Madison.

Duarte, I. and Matos, G. (2000) Romance clitics and the minimalist program. In J. Costa (ed.) *Portuguese Syntax: New Comparative Studies* (pp. 116–142). Oxford: Oxford University Press.

Ezeizabarrena, M.J. (1996) Adquisición de la morfología verbal en euskera y castellano por niños bilingües. PhD dissertation, University of the Basque Country.

Fujino, H. and Sano, T. (2002) Aspects of the null object phenomenon in child Spanish. In A.T. Pérez-Leroux and J. Muñoz Liceras (eds) *The Acquisition of Spanish Morphosyntax* (pp. 67–88). Dordrecht: Kluwer.

Gavarró, A., Mata, M. and Ribera, E. (2006) L'omissió dels clítics d'objecte i partitius en el català infantil: dades espontànies. In C. Pusch (ed.) *La gramàtica pronominal del català – Variació, evolució, funció/The Grammar of Catalan Pronouns – Variation, Evolution, Function* (pp. 27–46). Aachen: Shaker Verlag.

Granfeldt, J. and Schlyter, S. (2004) Cliticization in the acquisition of French as L1 and L2. In P. Prévost and J. Paradis (eds) *The Acquisition of French in Different Contexts* (pp. 333–370). Amsterdam: John Benjamins.

Grüter, T. (2005) Comprehension and production of French object clitics by child second language learners and children with specific language impairment. *Applied Psycholinguistics* 26 (3), 363–391.

Haiden, M. (2011) *La prédication*. Habilitation thesis, Université François Rabelais de Tours.

Hamann, C. (2004) Comparing the development of the nominal and the verbal functional domain in French language impairment. In P. Prévost and J. Paradis (eds) *The Acquisition of French in Different Contexts* (pp. 109–144). Amsterdam: John Benjamins.

Hamann, C., Rizzi, L. and Frauenfelder, U. (1996) On the acquisition of the pronominal system in French. In H. Clahsen (ed.) *Generative Perspectives on Language Acquisition* (pp. 309–334). Amsterdam: John Benjamins.

Hamann, C., Ohayon, S. Dubé, S., Frauenfelder, U.H., Rizzi, L., Starke, M. and Zesiger, P. (2003) Aspects of grammatical development in young French children with SLI. *Developmental Science* 6 (2), 151–158.

Hamann, C. and Belletti, A. (2006) Developmental patterns in the acquisition of complement clitic pronouns: Comparing different acquisition modes with an emphasis on French. *Rivista di Grammatica Generativa* 31, 39–78.

Hulk, A. (2000) L'acquisition des pronoms clitiques français par un enfant bilingue français-néerlandais. *Revue Canadienne de Linguistique* 45, 97–117.

Ilic, T. and Ud Deen, K. (2004) Object raising and cliticization in Serbo-Croatian child language. In J. Van Kampen and S. Baauw (eds) *Proceedings of GALA 2003* (Vol. 1; pp. 235–243). Utrecht: LOT.

Jacobson, P.F. and Schwartz, R.G. (2002) Morphology in incipient bilingual Spanish-speaking preschool children with specific language impairment. *Applied Psycholinguistics* 23 (1), 23–41.

Jakubowicz, C., Nash, L., Rigaut, C. and Gerard, C.-L. (1998) Determiners and clitic pronouns in French-speaking children with SLI. *Language Acquisition* 7 (2–4), 113–160.

Jakubowicz, C. and Rigaut, C. (2000) L'acquisition des clitiques nominatifs et des clitiques objets en Français. *The Canadian Journal of Linguistics* 45, 119–158.

Kayne, R.S. (1975) *French Syntax*. Cambridge, MA: MIT Press.

Larrañaga, P. (2000) *Ergative Sprachen, akkusative Sprachen. Der Erwerb des Kasus bei bilingualen Kindern*. Frankfurt am Main: Vervuert.

Manika, S., Varlokosta, S. and Wexler, K. (2011) The lack of omission of clitics in Greek children with SLI: An experimental study. In N. Danis, K. Mesh and H. Sung (eds) *Proceedings of the 35th Annual Boston University Conference on Language Development* (pp. 427–439). Somerville, MA: Cascadilla Press.

Paradis, J. (2004) The relevance of specific language impairment in understanding the role of transfer in second language acquisition. *Applied Psycholinguistics* 25 (1), 67–82.

Paradis, J., Crago, M. and Genesee, F. (2005/2006) Domain-general versus domain-specific accounts of specific language impairment: Evidence from bilingual children's acquisition of object pronouns. *Language Acquisition* 13 (1), 33–62.

Perez-Leroux, A., Pirvulescu, M. and Roberge, Y. (2008) Children's interpretation of null objects under the scope of negation. In S. Jones (ed.) *Proceedings of the 2008 Annual Conference of the Canadian Linguistic Association.*

Petinou, K. and Terzi, A. (2002) Clitic misplacement in normally developing and language impaired Cypriot-Greek speaking children. *Language Acquisition* 10 (1), 1–28.

Schaeffer, J. (1997) *Direct object scrambling in Dutch and Italian child language*. UCLA Dissertations in Linguistics, Number 17.

Smith, N., Edwards, S., Stojanovik, V. and Varlokosta, S. (2008) Object clitics, definite articles and genitive possessive clitics in Greek specific language impairment (SLI): Deficits and explanations. In T. Marinis, A. Papangeli and V. Stojanovik (eds) *Proceedings of the Child Language Seminar 2007 – 30th Anniversary* (pp. 151–162). Reading: The University of Reading.

Stavrakaki, S., Chrysomallis, M.A. and Petraki, E. (2011) Subject-verb agreement, object clitics, and wh-questions in bilingual French-Greek SLI: The case study of a French-Greek speaking child with SLI. *Clinical Linguistics and Phonetics* 25 (5), 339–367.

Tryzna, M.M. (2009) *Acquisition of object clitics in child Polish: A deficiency at the syntax–pragmatics interface or evidence for D-linking.* Doctoral dissertation, University of Iowa.

Tsakali, V. and Wexler, K. (2004) Why children omit clitics in some languages, but not in others: New evidence from Greek. In J. Van Kampen and S. Baauw (eds) *Proceedings of GALA 2003* (Vol. 2; pp. 493–504).Utrecht: LOT.

Tsimpli, I.M. (2010) The effects of bilingualism on clitics and gender agreement. Paper given at The Romance Turn IV, University of Tours, France, 27 August 2010.

Tsimpli, I.M. and Mastropavlou, M. (2007) Feature interpretability in L2 acquisition and SLI: Greek clitics and determiners. In H. Goodluck, J. Liceras and H. Zobl (eds) *The Role of Formal Features in Second Language Acquisition* (pp. 143–183). London: Routledge.

Tuller, L., Delage, H. and Monjauze, C. (2011) Clitic pronoun production as a measure of atypical language development in French. *Lingua* 121 (3), 423–441.

Varlokosta, S., Belletti, A., Costa, J., Friedmann, N., Gavarró, A., Grohmann, K.K., Guasti, M.-T., Tuller, L., Lobo, M. et al. (submitted). A cross-linguistic study of the acquisition of clitic and pronoun production. *Language Acquisition.*

Wexler, K., Gavarró, A. and Torrens, V. (2004) Feature checking and object clitic omission in child Catalan and Spanish. In R. Bok-Bennema, B. Hollebrandse, B. Kampers-Manhe and P. Sleeman (eds) *Romance Languages and Linguistic Theory 2002* (pp. 253–270), Amsterdam: John Benjamins.

White, L. (1996) Clitics in child L2 French. In H. Clahsen (ed.) *Generative Approaches to First and Second Language Acquisition* (pp. 335–368). Amsterdam: John Benjamins.

Zesiger, P., Chillier-Zesiger, L., Arabatzi, M., Baranzini, L., Cronel-Ohayon, S., Franck, J., Frauenfelder, U.H., Hamann, C. and Rizzi, L. (2010) The acquisition of pronouns by French children: A parallel study of production and comprehension. *Applied Psycholinguistics* 31 (4), 571–603.

Appendix A: The Object Clitic Elicitation Task

Warm-up

1.		Look! Here is a boy and here is a ball. Tell me: What is the boy doing with the ball? Target verb: throw
2.		Look! Here is a bear and here is a dog. Tell me: What is the dog doing with the bear's paw? Target verb: bite

Main task

1.		Look! Here is the mother and here is a girl. Tell me: What is the mother doing with the girl? Target verb: comb
2.		Look! Here is a boy, a thread of wool and some scissors. Tell me: What is the boy doing with the thread of wool? Target verb: cut
D1.		Look! Here is a tree and here is a tree. Tell me: What is the girl doing? Target verb: hide
3.		Look! Here is a girl and here is a giraffe. Tell me: What is the girl doing with the giraffe? Target verb: wash
4.		Look! Here is a boy and here is a hippo. Tell me: What is the boy doing with the hippo? Target verb: dry

D2.

Look! Here is a little girl and here is a comb. Tell me: What is the little girl doing?
Target verb: comb

5.

Look! Here is a dog and here is a cat. Tell me: What is the dog doing with the cat?
Target verb: lick

6.

Look! Here is a drawer and here is a girl. Tell me: What is the drawer doing with the girl?
Target verb: draw

D3.

Look! Here is a boy and here is a cat. Tell me: What is the boy doing with the cat?
Target verb: cut

7.

Look! Here is a boy and here is a cat. Tell me: What is the boy doing with the cat?
Target verb: wet

8.

Look! Here is a man and here is a house. Tell me: What did the man do with the house?
Target verb: paint

D4.

Look! Here is a duck and here is a bar of soap. Tell me: What is duck doing?
Target verb: wash

9.

Look! Here is a princess and here is a soldier. Tell me: What is the princess doing with the soldier?
Target verb: push

10.   Look! Here is a bee and here is a grasshopper in a cart. Tell me: What is the bee doing with the grasshopper? Target verb: pull

D5.   Look! Here's a giraffe. Tell me: What is the giraffe doing? Target verb: lick

11.   Look: here is a girl and here is a boy. Tell me: What is the girl doing with the boy? Target verb: wake up

12.   Look! Here is a cat and here is a fish. Tell me: What is the cat doing with the fish? Target verb: eat

Key: D=distractor.

Appendix B: Answer Sheet

Production of third person clitic pronouns: Answer sheet

Name _____   Participant # or code _____
Date _____   Age _____

Warm-up	Child's response
throw	
bite	

Target verb	Target sentence	Child's response
comb	1.	
cut	2.	
hide	D1.	
wash	3.	
dry	4.	
comb	D2.	
lick	5.	
draw	6.	
cut	D3.	
wet	7.	
paint	8.	
wash	D4.	
push	9.	
pull	10.	
lick	D5.	
wake up	11.	
eat	12.	

Key: D=distractor.

4 Comprehension of Exhaustive Wh-Questions

Petra Schulz

Introduction

Exhaustivity is a central feature of the semantics of wh-questions like 'Who is reading a book?', 'Who is eating what?' or 'Who is giving what to whom?'. Under an exhaustive reading of a wh-question, the answer exhausts the relevant set of elements satisfying the predicate. This is also referred to as the mention-all-reading. For example, in a situation in which Jane, Sue and Peter are reading a book, the exhaustive answer to 'Who is reading a book?' is 'Jane, Sue and Peter' and not just 'Peter'. Presumably, exhaustive wh-questions exist in all languages, and the rules for their interpretation seem to be universal. There is, nevertheless, cross-linguistic variation regarding the availability of multiple wh-questions as well as the type of wh-movement and the presence of overt exhaustivity markers. The exhaustivity task described in this chapter assesses the interpretation of several types of exhaustive wh-questions. Data from about 400 five- and six-year-old typically developing (TD) children across 19 languages coming out of two EU projects (COST Action A33, COST Action IS0804) support the hypothesis that acquisition of this structure is cross-linguistically robust, with mastery of single wh-questions such as 'Who is reading a book?' preceding mastery of multiple wh-questions such as 'Who is eating what?' or 'Who is giving what to whom?'. This confirms earlier results for German and English. Cross-linguistic robustness is also mirrored in the types of typical non-target answers. They reflect children's initial inability to take features like universal quantification, which are assumed to underlie wh-question meaning, into consideration when interpreting the question. Most importantly, exhaustivity in single and especially in multiple wh-questions has been found to be problematic for monolingual children with specific language impairment (SLI). Recent results from bilingual children provide evidence that exhaustivity in wh-questions is problematic in bilingual SLI as well. Thus, the vulnerability of exhaustivity in SLI together with its cross-linguistically robust acquisition path makes this structure a very good candidate for disentangling typical from impaired bilingual acquisition.

This chapter is organised as follows: the first section provides an overview of the phenomenon of exhaustivity in wh-questions and of central findings on its acquisition in TD monolingual and bilingual children and those with SLI. The motivation for the particular task design is described in the second section. After outlining considerations in using the exhaustivity task with bilingual children in the third section, the following section describes the task in detail including issues of procedure and scoring. The concluding section offers suggestions for adopting this task to other languages.

Exhaustive Wh-Questions and Their Acquisition

Exhaustive wh-questions across languages

The rules for interpreting exhaustive wh-questions seem to be uniform across languages. In general, to know the meaning of a question is equivalent to knowing what counts as an answer (Hamblin, 1973). Following the semantic account outlined in Schulz and Roeper (2011), wh-expressions are ambiguous, with the exhaustive interpretation being the default in a more-than-one-answer context. For example, in a situation in which Jane, Sue and Peter are reading, in the default case question (1a) has to be answered with the exhaustive list in (1b) rather than with the singleton list in (1c).

(1) (a) Who is reading?
     (b) Jane, Sue and Peter.
     (c) # Jane.

Using Krifka's (2001) structured meaning approach as the framework for our semantic account, we understand question meanings as functions that when applied to the meaning of the answer yield a proposition. In this approach, wh-expressions such as 'who' denote atomic individuals and plural individuals, marked by the plurality operator *, who all belong to the domain of human beings, expressed as PERSON, as illustrated in (2):

(2) $[[who]]$ $= \{x \mid x \in {}^*PERSON\}$
     $= \{Jane, Sue, Peter, Sue+Jane, Peter+Sue, Peter+Jane+Sue, ...\}$

Wh-questions denote structured propositions, where the wh-expression (e.g. who) specifies the focused question domain and the remainder of the question specifies the background of the structured proposition:

(3) $[[Who\ is\ reading?]]$ $= < \lambda x.x\ read, \{x \mid x \in {}^*PERSON\}>$

Informally, in the semantic account the default exhaustive reading is derived when the question domain is universally exhausted; a mention-some reading is derived from an existential quantification over the question domain. The exhaustivity feature that is needed to yield the exhaustive reading could be modelled in different ways. Following Nelken and Shan (2004) and Nishigaushi (1999), we assume that the wh-element in questions contains a variable that is universally quantificational in nature.

Regarding multiple wh-questions, in a situation in which Jane, Sue and Peter each ate something, the paired wh-question (4a) requires an exhaustive paired list (PL) answer as in (4b) and not a single pair (SP) answer as in (4c).[1] Finally, triple wh-questions like (5) require exhaustive triple list answers as in (5b) and not just one triple as in (5c). Importantly, complete answers to multiple wh-questions require exhausting the domain of pairs or triples; i.e. they require forming the respective pairs and triples and universally exhausting the question domain. Put differently, in most languages multiple questions generally presuppose that there is more than one answer and hence an SP answer is ruled out (Krifka, 2001). If pairing or tripling does not take place, non-target-like exhaustive lists of individuals may be formed, as illustrated in (4d) and (5d) with subject lists, marked as #.

(4)　　(a)　　Who is eating what?
　　　　(b)　　Jane (ate) an apple, Sue a banana and Peter a hamburger.
　　　　(c)　　# Jane an apple.
　　　　(d)　　# Jane, Sue and Peter.

(5)　　(a)　　Who is giving what to whom?
　　　　(b)　　Jane is giving a book to Sue, and Peter a necklace to Amanda.
　　　　(c)　　# Jane is giving a book to Sue.
　　　　(d)　　# Jane and Peter.

PL answers are derived semantically as follows. The multiple wh-question is answered via a function, i.e. a mapping procedure from a given domain to values. The multiple wh-question (4), repeated here as (6), is transformed by the operators in (7) to a question that asks for a mapping procedure (Krifka, 2001: 23):

(6)　　Who is eating what?

　　　　(a)　　$<\lambda<x,y>[eat(y)(x)]$, person × thing>

(7)　　(a)　　$FUN(R) = \lambda f \forall x\ [x \in DOM(f) \rightarrow R(<x,f(x)>)]$, the set of functions f such that every x in the domain of f stands in the R-relation to f(x)

　　　　(b)　　$FUN'(A \times B)$ = the set of functions from A to B

The answer specifies a function by enumeration, such as 'Jane an apple', 'Sue a banana', and 'Peter a Hamburger', as illustrated in (8):

(8)　　f:　　{Jane, Sue, Peter} → {apple, banana, hamburger},
　　　　　　　Jane → apple
　　　　　　　Sue → banana
　　　　　　　Peter → hamburger

In the default case, single wh-questions (1) as well as multiple wh-questions (4) and (5) are assumed across languages to contain an underlying universal quantifier, triggering the exhaustive interpretation (cf. Schulz and Roeper [2011] for a summary of the various accounts).

In contrast to their uniform interpretation, wh-questions exhibit cross-linguistic variation with regard to their syntactic and lexical properties (Bošković, 2003; Dayal, 2005; Grohmann, 2003; Hagstrom, 2003; cf. Schulz et al., in prep. for a discussion). First, while single wh-questions as in (1a) are present in all languages, in some languages like Irish and Italian multiple wh-questions like (4a) and (5a) are not allowed. Second, some languages employ quantifying question particles such as 'allemaal' in Dutch, 'all' in Irish English, 'ne`e' in Hausa, and 'alles' (all) in German, which function as exhaustivity markers in wh-questions, as illustrated in (9) (cf. Zimmermann, 2007).

(9)   Wer sitzt alles auf einem Stuhl?
       Who sits all on a chair?

Third, in some languages plural marking on the wh-pronoun and/or on the verb can be used to signal a non-singleton reading. In Turkish for example, the wh-pronoun itself can be marked for singular or plural, as illustrated in (10) (Grimm et al., 2010). In Dutch, the verb can be marked for singular or plural, even though the subject wh-pronoun is singular, as shown in (11a) and (11b) (Hollebrandse, 2003).

(10)   (a)   Kim sandalyede oturuyor?
              Who_SG sits on a chair
       (b)   Kimler sandelyenin üzerinde oturuyor?
              Who_PL are sitting on a chair
(11)   (a)   Wie leest er een boek?
              who reads_SG a book
       (b)   Wie lezen er een boek?
              who read_PL a book

Fourth, wh-questions differ regarding wh-movement. They may require fronting of all wh-words (e.g. Bulgarian, Polish, Romanian, (12)), or fronting of one wh-word (e.g. German, English, Hebrew), or may require the wh-words to be left *in situ* (e.g. Japanese). Interestingly, these differences do not result in different interpretations.

(12)   Kto   co   je?
       Who   what eats
       'Who is eating what?'

Finally, although in most languages wh-elements seem to be used only for question formation, in some languages like German several wh-elements are homophonous between question-words and indefinites, as illustrated in (13) for the object wh-word. In German, stressing the wh-element, expressed via capitals, disambiguates the meaning.

(13)   (a)   Wer isst WAS?
               'Who is eating what?'
        (b)   Wer isst (et)was?
               'Who is eating something?'

Acquisition of exhaustive wh-questions across languages and acquisition types

Investigation of the acquisition of exhaustivity in wh-questions originated with Roeper and de Villiers' (1991) pioneering study on multiple wh-questions, looking at monolingual English TD children. Using a question-with-picture task, Roeper and de Villiers (1991) found that while adults consistently responded to multiple wh-questions like (4) with exhaustive paired lists, 4- to 6-year-olds did so in about 80% of the cases and younger children in only 30% of the cases. Subsequent studies in English, Spanish, German and Swiss-German confirmed that the exhaustivity property of wh-questions is recognised by TD children around age 5–6 (Gavarró *et al.*, 2010; Heizmann, 2012; Hollebrandse, 2003; Oiry & Roeper, 2009; Penner, 1994; Pérez-Leroux, 1993; Roeper & de Villiers, 1991; Roeper *et al.*, 2007; Schulz & Roeper, 2011; Stangen, 2008; Wojtecka, 2010).

The exhaustivity task, used in COST Actions A33 and IS0804, assesses the interpretation of single, paired and triple exhaustive wh-questions. Up to now, data from 415 four- to six-year-old TD children across 19 languages have been collected (Afrikaans, Basque, Catalan, Cypriot Greek, Danish, Dutch, English, Estonian, French, German, Greek, Hebrew, isiXhosa, Polish, Portuguese, Romanian, Serbian, Swedish and Turkish). The results confirm the hypothesis that acquisition of this structure is cross-linguistically robust, with mastery of single wh-questions (around age 5) preceding mastery of multiple wh-questions (around age 6) and no difference between paired and triple wh-questions (for cross-linguistic comparisons: Schulz, 2010a, 2013b; Schulz *et al.*, in prep.; for specific languages, cf. also Forys, 2013; Haznedar *et al.*, 2012; Koch *et al.*, 2012; Southwood, 2011, 2013; Vuksanović *et al.*, 2012). Cross-linguistic uniformity was also found regarding the most frequent non-target answers: singleton responses as (1c) to single and multiple wh-questions, and exhaustive lists of subjects or objects to multiple wh-questions as (4d) and (5d). These error types indicate that the underlying universal quantifier(s) (and mapping procedure) were not taken into consideration when interpreting the question (cf. Schulz & Roeper [2011] for details).

Most importantly, results from several studies indicate that exhaustivity in single and especially in multiple questions is problematic in monolingual children with SLI (Afrikaans: Southwood, 2011; English: Roeper, 2004; French: Chondrogiani & Roesch, 2012; German: Schulz, 2013c; Schulz & Roeper, 2011; Serbian: Vuksanovic *et al.*, 2012), confirming that SLI can also affect the domain of sentential semantics (cf. Schulz, 2010b). Recently, studies initiated by COST IS0804 have been started with bilingual TD and SLI children who are acquiring typologically diverse languages as their first language (L1) combined with typologically different second languages (L2s) (e.g. Hungarian L1 and Serbian L2, Russian L1 and Hebrew L2, English L1 and French L2, Arabic L1 and French L2, Turkish L1 and German L2). Bilingual TD children have been found to master single and multiple wh-questions about a year later than their monolingual peers, which is expected given their often later age at onset of acquisition. However, bilingual TD learners differed from bilingual children with SLI who showed persistent difficulty with exhaustive wh-questions (Armon-Lotem *et al.*, 2013; Prévost 2012; Schulz, 2013b, 2013c; Vuksanovic & Bjekic, in prep.). In sum, evidence available to date seems to indicate that exhaustivity in multiple questions is problematic in bilingual SLI, just as in monolingual SLI.

Motivation for the Particular Task Design

The task aims at tapping into children's understanding of single and multiple wh-questions that require an exhaustive reading. Developed first for German, the exhaustivity task was then adopted in the COST Action A33 successfully for 13 different languages and tested with 5-year-old monolingual TD children. In the COST Action IS0804 it was used with monolingual and multilingual TD and SLI children aged 4–10 from language backgrounds as diverse as Hebrew and isiXhosa. The task employs the method of question-with-picture (cf. Schulz & Roeper, 2011). A child sees a picture and simultaneously hears a question to which he/she has to respond verbally. The simultaneous presentation of picture and test question enables the child to access the visual information while processing the question and planning the response.

Construction of the exhaustivity task

In constructing the task, the underlying structure of the event depicted, the wording of the wh-questions and the pictures were carefully controlled. First, all events involve six individuals some of whom share a certain property like EAT AN APPLE, while others are not involved in any visible activity. This contrast makes the task as easy as possible in terms of visually processing the depicted actions. To achieve comparability across items, all items show a one-to-one mapping between the individuals having the property being asked about in the wh-question and the object(s) participating in the activity. Across all wh-questions, pictures were constructed so that the answer lists would not contain the same object twice or contain objects from the same category. This served to avoid collective answers. For the paired question 'Who is eating what?', for example, the picture shows a girl, mom, dad and grandma eating an apple, ice cream, a banana and a piece of cake, respectively, in contrast to all of them eating an apple or all of them eating some type of fruit. In the test items, the number of individuals having the property in question varies between two and five out of the total of six. This variation ensured that children could not develop guessing strategies, such as listing all individuals in the picture or consistently responding with the same number of individuals. Results from this task as well as from the similar task used in Schulz and Roeper (2011) indicate that the number of individuals that have to be listed by the child does not influence his/her response patterns in any systematic way. In other words, children did not tend to give exhaustive list answers depending on the number of individuals, with small numbers favouring exhaustive lists. Note that this is contrary to the purely cognitive hypothesis that processing load associated with the need to produce longer lists would lead to avoidance of exhaustivity. In addition, a previous version of this task (Stangen, 2008; cf. summary in Schulz & Roeper, 2011) tested whether changes in the absolute number of individuals across pictures influence children's response behaviour. In that design, there were between three and six individuals of whom between two and four shared the property under question. In the multiple wh-condition, pictures displayed between two and four individuals sharing the same property. It was found that these changes did not influence children's response patterns: a smaller answer list did not alter children's willingness to give exhaustive responses, and a larger answer list did not lead to repeating elements (single items, pairs, triples) of the list or leaving some elements out.

Second, wording of the test questions was carefully controlled. The range of wh-words used in the wh-questions was limited to achieve comparability across items. All wh-questions are subject-questions or – in case of multiple questions – contain as the first wh-word a subject. Multiple wh-questions contain as the second (or third) wh-word 'what', 'where' and '(to) whom', which in English function as direct and indirect objects, marked as accusative and dative. Note that superiority effects were not tested in this design; therefore, the order of wh-words was always wh1-subject and wh2-non-subject. There is general cross-linguistic consensus that object-questions are more difficult and are acquired later than subject-questions in TD monolingual children and those with SLI (e.g. Friedmann & Novogrodsky, 2011; Schulz, 2013c), and in multilingual children (cf. Schulz [2013a] for early L2 learners of German). Therefore, subject wh-questions are used rather than object wh-questions to avoid additional complexity. Moreover, as complex wh-phrases have been found to be more difficult and to be acquired later in TD children and those with SLI (Friedmann *et al.*, 2009; Friedmann & Novogrodsky, 2011), wh-words rather than complex wh-phrases like 'which person' or 'which people' are used throughout the test items. In this way, interference with additional factors like complexity of wh-words is avoided. All verbs used in the wh-structures are inflected for present tense (or present progressive, depending on the particular language). They require one or two arguments (e.g. feed, build, show, give) and fall into different semantic classes: stative (e.g. have), process (e.g. play) and telic (e.g. sell). Moreover, the verbs used in the stimuli met the following criteria: They were easy to illustrate within a one-picture set-up, and they are part of the lexicon of pre-schoolers. Finally, minimal verbal discourse contexts were given before each question to make the wh-question felicitous. As a lead-in, general questions like 'Look, what is happening here?' were used. More specific introductory sentences like 'Look, they are hungry' before asking 'Who is eating what?', used by Schulz and Roeper (2011), were avoided in order to not prompt the child with the plural of verb and pronoun.

Third, the pictures were designed in a way to minimise children's burden of processing the visual scenes. Each picture displays several family members involved in everyday activities. Family members, referred to with generic terms (mother, father, grandfather, grandmother, boy, girl), rather than individuals with real names or characters that differed across pictures, were chosen to minimise memory effects. The characters are portrayed in a way to facilitate recognition of their family member role. Hence, stereotypical role models were chosen that in both COST Actions proved acceptable and identifiable across different cultural settings found in the 17 countries in which the task has been used so far. Similarly, the actions depicted in the scenes and referred to in the wh-questions involve everyday activities like eating, drinking and bike riding, and were chosen with the aim of being easily visually identifiable and known in different cultural settings.

Considerations in Using the Task with Bilingual Children

The exhaustivity task can be used with bilingual children of different acquisition types (simultaneous, and sequential, with different ages at onset of acquisition of L2). As described above, attempts were made to keep language demands beyond the phenomenon under investigation to a minimum. A vocabulary check has been added, which contains all objects that are used in a given question or are needed to answer test questions ($n=40$). This vocabulary check does not serve as a pretest; rather it can be used to ensure that the child knows the object words and is familiar with the way objects like BIKE or BUTTERFLY are depicted in the main task. The child is asked to name objects one by one. In order to keep track of how many objects the child can name at the first round, the experimenter may count the number of known items. If a child does not know an object or its name, the experimenter supplies the correct answer and then presents the child again with the picture.

The exhaustivity task can be administered in one or all of the child's languages. As in other multilingual test contexts, it is crucial that the experimenter addresses the child only in the language being tested to facilitate a monolingual communication mode. Code-switching or responses in the other language may be noted separately as they may shed light on the child's language dominance or lexical gaps. However, for quantitative analyses, we evaluated those responses together with responses in the tested language. One reason is that in our experience, code-switching and non-target language responses rarely happen in 'monolingual mode' test situations.

Description of the Exhaustivity Task

Materials

In the main test, the question-with-picture method is used. As illustrated in Table 4.1, there are four conditions: single wh-questions, paired wh-questions, triple wh-questions and single wh-ALL-questions. The items are ordered in a block design to avoid interference between the different test conditions and to ensure comparability across languages: In languages without multiple wh-questions like Italian or without overt lexical exhaustivity markers like French, the experiment ends after Part A-1 and Part A-3, respectively. Part A contains 20 test items and 10 control items. Part B contains eight test items and four controls. Within a block, test and control items are presented in a random but fixed order.

Table 4.1 Experimental stimuli and number of items in the exhaustivity task by condition

Part	Condition	No. of items
A-1	Single wh	8
	Single wh controls	4
A-2	Paired wh	8
	Paired wh controls	4
A-3	Triple wh	4
	Triple wh controls	2
B	Single wh-alles	8
	Single wh-alles controls	4

Typical test items for single wh-questions and single wh-alles-question are illustrated for German in (14) and Figure 4.1.

(14) Guck mal, was ist denn hier los?
      'Look, what is happening here?'
      (a)   Wer hat einen Fußball?
            who has a   soccer ball
            'Who is holding a   soccer ball?'
      (b)   Wer hat alles   einen Fußball?
            who has all   a   soccer ball
            'Who (all) is holding a soccer ball?'

Figure 4.1 Example picture for a single wh-question (Who is holding a soccer ball?)

Typical test items for paired wh-questions are given in (15) and Figure 4.2 and triple wh-questions are given in (16) and Figure 4.3, respectively.

(15)   Look. What is happening here?
        Wer isst was?
        who eats what
        'Who is eating what?'

Figure 4.2 Example picture for a paired wh-question (Who is eating what?)

(16)   Look. What is happening here?
        Wer gibt wem was?
        who gives whom what
        'Who is giving what to whom?'

Figure 4.3 Example picture for a triple wh-question (Who is giving what to whom?)

Each picture displays a group of people, who are introduced in an initial picture as a family. Individuals are referred to as mother, father, grandfather/

granddad, grandmother/grandma, boy, girl to minimise memory effects. In the single wh and the single wh-alles test conditions, there are always six individuals of whom between two and five share the property in question, such as holding a soccer ball. This variation ensures that children cannot easily develop guessing strategies, such as consistently responding with the same number of individuals or listing all individuals in the picture. The four single wh control items require a singleton answer and serve to prevent the child from assuming that he/she always has to respond with more than one individual. Recall that all wh-questions contain as the first wh-word a subject. As single subject wh-questions are mastered around age 3–4, the single wh control items should not pose any difficulties; children could assume a gap or a variable to answer with the correct subject. In the paired wh test conditions, the pictures display six individuals of whom between two and five share the same property such as eating something or reading something. The four paired wh control items (e.g. Who is building what?) depict six individuals as well, one of whom is engaged in the activity in question, such as building something, requiring an SP answer like 'The boy is building a tower'. Likewise, in the triple wh test conditions, six individuals are depicted, of whom between two and four are sharing the property in question like giving something to somebody. In the two triple wh controls (e.g. Who is putting what where?), one individual is engaged in the activity in question, requiring a single triple response like 'Mom is putting the fork on the table'. Even though in most languages multiple wh-questions semantically presuppose a list answer (cf. Krifka, 2001), the paired and triple wh control items are included to prevent the child from assuming that he/she always has to respond with more than one pair or triple, respectively. Note that, unlike single wh controls, paired and triple control items were not expected to be mastered by all children around age 4, as more than one variable or gap has to be represented.

Procedure

Each of the participants is tested individually in a quiet room. If children receive both parts of the experiment, two sessions are needed that are about one week apart. In Session 1, children receive the pictures of all family members, the vocabulary check and Part A of the main experiment. In Session 2, Part B of the main experiment is administered. All sessions should be audio- or ideally video-recorded for later data check against the on-site coding and for further individual analyses.

All pictures are integrated in a PowerPoint presentation, shown typically on a portable computer. The experimenter shows the child one picture at a time and then asks the test question while the child is looking at the picture. The child is encouraged from the very beginning to respond verbally rather than by pointing, because pointing is possible as a response to single, but not to multiple wh-questions. As usual, no response-contingent feedback is given by the experimenter. Importantly, the child should not be prompted after giving his/her initial response, e.g. by asking 'And who else?' or 'And what are they eating?'. Repetition of the test question is allowed if the child does not react or is not concentrating on the task. If the child corrects himself/herself, scoring is based on the self-corrected response.

In order to guarantee comparability across experimenters, a script was created for how to introduce the different parts of the experiment. In addition, to motivate younger or shy children to cooperate a story context was developed centred around a dog that likes taking pictures of his host family and now needs the child to explain the pictures to him. The dog-story context may be left out; all other prompts are obligatory. (17) illustrates the complete script:

(17)   Exhaustivity script
        This is x (name of dog or other animal puppet). He is pretty young and he lives with family Y. He brought some pictures from the family on the computer. Let's look at them, ok?
        (a)   Introduction of test figures
               Look, here's a girl. Here's a boy, etc. (E. shows the child the pictures of the single family members). Look, here they are all together (E. shows the family picture and points). This is …? (child should name the person).., and this is.. ?, etc.
        (b)   Vocabulary check
               Look, these are all things that family Y has. What is this? (E. points)
        (c)   Main test
               Family Y lives in a house with a garden. They do lots of different things together, and sometimes the things they do are a little funny. X lives there and likes taking pictures. Because he is so young, he doesn't always understand what is going on. He brought more pictures and would like to look at them with us. I'm sure he has questions about every picture. He recorded/wrote down the questions because he is a little shy and because he didn't want to forget any of the questions. He really wants to know what his family is doing there. Let's look at the picture together, ok?
        (d)   Lead in for each picture
               Oh, look, what are they doing here? or Look, what is happening here? (i.e. the family characters, activities or objects are not verbally introduced).

The wh-questions should be spoken at the same pace and with the same prosodic marking (with stress on each of the wh-words) throughout the experiment. Therefore, all test stimuli may be pre-recorded and checked for pace and intonation, or – if this is not feasible – experimenters need to practice phrasing the wh-questions.

Coding

Children's responses are coded as correct when they contain the required lists of individuals, pairs or triples, depending on the test condition. Thus, grammatical errors like incorrect case marking or inflections, missing determiners, etc., are not counted. Likewise, responses where the verb or the referent names have been altered do not lead to classification as incorrect as long as the event referred to remains identifiable. Furthermore, note that in single wh-questions no difference was made between verbal responses and non-verbal responses via pointing. Table 4.2 summarises

Table 4.2 Types of correct responses to the test items

Condition	Response type	Example
Single wh (+wh-all)	Verbally listing the subjects with VPs	The dad has a soccer ball, the girl has a soccer ball, the boy has a soccer ball, and the grandpa has a soccer ball.
	Verbally listing the subjects without verb	The dad, the girl, the boy and the grandpa.
	Pointing to the subjects	This, this, this and this one (points).
	Combination of pointing and verbal response	This, this, this and this one (points), this girl, this boy, this dad and this grandpa.
	Listing by exclusion	Everybody but these two (points)./Everybody but the mum and the grandma.
Paired wh	Verbally listing pairs with verb	The girl is eating an apple, the dad is eating a banana, the grandma is eating a cake and the mum is eating an ice cream.
	Verbally listing pairs without verb	The dad a banana, the mum an ice cream, the girl an apple and the grandma a cake.
	Pointing and verbally listing the pairs	The dad a banana, the girl an apple, the grandma a cake and the mum an ice cream (points to the individuals while speaking).
Triple wh	Verbally listing triples with verb	The mum is giving a watering can to the girl, the dad is giving a bone to the dog and the grandma is giving a teddy bear to the boy.
	Verbally listing triples without verb	The mum a watering can to the girl, the dad a bone to the dog and the grandma a teddy bear to the boy.
	Pointing and verbally listing the triples	The mum is giving a watering can to the girl, the dad a bone to the dog and the grandma a teddy bear to the boy (points to the individuals while speaking).

cf. Schulz and Roeper (2011: 396)

the most frequent types of responses coded as correct, illustrated with examples (1), (4) and (5).

In principle, responses can be incorrect in many different ways. However, results from previous versions of this experimental design (cf. summary in Schulz & Roeper, 2011) as well as data from the design described here across typologically different languages provide robust evidence that children's non-target-like responses fall into distinct categories. As for single wh-questions, children may answer by naming one individual rather than by giving the exhaustive list; this is referred to as a singleton response. Rarely do children list more than one but not all individuals; this is referred to as a plural response. Children who have not yet mastered paired wh-questions typically respond with exhaustive lists of subjects, like 'the girl, dad, grandma, mom' in response to the question 'Who is eating what?' (cf. Figure 4.2). In some cases, exhaustive lists of objects are given; in our example, 'apple, banana, cake and ice cream'. Both response types show that children have acquired universal quantification over one wh-variable, but not over two. Formulated in terms of Krifka's (2001) structured meaning approach, the mapping procedure from a given and identifiable domain to values is not in place, but the universal quantifier exhausting either the domain or the range is. Children who have not mastered universal quantification respond with singleton answers, restricted to the subject (e.g. the girl) or the object (e.g. an apple). One pair responses, pointing to mastery of pairing, i.e. the mapping function, without mastery of universal quantification, like 'the girl is eating an apple', are rarely given. Incorrect responses to triples fall mainly into the same categories as described for paired wh-questions: exhaustive lists of subject, of direct or indirect objects or one singleton answers, naming one subject, direct or indirect object.

How to Adopt This Task to Other Languages

When adopting the exhaustivity task in a different language, language-specific properties of exhaustive wh-questions in that language have to be considered as well as what is already known about the language abilities of bilingual (un)impaired children in that language.

While the interpretation of exhaustive wh-questions seems to be cross-linguistically robust, as sketched in the first section, their form systematically differs across languages in several respects. First, the range of wh-question types allowed in a language varies. Paired and triple wh-questions may be ungrammatical, as in Italian and Irish English. In that case, Parts A-2 and A-3 cannot be used. If conjoined wh-questions (e.g. Who is eating and what [is he eating]?) are preferred over multiple wh-questions, it is crucial to clarify whether this is due to grammaticality or to preference issues, as has been suggested for example for Xhosa (Frenette Southwood, p.c.). Likewise, in languages without overt exhaustivity markers like Standard English,

Part B cannot be used. However, in languages with plural wh-pronouns like 'which ones' (e.g. Turkish, Russian), Part B can be used with these structures, combined with either a plural or singular verb, depending on the language. Second, the type of wh-movement (overt or covert, fronting of one or of all wh-pronouns) determines the serialisation of the wh-pronoun(s) in the sentence. Consequently, in languages with multiple fronting like Polish, the question 'Who is eating what?' is translated as shown in example (12) in the first section. Third, in most languages obligatory subject–verb agreement regarding number exists between wh-pronoun subject and the verb. In that case, both should be marked for singular to avoid priming non-singleton responses. However, in some languages like Dutch, a singular wh-pronoun subject can occur with both a singular and plural verb. In that case, Part A may be administered with singular marking to ensure comparability across languages, and Part B may be used with verbs with plural marking. Finally, in a few languages like German, some wh-elements are homophonous with the respective indefinite pronouns. The potential ambiguity arising for the non-fronted wh-elements (e.g. Who is eating what? vs Who is eating something?) can be avoided by stressing these words.

If little is known about how to interpret exhaustive wh-questions in a given language, the adaptation should first be administered to a control group of adults, who are expected to perform at ceiling. In the bilingual settings tested so far, i.e. early successive language learners with an age of onset of around 3 years and simultaneous bilinguals, the task proves suitable for ages 5–10. Our results suggest that multiple wh-questions are as problematic for bilingual SLI children as they are for monolingual children with SLI.

In conclusion, the attested vulnerability of exhaustivity in SLI together with its cross-linguistically robust acquisition path makes this structure a very good candidate for disentangling typical from impaired bilingual acquisition. Furthermore, research on exhaustivity in wh-questions may add to the evidence already available that SLI can also affect the domain of sentential semantics (cf. Schulz, 2010b).

Acknowledgements

The research reported here has been supported by COST Action IS0804 'Language impairment in multilingual societies: Linguistic patterns and the road to assessment', by COST Action A33 'Crosslinguistic robust stages of children's linguistic performance with application to language assessment' and by the project MILA at the Research Center IDEA, funded by the LOEWE programme for excellence from the State of Hesse. I thank the working group members of both COST Actions for their valuable support, both theoretical and practical, that led to adoptions of this task in diverse languages, especially Anna Gavarro, Philippe Prévost and Naama Friedmann.

I also thank all researchers who used the exhaustivity task and shared their data and insights with me (Reili Argus, Larisa Avram, Sharon Armon-Lotem, Jovana Bjekic, Vasiliki Chondrogianni, Joao Costa, Marie-José Ezeizabarrena, Małgorzata Foryś, Naama Friedmann, Sharon Garner, Anna Gavarro, Angela Grimm, Kleanthes Grohmann, Ewa Haman, Belma Haznedar, Bart Hollebrandse, Kristine Jensen de Lopez, Maria Kambanaros, Napoleon Katsos, Corinna Koch, Maria Lobo, Natalia Meir, Michaela Nerantzini, Fernanda Pratas, Philippe Prévost, Athina Skordi, Anne Rösch, Rabea Schwarze, Irena Shnaiderman, Magdalena Smoczynska, Frenette Southwood, Laurie Tuller, Ianthi Tsimpli, Angeliek van Hout, Heather van der Lely, Spiridoula Varlokosta, Jasmina Vuksanovic, Christian Waldmann, John Weston and Magdalena Wojtecka). Finally, I thank the reviewer and the editors for helpful suggestions. I am indebted to Tom Roeper with whom I developed various versions of the exhaustivity task and who encouraged its cross-linguistic adoption. Thanks to Magdalena Wojtecka who created the pictures.

Note

(1) Note that in most languages, multiple wh-questions like (4a) are not felicitous in SP contexts, and hence never allow SP answers like (4c) (Bošković, 2003; Grohmann, 2002, 2003; Hagstrom, 1998). However, in Serbo-Croatian, Japanese (Bošković, 2003) and Malayalam (Grebenyova, 2006), multiple wh-questions have been argued to be felicitous in both PL and SP contexts, hence allowing SP answers like (4c) in an SP context.

References

Armon-Lotem, S., Granner, S., Shnaiderman, I. and Meir, N. (2013) Exhaustivity as a measure of typical development in the L2 of Russian-Hebrew children. Poster presented at the final conference of COST IS0804, Krakow, Poland.

Bošković, Z. (2003) On the interpretation of multiple questions. In P. Pica (ed.) *Linguistic Variation Yearbook 1* (pp. 1–15). Amsterdam: Benjamins.

Chondrogiani, V. and Roesch, A. (2012) Exhaustivity in French-German L1-TD, L1-SLI, 2L1-TD and L2-TD children. Paper presented at the COST IS0804 Meeting, Berlin, Germany.

Dayal, V. (2005) Multiple wh questions. In M. Everaert and H. van Riemsdijk (eds) *The Blackwell Companion to Syntax 3* (pp. 275–327). Malden, MO: Blackwell.

Foryś, M. (2013) Syntactic and semantic correlates of exhaustivity in single and multiple wh-questions. A study of Polish monolingual children. Unpublished master's thesis, University of Warsaw.

Friedmann, N., Belletti, A. and Rizzi, L. (2009) Relativized relatives: Types of intervention in the acquisition of A-bar dependencies. *Lingua* 119 (1), 67–88.

Friedmann, N. and Novogrodsky, R. (2011) Which questions are most difficult to understand? The comprehension of wh questions in three subtypes of SLI. *Lingua* 121 (3), 367–382.

Gavarró, A., Lewandowski, W. and Markova, A. (2010) An approach to multiple interrogatives in child Bulgarian and Polish. In J. Costa, A. Castro, M. Lobo and F. Pratas (eds) *Language Acquisition and Development Proceedings of GALA 2009* (pp. 170–181). Newcastle: Cambridge Scholars Press.

Grebenyova, L. (2006) Multiple Interrogatives: Syntax, Semantics, and Learnability. PhD dissertation, University of Maryland.

Grimm, A., Wojtecka, M., Ritter, A. and Schulz, P. (2010) Comprehension of exhaustive wh-questions in eL2 and L1 learners of German – cross-linguistically uniform or language-specific acquisition? Poster presented at Boston University Conference on Language Development (BUCLD), Boston, MA.

Grohmann, K.K. (2002) Multiple wh-fronting and the left periphery: German=Bulgarian+Italian. *Georgetown University Working Papers in Theoretical Linguistics* 2, 83–115.

Grohmann, K.K. (2003) German is a multiple wh-fronting-language! In C. Boeckx and K.K. Grohmann (eds) *Multiple Wh-Fronting* (pp. 99–130). Amsterdam: John Benjamins.

Hagstrom, P.A. (1998) Decomposing Questions. PhD dissertation, Massachusetts Institute of Technology.

Hagstrom, P.A. (2003) What questions mean. *GLOT International* 7/8, 188–201.

Hamblin, C.L. (1973) Questions in Montague English. *Foundations of Language* 10, 41–53.

Haznedar, B., Schulz, P. and Wojtecka, M. (2012) Exhaustive wh-questions across acquisition types: Comparing Turkish and German in monolingual and eL2-children. Paper presented at the COST IS0804 Meeting, Berlin, Germany.

Heizmann, T. (2012) Exhaustivity in questions and clefts, and the quantifier connection. A study in German and English. Unpublished PhD thesis, University of Massachusetts.

Hollebrandse, B. (2003) Distributive qualities of wh-words in Dutch child language. Paper presented at Taalkunde in Nederland dag (TIN-dag), Utrecht, Netherlands.

Krifka, M. (2001) For a structured meaning account of questions and answers. In C. Fery and W. Sternefeld (eds) *Audiatur vox sapentia. A Festschrift for Arnim von Stechow* (pp. 287–319). Berlin: Akademie Verlag.

Koch, C., Waldmann, C. and Schulz, P. (2012) On the acquisition of exhaustive wh-questions in Swedish. Paper presented at the COST IS0804 Meeting, Berlin, Germany.

Nelken, R. and Shan, C.-C. (2004) A logic of interrogation should be internalized in a modal logic for knowledge. Paper presented at the Conference on Semantics and Linguistic Theory (SALT 14), Chicago, IL. See http://semarch.linguistics.fas.nyu.edu/Archive/mEwOTFlO/nelken-shan-salt14.pdf.

Nishigauchi, T. (1999) Some preliminary thoughts on the acquisition of the syntax and semantics of wh-constructions. *Theoretical and Applied Linguistics at Kobe Shoin* 2, 35–48.

Oiry, M. and Roeper, T. (2009) How language acquisition reveals minimalist symmetry in the wh-system. In K.K. Grohmann and P. Phoevos (eds) *Selected Papers from the Cyprus Syntaxfest* (pp. 11–28). Cambridge: Cambridge Scholars Publishing.

Penner, Z. (1994) Ordered Parameter Setting in First Language Acquisition. The Role of Syntactic Bootstrapping and the Triggering Hierarchy in determining the Developmental Sequence in Early Grammar. A Case Study in the Acquisition of Bernese Swiss German. Habilitation thesis, University of Bern.

Pérez-Leroux, A.-T. (1993) Empty Categories and the Acquisition of Wh-Movement. PhD dissertation, University of Massachusetts.

Prévost, P. (2012) Exhaustive wh-questions in French. Paper presented at the COST IS0804 Meeting, Berlin, Germany.

Roeper, T. (2004) Diagnosing language variations: Underlying principles for syntactic assessment. *Seminars in Speech and Language* 25 (1), 41–55.

Roeper, T. and de Villiers, J. (1991) The emergence of bound variable structures. In T.L. Maxfield and B. Plunkett (eds) *Papers in the Acquisition of WH. Proceedings of the*

University of Massachusetts Roundtable (UMOP) (pp. 225–266). Amherst, MA: GLSA Publications.

Roeper, T., Schulz, P., Pearson, B. and Reckling, I. (2007) From singleton to exhaustive: The acquisition of wh-. In M. Becker and A. McKenzie (eds) *Proceedings of SULA 3: Semantics of Under-Represented Languages in the Americas* (pp. 87–102). Amherst, MA: GLSA Publications.

Schulz, P. (2010a) Who answered what to whom? On children's understanding of exhaustive questions. Paper presented at the final conference of COST Action A33, London.

Schulz, P. (2010b) Some notes on semantics and SLI. In J. Costa, A. Castro, M. Lobo and F. Pratas (eds) *Language Acquisition and Development. Proceedings of GALA 2009* (pp. 391–406). Cambridge: Cambridge Scholars Press.

Schulz, P. (2013a) Wer versteht wann was? Sprachverstehen im frühen Zweitspracherwerb des Deutschen am Beispiel der w-Fragen. In A. Deppermann (ed.) *Das Deutsch der Migranten. Jahrbuch 2012 des Instituts für deutsche Sprache Mannheim* (pp. 313–337). Berlin: de Gruyter.

Schulz, P. (2013b) Differences between typically developing children and children with SLI in a bilingual context: Exhaustivity. Paper presented at the final conference of COST IS0804 Krakow, Poland.

Schulz, P. (2013c) Früher Zweitspracherwerb und Spezifische Sprachentwicklungsstörungen: Von der Grundlagenforschung zur Diagnostik. Invited paper presented at the 14th DBS Symposium 'Mehrsprachig – mehr möglich?! Multilingualismus im Kontext der Sprachtherapie', Cologne, France.

Schulz, P. and Roeper, T. (2011) Acquisition of exhaustivity in wh-questions: A semantic dimension of SLI? *Lingua* 121 (3), 383–407.

Schulz, P., Gavarro, A., Prévost, P., Friedmann, N. *et al.* (in prep.) Children's understanding of exhaustivity in wh-questions: Evidence for universal acquisition principles across 14 languages.

Southwood, F. (2011) Comprehension of exhaustive Wh questions: MON-TD, BI-TD Afrikaans/isiXhosa-speaking children/adults. Paper presented at the Fifth Meeting of COST Action IS0804, St Paul's Bay, Malta.

Southwood, F. (2013) Wh exhaustivity in Afrikaans-speaking children: Preliminary results from MoTD, BiTD and SLI children. Paper presented at the Eighth Meeting of COST Action IS0804, Lisbon, Portugal.

Stangen, I. (2008) WER WIE WAS? Die Interpretation von w-Fragen bei fünfjährigen Kindern mit Deutsch als Muttersprache. Unpublished BA thesis, University of Frankfurt.

Vuksanović, J., Avramović-Ilić, I., Avramović, I. and Bjekić, J. (2012) Razumevanje svojstva iscrpnosti u višestrukim pitanjima kod predškolske dece tipičnog razvoja (Comprehension of exhaustive wh- questions of typically developing preschool children). *Zbornik Instituta za pedagoška istraživanja* 44 (2), 368–384. DOI: 10.2298/ZIPI1202368V.

Vuksanović, J. and Bjekić, J. (in prep) Is exhaustivity vulnerable in bilingual SLI? Evidence from second language learners of Serbian with L1 Hungarian.

Wojtecka, M. (2010) Eine experimentelle Studie zum Verstehen von exhaustiven W-Fragen bei Vorschulkindern mit Deutsch als Muttersprache. Unpublished magister thesis, Goethe University.

Zimmermann, M. (2007) Quantifying question particles in German: Syntactic effects on interpretation. In E. Puig-Waldmueller (ed.) *Proceedings of Sinn und Bedeutung (SuB 11)* (pp. 627–641). Barcelona: Universitat Pompeu Fabra.

5 Sentence Repetition

Theodoros Marinis
and Sharon Armon-Lotem

Introduction

Sentence repetition (SRep) tasks have been shown to be very sensitive and specific in identifying children with language impairment in monolingual populations (Conti-Ramsden *et al.*, 2001) among others. Sensitivity measures the proportion of children who have language impairment and score very low in a specific task; specificity, in contrast, measures the proportion of children with typical language development (TLD) who do not score low in a specific task. Poor sensitivity may lead to under-diagnosis of specific language impairment (SLI), whereas poor specificity may lead to over-diagnosis. In a seminal paper, Conti-Ramsden *et al.* (2001) showed that sentence recall from Clinical Evaluation of Language Fundamentals 3 (CELF-3) (Semel *et al.*, 1995) had 90% sensitivity and 85% specificity, much higher than measures for non-word repetition (78% sensitivity, 87% specificity), past tense (74% sensitivity, 89% specificity) and third singular –s (63% sensitivity, 90% specificity). These figures illustrate nicely that SRep tasks are more challenging for children with language impairment than other tasks and this is why 90% of children with language impairment score below the cut-off point. At the same time, they are more challenging for some children with TLD as well and this is why 15% of monolingual children with TLD score below the cut-off point, a higher proportion than on all other tasks. If SRep tasks are challenging for some monolingual children with TLD, will bilingual children find them even more challenging if they are tested in their second and non-dominant language?

SRep tasks have been used in bilingual children with variable success when the language tested was the children's second and non-dominant language. Some but not all studies so far have shown the effects of language dominance, age of onset (AoO) and/or length of exposure (LoE). Verhoeven *et al.* (2012) report language dominance effects on children's SRep performance, while Elin Thordardottir and Brandeker (2013) explore the effect of external factors such as LoE. Armon-Lotem *et al.* (2011) report that Russian–Hebrew and Russian–German bilingual groups already performed within the monolingual range on SRep tests in Hebrew as a second language

(L2) and German as an L2 after two years of exposure. Chiat *et al.* (2013) report the effects of AoA and LoE only for a Russian–Hebrew bilingual group, whereas for Turkish–English and Russian–German groups, AoA and LoE were not predictive of the children's SRep performance. Finally, Gutiérrez-Clellen *et al.* (2006) show that there is no gap in the global score of Spanish-dominant bilingual children with TLD when compared to monolingual speakers of Spanish.

The variable performance in bilingual children could be caused by a range of factors not only related to the populations tested, but also to the tasks used. The vocabulary used in the SRep tasks may not have been controlled in terms of widely used psycholinguistic factors, such as frequency, age of acquisition and imageability; the length of words and sentences may have been different across studies; and the tasks may have included different ranges of structures or structures that tap into different underlying grammatical processes. Whatever the differences in findings and possible reasons for these, it is clear that if bilingual children are being tested in their L2, low performance may reflect low language proficiency because of late AoO and limited LoE rather than language impairment. To rule this out, it is important to assess both of the children's languages, since SLI should manifest itself in all languages spoken by the child. A detailed language history is also necessary in order to ascertain the AoO and LoE in all languages spoken by the child (see Tuller, this volume).

To date there is a lack of bilingual/multilingual assessments for children in general and also bilingual/multilingual SRep tasks. COST Action IS0804 addressed this gap by developing a range of language tasks including SRep tasks across a large number of languages. The SRep tasks were constructed using a set of principles to provide comparable results across languages. This allows bilingual children to be assessed in both languages they speak. Difficulties in both languages would strongly indicate language delay or impairment; typical performance in their dominant language and difficulties in their non-dominant (often L2) language would indicate low proficiency in that language but no language impairment.

This chapter will start with a section on the rationale of SRep tasks and the domains they are tapping into. This will motivate the principles and designs used for the SRep tasks developed within the COST Action that will be presented in the second section. The following section will present and discuss examples of designs across a number of languages to illustrate how cross-linguistic differences were taken into account when the parallel versions were created. The fourth section will present the procedure and scoring schemes used and the fifth section will present pilot data. The chapter will conclude with a section which includes a discussion of the strengths and limitations of the tasks, future directions and recommendations of aspects that need to be taken into account when using the SRep tasks with bilingual children for research purposes and also within a clinical setting.

Rationale of SRep Tasks

There is a long tradition of using SRep tasks to assess whether or not children or adults have acquired specific structures in their first language (L1) or their L2, to measure language proficiency in a foreign language teaching setting (Bley-Vroman & Chaudron, 1994; Jessop et al., 2007; Lust et al., 1996) and to measure language abilities in a speech and language therapy setting (Conti-Ramsden et al., 2001) with clinical assessments of language often including a sentence recall subtest. Imitating someone else's behaviour, including their language, is an innate ability of humans and other species, and repeating sounds, words and sentences is often part of uninstructed and instructed teaching and learning processes. One important issue that has attracted a lot of attention is whether SRep is a passive echoing (parroting) of the stimulus, in which case it would not be informative about the participant's language abilities, or whether it is a productive process that involves the participant's grammatical system, in which case it would provide a window into the participant's language competence. Research from the 1970s onwards (Slobin & Welsh, 1973) has addressed this issue and has shown that SRep taps into the learners' implicit knowledge (Ellis, 2005; Erlam, 2006), although test design and in particular sentence length are crucial in this respect. If sentences are long enough to disallow passive copying, participants draw on their grammatical system to repeat the sentences; this requires processing of the incoming stream, analysis and reconstruction of the meaning of the sentence using their own grammatical and memory systems. As a result, they are not able to repeat sentences if they have not acquired the specific structures that are being elicited. However, if the sentences are very short, participants can bypass the decoding/encoding process and repeat sentences using passive copy, in which case SRep will measure only the participants' memory capacity. This is why SRep tasks usually include sentences that are relatively long. It has to be noted that length is relative to age, memory capacity and language abilities. For example, 5-year-old children with TLD may be able to repeat three-word utterances of a structure they have not yet fully acquired if they have good memory skills and the words are familiar to them, so they have strong lexical representations of the words; this does not mean that children with SLI of the same age will be able to bypass the decoding/encoding process and repeat sentences using passive copying; their memory capacity may not be able to support passive copying of a sentence, the structure of which has not been acquired (Fattal et al., 2011) and they may also have weaker lexical representations. We will now turn to the processes involved when participants take part in an SRep task that involves relatively long sentences, and thus taps into the children's grammatical system.

SRep involves listening to sentences and repeating them verbatim. To perform a SRep task, participants have to be able to process/analyse the sentence in terms of all levels of representation (phonological, morphosyntactic, semantic), extract its meaning and then use the production system to regenerate the meaning of the sentence from activated representations in long-term memory (Lombardi & Potter, 1992; Potter & Lombardi, 1990, 1998). Therefore, accuracy in repeating sentences verbatim depends on all processes and levels of representation related to comprehension and production and the ability to store and retrieve language material from memory. Within Baddeley's (2000) Multicomponent Working Memory model, in SRep tasks the episodic buffer plays an important role along with the phonological loop, the central executive and long-term memory. The episodic buffer is a temporary storage system with limited capacity that holds integrated chunks or episodic representations in a multidimensional code (Baddeley, 2000, 2012). Due to its limited capacity, the episodic buffer has been suggested to represent a constraint in language processing (Boyle et al., 2013).

The interaction between different levels of representation and memory has recently been explored by Polišenská (2011) and Polišenská et al. (under review) using SRep tasks in English and Czech. The tasks investigated the effect of prosodic structure, semantic plausibility, syntactic well-formedness and use of pseudo-sentences (with all lexical items or only content words/function words replaced by non-words) on children's ability to repeat sentences. Polišenská's study revealed that each one of these factors affects accuracy in SRep independently, and thus indicates a close linkage between different levels of representation and memory. Interestingly, the largest effects were observed in the conditions related to vocabulary and morphosyntax. Given that SRep tasks involve language processing at all levels of representation in both comprehension and production and also several working memory components, deficits in one or more of those domains and processes may affect performance on this task. Therefore, it is not surprising that children with language impairment score low in SRep tasks.

Principles and Design of the LITMUS-SRep Tasks

The principles and design of the LITMUS-SRep tasks were based on previous research using SRep tasks, on the theoretical understanding of the domains that SRep tasks are tapping into and also on previous research on the way SLI manifests itself across languages (Leonard, 1998). Cross-linguistic studies have shown that, on the one hand, syntactic complexity affects children with SLI across languages, and as a result, structures that are syntactically complex are vulnerable cross-linguistically. On the other hand, there are also important cross-linguistic differences in the way SLI manifests itself across languages, which relate to a large extent to the morphophonological properties of each language. This creates a challenge when trying to create parallel versions across languages. To address these issues and to establish parallel versions across languages, we used the following two principles:

(1) Include in all SRep tasks a set of syntactically complex structures that have been shown to be difficult for children with SLI across languages and involve embedding and/or syntactic movement along with a set of syntactically simple structures as control structures (language-independent structures).
(2) Include a set of structures for each language that have been shown to be difficult for children with SLI in the specific language (language-specific structures).

The language-independent structures include object wh-questions (Friedmann & Novogrodsky, 2011) and relative clauses (Adani et al., 2010; Friedmann & Novogrodsky, 2004) that have been shown to be challenging in children with SLI across languages along with conditionals that are not only syntactically but also semantically complex (Daniel & Klaczynski, 2006). Monoclausal sentences and biclausal sentences with coordination and subordination were included across languages as control conditions matched to the syntactically complex sentences in terms of length.

Language-specific structures were selected on the basis of previous research showing that a structure is vulnerable in a specific language in children with SLI, but not in bilingual children with TLD. For example, for English we selected sentences with auxiliaries and modals because difficulties with tense marking constitute one of the hallmarks of SLI in English (Rice & Wexler, 1996), but auxiliaries are a relative strength in bilingual children with TLD compared to the bound tense marking morphemes –ed and third singular –s (Paradis, 2005). Passives were also selected for English because children with SLI have been found to have difficulties with passives (Marinis & Saddy, 2013; Marshall et al., 2007; Montgomery & Evans, 2009; van der Lely, 1996). Passives were also targeted by the French version in addition to object clitics which are difficult for French-speaking children with SLI but are not expected to be difficult for bilingual children with TLD (see Prévost, this volume). By contrast, in Hebrew, passives are difficult for all speakers being rather infrequent (Ravid et al., 2003), and in Russian they are particularly difficult for bilinguals due to difficulties with the case system which is essential for comprehending passives (Polinsky, 2006). In Hebrew and Russian, some aspects of morphosyntax (e.g. present tense feminine plural verb morphology in Hebrew or number and gender morphology in Russian) are central for discriminating children with SLI from children with TLD because they are sensitive to language impairment but not to bilingualism (Armon-Lotem, 2014); therefore, they were included in the SRep task developed (see the section on the Hebrew and Russian SRep tasks).

In addition to these two principles, we controlled for the length of the sentences and the vocabulary used to ensure consistency within and between languages and to ensure that the children's memory capacity will not be disproportionately affected in particular structures or languages. The length was controlled in terms of the number of clauses (inclusion of monoclausal and biclausal sentences), the number of words/morphemes and the number of syllables in each sentence. In terms of psycholinguistic factors, word frequency, age of acquisition and imageability were controlled when such ratings were available in the languages. Since vocabulary is often a source of difficulty for bilingual children and could jeopardise their ability to repeat sentences (see Haman *et al.*, this volume), vocabulary was restricted to frequent early-acquired words rather than vocabulary for age-matched monolingual children.

Finally, several grammatical properties were controlled in each language depending on the properties of the specific language. For example, in languages with gender marking (e.g. French and Greek), gender was balanced across the task.

Examples of LITMUS-SRep Tasks Across Languages

LITMUS-SRep tasks have been developed so far in Albanian, Lebanese Arabic, Catalan, Croatian, Dutch, English, French, German, Standard and Cypriot Greek, Hebrew, Italian, Lithuanian, Polish, European Portuguese, Russian, Serbian and Turkish; Danish, Irish, Malay, Swedish and Welsh versions are currently in progress.

SRep tasks were developed in two stages. At the first stage, a large number of sentence types and sentences (approximately 60) were created in each language based on the principles outlined in the second section. These were based on the School-Age Sentence Imitation Test (SASIT) (Marinis *et al.*, 2010) and the SRep task by Fattal *et al.* (2011). The initial SRep tasks were piloted with monolingual and/or bilingual children with TLD and/or children with SLI. Reliability analyses for items were used to shorten the tasks and also analyses showing which structures differentiated maximally between children with TLD and children with SLI. At the second stage, a smaller number of sentences (approximately 30 in each language) were selected based on the reliability analyses and evidence of maximum differentiation between children with TLD and children with SLI. The second stage is ongoing; therefore, this section will provide examples from the first stage only. We will start by presenting the design of the English task and compare it with tasks developed in three typologically different languages, Hebrew, Russian and French. Each of these languages represents a different language family with its unique morphosyntactic properties: rich verbal inflection in Hebrew (a Semitic language), rich case system in Russian (a Slavic language) and clitics in French (a Romance language). This variety further allows different degrees of flexibility in word order, while allowing similar complex structures such as relative clauses.

English SRep task

The English SRep task (Marinis *et al.*, 2010) had 60 sentences targeting 15 structures (4 sentences per structure). The task was organised around three blocks with increasing difficulty, as shown in Table 5.1.

The language-independent structures were monoclausal subject-verb-object (SVO) structures (–embedding, –movement), object wh-questions (–embedding, +movement), biclausal sentences with coordination or subordination (+/–embedding, –movement), object relative clauses (+embedding, +movement) and conditionals (+embedding, –movement). Object clefts (+embedding, +movement) were included because they involve movement, like object wh-questions and object relative clauses. This predicted similar difficulties in all three structures. Subject clefts with passives tested whether or not children with SLI have difficulties with sentences involving passives across the board. Sentences with nouns taking complements (+embedding, –movement) tested whether embedding without movement within the noun phrase (on a par with relative clauses) would be challenging for children with SLI. The language-specific structures were the sentences with auxiliaries/modals (with and without negation) and short and long passives (–embedding, +movement) because, as mentioned earlier, they have been shown to be difficult for monolingual English children with SLI (Marinis & Saddy, 2013; Marshall *et al.*, 2007; Montgomery & Evans, 2009; Rice & Wexler, 1996; van der Lely, 1996).

To ensure that word frequency and age of acquisition did not act as confounding factors, the words used in the three blocks were matched in terms of word frequency and age of acquisition using the CELEX database (Baayen *et al.*, 1995) and the MRC Psycholinguistic database (Fearnley, 1997). The sentences in Blocks 1 and 2 were also matched in terms of number of words and number of syllables per sentence, but the sentences in Block 3 were slightly longer in the number of words and syllables than Blocks 1 and 2, to accommodate their syntactic complexity. Finally, the

Table 5.1 Structures tested in the English SRep task with examples

Block	Structure	Example
1	Subject-verb-object (SVO) with one auxiliary or modal (4)	The kitten is chasing the rat up and down. She can bring the glass to the table.
	SVO with negation and one auxiliary or modal (4)	The man wasn't driving the lorry to town. He shouldn't draw the tiger in the tree.
	Short actional passives (4)	She was stopped at the big red lights.
	Wh-who/what object questions (4)	Who did the monkey splash near the water? What did they find yesterday in the snow?
	Biclausal sentences: coordination or complement clauses (4)	His sister ran and his father walked. The cook tried to make the soup in the kitchen.
2	SVO with two auxiliaries or one auxiliary and one modal (4)	The policeman has been looking at us. She could have waited for them in the street.
	SVO with negation, one auxiliary and one modal (4)	John won't have talked about it with his father. They couldn't have chased the goose by the river.
	Long actional and non-actional passives (4)	The sandwich was eaten by the postman. She was seen by the doctor in the morning.
	wh-object which questions and oblique wh-questions (4)	Which picture did he paint at home yesterday? Who did she give the beautiful rose to?
	Biclausal sentences: complement or adjunct clauses (4)	She thinks that the spider is very small. The child ate breakfast after he washed his face.
3	Object relative clauses – sentence final (4)	The children enjoyed the sweets that they tasted. He should wash the baby that the child is patting.
	Object relative clause – centre embedded (4)	The swan that the deer chased knocked over the plant. The horse that the farmer pushed kicked him in the back.
	Conditionals (4)	The people will get a present if they clean the house. If the kids behave we will go in the garden.
	Object clefts with actives and subject clefts with passives (4)	It was the boy that the man splashed in the sea. It was the paper that was damaged by the fire.
	Sentences with nouns taking complements (4)	Peter had a dream of becoming a bus-driver. The promise of going to Paris made them happy.

Note: Number of sentences per structure in brackets.

type of nominal expression was controlled between the sentence types with the sentences having an equal number of full noun phrases and pronouns within each sentence type. The sentence types were pseudorandomised within each block to ensure that two consecutive test items did not elicit the same structure. Stimuli sentences varied in length from 7 to 13 syllables and from 7 to 13 words.

Russian SRep task

The SRep task in Russian (Meir & Armon-Lotem, 2015) has 56 items of varying complexity and length. Special attention was given to language-specific aspects of verbal and nominal morphology which are central in Russian and known to be difficult for monolingual children with SLI. For verb morphology, gender and number were controlled; for nominal morphology, prepositions and cases were selected to represent a wide range of cases.

The 56 items were chosen from a larger pool of sentences which were tested on Russian–Hebrew bilingual children with TLD aged from 5;08 to 6;07 (mean=6;01). All children grew up speaking Russian at home and Hebrew in their preschool from age 3, and scored within monolingual norms in at least one of their languages (Armon-Lotem, 2011). The pilot study showed poor performance of the bilingual children on a number of syntactic structures (e.g. passives with the agent-phrase, complex sentences with temporal clauses, oblique relatives, complex sentences with advanced conjunctions). Thus, it was decided to eliminate these structures as they pose great difficulties to typically developing bilingual children aged 6. Eleven structures were selected, as shown in Table 5.2. The structures vary in terms of embedding and syntactic movement, including sentences without embedding and movement (simple monoclausal sentences), sentences with embedding but without movement (biclausal sentences involving coordination vs subordination), sentences with movement but without embedding (object and oblique which-questions, object-verb-subject [OVS]) and sentences with embedding and movement (object relative clauses). These structures made the task comparable with the other languages. Conditionals were added to tap into semantic knowledge. The structures were grouped by length and complexity into three blocks and pseudorandomised within each block so that two consecutive test items did not contain the same target structure or the same lexical items. There were 8 sentences with SVO, the basic word order in Russian, to enable independent testing of morphosyntax and prepositions and 12 more structures with 4 sentences in each. The same lexical items were deployed across different syntactic structures to minimise the effect of specific lexical items. Stimulus sentences varied in length from four to nine words.

Table 5.2 Structures tested in the Russian SRep task with examples

Block	Structure	Example
1	SVO (8)	kotjonok našjol tapočki pod krovat'ju. kitten.NOM found slippers.ACC under bed.INSTR 'The kitten found the slipper under the bed'.
	SOV (4)	devočka mal'čika udarila v sadu. girl.NOM boy.ACC hit in gadern.LOC 'The girl hit the boy in the garden'.
	OVS (4)	mamu poceloval syn pered snom. mother.ACC kissed son.NOM before sleeping.INSTR 'The son kissed the mother before sleeping'.
2	Biclausal sentences with coordination (4)	tjotja pomyla posudu, a djadja svaril sup. aunt.NOM washed dishes.ACC and/but uncle.NOM cooked soup.ACC 'The aunt did the dishes and the uncle made soup'.
	Biclausal sentences with subordination (4)	oni uslyšali, čto ja prišjol iz magazina. they.NOM heard that i.NOM came from shop.GEN 'They heard that I came-back from the shop'.
	Object questions (4)	kakuju zebru lošad' dognala v cirke? which.ACC zebra.ACC horse.NOM caught-up in circus.PREP? 'Which zebra did the horse catch up with in the circus?'
	Oblique questions (4)	ot kakoj sobaki ubežala koška? from which.GEN dog.GEN ran-away cat.NOM 'From which dog did the cat run-away?'

Block	Structure	Example
3	Real conditionals (4)	esli ona pročitaet skazku, my pojdjom v park. if she.NOM will-read story.ACC we.NOM will-go in park.ACC 'If she reads the fairy-tale, we will go to the park'.
	Unreal conditionals (4)	my by pošli v kino, esli by sdelali uroki. we.NOM SUBJ went in cinema if SUBJ did lessions.ACC 'We would have gone to the cinema, if the brother had done homework'.
	Subject relatives (8)	jeto žiraf, kotoryj tolknul krokodila. this giraffe.NOM which.NOM pushed crocodile.ACC 'This is a giraffe that pushed the crocodile'.
	Object relatives (8)	jeto devochka, kotoruju narisovala mama. this girl.NOM which.ACC drew mother.NOM 'This is the girl that the mother drew'.

Note: Number of sentences per structure in brackets.

Hebrew SRep task

The Hebrew SRep task (Meir *et al.*, under review) also has 56 items of varying complexity and length. For language-specific morphosyntax, verb morphology included person morphology and plural morphology, which were reported to be difficult for Hebrew-speaking children with SLI (Dromi *et al.*, 1993, 1999) but not for bilingual children in their L2 Hebrew (Armon-Lotem, 2014). Special attention was given to prepositions, which were found to better discriminate SLI in Hebrew (Armon-Lotem *et al.*, 2008). The 56 items were chosen from a larger pool of sentences which were tested on Russian–Hebrew bilingual children with TLD aged from 5;08 to 6;07 (mean=6;01). All children were born in Israel and grew up speaking Russian at home and Hebrew in their preschool from age 3. All children scored within the monolingual norm in at least one of their languages (Armon-Lotem, 2011). The pilot study showed that bilingual children with TLD had difficulties with object clefts, passive constructions with the agent-phrase and complex sentences of dual complexity (e.g. questions containing a passive construction). Thus, it was decided to eliminate these structures as they pose great difficulties to typically developing bilingual children aged 6.

The 56 sentences selected vary in terms of embedding and syntactic movement, including sentences without embedding and movement (simple monoclausal sentences with a range of inflections and prepositions), sentences with embedding but without movement (biclausal sentences involving coordination vs subordination), sentences with movement but without embedding (object and oblique which-questions, verb-subject-object [VSO]) and sentences with embedding and movement (relative clauses). Following these principles made the task comparable with the other languages. Biclausal sentences with advanced conjunctions as well as conditionals were added to tap into semantic complexity. Eleven structures were grouped into three blocks, as shown in Table 5.3, by length and complexity and were pseudorandomised within each block so that two consecutive test items did not contain the same target structure or the same lexical items. There were 8 sentences with SVO, the basic word order for Hebrew, to enable independent testing of morphosyntax and prepositions and 10 more structures with 4–8 sentences in each. The same lexical items were deployed across different syntactic structures to minimise the effect of specific lexical items. Stimuli sentences varied in length from 5 to 11 words.

French SRep task

The French SRep task (Prévost *et al.*, 2012) has 56 items of varying complexity and length. Special attention was given to language-specific

Table 5.3 Structures tested in the Hebrew SRep task with examples

Block	Structure	Example
1	SVO (8)	ha- kelev maca et ha-ecem mitaxat la-mita DET- dog found ACC DET-bone under to+DET-bed 'The dog found the bone under the bed'.
	Biclausal sentences with coordination (4)	ha-yeladot oxlot glida ve ha-imahot šotot qafe. DET-girls eat ice-cream and DET-mothers drink coffee. 'The girls eat ice-cream and the mothers drink coffee'.
	Biclausal sentences with subordination (4)	ha-yeled xashav še- halaxta la- mesiba. DET-boy thought that- went.2P.MASC.SG to+DET- party 'The boy thought that you went to the party'.
2	Object questions (4)	eyze yeled ha-more hifxid etmol which.MASC boy DET-teacher.MASC frightened.3P.MASC.SG yesterday 'Which boy did the teacher frighten?'
	Oblique questions (4)	le- eyzo mora ha-yalda hevi'a perax to which.FEM teacher.FEM DET-girl brought.3P.FEM.SG flower 'Which teacher did the girl bring a flower to?'
	Object relatives (4)	ra'iti et ha-kelev še ha-sus daxaf saw.1P.SG ACC DET-dog that DET- horse pushed.3P.MASC.SG 'I saw the dog that the horse pushed'.
	Oblique relatives (4)	ze ha-tinoq še ha-xatul meciq lo this DET- baby that DET-cat annoy.3P.MASC.SG to+him 'This is the baby that the cat annoys'.

(Continued)

Table 5.3 (Continued)

Block	Structure	Example
3	Real conditionals (4)	im ha-boc yityabeš nece lesaxeq if DET- mud cry.3P.MASC.SG.PRES go-out.2P.PL to+play ba-xacer in+DET-yard. 'If the mud dries, we will go to play in the yard'.
	Unreal conditionals (4)	im hayiti mištatef ba-meroc hayiti if was.1P.SG take+part.PRES.MASC.SG in+DET-race was.1P.SG zoxe win.RES.MASC.SG 'If I had taken part in the race, I would have won'.
	Biclausal sentences with advanced conjunctions (8)	lamrot še ha-yalda nafla hi even+thought =hat DET-girl fell.3P.FEM.SG she himšixa ba-taxarut continued.3P.FEM.SG in+DET competition 'Even though the girl fell down, she continued (participating) in the competition'.
	VSO (8)	ba- boqer qar'a ha-yalda sefer in+DET morning read.3P.FEM.SG DET-girl book. 'In the morning the girl read a book'.

Note: Number of sentences per structure in brackets.

features of verbal morphology which are central in French and known to be difficult for monolingual children with SLI, focusing on present and past tense singular and plural. With French being a Romance language, masculine and feminine object clitics were also targeted as these have been found to be sensitive to SLI (Prévost, this volume). The 56 items were chosen from a larger pool of sentences which were tested on bilingual children with TLD aged 5–6. The pilot study showed poor performance of the bilingual children on a number of syntactic structures. Thus, it was decided to eliminate these structures as they pose great difficulties to bilingual children aged 6 with TLD. The 56 sentences selected vary in terms of embedding and syntactic movement, including sentences without embedding and movement (simple monoclausal sentences), sentences with embedding but without movement (biclausal sentences involving subordination with finite and non-finite sentential complements), sentences with movement but without embedding (who and which object wh-questions, short and long passives, right dislocation with clitics) and sentences with embedding and movement (relative clauses). These structures made the task comparable with the other languages. Seven structures with eight items each, as shown in Table 5.4 (some structures divided in two types with four sentences each, such as subject and object relative clauses) were ordered by length and complexity and pseudorandomised so that two consecutive test items did not contain the same target structure or the same lexical items. The same lexical items were deployed across different syntactic structures to minimise the effect of specific lexical items. Stimuli sentences varied in length from 4 to 10 words.

Procedure and Scoring

The sentences in all languages were pre-recorded by native speakers of the language, tested and incorporated into PowerPoint presentations for administration of the tasks to ensure that all children listen to the sentences in exactly the same way. PowerPoint presentations were created for both the first and second stage of development of the SRep tasks. For the first stage, a number represented each sentence and a smiley was used at the end of each group of 10 sentences to provide positive feedback and encourage participants to continue the task. Figure 5.1 shows a slide from the PowerPoint of the English task that consisted of 60 sentences.

For the languages in which the task was organised in three blocks with rising complexity, the three blocks were presented consecutively, as shown in Figure 5.1 (the patterns shades, dots and lines representing different blocks). For the languages that did not include levels of complexity (e.g. French), all sentences were presented in one block.

Table 5.4 Structures tested in the French SRep task with examples

Structure	Example
SVO, present tense (8)	Le bébé boit du lait. the.MASC.SG baby drinks some.MASC milk The baby drinks some milk.
SVO, passé composé (8)	La maman a fermé la fenêtre. the.FEM mother has closed the window The mother closed the window
Passives (8) Short (4)	Ce matin, le cheval a été brossé. this morning the.MASC.SG horse has been brushed This morning, the horse was brushed
Long (4)	La dame a été poussée par le garçon. the.FEM.SG woman has been pushed by the.MASC.SG boy The woman was pushed by the boy
Accusative clitics (right dislocation) (8)	Je le remplis toujours ce verre. I CL.ACC.3sg.masc fill always this.SG.MASC glass The glass, I always fill it
Biclausal sentences with subordination (8) Non-finite sentential complements (4)	Le papa sait très bien conduire la voiture the.MASC.SG daddy knows very well to+drive the.FEM car The father knows to drive the car very well
Finite sentential complements (4)	Le garçon dit que la maman a lu the.MASC.SG boy says that the.FEM mommy has read un livre. a.MASC book The boy says that the mother has read a book.

Structure		Example
Relatives (8)	Subject (4)	Je vois la fille qui a poussé le garçon.
		I see the.FEM girl that(subject) has pushed the.MASC boy
		I see the girl that pushed the boy.
	Object (4)	Je vois le garçon que la fille a poussé.
		I see the.MASC.SG boy that(object) the.FEM girl has pushed
		I see the boy that the girl pushed.
Object which-questions (8)	Who (4)	Qui la dame dessine?
		who the.FEM lady draws
		Who does the woman draw?
	Which (4)	Quel enfant la maîtresse punit?
		which child the.FEM teacher punishes
		Which child does the teacher punish?

Note: Number of sentences per structure in brackets.

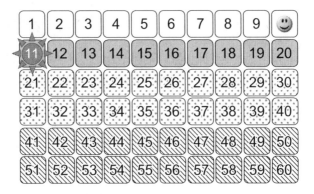

Figure 5.1 Slide from PowerPoint of the English SRep task (first stage, long SRep task)

Figure 5.2 Slide from PowerPoint of the English SRep task (second stage, short SRep task)

For the second stage, the SRep tasks were embedded into a treasure hunt in order to make the task more engaging. A bear was shown in a PowerPoint presentation going through several locations in search of a treasure. Figure 5.2 provides an example with the bear going towards a cave.

In this version, the bear moved from stone to stone. On each stone, the child heard a sentence and had to repeat the sentence for the bear to move to the next one. This proved to be very motivating for children who were eager to repeat the sentences in order to find out where the bear would go and what the treasure was going to be.

The sentences were presented through headphones to ensure good and consistent quality of input. External speakers were used for presentation in a very few cases in which the child objected to the headphones. The children's responses were recorded with high-quality microphones to allow detailed scoring after testing.

Children were seated in front of a computer screen showing the PowerPoint presentation. They were instructed to listen carefully to the sentences and say exactly what they heard. A practice session presented two to four sentences to demonstrate the task to the children and to ensure that the children understood what they had to do. If children did not repeat the sentences spontaneously, the experimenter explained the task again and encouraged them to repeat what they heard. The practice sentences could be repeated several times until the children understood what they had to do. Most children understood the task quickly and easily.

For the experimental sentences, children listened to each sentence only once unless there was a loud noise in the room or another interruption. Oral praise ('well done') was used irrespective of whether or not the children were repeating the sentences accurately in order to motivate the children to continue. If the child self-corrected, his/her final response was scored (whether correct or incorrect).

The children's responses were audio recorded and marked on an answer sheet during the testing. They were further transcribed and scored off-line on the basis of the recording. Figure 5.3 illustrates the first page of the scoring sheet of the English SRep task.

SRep tasks can be scored in different ways depending on whether they are being used for research or clinical purposes, the focus of the study and practical reasons, such as the amount of time available. For the LITMUS-SRep tasks, we initially used six scoring schemes and compared them with each other at the pilot phase of the studies.

The first two schemes, 0–1 and 0–3 schemes, calculate sentence scores (column S in the scoring sheet in Figure 5.3). The 0–1 scheme allocated a score of 1 if the sentence was repeated entirely verbatim and a score of 0 if there were one or more changes in the children's response. This scoring was based on the Test of Language Development-Primary (TOLD-P-4) (Newcomer & Hammill, 2008). The 0–3 scheme allocated a score of 3 if the sentence was repeated entirely verbatim, a score of 2 if there was one change, a score of 1 if there were two to three changes and a score of 0 if there were four or more changes in the children's response. This scoring was based on the CELF-3 (Semel et al., 1995).

The third scheme counted the number of content words (content word score) and function words (function word score) correct and noted the number of omissions, substitutions and additions. It was used to explore differences between word and error types. To facilitate scoring, content

		Year	Month	Day
Child name/ID number:	Date:	___	___	___
Tester:	Child date of birth:	___	___	___
	Child Age:	___	___	___

Practice items:
The girl is flying the balloon in the sky
The lion is drinking water at the zoo
They must paint the fence in the garden
He can play football in the park

					Omis		Sub		Add		Gram	Synt. struct
ITEM	TARGET	S	Cont	Funct	C	F	C	F	C	F		Aux
1	The kitten *is* chasing the rat up and down. (9)	3	6									
												Aux+neg
2	She *is n't* feeding the sheep on the farm. (9)	3	6									
												Mod+neg
3	He *should* n't draw the tiger in the tree. (9)	3	6									
												Mod+neg
4	The farmer *could* n't ride the horse in the river. (10)	4	6									
												Passive
5	The child *was* helped in the sweet shop. (8)	4	4									
												Passive
6	The books *were* taken to the office. (7)	3	4									
												Aux+neg
7	The man *was* n't driving the lorry to town. (9)	4	5									
												Modal
8	The boy *must* sweep the floor in the kitchen. (9)	4	5									
												Modal
9	She *can* bring the glass to the table. (8)	3	5									
												Passive
10	She *was* stopped at the big red lights. (8)	4	4									
												Wh-obj
11	Who *have* they seen near the steps? (7)	2	5									
												Complem
12	The cook tried to make the soup in the kitchen. (10)	5	5									
												Complem
13	She wants to eat a large sandwich. (7)	4	3									

Figure 5.3 Scoring sheet of English 60 item SRep task

words were highlighted in blue and function words were highlighted in yellow, as shown in Figure 5.3. This scoring scheme was based on the Sentence Imitation Test (SIT) (Seeff-Gabriel *et al.*, 2008).

The fourth was a grammaticality scheme. It allocated 1 point if the sentence had no grammatical errors, regardless of whether or not it was a verbatim repetition of the target sentence and a mark of 0 if the sentence had one or more grammatical errors.

The fifth scheme was a sentence structure score. It allocated 1 point if the child used the structure targeted irrespective of whether or not there were changes in other parts of the sentence. A score of 0 was given if the child made an error in the sentence structure that was targeted, e.g. omission of an auxiliary in sentences targeting auxiliaries. A score of 0 was also given if the child did not produce the sentence structure targeted and substituted it with another structure, e.g. substituting an object relative clause (The swan that the deer chased knocked over the plant) with a subject relative clause (The swan that chased the deer knocked over the plant) or substituting a passive (The child was helped in the sweet shop) with an active (The child was helping in the sweet shop). The score sheet indicated the structure that was targeted in the column 'syntactic structure'.

The sixth scoring scheme calculated the number of changes between the target and the repeated structure using the Levenshtein distance algorithm (Levenshtein, 1966) which measures the distance between the target and the response. This scheme was based on Riches *et al.* (2010) and was calculated automatically in an Excel spreadsheet.

In all schemes, allowances were given for self-corrections, consistent phonological processes, e.g. fronting, dialectal variation, contractions (they're for they are) and expansions (John will not for John won't).

Pilot Data

English

A pilot study of the English long SRep task was conducted with 100 six- to eight-year old children (60 monolingual children with TLD, 20 Polish–English children with TLD and 20 monolingual English children with SLI). All scoring schemes were used in order to identify which scoring schemes differentiated maximally the groups of children with TLD from the group of children with SLI. The 0–1, 0–3 and the grammaticality scheme were best in separating the monolingual and bilingual children with TLD from the children with SLI. In terms of the structures targeted, the monolingual and bilingual children with TLD outperformed the children with SLI on all sentence types, but some structures showed no overlap between the children with SLI vs the groups with TLD, whereas some other structures showed partial overlap because they were difficult also for the monolingual and bilingual children with TLD. The structures showing no overlap between the monolingual and bilingual children with TLD on the one hand and the children with SLI on the other hand were the SVO sentences with one auxiliary/modal, two auxiliaries or one auxiliary and one modal, the short and long passives, the who/what wh-questions, the right branching object relative clauses, the sentences with conditionals and the sentences with nouns taking complements. SVO sentences with negation and an auxiliary/modal, object clefts and subject clefts with passives were difficult for all groups of children and as a result showed overlap between the two groups of children with TLD and the children with SLI. Finally, some structures were difficult for the bilingual children with TLD and as a result showed overlap between this group and the group of children with SLI. These were the biclausal sentences with coordination and infinitival clauses, the sentences with negation, one auxiliary and one modal, which-object and oblique object questions, biclausal sentences with subordination and centre embedded object relative clauses.

Russian–Hebrew

In a pilot study, Meir (2010) tested 12 bilingual children with TLD (six female) aged from 5;6 to 6;5 (mean=6;08) in L1 Russian and L2 Hebrew. All children were born in Israel. Two scoring methods were applied: correct full sentence (1: correct repetition, 0: erroneous repetition) and correct target structure (1: correctly preserved target structure, 0: target structure was modified/omitted). The pilot identified the syntactic structures in which bilingual children with TLD performed poorly (e.g. passives with the agent-phrase in Russian and Hebrew, object clefts in Hebrew) and helped to decide which structures should be eliminated from the current version of the Russian and Hebrew SRep tasks on the grounds that they posed difficulties for bilingual children with TLD. The Russian and Hebrew tasks were administered to 38 sequential bilingual children with L1 Russian and L2 Hebrew (10 with SLI) (Meir *et al.*, under review). The bilingual group with TLD significantly outperformed the bilingual SLI group on most morphosyntactic structures in both languages. In L1 Russian, children with TLD showed better performance than the children with SLI on sentences with the VSO, OVS and subject-object-verb (SOV) word orders, biclausal sentences with coordination and subordination, oblique questions, subject and object relatives and real conditionals. However, object questions and unreal conditionals posed difficulties for all children. In Hebrew, the group with TLD repeated sentences containing object and oblique questions, object and oblique relatives, sentences with VSO word order, real and unreal conditionals and biclausal sentences with advanced conjunctions more accurately than their SLI peers. However, both groups showed a ceiling effect on sentences with SVO word order and biclausal sentences with coordination and subordination. Moreover, four error patterns distinguished the SLI group from the group with TLD: avoiding a response altogether, omitting coordinators, subordinators and prepositions and using simple clauses rather than relative clauses.

Discussion of Strengths, Limitations and Recommendations for Using the LITMUS-SRep Tasks

SRep tasks have several advantages compared to other types of tasks. They are quick and easy to administer, they have clear target sentences and can include a large range of sentence types, and they can be scored in several ways depending on the focus of the analysis (Gabriel *et al.*, 2010). The LITMUS-SRep tasks have all these strengths. In terms of the length of the tasks, the first version of the LITMUS-SRep tasks included approximately 60 sentences for each language including a large range of sentence structures. The task took around 20–30 minutes to administer. There is a tension between the length of a task and how comprehensive it is in providing data for a range of structures. Long SRep tasks can be less engaging for children and less appropriate within a clinical setting. Therefore, shorter versions of the LITMUS-SRep tasks including approximately 30 sentences were created based on pilot data. The shorter tasks take approximately 10 minutes to administer. The tasks were shortened not only on the basis of inter-item reliability and internal consistency measures, but also on empirical evidence about which structures are better in differentiating between monolingual and bilingual children with TLD and children with SLI.

The procedure of the LITMUS-SRep tasks was standardised between languages using pre-recorded sentences and the same PowerPoint slides in both stages across languages. Therefore, differences between languages cannot be attributed to differences in the task procedure. Scoring was also standardised across languages and includes a range of scoring schemes. These scoring schemes provide quantitative scores that can be used to compare the participants' performance between structures and between languages. In addition, qualitative analyses can be conducted by analysing the error patterns. Qualitative analyses can be tailored to research and/or clinical needs. They can provide invaluable information about the cause of the breakdown in repeating sentences and can be extremely helpful when designing language intervention protocols.

SRep tasks also have important limitations that need to be kept in mind. The most important limitation concerns the relationship between the developmental stage of the participant and the sentence length. If sentences are too short for the participant's language abilities, he/she may be able to repeat them passively (parroting) and the results will not reflect the participant's language abilities. To avoid this limitation, the LITMUS-SRep sentences are relatively long. However, the opposite effect may also occur. If the sentences are too long, they may exceed the participant's memory capacity and may lead to a floor effect. Participants may fail to repeat sentences not because they have not acquired a particular structure, such as auxiliaries in the English task, but for different reasons, for example because of the length of the sentence or the lexical items used. This can be partially addressed through the structural scoring, which identifies if participants were able to use the specific structure irrespective of whether or not they repeated the sentence verbatim.

A second important limitation is that it does not assess all aspects of language ability and all levels of representation. While it is extremely informative about lexical, morphosyntactic and syntactic skills, it does not separate comprehension from production and it does not assess the children's pragmatic skills. Therefore, despite its strengths, it should be supplemented by other language assessments.

When the LITMUS-SRep task is administered to bilingual children, it should be used in conjunction with a detailed language history questionnaire, such as the PABIQ questionnaire (see Tuller, this volume). This is crucial because differences in the participants' language history, such as AoO, LoE and quantity and quality of input may affect the participants' performance on the LITMUS-SRep tasks in the two languages. For example, a very short LoE in one of the two languages may result in a very low performance in that specific language. In fact, it would not be recommended to use the SRep task in a specific language if the LoE in a specific language is less than 12 months since we would expect performance to be very low with very limited LoE. Furthermore, the task may be frustrating for children with such limited exposure.

The tasks should be administered following the protocols developed. When both languages spoken by the child are tested, these should be tested in separate sessions and instructions should be given in the language tested. In each SRep task, instructions are included in the PowerPoint presentation. The task protocols should be followed carefully on the basis of the task manuals. Giving allowances consistently for self-corrections, phonological processes and expansions is crucial, as well as calculating inter-rater reliability scores for transcription and scoring. Finally, it is very important to keep the children engaged in the task by praising them for their responses irrespective of whether or not they repeat the sentences verbatim.

Acknowledgements

The sentence repetition tasks were developed within the COST Action IS0804 'Language Impairment in a Multilingual Society'. At the time of writing, Theodoros Marinis was supported by an Onassis Fellowship and Sharon Armon-Lotem was supported by the German-Israel Foundation (Grant No. 1113/2010). We would like to thank all members of the Sentence Repetition group for developing tasks in a range of languages and Vicky

Chondrogianni, Enkeleida Kapia and Aneta Miekisz for working on the PowerPoint presentation of the short SRep task.

References

Adani, F., van der Lely, H.K., Forgiarini, M. and Guasti, M.T. (2010) Grammatical feature dissimilarities make relative clauses easier: A comprehension study with Italian children. *Lingua* 120 (9), 2148–2166.

Armon-Lotem, S. (2011) Design and data of English-Hebrew and Russian-Hebrew sentence repetition tasks. Paper presented at COST IS0804 WG and MC Meeting, Malta, November.

Armon-Lotem, S. (2014) Between L2 and SLI: Inflections and prepositions in the Hebrew of bilingual children with TLD and monolingual children with SLI. *Journal of Child Language* 41 (1), 1–31.

Armon-Lotem, S., Danon, G. and Walters, J. (2008) The use of prepositions by bilingual SLI children: The relative contribution of representation and processing. *Proceedings of the Generative Assembly on Language Acquisition* (pp. 41–46).

Armon-Lotem, S., Gagarina, N. and Walters, J. (2011) The impact of internal and external factors on linguistic performance in the home language and in L2 among Russian-Hebrew and Russian-German preschool children. *Linguistic Approaches to Bilingualism* 1 (3), 291–317.

Baayen, R.H., Piepenbrock, R. and Gulikers, L. (1995) The CELEX lexical database (CD-ROM). Paper presented at the Linguistic Data Consortium, University of Pennsylvania, PA.

Baddeley, A. (2000) The episodic buffer: A new component of working memory? *Trends in Cognitive Sciences* 4 (11), 417–423.

Baddeley, A. (2012) Working memory: Theories, models, and controversies. *Article in Annual Review of Psychology* 63, 1–19.

Bley-Vroman, R. and Chaudron, C. (1994) Elicited imitation as a measure of second-language competence. In E.E. Tarone, S.M. Gass and A.D. Cohen (eds) *Research Methodology in Second-Language Acquisition* (pp. 245–262). Hillsdale, NJ: Lawrence Erlbaum.

Boyle, W., Lindell, A.K. and Kidd, E. (2013) Investigating the role of verbal working memory in young children's sentence comprehension. *Language Learning* 63, 211–242.

Chiat, S., Armon-Lotem, S., Marinis, T., Polisenska, K., Roy, P. and Seeff-Gabriel, B. (2013) Assessment of language abilities in sequential bilingual children: The potential of sentence imitation tasks. In V.C. Mueller Gathercole (ed.) *Issues in the Assessment of Bilinguals* (pp. 56–89). Bristol: Multilingual Matters.

Conti-Ramsden, G., Botting, N. and Faragher, B. (2001) Psycholinguistic markers for specific language impairment. *Journal of Child Psychology and Psychiatry* 42 (6), 741–748.

Daniel, D.B. and Klaczynski, P.A. (2006) Developmental and individual differences in conditional reasoning: Effects of logic instructions and alternative antecedents. *Child Development* 77 (2), 339–354.

Dromi, E., Leonard, L. and Shteiman, M. (1993) The grammatical morphology of Hebrew speaking children with specific language impairment: Some competing hypotheses. *Journal of Speech and Hearing Research* 36 (4), 760–771.

Dromi, E., Leonard, L., Adam, G. and Zadunaisky-Ehrlich, S. (1999) Verb agreement morphology in Hebrew-speaking children with specific language impairment. *Journal of Speech, Language and Hearing Research* 42 (6), 1414–1431.

Elin Thordardottir, E. and Brandeker, M. (2013) The effect of bilingual exposure versus language impairment on nonword repetition and sentence imitation scores. *Journal of Communication Disorders* 46 (1), 1–16.

Ellis, R. (2005) Measuring implicit and explicit knowledge of a second language: A psychometric study. *Studies in Second Language Acquisition* 27 (2), 141–172.

Erlam, R. (2006) Elicited imitation as a measure of L2 implicit knowledge: An empirical validation study. *Applied Linguistics* 27 (3), 464–491.

Fattal, I., Friedmann, N. and Fattal-Valevski, A. (2011) The crucial role of thiamine in the development of syntax and lexical retrieval: A study of infantile thiamine deficiency. *Brain* 134 (Pt. 6), 1720–1739.

Fearnley, S. (1997) MRC Psycholinguistic Database search program. *Behavior Research Methods, Instruments, & Computers* 29 (2), 291–295.

Friedmann, N. and Novogrodsky, R. (2004) The acquisition of relative clause comprehension in Hebrew: A study of G-SLI and normal development. *Journal of Child Language* 31, 661–681.

Friedmann, N. and Novogrodsky, R. (2011) Which questions are most difficult to understand? The comprehension of Wh questions in three subtypes of SLI. *Lingua* 121, 367–382.

Gabriel, B., Chiat, S. and Dodd, B. (2010) Sentence imitation as a tool in identifying expressive morphosyntactic difficulties in children with severe speech difficulties. *International Journal of Language and Communication Disorders* 45 (6), 691–702.

Gutiérrez-Clellen, V.F., Restrepo, M.A. and Simon-Cereijido, G. (2006) Evaluating the discriminate accuracy of a grammatical measure with Spanish-speaking children. *Journal of Speech, Language and Hearing Research* 49 (6), 1209–1223.

Jessop, L., Suzuki, W. and Tomita, Y. (2007) Elicited imitation in second language acquisition research. *The Canadian Modern Language Review* 64, 215–238.

Leonard, L. (1998) *Children with Specific Language Impairment*. Cambridge, MA: MIT Press.

Levenshtein, V.I. (1966) Binary codes capable of correcting deletions, insertions, and reversals. *Soviet Physics Doklady* 10, 707–710.

Lombardi, L. and Potter, M.C. (1992) The regeneration of syntax in short term memory. *Journal of Memory and Language* 31 (6), 713–733.

Lust, B., Flynn, S. and Foley, C. (1996) What children know about what they say: Elicited imitation as a research method for assessing children's syntax. In D. McDaniel, C. McKee and S. Cairns Helen (eds) *Methods for Assessing Children's Syntax* (pp. 55–76). Cambridge, MA: MIT Press.

Marinis, T., Chiat, S., Armon-Lotem, S., Gibbons, D. and Gipps, E. (2010) *School-Age Sentence Imitation Test (SASIT)*. Reading: University of Reading.

Marinis, T. and Saddy, D. (2013) Parsing the passive: Comparing children with specific language impairment to sequential bilingual children. *Language Acquisition* 20 (2), 155–179.

Marshall, C., Marinis, T. and van der Lely, H. (2007) Passive verb morphology: The effect of phonotactics on passive comprehension in typically developing and grammatical-SLI children. *Lingua* 117 (8), 1434–1447.

Meir, N. and Armon-Lotem, S. (2015) Disentangling bilingualism from SLI in Heritage Russian: The impact of L2 properties and length of exposure to the L2. In C. Hamann and E. Ruigendijk (eds) *Language Acquisition and Development: Proceedings of GALA 2013*. Cambridge Scholars Publishing: Newcastle.

Meir, N., Armon-Lotem, S. and Walters, J. (under review) Disentangling SLI and bilingualism using Sentence Repetition Tasks: the impact of L1 and TL properties. *International Journal of Blingualism*.

Montgomery, J. and Evans, J. (2009) Complex sentence comprehension and working memory in children with specific language impairment. *Journal of Speech, Language, and Hearing Research* 52 (2), 269–288.

Newcomer, P. and Hammill, D.D. (2008) *Test of Language Development: Primary* (4th edn). Austin, TX: Pro-ed.

Paradis, J. (2005) Grammatical morphology in children learning English as a second language: Implications of similarities with specific language impairment. *Language, Speech and Hearing Services in the Schools* 36 (3), 172–187.

Polinsky, M. (2006) Incomplete acquisition: American Russian. *Journal of Slavic Linguistics* 14, 191–262.

Polišenská, K. (2011) The influence of linguistic structure on memory span: Repetition tasks as a measure of language ability. Unpublished doctoral thesis, City University London.

Polišenská, K., Chiat, S., and Roy, P. (2015). Sentence repetition: What does the task measure? *International Journal of Language and Communication Disorders*, 50, 106–118.

Potter, M.C. and Lombardi, L. (1990) Regeneration in the short-term recall of sentences. *Journal of Memory and Language* 29, 633–654.

Potter, M.C. and Lombardi, L. (1998) Syntactic priming in immediate recall of sentences. *Journal of Memory and Language* 38 (3), 265–282.

Prévost, P., Tuller, L. and Zebib, R. (2012) *LITMUS-SR-French.* Tours.

Ravid, D., Landau, H., and Lovetski, M. (2003) Passive morphology in the school years: An example of later language acquisition (in Hebrew). *Script* 5–6, 129–158.

Rice, M.L. and Wexler, K. (1996) Toward tense as a clinical marker of specific language impairment in English-speaking children. *Journal of Speech and Hearing Research* 39, 1239–1257.

Riches, N.G., Loucas, T., Baird, G., Charman, T. and Simonoff, E. (2010) Sentence repetition in adolescents with specific language impairments and autism: An investigation of complex syntax. *International Journal of Language and Communication Disorders* 45 (1), 47–60.

Seeff-Gabriel, B., Chiat, S. and Roy, P. (2008) *Early Repetition Battery.* London: Pearson Education, Inc.

Semel, E., Wiig, E. and Secord, W.A. (1995) *Clinical Evaluation of Language Fundamentals 3 (CELF-3).* San Antonio, TX: The Psychological Corporation.

Slobin, D.I. and Welsh, C.A. (1973) Elicited imitation as a research tool in developmental psycholinguistics. In C.A. Ferguson and D.I. Slobin (eds) *Studies in Child Language Development* (pp. 485–497). New York: Holt, Rinehart, & Winston.

van der Lely, H.K.J. (1996) Specifically language impaired and normally developing children: Verbal passive vs. adjectival passive sentence interpretation. *Lingua* 98 (4), 243–272.

Verhoeven, L., Steenge, J. and van Van Balkom, H. (2012) Linguistic transfer in bilingual children with specific language impairment. *International Journal of Language and Communication Disorders* 47 (2), 176–183.

Part 2
Phonological and Lexical Processing

6 Non-Word Repetition

Shula Chiat

Introduction

In the quest for assessments that will address the challenges of diagnosing language impairment (LI) in bilingual children, non-word repetition appears to have an advantage over other assessment tasks. In non-word repetition tasks, children are asked to repeat items that, by definition, they have not heard before and are not part of their learned vocabulary. From this, we might infer that children cannot benefit from stored knowledge of the target item, and that children will therefore not be disadvantaged if they have had limited exposure to the target language and have limited knowledge of words in the language. A small body of research has found that differences in language experience among monolingual children have less effect on non-word repetition tests than on tests of vocabulary and grammar (Campbell *et al.*, 1997; Engel *et al.*, 2008; Roy & Chiat, 2013).

At the same time, extensive research on non-word repetition in English has found that children diagnosed with primary or specific language impairment (SLI) show deficits in non-word repetition, leading to the proposal that non-word repetition may serve as a clinical marker of LI in children (Bishop *et al.*, 1996; Conti-Ramsden *et al.*, 2001). Similar findings have emerged from studies in many languages, often typologically distinct, for example, Italian (Casalini *et al.*, 2007; Dispaldro *et al.*, 2013), Dutch (de Bree *et al.*, 2007), Spanish (Girbau & Schwartz, 2007), Russian (Kavitskaya *et al.*, 2011), Swedish (Sahlén *et al.*, 1999), Icelandic (Elin Thordardottir, 2008) and French (Elin Thordardottir & Brandeker, 2013). The only exception to date is one study of Cantonese which found no difference between groups of children diagnosed with SLI and chronologically age-matched typically developing (TD) children (Stokes *et al.*, 2006).

To the extent that non-word repetition is less affected by language knowledge than other language assessments, and is effective in identifying children with LI, it offers a unique tool for diagnosing LI in children with limited experience and knowledge of the target language. However, these qualifications are important. While non-word repetition, unlike other language assessments, does not draw directly on knowledge of vocabulary and syntax, it is still influenced by language-specific (LS) knowledge. The evidence is that children are better able to repeat non-words that share phonological characteristics of real words in their language. Since such knowledge necessarily relies on language exposure and experience, we might expect bilingual children to vary in their non-word repetition performance depending on their familiarity with lexical phonology in the target language. Findings to date are mixed.

Some studies find no effects of language experience. Elin Thordardottir and Juliusdottir (2013), for example, report that a second language (L2) Icelandic group (aged from just under 5 to just over 17 years) gained very high scores on an Icelandic non-word repetition test, in contrast to their very low scores on a measure of language. Armon-Lotem et al. (in preparation) found that 4- to 6-year-olds with first language (L1) Russian and L2 Hebrew did not differ from their monolingual peers. Likewise, Lee and Gorman (2013) found that three groups of bilingual 7-year-olds, with L1/Korean, L1/Chinese and L1/Spanish, and varying length of exposure to English, achieved overall accuracy on an English non-word repetition test comparable to that of monolingual English-speaking peers. Lee et al. (2013) investigated the performance on a Korean non-word repetition test in monolingual 3- to 5-year-olds living in Korea and bilingual peers with L1 Korean living in the USA, and again found no significant differences between groups. Elin Thordardottir and Brandeker's (2013) study of non-word repetition in monolingual and bilingual 5-year-olds acquiring French and English simultaneously, but with varied levels of exposure to the two languages, revealed very little effect of language experience on the bilingual children's performance. Furthermore, this study found good differentiation between TD bilingual children and monolingual children with LI. In contrast, other studies of non-word repetition in children's L1 and/or L2 have found that language experience does affect non-word repetition. Sharp and Gathercole (2013) compared the performance of Welsh–English bilingual children with varying levels of exposure to Welsh in the home and found that children's performance, especially on sounds unique to Welsh, was affected by the amount of exposure to the language. Likewise, Lee and Gorman (2013) report that sound inventory (both of consonants and vowels) in L1 is linked to children's ability to repeat non-words.

Engel de Abreu (2011) found that bilingual children, with a variety of European languages as their L1, performed less well than monolingual children on a Luxembourgish test of non-word repetition. Interestingly, though, the group difference disappeared once vocabulary was controlled, suggesting that reduced language experience was responsible for the difference in non-word repetition. Messer et al. (2010) found that Turkish–Dutch 4-year-olds had lower scores than their Dutch monolingual peers on a Dutch non-word repetition test, but higher scores on a Turkish test, reflecting differences in the two groups' language experience. Studies of the Hispanic population in the USA have been most consistent in finding language and/or group differences. Summers *et al.* (2010) administered Spanish and English non-word repetition tests to TD Spanish–English bilingual children aged 4;6–6;5 and found their performance to be significantly better in Spanish. However, a comparison of performance across languages must be made with caution, since tests in the two languages are not necessarily matched in phonological difficulty (see further discussion below). Comparing bilingual with monolingual performance on the same English test, Kohnert *et al.* (2006) and Windsor *et al.* (2010) found that bilingual Spanish–English children (age ranges 7;10–13;11 and 6;0–11;6, respectively) performed significantly below monolingual English children on an English non-word repetition test. The TD bilingual groups nevertheless outperformed the groups with LI, monolingual as well as bilingual. This finding is encouraging for the diagnostic potential of non-word repetition. However, this potential is greater where bilingual groups are found to perform on a par with their monolingual peers, as in Elin Thordardottir and Brandeker's (2013) study.

This heterogeneity in findings for bilingual children is unsurprising, given the multiple differences between studies. These involve linguistic factors in terms of the particular languages studied and the ways in which non-word repetition tests are constructed in those languages. Social and individual factors also vary between studies, with differences in the socio-economic and cultural characteristics of bilingual communities, in the status of children's L1 and L2 and in children's age, length and intensity of exposure to their L2. Unpicking the contribution of these factors will require many studies. This chapter focuses on just one of these factors, the construction of non-word repetition tests.

Work on non-word repetition within COST Action IS0804 has given us new insights into the types of LS knowledge that may contribute to non-word repetition, and the need to consider these when constructing non-word repetition tasks. Combining previous research findings with our consideration of linguistic factors relevant to non-word repetition, we have developed a framework for designing non-word repetition tests that may be applied across typologically diverse languages, with appropriate adaptations, and with careful attention to the possible impact of children's L1 and their exposure to the target language if this is not their L1.

In considering the potential of these tests for diagnosing LI in bilingual children and children with limited exposure to the target language, a further note of caution must be sounded. By and large, studies of non-word repetition have compared the performance in TD children and children already diagnosed with LI, and almost always these children are aged at least 4 years if not older. Finding that a non-word repetition test differentiates between these groups, and reveals a deficit in the LI group, is important. But even in studies of already defined groups, there is usually some overlap. In the few studies of non-word repetition in a population rather than in defined groups, the overlap increases. So, for example, a test that yielded excellent discrimination between already identified TD and SLI groups (Dollaghan & Campbell, 1998) did much less well in a large population study (Ellis Weismer *et al.*, 2000). In the case of bilingual children, this may be further compounded by differences in language experience. Indeed, Gutiérrez-Clellen and Simon-Cereijido (2010) found that diagnostic accuracy in Spanish–English bilingual children increased if their performance on both English and Spanish non-word repetition tests was considered. Thus, while children with LI are at risk of non-word repetition deficits, non-word repetition performance is not a litmus test for LI, a qualification that must be borne in mind when using non-word repetition as a diagnostic tool in both monolingual and bilingual children.

Having highlighted the unique potential of non-word repetition for cross-linguistic clinical assessment, as well as reasons for caution in its use, this chapter presents the non-word repetition framework we have developed. The chapter starts with a brief review of the nature of non-word repetition tasks and the factors that influence performance, the relevance of these factors across different languages, and the characteristics of non-word repetition tasks that make them more or less effective in differentiating children with and without LI. This provides the background and motivation for the COST IS0804 non-word repetition framework. The aim of the framework, fundamental to the project of developing assessments for bilingual children, is to identify tests that, on the one hand, maximise the gap between the performance of children with and without LI, and on the other hand, minimise the gap between TD children with more vs less experience of the target language. In order to explore which types of non-words achieve the best trade-off between these objectives, our framework incorporates three sets of items that vary in proximity to the phonology of the target language:

(1) *Quasi-universal (QU) items with quasi-neutral prosody:* Phonological content is selected to be compatible with the phonologies of diverse languages.
(2) *Quasi-universal (QU) items with language-specific prosody:* The items are the same as (1), but with LS prosody applied.
(3) *LS items:* Phonological content is compatible with and representative of lexical phonology in the target language, with systematic manipulation of phonological factors known to influence performance in monolingual children.

Theoretical and Empirical Influences on Non-Word Repetition Test Development

Factors influencing non-word repetition performance in typically developing children

The first factor that was observed to influence non-word repetition performance was item length. Effects of length, indicating declines in performance as item length increased, were taken as evidence that non-word repetition was a measure of short-term memory capacity. However, it was not long before the influence of the prosodic and segmental structure of items became evident. Furthermore, the influence of these factors depended in part on the characteristics of the target language. These findings led to non-word repetition being considered a test of phonological abilities rather than pure memory. Some would argue that the two are inseparable, in that memory capacity will depend on the strength of processing of the material to be stored in memory. A keynote paper by Gathercole (2006) together with commentaries by many researchers in the field provides a good overview of debates about the nature of non-word repetition and evidence bearing on these. For our purposes of test development, we look to this research for evidence of characteristics of non-words that influence performance and are informative about children's language abilities.

Length: Length effects have been observed in many languages apart from English, including Cantonese (Stokes *et al.*, 2006), Hebrew and Russian (Armon-Lotem *et al.*, in preparation). To our knowledge, they have been found in every language in which the length of non-words has been considered.

Prosodic structure: Few studies have investigated the effects of prosodic structure, but those that have done so have found significant effects on performance in Swedish (Sahlén *et al.*, 1999) and English (Chiat & Roy, 2007; Roy & Chiat, 2004; Williams *et al.*, 2013). These studies show children having particular difficulties with initial unstressed syllables which are atypical in words of their language. The broader effects of prosody are most clearly revealed in a study by Archibald and Gathercole (2007) which compared repetition of the same syllable sequences in two conditions: in one, the sequence of syllables was produced as a list, with even stress on each (e.g. *fow . . . moy . . . chee*); in the other, the syllables were produced with the rhythmic pattern of a single non-word (e.g. *fowmoychee*). The only difference between conditions, then, was in the prosody assigned to the string of syllables, and this was found to facilitate children's repetition.

Segmental complexity: Segmental complexity has emerged as a key factor, with children's performance consistently better for non-words containing only single consonants compared with non-words containing clusters

(English: Archibald & Gathercole, 2006; Jones *et al.*, 2010; Hebrew and Russian: Armon-Lotem *et al.*, in preparation).

Phonotactic probability: A number of studies have established that non-word repetition is affected by the relative frequency of phoneme sequences within items, with performance better for items that have higher phonotactic probability (Jones *et al.*, 2010; Munson, 2001; Munson *et al.*, 2005a). It should be pointed out that the calculation of phonotactic probability is normally derived from bigram frequencies, that is, the frequency of each pair of adjacent phonemes making up the non-word. The frequency of co-occurrence can be calculated for longer sequences, for example trigrams. The most comprehensive measure of phonotactic probability, n-gram frequency, takes into account the frequency of co-occurrence of successively longer sequences of phonemes in an item, from the smallest (bigrams) to the largest (full sequence of phonemes making up the item). It should also be noted that phonotactic probability does not take into account the position of phonemes within the prosodic and syllabic structure of the word, for example whether two phonemes form an initial cluster of a stressed or unstressed syllable or a sequence of singleton coda and singleton onset crossing a syllable boundary.

The properties of non-words that have been systematically investigated reflect the lexical typology of languages studied to date (largely Germanic and Romance). Length and segmental complexity are the most consistently represented variables in these language families. Prosody is more variable: some languages such as English, Swedish, Greek and Russian have variable word stress and therefore more vs less typical stress patterns; others have fixed stress, for example, French, Finnish, Hebrew and Polish. Furthermore, some languages reduce vowels in unstressed syllables, as in English, Swedish and German, while others preserve vowel quality, as in Greek, Italian and Spanish. It is striking that prosodic effects on non-word repetition have been investigated in English and Swedish, but not to our knowledge in Romance languages. It follows from these observations that we may have overlooked potentially influential factors that do not arise in the language families studied to date. A striking example is *tone*, which is a critical feature of lexical phonology in Chinese languages. In Stokes *et al.*'s (2006) study of Cantonese, non-words at each length were assigned a single tonal pattern that was characteristic of real words of the same length, hence tone was not manipulated in this study.

All the factors that we have considered above are objective properties of lexical phonology. One other characteristic of non-words that has been investigated is *wordlikeness*. This is a measure of native speakers' judgement about the extent to which a non-word resembles a real word. It is therefore a subjective rating rather than an inherent property of the non-word. We might assume that the objective properties of non-words we have considered will contribute to these subjective judgements of wordlikeness:

that items with more typical length and prosody, and higher-frequency phoneme sequences, will be judged more wordlike, and these factors are indeed found to correlate with wordlikeness judgements (Polišenská *et al.*, in preparation). However, other factors may contribute, for example whether items contain syllables or syllable sequences that are real morphemes, which may be whole words or affixes (see Casalini *et al.*, 2007, and below). A comparison of children's performance on more vs less wordlike items has revealed significant effects (Gathercole, 1995). Casalini *et al.* report better performance on items containing Italian roots and affixes than those with no constituent morphemes. Likewise, Armon-Lotem and Chiat (in preparation) found significant effects of morphemes in both Russian (where wordlike items contained real affixes) and Hebrew (where wordlike items contained the root-pattern structure characteristic of real words in Semitic languages).

Relevance of Factors in Different Languages

Human languages vary dramatically in the way they deploy the human phonetic capacity to create word phonologies, and the way phonology links with the semantic and syntactic properties of words. The phonological and morphological characteristics of words particular to a language determine potential influences on non-word repetition.

We might well assume that variations in word length are universal, but even this factor is not consistent across languages. In Cantonese, words are normally monosyllabic; most polysyllabic words are compounds, phrases or English loanwords (see Stokes *et al.*, 2006). In English, most *monomorphemic* words are monosyllabic or bisyllabic, though polysyllabicity is common once words contain derivational morphemes. Thus, children's experience of word length varies according to their language. It is possible that this experience will influence the extent of length effects on non-word repetition, for example it may be that children who are exposed to words of three or more syllables from an early age will be better able to repeat longer non-words than children whose early experience is largely confined to words of one and two syllables. Indeed, this is put forward by Dispaldro *et al.* (2013) as a possible reason for the very high scores attained by TD children on their Italian non-word repetition test, and by Summers *et al.* (2010) as one possible reason why scores on their Spanish non-word repetition were higher than on their English non-word repetition test (as reported above). However, other phonological factors may be responsible for these cross-language differences, and it is possible that, all other things being equal, the effects of length would override the frequency of exposure to polysyllabic items in the target language. In order to address this issue, we would need to compare the performance of children exposed to lexicons with opposite length biases, using tests that are the same on all variables apart from length. However, this theoretically interesting question may defy empirical investigation because length is conflated with other variables.

We have already seen that languages treat polysyllabic words in a variety of ways. In some, polysyllabic words are temporally like sequences of monosyllables, with even stress on each, and tone of syllables is contrastive; in some, the position of word stress is fixed, while others show complex patterns of stress. In stress-marking languages, some reduce unstressed vowels rendering unstressed syllables shorter than stressed syllables. Thus, increases in word length cannot be separated from prosodic structures which vary between languages. While we have some evidence that prosodic organisation of syllables facilitates repetition in English and Swedish (see above), these languages both favour trochaic patterns (in which unstressed syllables attach to a previous stressed syllable), making initial unstressed syllables atypical. We do not know how prosodic factors influence performance in typologically different languages, for example, if prosody has less or no effect in languages which do not reduce unstressed syllables. It may be that prosodic organisation of syllables is only helpful to children if this follows familiar prosodic patterns, but it is also possible that prosodic organisation facilitates recall regardless of children's particular language experience. This is an empirical question that COST Action IS0804 data will help to resolve.

Languages are similarly diverse in syllabic structure, varying in the number of consonants that may occur in onset and coda positions (i.e. before and after the vowel). Cantonese, for example, only allows singleton consonants, and the range of consonants that can occur in coda position is very limited. Finnish does not allow clusters, though some loanwords contain clusters in onset position; it does, on the other hand, employ geminate (long) consonants. Hebrew allows clusters in onset but not coda position, and Turkish the reverse. Many languages, including Polish, Russian, English, German and French, allow clusters of two or three consonants in one or both positions. We have extensive evidence that syllable complexity affects non-word repetition in languages that allow clusters, but we do not know whether children nevertheless benefit from familiarity with complex syllabic structures and are better able to repeat clusters if these occur in their language.

In addition to suprasegmental and syllabic differences, languages differ in their segmental repertoires, that is, in the numbers and types of consonant and vowel contrasts they deploy to create words. A few examples serve as a reminder of this point. Romance and Germanic languages share a range of fricative contrasts, but while German and Castilian Spanish, for example, use the voiceless fricative /x/, French and English do not; English and Castilian Spanish use /θ/, German and French do not. In contrast to English, which has around 20 vowels (depending on accent), Greek has just 5. Even when languages employ a similar set of contrasts, for example voiced and voiceless plosives, the phonetic realisation of these contrasts is specific to the language, for example initial voiceless stops are aspirated in English but not in Spanish. The ways in which these segments combine with each other are also specific to the language. For example, French and English both allow word-initial /fr/, but only French allows [vr], and neither allow /pf/ which is legal in German. Finally, the frequency with which languages deploy segments and segmental combinations in their lexicon varies. Hence, phonotactic legality and probability are specific to a language.

The points made in this section are well known, and every reader will no doubt be able to think of segmental differences between languages with which they are acquainted and segments which are missing from their native repertoire and therefore difficult to produce. The purpose of drawing attention to these differences is to highlight the extent to which properties of non-words known to influence non-word repetition are LS. However we construct non-words, they will be more or less like real word phonology in different languages with respect to length, prosody, segmental constituents and their frequency, segmental combinations and their frequency, and phonetic realisation of segments. A particular length or prosody that is typical in one language may be disallowed or atypical in another; a syllable structure that is the norm in one language may be exceptional in another. Since non-words necessarily carry these LS properties, a truly universal non-word test is not a possibility. This was an important issue for the development of the COST Action IS0804 non-word repetition framework described below.

Manipulation of Factors in Non-Word Repetition Tests

Non-word repetition tests vary in the methods used to construct non-words and the factors that are systematically manipulated. Length appears to be the only factor manipulated in all tests. Predictably, the widest range of tests and factors investigated is found in English. Indeed, the two most widely used English tests, the Children's Test of Nonword Repetition (CNRep; Gathercole & Baddeley, 1996) and the Nonword Repetition Test (NRT; Dollaghan & Campbell, 1998), lie at opposite ends of the spectrum with regard to a number of these factors. Both manipulate length of items, but beyond this, they diverge. Items in the CNRep incorporate many real English morphemes (e.g. *stoppograttic* contains the real word *stop* and adjectival suffix *-ic*). All items carry prosodic structure that is typical for English words, and prosody is not controlled. Items vary in segmental complexity, with many containing clusters (e.g. *skiticult*), and again, this factor is not controlled. Nor is the perceptual or articulatory complexity of segments considered. In contrast, items in the NRT deliberately exclude any syllables that are real words or morphemes in order to eliminate any possible benefit from lexical knowledge. All syllables in NRT items contain tense vowels, and are produced with even stress, for example /dɔɪtɑuvæb/, /tævɑtʃinɑɪg/. Their prosody makes items in the NRT quite different from real words in English, which are characterised by alternation of stressed and unstressed syllables, with unstressed syllables undergoing vowel reduction. In addition, NRT items are made up of simple consonant-vowel-consonant-vowel (CVCV) structures, with no clusters, and do not include segments that are known to be challenging for children and emerge relatively late. In a further simplified test which aimed to eliminate any confounds from difficulties with speech sounds in non-words, Shriberg et al. (2009) created a set of items that contained only four of the earliest occurring consonants and one early occurring vowel. Below, we consider how these differences between English non-word repetition tests influence their power to discriminate children with and without LI.

Few studies have pitted different factors against one another to determine whether these have independent or convergent effects (though effects of length, complexity and phonotactic probability are considered by Jones et al. [2010]; effects of length and prosodic structure by Roy and Chiat [2004] and Chiat and Roy [2007]; and effects of prosody and complexity by Marshall and van der Lely [2009]). It would be difficult, if not impossible, to manipulate all relevant factors in a single test, since some factors cannot be disentangled from others. For example, more complex segmental structures are likely to be of lower phonotactic probability and/or more difficult to perceive or articulate. However, manipulation of factors through test design is not the only way to investigate their relative effects. The Polish team in the COST Action IS0804 project (Szewczyk and Wodniecka; see Szewczyk, 2012) is using a different methodology to address this issue. Rather than manipulating selected factors to create Polish and English non-word repetition tests, Szewczyk computer-generated non-words from real words, yielding items that vary on multiple parameters. Regression analyses can then be used to determine which factors make an independent contribution to children's performance, and the extent of that contribution. A key aim of this investigation is to throw more light on the skills that underpin non-word repetition and the role these play for different groups of children, monolingual and bilingual, with and without SLI.

Other teams within the COST Action IS0804 project have started from theories of phonological complexity, and used theoretically motivated parameters to drive the construction of non-words, taking into account cross-linguistic differences that have emerged through the project. In particular, the French and German teams (Ferré & dos Santos,

2012; Grimm, 2012) have collaborated in developing tests that focus on the segmental content of non-words, systematically varying complexity in terms of segments (more vs less difficult to produce) and syllable structure (with vs without clusters). In line with the broader COST Action IS0804 framework, these factors are manipulated in two sets of items, one designed to be maximally independent of the target language, and the other more language dependent due to the incorporation of LS features. Tests following these principles have been developed in collaboration with dos Santos and Ferré for Lebanese Arabic (Abi-Aad et al., 2013), Luxembourgish (Engel & dos Santos, 2012) and Serbian (Vuksanovic et al., 2013).

Other COST Action IS0804 researchers have developed tests controlled for one or more of the factors discussed above. These include Hebrew (Armon-Lotem et al., in preparation), Lithuanian (Dabašinskienė & Krivickaitė, 2012; Krivickaitė & Dabašinskienė, 2013), Slovakian (Kapalková et al., 2013) and Turkish (Topbaş & Kaçar, 2013).

The framework presented in this chapter (see next section) was designed to be compatible with the full range of language typologies represented in the group, with manipulation of universally applicable and LS factors. This framework is currently being applied in Finnish (Kunnari, personal communication), Greek-Cypriot (Kambanaros, 2011), Maltese and Maltese English (Grech & Calleja, personal communication), Serbian (Bjekic & Vuksanovic, 2012), English (Chiat, this chapter) and Irish English (Antonijevic-Elliott, personal communication). While typologically wide-ranging, these languages are far from fully representative of phonologies worldwide. We may therefore have overlooked factors that need to be considered in languages that are not represented in the working group, and exaggerated the importance of factors that are.

Relative Effects of Factors on Children with LI and Bilingual Children

The variety of factors manipulated in non-word repetition tests begs questions about what type of non-word items best differentiate children with LI from TD children. It was important to take account of research addressing this question in creating our non-word repetition framework. Unsurprisingly, given the variety of non-word repetition tests and the plethora of research studies in English, most of the evidence to date comes from English. In drawing on this evidence, it must be emphasised that outcomes may be specific to English language typology.

Findings on non-word repetition in English-speaking children with vs without LI have been reviewed in a number of papers (Coady & Evans, 2008; Gathercole, 2006). A meta-analysis conducted by Graf-Estes et al. (2007), collating the results of 23 studies employing four different non-word repetition tests, is particularly pertinent. This meta-analysis revealed that the performance of SLI groups was on average 1.27 standard deviations below that of TD groups, and this did not change with age. However, the gap between TD and SLI groups varied considerably between tests. The most discriminating test was the CNRep (average effect size 1.94), and the least discriminating was the NRT (average effect size 0.9). This outcome is in line with findings of a study in which Archibald and Gathercole (2006) directly compared performance on these two tests in a group of 7-to 11-year-olds. Both groups of children gained higher scores for percentage phonemes correct on the CNRep than on the NRT, but the CNRep produced a greater *discrepancy* between groups. Indeed, when children's *cognitive* ability was controlled, the group difference disappeared for the NRT, but was still present for the CNRep. We might infer that the CNRep taps into more LS skills and knowledge than the NRT (which makes sense when we consider the different characteristics of the two tests outlined above). The test that relies more on knowledge of the language is more challenging for children with language deficits.

As pointed out, the CNRep and NRT differ on a range of relevant parameters, so the greater deficit observed in the CNRep could arise from one or more of the parameters that differentiate it from the NRT. Many studies have examined the relative effect of particular parameters on children with vs without SLI. Interestingly, the prosodic factor on its own seems to produce a pattern of results similar to that observed for the CNRep vs NRT. In Archibald and Gathercole's (2007) study comparing repetition of syllables that were produced either as a list or as a single non-word (see above), the single non-word condition yielded higher scores in both groups of children (with and without SLI), but the difference between groups was greater in this condition, i.e. the SLI group showed a larger deficit in the single non-word than the list condition. It seems that both groups of children gain from having syllables prosodically organised in a single unit, but TD children benefit more than those with SLI. This is an interesting finding, and one which might throw light on the unique findings on non-word repetition in Cantonese. Stokes *et al.* (2006) point out that Cantonese lacks the prosodic and phonotactic complexity of languages such as English and Swedish. The Cantonese non-words are therefore more like non-words in the English NRT, but with the difference that they are like real polysyllabic words in Cantonese (characterised by even stress on syllables); this presumably makes them more familiar to Cantonese speakers compared with the NRT items whose prosody is uncharacteristic of English. It is also possible that the characteristics of the Cantonese non-words make repetition more dependent on cognitive abilities, less dependent on phonological abilities and therefore less vulnerable to deficits in phonological processing, as was found for the NRT (see Stokes *et al.* [2006] for further evidence).

When we look at the effects of other parameters on performance in children with and without SLI, the picture is mixed. Each parameter has been found to affect both groups. However, findings on the *relative effects* on children with and without SLI vary between factors and studies. In most cases, factors that make non-words more difficult for TD groups make them disproportionately difficult for SLI groups. Thus, children with SLI have a greater deficit on items containing clusters (Archibald & Gathercole, 2006; Jones et al., 2010) and on longer items (Graf-Estes et al., 2007), though findings may vary according to the range of item lengths that are compared. Children with SLI have also been found to have a greater deficit on items with low phonotactic probability (Munson et al., 2005b), but findings are not consistent (Jones et al., 2010).

If monolingual children with SLI are disproportionately affected by particular characteristics of non-words such as length or syllable complexity, an important question is how these characteristics affect non-word repetition in bilingual children. Elin Thordardottir and Brandeker (2013), for example, found that non-word length had particular effects on performance in their monolingual language-impaired group, but not in their TD bilingual group.

Evidence of how relevant factors affect language-impaired vs bilingual groups is currently very limited. This question merits further investigation: if bilingual children are less affected by length and/or syllable complexity than those with LI, these factors may help with clinical diagnosis in bilingual children when their overall scores fall below those of monolingual children.

The Cost Action IS0804 Non-Word Repetition Framework

We have seen that items are more effective for detecting LI (in English) if they are prosodically structured, are longer, have more complex segmental structures and perhaps if they contain lower frequency phoneme sequences. As pointed out above, these factors play out in different ways in the lexical structure of different languages. It is therefore possible that their effects on children with and without LI may vary according to the properties of real words that children have experienced. This encapsulates the challenges of constructing cross-linguistic non-word repetition tests. The QU and LS components that make up the COST Action IS0804 non-word repetition framework represent different reconciliations between the competing demands of maximum applicability across languages and maximum discrimination between children with and without SLI. They will enable us to evaluate the potential contribution of each type of test to the diagnosis of LI in bilingual children and children with limited experience of the target language.

Quasi-universal tests

We have already established the impossibility of a universal non-word repetition test. We have furthermore established that non-word repetition tests are informative because they tap children's phonological processing and representations, which are LS, and that tests and items containing more complex phonology are more informative about skills and deficits. Nevertheless, the COST Action IS0804 project provides a unique opportunity to run a set of almost identical non-words across languages and find out if such a test discriminates TD and LI groups across languages, and how this compares with outcomes on LS tests. This was the rationale for creating the QU tests. Items in these tests were designed to be compatible with the cross-linguistically diverse constraints on lexical phonology discussed above. We designate the items *quasi*-universal because they necessarily have some LS characteristics, and even their shared properties are necessarily more or less characteristic of different languages.

The test contains 16 items, with equal numbers at two, three, four and five syllables. The items contain a limited range of consonants /p, b, t, d, k, g, s, z, l, m, n/ and vowels /a, i, u/, combined into simple CVCV structures. This makes them compatible with word phonology in most languages regardless of the further segmental contrasts and syllable structures that particular languages allow. Since any particular sequence of consonants and vowels may be a real word in a particular language, or contain a real word inflection, the test offers a set of options for each item. These are shown in Appendix A. Once selected, the consonants and vowels in these items have to be produced with particular phonetic qualities, and these necessarily vary between languages. In the QU tests, consonants and vowels are assigned phonetic realisations that are characteristic of the dominant language in the child's environment (which may of course be distinct from the child's L1). In this respect, then, the items are language specific.

Quasi-universal (QU) items with quasi-neutral prosody: We have established that prosody varies between languages. This means that it is not possible to assign a truly language-neutral prosody to QU items. However, we might assume that the most neutral prosody will be one that avoids any particular prosodic pattern by stressing all syllables equally. This reduces the possible influence of LS prosodic knowledge, and is the option we selected for the QU test with quasi-neutral prosody. Syllables in these items are produced with even length and pitch, apart from final syllable lengthening which characteristically marks the end of an utterance. It should be clear, though, that this even prosody is not truly neutral between languages: while it is close to the typical prosody for polysyllabic words in a language such as Cantonese (though lacking the tones that characterise Cantonese words), it is remote from prosody in languages such as English that reduce unstressed syllables, typically reducing the vowel to a schwa.

Quasi-universal (QU) items with language-specific prosody: A second QU test, the QU test with language-specific prosody, presents the same 16 items but with the prosodic pattern most typical for each word length in the target language. As pointed out above, we already have some evidence that lexical prosody benefits non-word repetition, and that non-words with lexical prosody may yield greater differences between children with and without SLI (Archibald & Gathercole, 2007). However, this evidence is confined to English-speaking children, so we don't know whether these advantages are specific to languages in which polysyllabic words carry word-level prosodic patterns which distinguish them from a sequence of monosyllables, or whether they arise from universal language-processing mechanisms that make it easier to process phonological material when it is 'chunked' by prosody. Comparing the performance on the two QU tests (with quasi-neutral vs language-specific prosody) in children exposed to languages that differ in their prosodic properties will help to address this question. The English QU tests with quasi-neutral and language-specific prosody (Chiat, Polišenská & Szewczyk, 2012) are presented in Appendix B.

Language-specific tests

The purpose of the LS tests within the COST Action IS0804 framework is to allow manipulation of phonological properties previously found to affect performance and relevant to particular languages. The LS framework includes 24 items, controlled for length, prosody and syllable structure. In order to allow investigation of these factors without making the test excessively long, prosody and syllable structure are manipulated separately, but not in combination. Broad specifications for each parameter are proposed, with flexibility to cater for properties of lexical items in the target language. Where metrics for phonotactic probability are available for the target language, this factor is also manipulated. Wordlikeness ratings, on the other hand, can be obtained for all languages to provide a broad measure of their phonological familiarity.

Items in LS tests are consistent with constraints on lexical phonology in the target language. They are constructed from a representative range of consonants and vowels that occur in the language, avoiding only late-emerging consonants that may pose articulatory challenges to some children, and deploy these in phonotactically legal combinations. To minimise the potential contribution of lexical knowledge, syllables that are real morphemes in the target language should be avoided. The constituent segments are phonetically realised in accordance with the target language.

Length: The 24 items in the LS test are equally divided between lengths of two, three and four syllables. Monosyllabic items are not generally included since they are likely to produce ceiling effects, and add little to the evidence provided by bisyllabic items (Graf Estes *et al.*, 2007). However, they should be included if real words in the language are typically monosyllabic. Conversely, five syllable items are not generally included because they are likely to produce floor effects in young children, and add little to evidence provided by four-syllable items, particularly if a language allows complex syllabic structures. However, five-syllable items should be included in languages where most lexical items are polysyllabic and five-syllable items are common in children's vocabulary, and in those which lack the additional complexity of consonant clusters.

Prosody: In languages with *variable* word stress, six items with simple CV structure (see segmental complexity below) are assigned atypical stress patterns, two at each length. The remaining 18 items bear typical stress patterns.

Segmental complexity: In languages that permit consonant clusters, items with typical stress have no cluster or have one initial/medial cluster (depending whether one or both of these positions tolerate clusters in the target language), with equal numbers of each. Given the different possible combinations of factors in different languages, numbers of items with clusters will vary. The English LS test contains 18 items with typical stress patterns, 6 at each length, and these are equally divided between items with no cluster, initial cluster and medial cluster, with 2 of each (see Appendix C) (Chiat et al., 2012). In languages with fixed word stress, manipulation of syllable structure applies to all 24 items, allowing for a wider representation of clusters. These include eight at each length, divided as evenly as possible between no cluster, initial cluster and medial cluster (according to positions in which clusters can occur).

In order to limit the number of factors and hence the length of tests, clusters are restricted to two consonants, but these should include several exemplars.

Phonotactic probability: Where metrics for phonotactic probability are available, subsets of items defined by length and, where applicable, prosody/segmental complexity, should be equally divided between high and low phonotactic probability, resulting in 12 of each.

Other lexical phonological factors: The factors specified so far reflect the lexical phonology of the languages most studied to date, with English obviously the most dominant. Lexical phonological parameters relevant to other languages will influence phonological familiarity and wordlikeness of non-words, and should be taken into account in the construction of LS tests. For example, Hebrew and Arabic words are made up of *roots* (consonant frames) which are filled by *patterns* (vowels); in these languages, non-words might be created from real root with non-pattern, non-root with real pattern or non-root with non-pattern (Armon-Lotem et al., in preparation). Turkish and Finnish words are characterised by vowel harmony, and non-words might be created with vs without harmony. In languages which inflect words according to their grammatical category, for example those that mark gender and/or case on nouns, non-word repetition tests may manipulate this factor, including items with and without recognisable inflections. However, it should be borne in mind that inclusion of real roots and patterns, vowel harmony or inflections makes items more wordlike and therefore more susceptible to the influence of knowledge and experience.

Wordlikeness: Wordlikeness of non-words is a subjective judgement of their similarity to real words. As pointed out, we might expect this to relate to the objective factors considered above, since native speakers presumably draw on their unconscious knowledge of typical prosodic and segmental patterns when they rate wordlikeness. Nonetheless, as a subjective judgement of similarity to real words, whatever the phonological and lexical factors influencing the judgement, wordlikeness is the one measure that may be truly cross-linguistic. For this reason, as well as the lack of lexicality metrics in some languages, it is useful to obtain wordlikeness judgements. To do this, all non-words are entered on a sheet for native speakers to rate using a 5-point rating scale, with 5 most wordlike and 1 least wordlike. There are two options for the order of items on the sheet: the full set of QU and LS items may be randomised and presented in a single block, or QU non-words with quasi-neutral and language-specific prosody and LS items may be randomised in three separate blocks, in which case the order of the three blocks is counterbalanced across raters.

Order of testing

As with the order of presentation for wordlikeness ratings, the COST Action IS0804 framework offers two options for the order of presentation of items to children. All items may be randomised in one single set. In this case, the resulting randomised set may still be broken into several blocks to allow for breaks if children require these. The alternative is to randomise QU items with quasi-neutral prosody, QU items with language-specific prosody, and LS items in three separate blocks. In this case, the order of blocks should again be counterbalanced. Running the tests in these different ways will allow us to determine whether the effects of different types of items (QU with quasi-neutral/language-specific prosody and LS) are influenced by the properties of surrounding items. This will help to decide the order of items when the test format is finalised for clinical use.

Administration of tests

Items are recorded and recordings are incorporated into a PowerPoint presentation. COST Action IS0804 teams have developed a variety of child-friendly formats. The Polish test uses aliens to introduce non-words (a format created by COST Action IS0804 member Engel de Abreu); the Finnish test (Kunnari) displays a set of stepping stones for each of the three tests, with one non-word attached to each stepping stone; the Turkish team (Topbaş and colleagues) use an animated parrot to deliver each non-word. The English test is available in two formats: the 'alien' format used in the Polish test, and a 'bead game' format developed by Polišenská and Kapalková (2014).

Whatever the format used, each item is played once, but a replay is allowed if the first recording is interrupted, if the child is momentarily distracted and for the first few items if the child gives no response to these. However, replays are not provided in response to children requesting another opportunity to hear the item again or improve on their first attempt.

Scoring

The COST Action IS0804 framework allows two levels of scoring: number of whole items correct and number of segments correct. Whole-item scoring is used in the CNRep and in the Preschool Repetition Test (Seeff-Gabriel et al., 2008). This has been found to be sufficiently discriminating, and is quicker and therefore more clinically practical (see also Dispaldro et al., 2013). Segmental scoring is used in the NRT and in some experimental studies using the CNRep. It is more time-consuming, but provides a more fine-grained measure of performance and may be more discriminating.

In the COST Action IS0804 framework, whole items are correct if they contain all and only the segments in the target in the correct order. Segments are correct if they fall within the target segmental category, even if they are phonetically distorted. Allowances are made for segmental substitutions that are relatively consistent in the child's productions and are characteristic of immature speech, for example, stopping of fricatives, fronting of velar stops in languages where these are observed in young children.

Conclusions and Next Steps

COST Action IS0804 work on the development of non-word repetition tests has thrown a spotlight on the diverse ways in which languages harness the human speech capacity to create words, evidenced by the rich cross-linguistic variation in lexical structure which must be considered when constructing non-words. We have selected phonological properties that are widely applicable across languages for the creation of our QU tests, and for LS tests, we have identified a range of parameters to be manipulated depending on the lexical typology of the target language. While motivated by evidence of cross-linguistic differences in lexical phonology and how these affect children's non-word repetition, our selection of properties and parameters is not necessarily optimal. It may be that the application of more abstract principles, with parametric variations appropriate to individual languages, would yield a more selective and informative set of items (dos Santos, Ferré and Grimm). Another possibility is that more comprehensive and sophisticated analyses of children's non-word repetition will reveal which factors contribute most to their performance and/or which differentiate best between children with and without SLI (Szewczyk). Outcomes of such research might guide us towards reductions in the number of parameters to be manipulated in non-word repetition tests, leading to maximally short and informative tests.

Research using the COST Action IS0804 framework will also contribute new insights, helping to address a number of important empirical and theoretical questions. Cross-linguistic comparison of the two QU tests will clarify whether the parameters manipulated within and between these tests have a similar influence on children's performance regardless of their language background, or whether their influence varies according to the way these parameters play out in the language(s) to which children have been exposed. Together with findings from LS tests, they will also help to determine what types of non-words are most informative about children's language abilities regardless of their language background.

Some caution is needed in making these cross-linguistic comparisons. Our non-word items are not identical across languages even in the QU tests. Different teams will be using different recordings of non-words and different formats for presenting these, administering tasks in different combinations and different settings, and scoring them independently. Hence, any cross-linguistic differences we observe could be due to differences in items and/or methods rather than influences of language background. Nonetheless, if we find that certain factors have consistent effects across language groups, including languages where these factors play out differently, the evidence for universality of these factors will be strengthened, with implications for the phonological processing that non-word repetition assesses. Conversely, if we find that certain factors have variable effects across languages, and these are consistent with the role played by these factors in the lexical phonology of the language, this will strengthen the evidence for LS contributions to non-word repetition. The most definitive evidence will come from collaborative studies employing the *same recordings* of the QU tests (e.g. those made for English or Finnish) with different language groups, such that the pronunciation of consonants and vowels in both tests, and the prosody in the QU test with language-specific prosody, will be alien to at least one group. In such comparisons, any cross-group similarities and differences cannot be due to materials or methods, and must be attributed to linguistic experience and/or processing.

Finally, research on children with LI, both monolingual and bilingual, will throw more light on the extent to which the factors manipulated in the QU and LS tests affect their repetition of non-words relative to their

TD peers, and which yield the most marked differences between groups. This will pave the way to identifying optimal non-word tests for our purposes: tests that yield the least difference between monolingual and bilingual children, and the greatest difference between children with and without LI.

References

Abi-Aad, K., Atallah, C., Ferré, S. and dos Santos, C. (2013) Lebanese study: BiSLI and biTD. In Chiat, S., Ferré, S., dos Santos, C. and Grimm, A. Nonword repetition tests for assessing bilingual children. Paper presented at COST Action IS0804 final conference, Krakow 27–29 May 2013.
Archibald, L.M.D. and Gathercole, S.E. (2006) Nonword repetition: A comparison of tests. *Journal of Speech, Language, and Hearing Research* 49 (5), 970–983.
Archibald, L.M.D. and Gathercole, S.E. (2007) Nonword repetition in specific language impairment: More than a phonological short-term memory deficit. *Psychonomic Bulletin & Review* 14 (5), 919–924.
Armon-Lotem, S., Meir, N. and Chiat, S. (in preparation) The role of language experience in a STM task: Evidence from nonword repetition in Russian and Hebrew monolingual and sequential bilingual children.
Bishop, D.V.M., North, T. and Donlan, C. (1996) Nonword repetition as a behavioural marker for inherited language impairment: Evidence from a twin study. *Journal of Child Psychology and Psychiatry* 37 (4), 391–403.
Bjekic, J. and Vuksanovic, J. (2012) Application of two quasi-universal nonword repetition tasks in Serbian SLI and TD children: A pilot study. Paper presented at COST Action IS0804 meeting held in Padova, 19–21 September 2012.
Campbell, T., Dollaghan, C., Needleman, H. and Janosky, J. (1997) Reducing bias in language assessment: Processing-dependent measures. *Journal of Speech, Language, and Hearing Research* 40 (3), 519–525.
Casalini, C., Brizzolara, D., Chilosi, A., Cipriani, P., Marcolini, S., Pecini, C., Roncoli, S. and Burani, C. (2007) Nonword repetition in children with specific language impairment: A deficit in phonological working memory or in long-term verbal knowledge? *Cortex* 43 (6), 769–776.
Chiat, S., Polišenská, K. and Szewczyk, J. (2012) Crosslinguistic Nonword Repetition Tasks: British English version. A part of LITMUS COST IS0804 Battery. Unpublished material.
Chiat, S. and Roy, P. (2007) The preschool repetition test: An evaluation of performance in typically developing and clinically referred children. *Journal of Speech, Language, and Hearing Research* 50 (2), 429–443.
Coady, J.A. and Evans, J.L. (2008) Uses and interpretations of non-word repetition tasks in children with and without language impairments (SLI). *International Journal of Language and Communication Disorders* 43 (1), 1–40.
Conti-Ramsden, G., Botting, N. and Faragher, B. (2001) Psycholinguistic markers for specific language impairment (SLI). *Journal of Child Psychology and Psychiatry* 42 (6), 741–748
Dabašinskienė, I. and Krivickaitė, E. (2012) Paper presented at COST Action IS0804 meeting held in Berlin, May 2012.
De Bree, E., Rispens, J. and Gerrits, E. (2007) Non-word repetition in Dutch children with (a risk of) dyslexia and SLI. *Clinical Linguistics & Phonetics* 21 (11–12), 935–944.
Dispaldro, M., Leonard, L.B. and Deevy, P. (2013) Real-word and nonword repetition in Italian-speaking children with specific language impairment: A study of diagnostic accuracy. *Journal of Speech, Language, and Hearing Research* 56 (1), 323–336.

Dollaghan, C. and Campbell, T.F. (1998) Nonword repetition and child language impairment. *Journal of Speech, Language, and Hearing Research* 41, 1136–1146.

Elin Thordardottir, E. (2008) Language-specific effects of task demands on the manifestation of specific language impairment: A comparison of English and Icelandic. *Journal of Speech, Language, and Hearing Research* 51, 922–937.

Elin Thordardottir, E. and Brandeker, M. (2013) The effect of bilingual exposure versus language impairment on nonword repetition and sentence imitation scores. *Journal of Communication Disorders* 46 (1), 1–16.

Elin Thordardottir, E. and Juliusdottir, A.G. (2013) Icelandic as a second language: A longitudinal study of language knowledge and processing by school-age children. *International Journal of Bilingual Education and Bilingualism* 16 (4), 411–435.

Ellis Weismer, S., Tomblin, J.B., Zhang, X., Buckwalter, P., Chynoweth, J.G. and Jones, M. (2000) Nonword repetition performance in school-age children with and without language impairment. *Journal of Speech, Language, and Hearing Research* 43, 865–878.

Engel, P. and dos Santos, C. (2012) Language bias in nonword repetition – towards a culture fair nonword repetition test. Paper presented at COST Action IS0804 meeting held in Berlin, 14–16 May 2012.

Engel, P.M.J., Santos, F.H. and Gathercole, S.E. (2008) Are working memory measures free of socioeconomic influence? *Journal of Speech, Language, and Hearing Research* 51, 1580–1587.

Engel de Abreu, P.M.J. (2011) Working memory in multilingual children: Is there a bilingual effect? *Memory* 19 (5), 529–537.

Ferré, S. and dos Santos, C. (2012) French NWRT: Inter-group comparison for French and Lebanese children. Paper presented at COST Action IS0804 meeting held in Padova, 19–21 September 2012.

Gathercole, S.E. (1995) Is nonword repetition a test of phonological memory or long-term knowledge? It all depends on the nonwords. *Memory and Cognition* 23 (1), 83–94.

Gathercole, S.E. (2006) Nonword repetition and word learning: The nature of the relationship. *Applied Psycholinguistics* 27 (4), 513–543.

Gathercole, S.E. and Baddeley, A.D. (1996) *The Children's Test of Nonword Repetition.* London: Psychological Corporation.

Girbau, D. and Schwartz, R.G. (2007) Non-word repetition in Spanish-speaking children with specific language impairment (SLI). *International Journal of Language and Communication Disorders* 42 (1), 59–75.

Graf Estes, K., Evans, J. and Else-Quest, N.M. (2007) Differences in the nonword repetition: Performance of children with and without specific language impairment: A meta-analysis. *Journal of Speech, Language and Hearing Research* 50 (1), 177–195.

Grimm, A. (2012) The French-German NRT: How do German MON-SLI differ from eL2-SLI? Paper presented at COST Action IS0804 meeting held in Padova, 19–21 September 2012.

Gutiérrez-Clellen, V.F. and Simon-Cereijido, G. (2010) Using nonword repetition tasks for the identification of language impairment in Spanish-English-speaking children: Does the language of assessment matter? *Learning Disabilities Research & Practice* 25 (1), 48–58.

Jones, G., Tamburelli, M., Watson, S.E., Gobet, F. and Pine, J.M. (2010) Lexicality and frequency in specific language impairment: Accuracy and error data from two nonword repetition tests. *Journal of Speech, Language, and Hearing Research* 53 (6), 1642–1655.

Kambanaros, M. (2011) Results of Greek Cypriot/Standard Greek test. Paper presented at COST Action IS0804 meeting held in Malta, 28–30 November 2011.

Kapalková, S., Polišenská, K. and Vicenová, Z. (2013) Non-word repetition performance in Slovak-speaking children with and without SLI: Novel scoring methods. *International Journal of Language and Communication Disorders* 48 (1), 78–89.

Kavitskaya, D., Babyonyshev, M., Walls, T. and Grigorenko, E. (2011) Investigating the effects of syllable complexity in Russian-speaking children with SLI. *Journal of Child Language* 38 (5), 979–998.

Kohnert, K., Windsor, J. and Yim, D. (2006) Do language-based processing tasks separate children with language impairment from typical bilinguals? *Learning Disabilities Research & Practice* 21 (1), 19–29.

Krivickaitė, E. and Dabašinskienė, I. (2013) Lithuanian nonword repetition test. Paper presented at COST Action IS0804 meeting held in Lisbon, 13–15 February 2013.

Lee, H.J., Kim, Y.T. and Yim, D. (2013) Non-word repetition performance in Korean-English bilingual children. *International Journal of Speech-Language Pathology* 15 (4), 375–382.

Lee, S.A.S. and Gorman, B.K. (2013) Nonword repetition performance and related factors in children representing four linguistic groups. *International Journal of Bilingualism* 17 (4), 479–495.

Marshall, C.R. and van der Lely, H.K.J. (2009) Effects of word position and stress on onset cluster production: Evidence from typical development, SLI and dyslexia. *Language* 85 (1), 39–57.

Messer, M.H., Leseman, P.P.M., Boom, J. and Mayo, A.Y. (2010) Phonotactic probability effect in nonword recall and its relationship with vocabulary in monolingual and bilingual preschoolers. *Journal of Experimental Child Psychology* 105 (4), 306–323.

Munson, B. (2001) Phonological pattern frequency and speech production in children and adults. *Journal of Speech, Language, and Hearing Research* 44 (4), 778–792.

Munson, B., Edwards, J. and Beckman, M.E. (2005a) Phonological knowledge in typical and atypical speech-sound development. *Topics in Language Disorders* 25 (3), 190–206.

Munson, B., Kurtz, B.A. and Windsor, J. (2005b) The influence of vocabulary size, phonotactic probability, and wordlikeness on nonword repetitions of children with and without specific language impairment. *Journal of Speech, Language, and Hearing Research* 48 (5), 1033–1047.

Polišenská, K., Chiat, S. and Szewczyk, J. (in preparation) An investigation of relations between objective properties of nonwords and subjective judgements of their wordlikeness.

Polišenská, K. and Kapalkova, S. (2014) Improving child compliance on a computer administered nonword repetition task. *Journal of Speech, Language, and Hearing Research* 57, 1060-1068. eScholarID:234227, DOI:10.1044/1092-4388(2013/13-0014)

Roy, P. and Chiat, S. (2004) A prosodically controlled word and nonword repetition task for 2- to 4-year-olds: Evidence from typically developing children. *Journal of Speech, Language, and Hearing Research* 47, 223–234.

Roy, P. and Chiat, S. (2013) Teasing apart disadvantage from disorder: The case of poor language. In C.R. Marshall (ed.) *Current Issues in Developmental Disorders* (pp. 125–150). Hove: Psychology Press.

Sahlén, B., Reuterskiöld-Wagner, C., Nettelbladt, U. and Radeborg, K. (1999) Nonword repetition in children with language impairment – pitfalls and possibilities. *International Journal of Language and Communication Disorders* 34 (3), 337–352.

Seeff-Gabriel, B., Chiat, S. and Roy, P. (2008) *The Early Repetition Battery.* London: Pearson Assessment.

Sharp, K.M. and Gathercole, V.C.M. (2013) Can a novel word repetition task be a language-neutral assessment tool? Evidence from Welsh–English bilingual children. *Child Language Teaching and Therapy* 29 (1), 77–89.

Shriberg, L.D., Lohmeier, H.L., Campbell, T.F., Dollaghan, C.A., Green, J.R. and Moore, C.A. (2009) A nonword repetition task for speakers with misarticulations: The Syllable Repetition Test (SRT). *Journal of Speech, Language, and Hearing Research* 52, 1189–1212.

Stokes, S.F., Wong, A., Fletcher, P. and Leonard, L.B. (2006) Nonword repetition and sentence repetition as clinical markers of specific language impairment: The case of Cantonese. *Journal of Speech, Language, and Hearing Research* 49 (2), 219–236.

Summers, C., Bohman, T.M., Gillam, R.B., Pen a, E.D. and Bedore, L.M. (2010) Bilingual performance on nonword repetition in Spanish and English. *International Journal of Language and Communication Disorders* 45 (4), 480–493.

Szewczyk, J. (2012) Subject- and item-related predictors of nonword repetition performance, based on the Polish NWR test. Paper presented at COST Action IS0804 meeting held in Berlin, May 2012.

Topbaş, S. and Kaçar, D.K. (2013) A comparative study: The implementation of a Turkish Nonword Repetition Test and Quasi-Universal Nonword Repetition Test with monolingual Turkish children with SLI. Paper presented at COST Action IS0804 meeting held in Lisbon, 13–15 February 2013.

Vuksanovic, J., Bjekic, J. and Zivanovic, M. (2013) Application of two nonword repetition tasks in TD bilingual Serbian-Hungarian children. Paper presented at COST Action IS0804 meeting held in Lisbon, 13–15 February 2013.

Williams, D., Payne, H. and Marshall, C.R. (2013) Non-word repetition impairment in autism and SLI: Evidence for distinct underlying cognitive causes. *Journal of Autism and Developmental Disorders* 43 (2), 404–417.

Windsor, J., Kohnert, K., Lobitz, K.F. and Pham, G.T. (2010) Cross-language nonword repetition by bilingual and monolingual children. *American Journal of Speech-Language Pathology* 19 (4), 298–310.

Appendix A: Construction of Quasi-Universal Tests

- For each item (1–16), select any one example in the row which is **not** a real word in the target language:

1	zibu	sibu	sipu	zipu		
2	lita	lida	dula	tula		
3	maki	naki	magi	nagi		
4	luni	lumi	nuli	muli		
5	sipula	zipula	sibula	zibula		
6	bamudi	banudi	pamudi	panudi	pamuti	panuti
7	malitu	malidu	nalitu	nalidu	malitu	malidu
8	lumika	lunika	lumiga	luniga		
9	zipalita	sipalita	zibalita	sibalita	zipalida	sipalida
10	mukitala	nukitala	mugitala	nugitala	mukidala	mugidala
11	kasulumi	gasulumi	kazulumi	gazulumi	kasuluni	gasuluni
12	litisaku	lidisaku	litisagu	lidisagu	litizaku	lidizaku
13	sipumakila	sibumakila	sipunakila	sibunakila	sipumagila	sibumagila
14	tulikasumu	dulikasumu	tuligasumu	duligasumu	tulikazumu	dulikasumu
15	malusikuba	maluzikuba	malusiguba	maluziguba	malusikupa	maluzikupa
16	litapimuti	lidapimuti	litabimuti	lidabimuti	litapimudi	lidabimudi

- Pronounce each item with vowel and consonant qualities appropriate to the target language.
- *QU with quasi-neutral prosody:* Produce items with even stress on each syllable, and if appropriate for target language, final lengthening on final syllable.
- *QU with language-specific prosody:* Produce items with the prosodic pattern most typical for each word length in the target language.

Appendix B: Quasi-Universal Tests for English (Chiat, Polišenská & Szewczyk, 2012)

	With language-specific prosody:
With quasi-neutral prosody: With English consonants and vowels	With English consonants and vowels, and prosody typical for word length
' even stress and pitch ˌfalling pitch	' primary stress ˌsecondary stress
/'ziˌbu/ /'duˌla/ /'naˌgi/ /'luˌmi/	/'zibə/ /'dulə/ /'nagi/ /'lumi/
/'si'puˌla/ /'ba'muˌdi/ /'ma'liˌtu/ /'lu'miˌga/	/'sipəˌla/ /'baməˌdi/ /'malɪˌtu/ /'lumɪˌga/
/'zi'pa'liˌda/ /'mu'ki'taˌla/ /'ka'su'luˌmi/ /'lidi'saˌku/	/'zipəˌlidə/ /'mukɪˌtalə/ /ˌkasə'lumi/ /ˌlidɪ'sakə/
/'si'pu'ma'kiˌla/ /'du'li'ga'suˌmu/ /'ma'lu'zi'guˌba/ /'li'ta'pi'muˌti/	/ˌsipəmæ'kilə/ /ˌdulɪgæ'sumə/ /ˌmalə'zigəbə/ /ˌlitə'piməti/

Appendix C: Language-Specific Test For English (Chiat, Polišenská & Szewczyk, 2012)

Transitional probability (TP)/Ngram frequency (NF)[1]

Stress	Complexity	No Syll	High Item no.	High Item TP/NF	Low Item no.	Low Item TP/NF
Typical	– cluster	2	1	ˈdallen ˈdælən 11 / 4.56	13	ˈrefap ˈrɛfəp 8.8 / 3.12
		3	2	ˈsannery ˈsænəri 16.8 / 3.42	14	ˈzummerlah ˈzʊmələ 4.6 / 2
		4	3	ˌponnerˈvayker ˌpɒnəˈveɪkə 13.9 / 2.5	15	ˌkefferˈmoyper ˌkɛfəˈmɔɪpə 10.7 / 1.6
	+ initial cluster	2	4	ˈspoddle ˈspɒdəl 9.6 / 2.96	16	ˈfrashek ˈfræʃək 7.1 / 2.72
		3	5	ˈstoffely ˈstɒfəli 15.9 / 2.79	17	ˈsmisherˌtow ˈsmɪʃəˌtaʊ 9.5 / 2.28
		4	6	ˌskoomerˈkider ˌskuməˈkaɪdə 10.4 / 1.94	18	ˌflahnerˈmoozer ˌflanəˈmuzə 8.8 / 1.79
	+ medial cluster	2	7	ˈnahsket ˈnɑskət 12 / 3.15	19	ˈlursnok ˈlɜsnɒk 5.6 / 2.44
		3	8	ˈmahsperˌdow ˈmɑspəˌdaʊ 8.8 / 2.25	20	ˈzeespegoy ˈzispəˌgɔɪ 4.8 / 1.35
		4	9	ˌtoskerˈleemer ˌtɒskəˈlimə 8.7 / 2.1	21	ˌvosnaˈrouder ˌvɒsnəˈraʊdə 7.6 / 1.81
Atypical	– cluster	2	10	reˈvike rɪˈvaɪk 12 / 3.63	22	naˈlorsh nəˈlɔʃ 3 / 2.28
		3	11	peˈzayner pəˈzeɪnə 11.7 / 2.88	23	leˈvooger ləˈvugə 9.4 / 2.05
		4	12	reˈnusedar rəˈnusədɑ 5.3 / 1.96	24	zeˈdahgenur zəˈdagən3 3.6 / 1.49

[1] Transitional probability and Ngram frequency were derived from the corpus biSubtlex-US (Brysbaert & New, 2009).

7 Using Parental Report to Assess Early Lexical Production in Children Exposed to More Than One Language

Daniela Gatt, Ciara O'Toole
and Ewa Haman

Introduction

A small expressive vocabulary in young children is considered to be the first warning signal of delayed language development (Ellis & Thal, 2008). In turn, early language delay may be the most obvious indication of later language impairment (Paul & Roth, 2011). However, the immense variability characterising language development in young children makes it difficult to predict the evolution of early language difficulties (Ellis & Thal, 2008). For instance, substantial proportions of late talkers have been reported to spontaneously overcome their language learning difficulties completely (e.g. Dale et al., 2003; Rescorla et al., 2000). In contrast, a series of research findings attest to late talkers' continuing speech and language difficulties through the preschool years (see Paul & Roth, 2011). Difficulties with language development may continue to manifest themselves in a subtle form in adolescence (Rescorla, 2009, 2013; Tomblin, 2008) or may even become more persistent and marked with increasing age (Rutter, 2008). It is therefore best to consider limited word production in young children as a 'red flag' for potential specific language impairment (SLI) (Ellis & Thal, 2008), the latter being diagnosed when children's persistent difficulties in language are discrepant with broadly typical abilities in other areas of cognitive, physical and socio-emotional development.

A cross-linguistic investigation of early lexical production in children exposed to more than one language

One of the challenges in dealing with bilingual children is the investigation of early lexical production across a series of language pairs, with a view to expanding the limited knowledge base on indicators of language delay in young children exposed to two languages. The relevant methodology adopted in this chapter[1] is based on the premise that the identification of early language delay relies heavily on the measurement of emergent lexical production as one aspect of linguistic competence. In this chapter, we document the productive vocabulary skills of young children exposed to varying bilingual environments, as a first step towards identifying normative measures for specific language pairs. We also aim to compare findings across the different bilingual contexts considered, with a view to identifying general vocabulary development trends in children exposed to more than one language.

The current chapter outlines the challenges posed by the measurement of early vocabulary production across different groups of children receiving bilingual exposure. It is purely methodological in approach, describing potential solutions for the assessment of young children for whom the effects of bilingual exposure may be readily confounded with the symptoms of language delay. In so doing, it paves the way for a series of planned publications which will present empirical findings generated by the research design documented here.

This is probably the first cross-linguistic endeavour to address early lexical development across various bilingual contexts and language pairs. The collective analysis of findings to be obtained for different language pairs has an important contribution to make to language acquisition theory. Importantly, it should help to clarify whether lower-end lexical production scores are specific to the language pairs being learnt, the social contexts or other external variables or whether they are more generally evident across designed languages and contexts.

To ensure the viability of cross-linguistic comparison, individual language pair studies call for a uniform methodological design. The latter also has to reflect considerations emerging from the empirical literature regarding the evaluation of early expressive vocabulary in children exposed to more than one language. This chapter starts with a review of theoretical viewpoints relevant to the identification of delay and risk for continuing language impairment in young children. This appraisal then leads to a set of guiding principles for assessing lexical expression in children exposed to different language pairs, which we present in the following section. These strategies should assist the measurement of early lexical expression across various bilingual contexts, facilitating subsequent cross-linguistic evaluation.

Identification of language delay and risk for language impairment

Different criteria are used to identify constrained lexical development. For instance, on the MacArthur–Bates Communicative Development Inventories (CDIs) (Fenson *et al.*, 2007) and its first edition (Fenson *et al.*, 1993), children are typically identified as late talkers when their vocabulary size falls below the tenth percentile for age. Moreover, Rescorla (1989) posited fewer than 50 words of spoken vocabulary at 24 months or, alternatively, the absence of two-word combinations at the same age, as indicators of language delay.

When employed in isolation, the comparison of young children's lexicon size to established clinical thresholds does not shed light on whether the identified delay will resolve or persist. Outcomes of the Early Language in Victoria Study (ELVS), which draws on a large community sample, clearly illustrate this point. Bavin and Bretherton (2013) report that late talker status, assigned to children whose expressive vocabulary scores fell at or below the US tenth percentile on the CDI: Words and Sentences (CDI: WS) at 2 years, only explained 23.6% and 30.4% of the variance in receptive and expressive language outcomes, respectively, at 4 years. Moreover, although 37.7% of late talkers identified at age 2 continued to have language difficulties at 4 years, 8.9% of non-late talkers unexpectedly presented with impaired language skills at age 4. While highlighting the limited predictive value of expressive vocabulary skills, these findings underscore the relevance of collecting biological and environmental information. Indeed, factors that co-occur with delayed language development can be indicative of increased risk for longer-term difficulties, warranting consideration (Paul & Roth, 2011). For example, Klee *et al.* (2000) found that by adding parental concerns regarding language development or more than six ear infections during the first two years of life to Rescorla's (1989) delay criteria, the positive predictive value of 24-month-old screening increased. A positive family history of language delay, male gender, prematurity and low birth weight have also been consistently and significantly associated with the late emergence of language (Nelson *et al.*, 2006; Reilly *et al.*, 2009; Taylor *et al.*, 2013). On the other hand, social and environmental risk factors, such as parental education, family size and birth order, have been less consistently linked to long-term language impairment in the empirical literature (Nelson *et al.*, 2006). Nonetheless, there is a body of research findings that shows parental socio-economic status (SES) to be closely associated with language learning difficulties. For instance, Tallal *et al.* (1991) reported that children presenting with SLI and having a positive family history of language delay also came from families with a lower SES. More recently, Chiat and Roy (2012) cited a substantial amount of evidence showing children from socio-economically disadvantaged backgrounds to perform significantly lower than their more advantaged peers on language measures.

Although it is established that SES is related to child-directed speech, in turn influencing children's early lexical expression (Hoff, 2003; Rowe, 2008), there is disagreement in the literature as to when experiential factors start to impact language learning. Reports of significant effects of SES on expressive vocabulary as early as 18 months (Fernald *et al.*, 2013) contrast with findings that show language outcomes at 24 months to be largely unrelated to social, family and environmental factors (Reilly *et al.*, 2009; Zubrick *et al.*, 2007). Nonetheless, Reilly *et al.* (2009) pointed out that the associations between the latter factors and diagnosed language impairment in older children may well be different, highlighting the need for further longitudinal research that addresses their predictive value. These considerations necessitate a holistic approach to assessment that not only evaluates early vocabulary production but also takes into account other risk markers for continuing language impairment.

The use of parental report to gather vocabulary data

The clinical thresholds for limited vocabulary development outlined in the previous section draw on parental report measures of children's expressive vocabulary skills. In fact, the parental report method is often chosen when measures of young children's lexical expression and emergent grammar are sought. It differs from the parental diary method, the latter frequently involving comprehensive note-taking and intensive recording of individual children's productive language (Behrens, 2008). Parental report, on the other hand, makes available protocols that encourage parents to focus on specific aspects of available language skill. Similar to the parental diary method, it draws on parents' or main caregivers' direct and intensive contact with young children across a range of daily settings (Feldman *et al.*, 2005), thus facilitating experiential reporting of early language abilities. Parental report has the added advantage of not relying on memory, as it focuses only on current language behaviours and encourages the recognition of vocabulary items, rather than their recall. Parents are typically provided with a comprehensive list of vocabulary items and are asked to identify the words their children produce spontaneously.

Patterson (2000) reports on a substantial body of evidence that confirms the validity and reliability of parental reports of young children's early language skills. However, parents may under- or overestimate their children's vocabulary and emergent grammar skills, particularly when they come from low socio-economic minority backgrounds (Roberts *et al.*, 1999). There is also evidence showing that structured parental reporting of early vocabulary production underestimates expressive lexical abilities when compared to more comprehensive diary records (Mayor & Plunkett, 2011; Robinson & Mervis, 1999). Acknowledging the potential shortcomings of parental reports of lexical ability, Fenson *et al.* (1994)

maintained that outcomes are best seen as indices rather than exhaustive measures of children's lexical repertoires. Accordingly, the strength of such vocabulary measures lies in their potential for comparison, enabling the ability of individual children and/or groups to be gauged in relation to others' performance. The MacArthur–Bates CDIs (Fenson *et al.*, 2007) and the Language Development Survey (Rescorla, 1989) are frequently used parental report tools that provide normative data, allowing children's reported expressive vocabulary skills to be measured against expectations for their age.

Identification of vocabulary delays in bilingual children

When objective normative data and standardised assessments are non-existent, early detection of limited word production is hampered. This is often the case with children in bilingual contexts, whose early vocabulary delays may be the first warning signal of bilingual language impairment (Gatt *et al.*, 2008), but are frequently overlooked as 'the child is bilingual' (O'Toole & Hickey, 2013). For children exposed to two languages, there is an urgent need for evidence documenting emergent vocabulary production skills so that the level of lexical expression that signals language delay for specific language pairs may be identified and disentangled from typical bilingual development.

Exposure to more than one language adds a series of challenges to early assessment practices, over and above those adopted for monolingual children. Firstly, the amount of exposure received in each language varies across children, with empirical evidence showing it to be strongly related to the corresponding vocabulary size (see Elin Thordardottir, 2011; Hoff *et al.*, 2012; Patterson & Pearson, 2012; Pearson *et al.*, 1997). In addition, vocabulary knowledge is likely to be distributed across both of the child's languages, so that some vocabulary is language specific and some is shared (Bedore *et al.*, 2005). Thus, exposure to more than one language increases the normal variation expected in vocabulary development. As a result, difficulties with language learning cannot be readily picked up on the basis of limited word production alone. Exposure to two languages produces differences in lexical expression that may easily be confounded with vocabulary delays. Early identification demands a clear distinction between core language learning deficits and differences in language development that stem from bilingual exposure.

Very little is known about the threshold of bilingual vocabulary size that suggests a potential language learning difficulty. Certainly, the bilingual child's vocabulary production in each language separately cannot be compared to monolingual norms (Elin Thordardottir, 2005). Yet, many studies continue to use monolingual norms as a basis for comparison (see Hoff *et al.*, 2012). The bilingual child's level of development in only one of her/his languages may appear to be at risk when compared to monolingual norms for the same language, since measurement of single-language skill underestimates overall language ability (Bedore & Peña, 2008). Nonetheless, recent findings suggest that monolingual and bilingual children's level of ability in a particular language may be compared, provided that equivalent amounts of exposure to that language are received by both groups (De Houwer, 2010). In a study by Elin Thordardottir (2011), expressive vocabulary scores of 5-year-old children receiving bilingual exposure to French and English were compared to the scores of monolinguals matched for SES and non-verbal cognition. Results showed that unbalanced bilinguals receiving more than 60% exposure in one language performed comparably to the corresponding monolingual group on expressive vocabulary. In contrast, balanced bilingual children had significantly lower vocabulary sizes when compared to monolinguals. These results imply that by the age of 5 years, over 60% cumulative exposure to one language supports achievement of a monolingual level of performance in that language. Amount of exposure therefore determines whether the comparison of bilingual children's single-language performance to monolingual norms may be relevant.

Core language learning difficulties manifest themselves across the board in all language-related activities encountered by the child rather than limiting themselves to one of the languages being learnt (e.g. Armon-Lotem, 2012; Bedore & Peña, 2008; Kohnert, 2010). Thus, difficulties restricted to one of the bilingual child's languages are not sufficient to indicate impaired language processing ability, although they may imply insufficient exposure to that language (Pearson et al., 1997). With young children receiving bilingual exposure, therefore, accurate identification of early language difficulties hinges on acknowledging vocabulary skills in both languages. Accordingly, Patterson and Pearson (2012) hold that assessment of bilingual vocabulary production must address the totality of expressive vocabulary distributed across both languages. This approach to assessment necessitates dedicated measures that tap into the child's composite lexical repertoire. In a study of expressive vocabulary development in Spanish–English bilingual children in the United States, Pearson et al. (1993) proposed two measures that fulfilled this purpose. Total vocabulary (TV) represented the sum of English and Spanish *words* reported for each child. Total conceptual vocabulary (TCV) counted the *concepts* shared between languages so that translation equivalents, or words from both languages having the same meaning, were counted only once. In recent years, TV and TCV scores have been widely employed to quantify the totality of early lexical expression in children receiving bilingual exposure while gauging the extent of lexical overlap emerging between each of their languages.

The popularity of these double-language measures has triggered a constructive debate on their measurement properties. For instance, Patterson and Pearson (2012) point out that semantic immaturities may not allow children to realise that synonyms across languages are equivalent, leading to a different conceptualisation for both terms. In such cases, TCV scores would underestimate the child's conceptual knowledge since equivalent labels would not overlap but have different conceptualisations. They use the example of a child saying 'boat' for one type of boat and 'barco' in Spanish for a very different type. Patterson and Pearson (2012) therefore recommend that TV scores are the preferred bilingual vocabulary measures for infants and toddlers, since they count all sound–meaning pairings as different concepts. Elin Thordardottir *et al.* (2006) called attention to the fact that TCV measures would be less appropriate for children whose proficiency in two languages is relatively balanced. Lower TCV scores, resulting when children know many translation equivalents, would act as a false alarm for language delay when comparison to monolingual norms is attempted.

From a different perspective, Bedore *et al.*'s (2005) study evaluated the classification accuracy of monolingual, total and conceptual scoring approaches when measuring the expressive vocabularies of typically developing Spanish–English children in the United States. The participants came from different backgrounds, namely Spanish dominant (using Spanish over 80% of the time), English dominant (using English over 80% of the time), bilingual Spanish (using Spanish 50%–80% of the time) and bilingual English (using English 50%–80% of the time). Findings showed conceptual scoring to have the best potential for accurately identifying participants as typically developing, suggesting that it would also reduce misidentification of language impairment in children receiving bilingual exposure.

Taken together, the theoretical viewpoints and empirical findings on TV and TCV scores attest to the strengths and weaknesses of both measures, suggesting that each one has value in gauging vocabulary skills that span two languages.

Bilingual and monolingual lexical development: Similarities and differences

The introduction of TV and TCV measures prompted a series of investigations that evaluated the expressive vocabulary shared between the two languages of bilingual children in relation to monolingual control groups. The evidence on bilingual vocabulary acquisition in relation to monolingual development is inconclusive. Similarities between TCV and monolingual scores have been reported for young Spanish–English bilinguals (Pearson *et al.*, 1993) and German–English bilinguals (Junker & Stockman, 2002). Elin Thordardottir *et al.* (2006) identified significantly lower TCV scores in bilingual French–English children when compared to English monolingual vocabulary counts. In contrast, the smaller monolingual French vocabularies were similar in size to the bilingual conceptual lexicons. It is possible that bilingual conceptual scores approximate monolingual vocabulary scores more consistently in children having unbalanced proficiency (Elin Thordardottir *et al.*, 2006). This tentative explanation assumes the relationship between double-language and monolingual measures to be influenced by the extent of overlap in conceptual knowledge between the child's two languages. More recently, Poulin-Dubois *et al.* (2012) found the expressive vocabularies of 24-month-old monolingual children speaking French or English to be larger than the TV size of their bilingual peers having French or English as their first language (L1), although this difference was not statistically significant.

Inconsistent findings do not necessarily imply a slower rate of vocabulary development in bilinguals, but point towards other variables that might impinge on bilingual vocabulary growth. Environmental variables determining language exposure patterns may potentially contribute to the discrepant results (Elin Thordardottir *et al.*, 2006). For example, Pearson and Fernández (1994) suggested that children's levels of exposure to their two languages may vary according to whether they learn both languages in the same or different contexts, and whether they receive exposure from the same or different individuals who may be monolingual or bilingual. Elin Thordardottir *et al.* (2006) identified the specific language pair being learnt as another potentially relevant factor, such that the various combinations of languages to which young children are exposed may result in different rates of lexical acquisition.

Wanted: Clinical thresholds for children exposed to more than one language

There is a growing body of research that addresses expressive vocabulary measurement in children exposed to more than one language, although the focus is noticeably on simultaneous bilingual children. Two approaches to assessment are suggested in this domain, both of which address the need for objective criteria to guide the detection of delay. The comparison of double-language measures, and specifically conceptual scores, to monolingual norms has been proposed as one route to the identification of early language delays (Junker & Stockman, 2002). However, evidence documenting limited comparability of conceptual and monolingual vocabulary scores has reduced the value of this suggestion (see Elin Thordardottir *et al.*, 2006). Another approach also draws on available monolingual norms, comparing them to the lexicon size in each of the languages of simultaneous bilinguals. De Houwer's (2010) findings for children exposed to Dutch and French from birth suggest that the comparison of single-language vocabulary scores to monolingual normative data for the respective languages may be sufficient to identify lower-performing children whose language learning difficulties span both languages.

It cannot be excluded that monolingual reference measures may also be useful in the assessment of young children who are markedly dominant in one language because exposure to the second language (L2) is as yet limited, or whose L2 ability becomes established after their L1. Remarkably, there is no empirical evidence that substantiates this proposal for young children who are as yet monolingual but are likely to develop sequential bilingualism at a later stage, or who are already sequential bilinguals. For these children, comparison of vocabulary ability in the dominant language to monolingual norms for the same language, if available, may provisionally gauge language performance and signal the need for in-depth monitoring. Further, for languages and language pairs lacking normative data, the possible presence of delay may be identified through cautious reference to clinical thresholds established for other languages, such as Fenson *et al.*'s (1993, 2007) tenth percentile scores at monthly intervals and Rescorla's (1989) criterion of fewer than 50 words at 24 months, both intended for American English-speaking children (Gatt *et al.*, 2013). In all cases, however, the utilisation of monolingual data sidesteps the limited availability of customised norms against which the performance of young simultaneous or (potential) sequential bilinguals should be evaluated. This stems from the limited research addressing the typical rate of development and the accompanying range of variation in these groups of children. Clinical identification of potential language impairments is therefore hindered. This fact points towards an imminent need for objective clinical thresholds that can differentiate potential SLI risk from the normal variation that accompanies bilingual exposure. For languages and language pairs that lack developmental norms and for which large-scale standardisation research is not immediately possible, an important first step towards establishing reference measures for lexical expression is the collection of mean, minimum and maximum vocabulary scores for small samples of typically developing children at specific ages (Gatt *et al.*, 2013). A preliminary delineation of the normal distribution of vocabulary size would allow lower-performing children to be identified and monitored.

Research findings show the prevalence rate of primary language delay to be approximately 6% of the childhood population (Law *et al.*, 2000). As we should not expect the incidence of language delay in children receiving bilingual exposure to be any different, this suggests that up to 6% of (potentially) bilingual children are also at risk for language learning difficulties. In turn, composite vocabularies that fall within the lowest 6% of the size range might signal core language deficits. On the other hand, the CDI threshold for small lexicon size that signals risk for persistent language impairment is the lower tenth percentile (Fenson *et al.*, 2007), which translates into approximately 1.5 SD below the mean. These contrasting values highlight the absence of a gold standard for identifying early language delay (Law *et al.*, 2000; Nelson *et al.*, 2006). They also point towards the relevance of normative data that are specific to the language(s) being acquired in the early years. Taking into account the total expressive vocabulary spanning both languages avoids over-identification of children performing poorly in one language only. Furthermore, comparison of productive vocabulary measures across children exposed to different bilingual environments allows insight as to whether lower-end scores are specific to the language pair being learnt or are common to various bilingual settings.

Methodology

The methodological design described in this section incorporates conclusions derived from the research literature regarding the measurement of early lexical development in children exposed to bilingual environments. Following an outline of the criteria for participant recruitment, an account of the proposed methodology, including tools and procedures for data collection and analysis, is given. This research design also reflects our recommendations for the optimal evaluation of productive vocabulary skills in young children receiving bilingual exposure, as well as a comparison of findings across language pairs and contexts. The assessment guidelines we propose can be applied to other studies utilising CDIs and CDI adaptations across various bilingual contexts. We exemplify the recommended methodology by describing the design of a cross-linguistic CDI study implemented in the COST Action, the results of which will be presented in a series of subsequent publications. This study involved six subgroups of participants who received exposure to one of the following language pairs: Maltese and English, Irish and English, Polish and English, French and Portuguese, Turkish and German as well as English and Hebrew.

Criteria for participant recruitment

Criteria for participant recruitment are a key consideration for a study aiming to demonstrate the gains in lexical production expected within the normal range of development, across different language pairs and bilingual contexts.

Age: According to Rescorla (1989), expressive vocabularies that count less than 50 words at 24 months signal a delay in language development, which in turn is a risk marker for continuing language impairment (Paul & Roth, 2011). This empirically tested threshold suggests that protracted language growth may be identified with confidence at the onset of children's third year of life. This could be an outcome of the decrease in variability in lexical production that accompanies the 24-month age point. CDI normative data for American English children reveal increasing variability in word production up to the age of 24 months, following which the range of variation in vocabulary scores shows a consistent drop (Fenson *et al.*, 1993, 2007). In a cross-linguistic CDI study by Bleses *et al.* (2008), monolingual children learning a range of languages were all reported to use over 150 words at 24 months, based on median scores. With evidence suggesting that most children at this age produce a substantial number of words, the resulting variance in vocabulary measures would be expected to decline. For this reason, we chose to consider 24 months as the lowest age point in our study. This does not imply, however, that younger children should not be considered in similar investigations. Since there is a need to identify delayed language development as early as possible (Law *et al.*, 2000), studies aiming to establish a threshold of risk for language impairment may opt to include children exposed to two languages who are younger than 24 months. The upper end of the age range should not be excessively restricted either. We suggest that the upper end of the age range may go beyond the 30-month margin intended for the vocabulary checklist of Fenson *et al.*'s (1993, 2007) CDI: WS form and its adaptations to other languages, which are recommended as data collection tools (see further 'Research tool 1' for a descriptive account of the CDI: WS and its adaptations for use with monolingual and bilingual children). The higher variability in vocabulary production that is expected in bilingual populations, coupled with the extensive numbers of words made available to caregivers when bilingual or parallel monolingual checklists are employed, should minimise the possibility of a ceiling effect on participants' composite vocabulary scores (see further 'Research tool 1' for more detail on available vocabulary assessment tools and Table 7.1 for total numbers of checklist entries available for each language pair). We therefore propose that participants are recruited up to the age of 36 months, while acknowledging that monolingual normative data for the CDI: WS and its adaptations, where available, do not usually surpass the 30-month age point, although this can vary across languages (see Dale & Penfold, 2011). Following these considerations, the age range of participants selected for our study was 24–36 months, although limited data were also collected from children aged between 19 and 23 months in three sub-studies, and from 37-month-olds exposed to another language pair.

Minimal exposure to L2: In selecting participants for our study, we also applied the criterion of a minimum of 6 months' exposure to L2. Given that the youngest children taking part in the study were 24 months old, this condition essentially meant that all children were exposed to their L2 at least by 18 months. The children's ages at onset of L2 exposure led us to consider the debate in the literature as to what constitutes simultaneous and sequential bilingualism. For example, McLaughlin (1984) proposed that exposure to two languages before 3 years of age constitutes simultaneous bilingual development while De Houwer (1995) employed a more stringent criterion of exposure to two languages within one month

Table 7.1 Research tool 1: Components of vocabulary checklist adaptations – L1 and L2 vocabulary and conceptual vocabulary per semantic category, where concept counts represent the sum of L1 and L2 words minus the number of translation equivalent pairs across each language pair (for bilingual Maltese-English and Irish-English adaptations, the number of non-specific language words [NSL] is included)

Components of vocabulary checklist adaptations

Semantic categories	*Maltese–English*				*Irish–English*				*Polish–English*		
	Maltese vocabulary	*English vocabulary*	*NSL vocabulary*	*Conceptual vocabulary*	*Irish vocabulary*	*English vocabulary*	*NSL vocabulary*	*Conceptual vocabulary*	*Polish vocabulary*	*UK English vocabulary*	*Conceptual vocabulary*
Sound effects, animal sounds	6	0	19	25	0	0	13	13	12	12	18
Animals	28	22	0	34	41	41	7	48	43	43	55
Vehicles	17	6	0	17	9	9	8	17	14	14	19
Toys	16	8	0	20	16	15	4	20	18	18	25
Food and drink	75	19	2	79	51	51	10	61	66	68	94
Clothing	35	11	0	35	29	29	3	32	24	28	35
Body parts	22	6	4	27	28	27	0	28	26	27	33
Body care/ functions	–	–	–	–	–	–	–	–	–	–	–
Small household items	65	17	3	73	48	48	5	53	48	50	69
Furniture and rooms	42	6	0	45	30	30	0	30	31	33	48
Outside things	31	8	0	33	38	38	0	38	30	31	42

Table 7.1 (Cont.)

Semantic categories

Components of vocabulary checklist adaptations

	Maltese–English				Irish–English				Polish–English		
	Maltese vocabulary	English vocabulary	NSL vocabulary	Conceptual vocabulary	Irish vocabulary	English vocabulary	NSL vocabulary	Conceptual vocabulary	Polish vocabulary	UK English vocabulary	Conceptual vocabulary
Places to go	13	5	1	17	20	20	2	22	18	22	29
People	18	10	4	25	24	24	6	30	27	29	36
Games and routines	23	7	5	32	28	28	3	31	19	24	32
Occasions	3	2	0	5	–	–	–	–	–	–	–
Action words	70	8	0	72	95	95	0	95	114	110	155
Descriptive words	31	10	1	35	62	62	0	62	33	65	86[1]
Adverbs	–	–	–	–	–	–	–	–	13	–	–
Adverbs – places	–	–	–	–	–	–	–	–	16	–	–
Words about time	27	24	0	26	12	12	0	12	18	12	22
Pronouns	32	25	0	29	20	18	0	20	17	25	32[2]
Prepositional pronouns	–	–	–	–	24	–	0	24	–	–	–
Demonstrative pronouns	–	–	–	–	–	–	–	–	9	–	–
Question words	9	7	0	9	7	7	0	7	13	7	13
Modal adverbs	–	–	–	–	–	–	–	–	8	–	–

(Continued)

Table 7.1 (Cont.)

Components of vocabulary checklist adaptations

Semantic categories	Maltese–English				Irish–English				Polish–English		
	Maltese vocabulary	English vocabulary	NSL vocabulary	Conceptual vocabulary	Irish vocabulary	English vocabulary	NSL vocabulary	Conceptual vocabulary	Polish vocabulary	UK English vocabulary	Conceptual vocabulary
Prepositions and locations	28	27	0	27	32	32	0	32	15[3]	27	52[4]
Pre-/post-positions	–	–	–	–	–	–	–	–	–	–	–
Quantifiers and articles	16	16	0	17	18	17	1	19	20[5]	17	29
Numbers/quantities	–	–	–	–	–	–	–	–	–	–	–
Helping verbs	3	0	0	3	17	14	0	17	9	21	28
Negatives	2	1	0	1	–	–	–	–	–	–	–
Connecting words	15	5	0	15	7	7	0	7	9	7	13
Prepositions/connectors	–	–	–	–	–	–	–	–	–	–	–
Total	627	250	39	701	658	624	61	718	670	690	965

[1] In computing the conceptual vocabulary count, translation equivalent pairs considered include items in the *Adverbs* category of the Polish adaptation.
[2] In computing the conceptual vocabulary count, translation equivalent pairs considered include items in the *Demonstrative Pronouns* category of the Polish adaptation.
[3] Category only includes prepositions in the Polish adaptation.
[4] In computing the conceptual vocabulary count, translation equivalent pairs considered include items in the *Adverbs – places* and *Modal adverbs* of the Polish adaptation.
[5] Does not include articles.

Table 7.1 (Cont.)

Components of vocabulary checklist adaptations

Semantic categories	German-Turkish			Hebrew-English			French-Portuguese		
	German vocabulary	Turkish vocabulary	Conceptual vocabulary	Hebrew vocabulary	American English vocabulary	Conceptual vocabulary	French vocabulary	Portuguese vocabulary	Conceptual vocabulary
Sound effects, animal sounds	0	13	13	15	12	17	13	21	25
Animals	27	41	47	46	43	52	43	44	59
Vehicles	15	14	21	15	14	18	14	18	20
Toys	13	20	27	22	18	24	18	21	28
Food and drink	33	66	78	68	68	92	73	77	104
Clothing	22	32	43	29	28	34	32	49	56
Body parts	21	27	32	26	27	31	28	37	42
Body care/functions	11	–	11	–	–	–	–	–	–
Small household items	34[1]	33	76	47	50	53	56	90	96
Furniture and rooms	0	27	–	31	33	37	33	39	54
Outside things	14	37	39	29	31	34	31	36	48
Places to go	0	25	25	19	22	27	23	33	42

(Continued)

Table 7.1 (Cont.)

Components of vocabulary checklist adaptations

Semantic categories	German-Turkish			Hebrew-English			French-Portuguese		
	German vocabulary	Turkish vocabulary	Conceptual vocabulary	Hebrew vocabulary	American English vocabulary	Conceptual vocabulary	French vocabulary	Portuguese vocabulary	Conceptual vocabulary
People	15	32	37	17	29	29	28	32	38
Games and routines	9	40	43	30	25	41	26	34	54
Occasions	–	–	–	103	103	119	–	–	–
Action words	34	146	171	–	–	–	102	122	170
Descriptive words	23	61	72	46	63	73	65	61	89
Adverbs	–	–	–	–	–	–	–	–	–
Adverbs – places	–	–	–	–	–	–	–	–	–
Words about time	0	13	13	14	12	17	11	19	19
Pronouns	15	21	32	12	25	25	23	37	48
Prepositional pronouns	–	–	–	–	–	–	–	–	–
Demonstrative pronouns	–	–	–	–	–	–	–	–	–
Question words	3	12	12	10	7	10	7	8	9
Modal adverbs	–	–	–	–	–	–	–	–	–

Table 7.1 (Cont.)

Components of vocabulary checklist adaptations

Semantic categories	German-Turkish			Hebrew-English			French-Portuguese		
	German vocabulary	Turkish vocabulary	Conceptual vocabulary	Hebrew vocabulary	American English vocabulary	Conceptual vocabulary	French vocabulary	Portuguese vocabulary	Conceptual vocabulary
Prepositions and locations	–	–	–	13	26	23	26	31	37
Pre-/post-positions	16	21	28	–	–	–	–	–	–
Quantifiers and articles	0	23	23	10	17	17	14	27	33
Numbers/quantities	6	–	6	–	–	–	–	–	–
Helping verbs	8	–	8	–	21	21	18	7	19
Negatives	–	–	–	–	–	–	–	–	–
Connecting words	–	–	–	–	6	6	6	10	9
Prepositions/connectors	0	7	7	–	–	–	–	–	–
Total	319	711	864	602	680	803	690	853	1099

¹Small household items and Furniture and rooms are merged into one semantic category in the German adaptation.

of birth. More recently, Pearson (2013) stipulated that both simultaneous and sequential bilingualism are possible during the first three years of life. While simultaneous bilingual children regularly experience two languages concurrently, sequential bilinguals' L1 becomes established before L2. This implies that, in sequential bilinguals, regular exposure to L2 commences only after the child receives consistent and substantial input in another language (L1) from very early on.

Alongside *timing* of initial exposure to two languages, *amount* of exposure to each language is another factor that appears to be directly related to the mode of bilingual development. For instance, a child receiving input primarily in one language and minimal exposure to the majority language at societal level would not be engaging in simultaneous bilingual development, despite concurrent exposure to two languages. Limited exposure to L2, the majority language, would imply monolingual development with potential for sequential bilingualism at a later stage. This is typically the case with infants and toddlers from immigrant environments, who have limited access to L2 until their regular involvement in nursery or day-care settings brings them in regular contact with L2 as the medium of communication. A similar outcome would be expected in settings where, despite the presence of bilingualism at a societal level, parents prefer one language for communicative exchanges in the home. Establishing a minimal amount of exposure to both L1 and L2 is therefore warranted when selecting participants. We suggest that an important participant selection criterion should be a minimal period of six months' exposure to L2. Longitudinal findings reported by Pearson *et al.* (1997) showed the proportions of vocabulary produced in each language by young bilingual children to reflect changes in the language environment with a delay of one month. We therefore deduced that the criterion of at least six months' bilingual exposure should ensure that children's developing lexical systems respond to the bilingual input received. As a result, the children whose lexical production was assessed in our study had all been receiving L2 input for a minimum of six months. They were either exposed simultaneously to both languages in their immediate environment from birth or else they received input primarily in one language at home, with exposure to L2 occurring through child care, television programmes as well as L2-speaking relatives and friends among others, thus paving the way for sequential bilingualism in the near future. The amount of L2 exposure received varied across language pairs.

Number of reporters: Most studies using parental report for assessment of early lexical production involve one reporter for each child. We suggest that expressive vocabulary skills in L1 are reported on by the main caregiver, provided that this person's language capabilities support reading of the vocabulary checklist and, where relevant, recognition of words as components of the child's lexical repertoire. In the event that the main caregiver has bilingual competence, L2 word production can also be reported. The validity of this method has been established in other bilingual studies where one reporter was used to report on the child's development in both languages (Marchman & Martínez-Sussman, 2002). Otherwise, it may be delegated to a person who regularly uses L2 as a medium of communication with the child and can therefore gauge the child's lexical expression in the language. Although the involvement of two or three adults in rating the same child's vocabulary skills has been recommended in both monolingual (De Houwer *et al.*, 2005) and bilingual environments (De Houwer, 2010) to enhance reliability of measures, this can be problematic. Vocabulary norms typically draw on data generated by a single informant per child. If multiple informants are claimed to significantly change the results for individual children, norms based on such composite measures should be derived in addition to single-informant norms. However, multiple reporters are usually not easily available. In most language contexts, having more than one informant per child may result in smaller sample sizes. It is easier to recruit children who have one caregiver willing to complete the vocabulary assessment. In the light of these facts, the option of having multiple reporters may be abandoned in favour of maximising the chances of identifying larger samples of children and therefore of increasing the statistical power of subsequent analyses. In our model study, this was an important consideration given the aim of identifying the normal distribution of children's lexicon sizes within and across different language pairs. We suggest that the number of participants should be considered to be more important than having multiple informants for one child. Nonetheless, the involvement of multiple reporters is recommended in situations where an informant is not familiar with both of the child's languages, to ensure that the vocabulary data reported for each of the child's languages are accurate. Such instances would lead to multiple-informant data for specific children being analysed together with single-informant measures for other participants within the same sample. This methodological limitation would be compensated for by reported vocabulary data that are sufficiently reliable for each of the children's languages.

Language exposure patterns: Participants can have a variety of language exposure patterns, highlighting the diverse bilingual environments that young children may experience. This heterogeneity should not undermine methodological rigour as it reflects the reality of acquiring more than one language. It can also ensure that outcomes for the individual sub-studies provide comparable reference measures for the various language pairs and types of bilingual context addressed. In addition, the diversity of language learning settings should make available an opportunity to observe whether thresholds for limited lexicon size identified for each group are specific to the language pairs being investigated or suggest a universal trend.

Information regarding the length of children's exposure to L1 and L2 as well as their social environment (including SES), family language usage, language dominance and age of initial exposure to L2 should be collected through a detailed questionnaire. Such a questionnaire was developed for the COST Action IS0804 study and is described in 'Proposed Data Coding System and Analysis' below.

Method and tools

The methodological design presented here seeks to generate two types of data. Expressive vocabulary measures are the primary focus. Developmental and language background information for each child complements the lexical data, placing them in context. In the model study, participating parents were asked to provide information on the words produced spontaneously by their child in daily contexts by ticking the relevant words on a vocabulary checklist, details of which are given in 'Research tool 1'. Parents were also asked to report on specific aspects of their child's development and language environment by completing a questionnaire (see 'Research tool 2').

Research tool 1: Vocabulary checklist adaptations

Since adaptations of the CDI: WS (Fenson et al., 1993, 2007) are now available for 61 languages (Dale & Penfold, 2011), we suggest that this is the optimal tool for research considering early lexical expression in bilingual populations. The American English language version of the CDI: WS, intended for children aged 16–30 months, incorporates a 680-item word production checklist and questions on the use of words in Part I (Words Children Use), together with an appraisal of emergent morphological and syntactic skills in Part II (Sentences and Grammar). A review of the research literature spanning the numerous publications related to the CDIs shows relatively high concurrent correlations between CDI expressive vocabulary scores and standardised and/or naturalistic measures across various samples of children, including children with delayed language and from low SES groups (Law & Roy, 2008). Similarly, predictive validity studies have shown high associations between CDI vocabulary scores and subsequent outcome measures based on parental report, direct observation or both (Miller et al., 1995; Reese & Read, 2000). The growing stock of CDI adaptations to languages other than American English, as attested by the outcomes of a survey of authorised adaptations (see Dale & Penfold, 2011), has been the driving force behind a series of cross-linguistic efforts addressing early language development. Earlier attempts at comparing monolingual children's performance in English and Italian (Caselli et al., 1995, 1999) have been followed up with more extensive studies that capitalise on the wider availability of CDI adaptations for various languages. For example, Bleses *et al.*'s (2008) study examined early vocabulary development in Danish children in relation to findings reported for CDI versions in 18 languages. Within-language and cross-language comparisons have been markedly facilitated by the recent launch of the web-based CLEX (Cross-Linguistic Lexical Norms) project (Jørgensen *et al.*, 2010), which has brought together norms for several CDI adaptations.

In addition to the abundance of studies investigating lexical expression in monolingual children through the various CDI adaptations, there is a small body of evidence that documents use of the CDI: WS and/or its adaptations to measure the expressive vocabularies of children exposed to more than one language. Often, these studies compare the composite expressive vocabularies of bilingual children to the single-language vocabulary scores obtained by monolingual children (see introductory section of this chapter). For instance, the series of investigations of the lexical development of Hispanic toddlers exposed to American English and Spanish by Pearson and colleagues (Pearson & Fernández, 1994; Pearson *et al.*, 1993, 1995, 1997) incorporated earlier versions of the English CDI vocabulary checklist as well as the Spanish CDI adaptation in parallel. Similarly, in Poulin-Dubois *et al.*'s (2012) investigation of the expressive lexical abilities of young children exposed to either French or English as L1 and to English, French, Hebrew, Turkish or Italian as L2, parents reported on their children's vocabularies by completing separate vocabulary checklists according to the language input received. The finding that measures of expressive L1 vocabulary and TV generated by parental report were strongly correlated with receptive vocabulary scores obtained through direct assessment, served to validate the methods and tools employed. Separate checklists have also been used to explore the similarities between single-language vocabulary measures obtained for bilingual children and those expected for children developing monolingually in the same language. For example, Tan (2010) employed standardised CDI vocabulary checklist adaptations to Singapore English, Mandarin and Malay in parallel to measure the vocabulary skills of children exposed to English, Mandarin or Malay, or a combination of these and other languages. Another study employing separate but parallel American English and Spanish CDI checklists showed that reported bilingual vocabulary measures could predict children's lexical abilities in spontaneous and structured contexts (Marchman & Martínez-Sussman, 2002).

In addition to the use of two vocabulary checklists in parallel, measurement of word production in children exposed to two languages has also employed single bilingual checklists, as in the case of the Maltese–English (Gatt, 2007) and Irish–English (O'Toole & Fletcher, 2010) versions. A Welsh–English CDI adaptation is also in preparation (see Dale & Penfold, 2011). Single bilingual checklists are considered appropriate in these settings as parents are usually competent in both languages, although possibly to varying degrees, and bilingualism is always present in children's language learning contexts. Although bilingual CDI versions are relatively scarce, the ample range of monolingual CDI adaptations now available is expected to bolster the investigation of expressive lexical development in a range of language pairs. Despite the numerous adaptations, there is a paucity of research evidence documenting expressive vocabulary skills in young children brought up in bilingual environments. The investigation described here represents an attempt at reducing this gap in the empirical literature. It differs from previous studies on early bilingual or multilingual acquisition in a single context (e.g. Poulin-Dubois et al., 2012; Tan, 2010) in attempting to bring together findings on vocabulary development in children exposed to different language pairs in diverse contexts.

Unlike other studies within COST Action IS0804, the cross-linguistic measurement of early lexical expression does not make use of novel assessments devised purposely for the study. Instead, the enquiry to which we relate in this chapter capitalises on tools that had been previously validated. This allows more effort to be directed towards ensuring uniformity in the methodological design and analytical procedures employed across the individual sub-studies. Our design employs original or adapted monolingual CDI vocabulary checklists utilised in parallel, or bilingual versions (as in the Maltese and Irish situations), depending on availability as well as on family and social contexts.[2] This allowed the measurement of productive vocabulary in L1, or both L1 and L2, depending on the extent of bilingual exposure received. Indeed, the lack of bilingual assessments often necessitates the pairing of monolingual protocols in order to obtain a reasonable estimate of bilingual ability.

Comparing CDI adaptations used to study bilingual lexical development

When employing bilingual or single language CDI adaptations in bilingual contexts for the purpose of cross-linguistic investigation, a detailed comparison of the contents of the protocols used is essential. We suggest that the semantic categories and the respective number of words and concepts for the checklist adaptations employed in each sub-study are compared. As we shall be showing in subsequent publications, the use of absolute measures of vocabulary production can be revealing in its own right (see also 'Proposed data coding system and analysis: Cheklist measures'). Side-by-side tabulation of the contents of each checklist adaptation employed therefore provides a baseline for statistical comparison. Table 7.1 illustrates this exercise for the IS0804 WG3 CDI study. The components of monolingual checklists/checklist adaptations used in parallel are listed alongside each other for easy identification of the L1 and L2 items presented to caregivers of children in each language pair subgroup.

Research tool 2: Questionnaires

Recent empirical literature on L2 acquisition in childhood has emphasised the relevance of information related to developmental and language input variables for a holistic appraisal of emergent bilingual skills. For instance, Paradis *et al.* (2010) reported that details on the early milestones, current L1 abilities, behaviour and activity preferences as well as a family history of children learning English as their L2 differentiated typically developing from language-impaired school-aged children. Furthermore, in an investigation addressing individual differences in children's acquisition of vocabulary and verb morphology, Paradis (2011) identified length of L2 exposure and richness of L2 input as significant predictors of lexical and morphosyntactic development in children aged between 4;10 and 7;0 years. The link between language background and bilingual development has been previously acknowledged by various other researchers. For instance, among the findings of a series of studies on Hispanic–English children aged between 5 and 10 years growing up in Miami was the significant effect of frequency of input on vocabulary development (Oller & Eilers, 2002). Interestingly, in a three-year longitudinal study on L2 English acquisition among Chinese child and adolescent immigrants, Jia and Aronson (2003) identified age of onset of L2 input as one of the environmental factors that contributed to language proficiency changes. Younger arrivals eventually became dominant in English while older arrivals maintained their L1 Chinese dominance. Together, these findings point towards the relevance of environmental and developmental factors to the study of bilingual acquisition. We suggest that cross-linguistic investigations of early lexical development in children receiving bilingual exposure consider language background and developmental details as important pieces of information that place vocabulary data in a meaningful context. Following this guideline, we designed a parental background questionnaire which is now described in detail.

The Questionnaire for Parents of Bilingual Children: Infants and Toddlers Version (PABIQ-IT) (Gatt *et al.*, 2011) was prepared especially for the purposes of the investigation we relate to in this chapter. It is a version of the Questionnaire for Parents of Bilingual Children (PABIQ), used within COST Action IS0804 (see Tuller, this volume), that is suitable for use with younger children. The questionnaire format was closely based on the Beirut-Tours Questionnaire (Tuller & Messarra, 2010), which was created and piloted by French and Lebanese members of COST Action IS0804 and was in turn based on the Alberta Language and Development Questionnaire (ALDeQ) (Paradis *et al.*, 2010) and the Alberta Language Environment

Questionnaire (ALEQ) (Paradis, 2011). The latter three questionnaires were purposely designed to assess language and environmental background in bilingual populations, but were intended for school-aged children. Our questionnaire adapted the Beirut-Tours protocol for use with children younger than 3 years. Several components of the original protocol were retained while others concerning the child's school language environment were replaced with questions focusing on potential risk markers for language impairment in early childhood. The latter were considered to be of greater significance to younger children. Areas of development thus addressed included eventful pre- and perinatal histories, age at first word production, the absence of word combinations, parental concerns regarding language development, the presence of specific medical conditions, as well as a history of frequent colds, allergies and/or ear infections. Parents were also asked to report on the language exposure pattern typically received by their child, i.e. whether the child was exposed to one language only, or one language with some words in another language, or approximately equal proportions of two languages, or two languages and an additional language. These questions were accompanied by others derived from the Beirut-Tours Questionnaire, targeting general information about the child, developmental history, languages used with and by the child, education and occupation of the parents, as well as a family history of speech, language and/or literacy difficulties. Most questions were intended to elicit a yes/no response or a tick next to the most appropriate descriptor. Other questions required parents to provide specific details such as the child's birth weight, or the age at which first steps were taken. In some instances, parents were invited to elaborate on their responses. For example, they were asked to briefly describe their concerns about the child's language development or to specify any medical conditions that the child presented with.

The changes made to the Beirut-Tours Questionnaire led to a substantial reduction in its length. In fact, the PABIQ-IT did not address the child's exposure to languages according to context, current skills in verbal comprehension and expression including speech intelligibility, vocabulary repertoire, grammatical and conversational ability, activities per week in each language and languages spoken at school, among others. The omission of most of these components was motivated by their limited relevance to the target age range or to the focus of the study. In hindsight, however, eliciting an account of the total waking hours spent by each child in different language environments would have provided more detail on the proportion of L1 and L2 exposure that the participants received. Besides current language exposure, questions addressing the sum of children's exposure over each year of life would have supplied useful information on *cumulative* exposure (see Unsworth, 2013; Unsworth *et al.*, 2011). These data would have not only served the purpose of better defining the language input patterns received by each group of participants, but would have also allowed measures of expressive lexicon size to be linked directly to the amount of cumulative exposure to each language, leading to more realistic expectations for vocabulary production. Regretfully, these notions only emerged when implementation of our model study was well underway. Appraisal of outcome is therefore not possible, although the collection of such information could be considered in future CDI studies involving children receiving bilingual exposure.

The PABIQ-IT was first developed in English and then translated to other languages[3] (see Appendix B for the English version of the questionnaire). COST IS0804 (2011) subsequently developed the PABIQ, which is a short version of the Beirut-Tours Questionnaire (Tuller & Messarra, 2010) (see Tuller, this volume, for more detail on the PABIQ). Although our questionnaire was already in use at the time, researchers who joined the investigation at a later stage could choose either version to employ in their language pair study. Methods of completion varied across individual studies. Like the ALDeQ and the ALEQ, the Beirut-Tours adaptation was intended for face-to-face administration to parents, with responses written on the form by the interviewer. This procedure was motivated by the needs of the population on which the tool was initially tested. There were, however, no contraindications for presenting the questionnaire to parents in written format for completion without interviewer intervention. In fact, our questionnaire adaptation for younger children was sent and received by mail, thus requiring unassisted written completion by caregivers, or administered through face-to-face or telephone interviews. The Methodology section describes the procedure followed in the model CDI study.

Procedure

In our model study, parents of children aged 24–36 months who were exposed to two languages were contacted through immigrant or bilingual communities, associations, websites, newspapers, preschools and population databases. When parents expressed an initial interest in the study, they were sent an information letter and consent form by mail, together with a copy of the vocabulary checklist adaptation(s) and the PABIQ-IT or the PABIQ. Two vocabulary checklists were forwarded for every child, one for each language she/he was exposed to, with the exception of children for whom a vocabulary checklist was available in a bilingual format, in which case one checklist that incorporated both languages was circulated (see introductory section of this chapter). For most sub-studies, two versions of the questionnaires were sent, reflecting the target languages. In some instances, however, the questionnaire was forwarded in a single language version which caregivers could respond to with ease. The information letter introduced the aims of the study and described the involvement that it would entail. Parents were invited to complete the checklist and questionnaire if they consented to their child's participation in the study. Contact details of the researcher(s) were provided so that specific queries could be clarified. The front page of every vocabulary checklist adaptation included a set of guidelines to assist completion, supplemented by examples that aimed to minimise misinterpretation. It was emphasised that only vocabulary items produced spontaneously were to be reported, conforming to the standard requirement of CDI completion. The forms were to be returned to the researcher(s) in the self-addressed envelopes provided or in person, depending on the specific circumstances of the study. Some questionnaires and checklists were completed during face-to-face or telephone interviews. Caregivers could opt for anonymity if they wished, with choice of method of completion being determined by the characteristics of the specific participant groups or individuals. Factors such as caregivers' expectations, as laid down by cultural norms, and educational and literacy levels, were taken into account. For instance, if the main caregiver was suspected or reported to present with literacy difficulties, an interviewer's assistance in completing the forms was necessary. The next section outlines the variables yielded for analysis by the vocabulary checklists and questionnaires. Subsequent papers (in preparation) will review the data emerging from this study.

Proposed Data Coding System and Analysis

We describe the data coding system and subsequent analysis adopted in our study to exemplify the implementation of the guidelines outlined above. Data for each language pair were coded separately and then pooled into a common database for collective analyses. A structured approach to the scoring of vocabulary checklist and questionnaire data allowed findings from the individual studies to be collated and compared cross-linguistically. This section describes the measures that would need to be derived from vocabulary and background data to be employed in inter-group comparisons.

Checklist measures

With bilingual vocabulary measurement being an issue for debate (see introductory section of this chapter), the choice of scoring approach for the present study was far from straightforward. Weighing the various arguments in favour and against total and conceptual scoring led to the conclusion that deriving both TV and TCV scores for each child would

- allow for the possibility of comparing conceptual scores to monolingual norms, depending on availability of the latter;

- compensate for the measurement error inherent in conceptual scoring should semantic immaturities be present;
- pave the way for identification of a threshold indicating composite lexicon sizes falling at the lower end of the normal range;
- enable the derivation of common scores for children having different bilingual backgrounds.

Checklist words available for each language pair, whether on separate or bilingual inventories, were mapped onto each other so that the available translation equivalent pairs were identified. By subtracting the number of translation equivalent pairs from the TV count comprising all available checklist words for each language pair, the maximum TCV score possible for each language pair was established. A relevant technical paper by Pearson (1992) provided the guiding principles for the mapping procedure. Every vocabulary checklist adaptation listed a different number of words, leading to concerns regarding the comparability of raw scores across individual studies. The option of expressing TV and TCV counts for each child as a proportion of the respective maximum scores possible for each language pair was explored. This approach to measurement controlled checklist length effects and allowed cross-linguistic comparison of results. Unexpectedly, however, use of percentage scores also revealed anomalies. Specifically, TCV percentage scores tended to be higher than TV percentages since the TCV counts were often expressed as a proportion of a smaller total. Conversely, when raw scores were considered, TCV was always smaller than TV. These issues led to the conclusion that the computation of raw mean scores was also of value as it allowed deeper insight into the language-specific trends in expressive vocabulary development. Monolingual vocabulary scores were also derived in order to gauge the relative dominance of each of the child's languages. These were then expressed as a percentage of the L1 and L2 vocabulary items available on the respective checklists across language pairs. In instances where the number of L2 checklist words was much smaller than the L1 lexical items, the L2 word proportion scores turned out to be higher than the percentage of L1 words. Again, this outcome pointed towards the relevance of including mean raw L1 and L2 word counts alongside proportion scores, for a more comprehensive account of children's vocabulary production in each of the languages to which they were exposed.

Not all words reported by parents could be confidently tallied as L1 and L2 words. Initially, a separate coding category was set up for cognate terms, which were identified as words having the same historical language source (Li Wei, 2000) e.g. *mama* and *mummy*. Coding attempts, however, revealed that there were several words other than cognates that could not be assigned L1 or L2 status. It was therefore decided that a more comprehensive count of non-specific language (NSL) words would also be computed for every child. Based on a measure proposed by Gatt (2010), this score represented the sum of

- cognate terms;
- homophones, that is, word forms that sound similar in the child's L1 and L2 so that they cannot be clearly attributed to either language; these included onomatopoeic terms that were not language specific e.g. the sound effect *moo*;
- proper nouns e.g. the child's name;
- lexical items indicated as family-specific words in the relevant vocabulary checklists. For instance, the CDI: WS and its adaptations flag children's body part names for male and female genital organs as words that vary across families. When ticked, such lexical items could not be counted as L1 or L2 words since the relevant lexical entries do not specify the actual word used by the child.

Lexical items that fitted these criteria were therefore excluded from the L1 and L2 vocabulary counts and tallied separately. The sum of L1 vocabulary, L2 vocabulary and NSL words represented the TV count. Further vocabulary measures were employed to represent the number of lexical items reported in each semantic category (see Table 7.1 for a list of semantic categories appearing across all vocabulary checklist adaptations). For each child, vocabulary scores were accompanied by background measures that attempted to quantify aspects of the child's development and language input. These questionnaire measures are described in the next section.

Questionnaire measures

In exploring the clinical significance of low expressive lexicon size in monolingual children, biological factors as well as environmental and social variables assume importance in predicting the risk of persistence of early language difficulties (see introductory section of this chapter). It seems reasonable to expect a similar trend in children exposed to two languages. By complementing lexical scores with additional measures of child-internal and child-external variables, we hoped to enhance the identification of lower levels of vocabulary size that are likely to evolve into persistent language impairments as children grow older. Factoring in data related to variables other than vocabulary size in statistical analyses should help to disentangle language difference from delay, leading to better identification of SLI risk. Thus, it is recommended that measures derived from questionnaire data related to child's gender, birth order, family history of language difficulties, birth weight, health problems (including ear infections) as well as parental concerns about language development, are used as additional variables in the analysis of lexicon size. With regard to children's ear infections, we opted to code only the questionnaire responses indicating frequent occurrences or otherwise rather than actual number of episodes (see Question 2.8(d) in the PABIQ-IT, Appendix B). From the data gathered in our study, we deduced that caregivers would be more accurate when reporting on general rather than specific frequency of occurrence. This coding decision also allowed conformity with the data generated by a similar question in the PABIQ which was concerned only with the presence or absence of frequent ear infections.

Research studies show parental education and occupation to relate to the outcomes of early vocabulary delays, although the strength of the evidence varies (see introductory section of this chapter). Ellis and Thal (2008) hypothesised that the risk for persistent language difficulties grows as the number of associated risk factors increases, which highlights the importance of including all potential factors in the relevant statistical models. Therefore, in our study, the highest level of education achieved by each child's mother and father was also recorded. Parental occupations were coded on the basis of the European Social Survey Round 5 Occupation Codes (Norwegian Social Science Data Services, 2010). An additional code category of 0 was set up to cater for parents who were homemakers or unemployed. It was also decided that for parents currently on maternity or paternity leave, habitual occupation would still be coded if this was reported in the questionnaire. Since there was no question directly addressing this issue, data corresponding to the homemaker category might have included parents fulfilling this role both on a temporary and on a permanent basis.

An additional variable was frequency of the child's exposure to L1 and L2, which was expected to impact directly on the size of children's L1 and L2 vocabularies (see introductory section of this chapter). Since the pattern of bilingual exposure received by each child is likely to account for a proportion of the variance in lexicon size, the amount of exposure is a crucial piece of information to include in the analysis of measures. A preliminary attempt at data analysis revealed that more of the available questionnaire measures related to language exposure should be included to better explore their role as variables influencing vocabulary production. Therefore, the frequency of main caregivers' L1 and L2 input was also coded, adding to the information on the extent of children's exposure to each language. This was supplemented by details on the language use patterns in child-directed communicative exchanges and among household members. The latter information sought to gauge the extent of mixing in children's input, so that this could be analysed in relation to the proportions of L1 and L2 employed in children's vocabularies.

We acknowledge that responses to questionnaire items are subject to interpretation by caregivers, particularly when interviewers do not assist completion. A case in point is the range of responses elicited by the question addressing the child's age at initial L1 exposure. Although most caregivers established this to be in the range of 0 and 2 months, others reported the ages of 6–9 months, which seems to be a highly unlikely occurrence. It might have been the case that parents were interpreting this question as to when the child began to respond to or use language as opposed to being exposed to language, which happens from birth. Such responses point to the need for a caveat concerning the accuracy of questionnaire responses completed independently by caregivers. Although assisted completion would be likely to enhance the reliability of questionnaire data, the involvement of interviewers would considerably increase the demands on human resources required for data collection. We therefore suggest that researchers attempt to balance accuracy and feasibility in the design of similar studies.

Conclusion

The present chapter's motivation was primarily methodological, in that it intended to provide a discussion of variables and measures which should be considered when lexical thresholds for identifying early language delays in children exposed to specific language pairs in different bilingual contexts are to be identified. We have documented tried and tested solutions to methodological problems arising in the cross-linguistic investigation of early lexical acquisition in children receiving bilingual exposure, conducted within the framework of COST Action IS0804. The course of action described in this chapter hopes to represent a feasible proposal for unravelling the effects of bilingual development and core language learning difficulties on productive vocabulary skills. Moreover, the reported methodology represents a cross-linguistic endeavour that tests the universality of identified thresholds across various language pairs. The considerations outlined in this chapter hope to guide the design of further cross-linguistic studies that address early lexical development in bilingual contexts, with the aim of producing a wider range of bilingual norms that facilitate identification practices. Objective thresholds that guide the prompt detection of risk for persistent bilingual impairment should instil confidence in decisions regarding the provision of early intervention services. For young children struggling to acquire the two languages they are exposed to, this represents an important step towards diminishing the adverse effects of continuing deficits.

Notes

(1) The methodological design was planned within COST Action IS0804 Working Group 3 (WG3).

(2) References to language-specific adaptations of the CDI employed in this study can be found in Appendix A.
(3) References to language-specific adaptations of the PaBiQ-IT employed in the study can be found in Appendix A.

References

Armon-Lotem, S. (2012) Introduction: Bilingual children with SLI – the nature of the problem. *Bilingualism: Language and Cognition* 15 (1), 1–4.
Bavin, E.L. and Bretherton, L. (2013) The Early Language in Victoria Study: Late talkers, predictors, and outcomes. In L.A. Rescorla and P.S. Dale (eds.) *Late Talkers: Language development, interventions, and outcomes* (pp. 67–87). Baltimore: Brookes.
Bedore, L.M., Peña, E.D., García, M. and Cortez, C. (2005) Conceptual versus monolingual scoring: When does it make a difference? *Language, Speech and Hearing Services in Schools* 36 (3), 188–200.
Bedore, L.M. and Peña, E.D. (2008) Assessment of bilingual children for identification of language impairment: Current findings and implications for practice. *The International Journal of Bilingual Education and Bilingualism* 11 (1), 1–29.
Behrens, H. (2008) Corpora in language acquisition research: History, methods and perspectives. In H. Behrens (ed.) *Corpora in Language Acquisition Research: History, Methods and Perspectives* (pp. xi–xxx). Amsterdam: John Benjamins.
Bleses, D., Vach, W., Slott, M., Wehberg, S., Thomsen, P., Madsen, T.O. and Basbøll, H. (2008) Early vocabulary development in Danish and other languages: A CDI-based comparison. *Journal of Child Language* 35 (3), 619–650.
Caselli, M.C., Bates, E., Casadio, P., Fenson, J., Fenson, L., Sanderl, L. and Weir, J. (1995) A cross-linguistic study of early lexical development. *Cognitive Development* 10 (2), 159–199.
Caselli, M.C., Casadio, P. and Bates, E. (1999) A comparison of the transition from first words to grammar in English and Italian. *Journal of Child Language* 26 (1), 69–111.
Chiat, S. and Roy, P. (2012) Teasing apart disadvantage from disorder: The case of poor language. In C. Marshall (ed.) *Current Issues in Developmental Disorders* (pp. 125–150). Hove: Psychology Press.
COST IS0804 (2011) *Questionnaire for Parents of Bilingual Children (PaBiQ)*. See http://www.bi-sli.org
Dale, P.S., Price, T.S., Bishop, D.V.M. and Plomin, R. (2003) Outcomes of early language delay I: Predicting persistent and transient language difficulties at 3 and 4 years. *Journal of Speech, Language and Hearing Research* 46 (3), 544–560.
Dale, P.S. and Penfold, M. (2011) Adaptations of the MacArthur-Bates CDI into Non-U.S. English Languages. See http://mb-cdi.stanford.edu/documents/AdaptationsSurvey7-5-11Web.pdf (accessed 11 December 2014).
De Houwer, A. (1995) Bilingual language acquisition. In P. Fletcher and B. MacWhinney (eds) *Handbook of Child Language* (pp. 219–250). Oxford: Basil Blackwell.
De Houwer, A. (2009) *Bilingual First Language Acquisition*. Bristol: Multilingual Matters.
De Houwer, A. (2010) Assessing lexical development in bilingual first language acquisition: What can we learn from monolingual norms? In M. Cruz-Ferreira (ed.) *Multilingual Norms* (pp. 279–322). Frankfurt am Main: Peter Lang.
De Houwer, A., Bornstein, M.H. and Leach, D.B. (2005) Assessing early communicative ability: A cross-reporter cumulative score for the MacArthur CDI. *Journal of Child Language* 32 (4), 735–758.
Elin Thordardottir. (2005) Early lexical and syntactic development in Quebec French and English: Implications of cross-linguistic and bilingual assessment. *International Journal of Language and Communication Disorders* 40 (3), 243–278.

Elin Thordardottir. (2011) The relationship between bilingual exposure and vocabulary development. *International Journal of Bilingualism* 15 (4), 426–445.

Elin Thordardottir, Rothenberg, A., Rivard, M. and Naves, R. (2006) Bilingual assessment: Can overall proficiency be estimated from separate measurement of two languages? *Journal of Multilingual Communication Disorders* 4 (1), 1–21.

Ellis, E.M. and Thal, D.J. (2008) Early language delay and risk for language impairment. *Language Learning and Education* 15 (3), 93–100.

Feldman, H.M., Dale, P.S., Campbell, T.F., Colborn, D.K., Kurs-Lasky, M., Rockette, H.E. and Paradise, J.L. (2005) Concurrent and predictive validity of parent reports of child language at ages 2 and 3 years. *Child Development* 76 (4), 856–868.

Fenson, L., Dale, P.S., Reznick, J.S., Thal, D., Bates, E., Hartung, J.P., Pethick, S.J. and Reilly, J.S. (1993) *The MacArthur Communicative Development Inventories.* San Diego, CA: Singular.

Fenson, L., Dale, P.S., Reznick, J.S., Bates, E., Thal, D. and Pethick, S.J. (1994) Variability in early communicative development. *Monographs of the Society for Research in Child Development* 59 (5, Serial No. 242).

Fenson, L., Marchman, V.A., Thal, D.J., Dale, P.S., Reznick, J.S. and Bates, E. (2007) *The MacArthur-Bates Communicative Development Inventories* (2nd edn). Baltimore, MD: Brookes.

Fernald, A., Marchman, V.A. and Weisleder, A. (2013) SES differences in language processing skill and vocabulary are evident at 18 months. *Developmental Science* 16 (2), 234–248.

Gatt, D. (2007) Establishing the concurrent validity of a vocabulary checklist for young Maltese children. *Folia Phoniatrica et Logopaedica* 59 (6), 297–305.

Gatt, D. (2010) Early Expressive lexical development: Evidence from children brought up in Maltese-speaking families. PhD thesis, University of Malta.

Gatt, D., Letts, C. and Klee, T. (2008) Lexical mixing in the early productive vocabularies of young Maltese children: Implications for intervention. *Clinical Linguistics and Phonetics* 22 (4), 267–274.

Gatt, D., O'Toole, C. and Haman, E. (2011) *Questionnaire for Parents of Bilingual Children: Infants and Toddlers Version (PaBiQ-IT).* See http://www.bi-sli.org/files_members/background-questionnaires/ *Questionnaire for Parents of Bilingual Children: Infants and Toddlers Version (PaBiQ-IT)* (accessed 11 December 2014).

Gatt, D., Grech, H. and Dodd, B. (2013) Early lexical expression in typically-developing Maltese children: Implications for the identification of language delay. *Clinical Linguistics and Phonetics* 27 (6–7), 459–471.

Hoff, E. (2003) The specificity of environmental influence: Socioeconomic status affects early vocabulary development via maternal speech. *Child Development* 74 (5), 1368–1378.

Hoff, E., Core, C., Place, S., Rumiche, R., Senor, M. and Parra, M. (2012) Dual language exposure and early bilingual development. *Journal of Child Language* 39 (1), 1–27.

Jia, G. and Aronson, D. (2003) A longitudinal study of Chinese children and adolescents learning English in the United States. *Applied Psycholinguistics* 24 (1), 131–161.

Jørgensen, R.N., Dale, P., Bleses, D. and Fenson, L. (2010) CLEX: A cross-linguistic lexical norms database. *Journal of Child Language* 37 (2), 419–428.

Junker, D.A. and Stockman, I.J. (2002) Expressive vocabulary of German-English bilingual toddlers. *American Journal of Speech-Language Pathology* 11 (4), 381–394.

Klee, T., Pearce, K. and Carson, D. (2000) Improving the positive predictive value of screening for developmental language disorder. *Journal of Speech, Language and Hearing Research* 43 (4), 821–833.

Kohnert, K. (2010) Bilingual children with primary language impairment: Issues, evidence and implications for clinical actions. *Journal of Communication Disorders* 43 (6), 456–473.

Law, J., Boyle, J., Harris, F., Harkness, A. and Nye, C. (2000) Prevalence and natural history of primary speech and language delay: Findings from a systematic review of the literature. *International Journal of Language and Communication Disorders* 35 (2), 165–188.

Law, J. and Roy, P. (2008) Parental report of infant language skills: A review of the development and application of the Communicative Development Inventories. *Child and Adolescent Mental Health* 13 (4), 198–206.

Li Wei (2000) Glossary. In Li Wei (ed.) *The Bilingualism Reader* (pp. 494–499). London: Routledge.

Marchman, V.A. and Martínez-Sussmann, C. (2002) Concurrent validity of caregiver/ parent report measures of language for children who are learning both English and Spanish. *Journal of Speech, Language and Hearing Research* 45 (5), 983–997.

Marchman, V.A., Martínez-Sussman, C. and Dale, P.S. (2004) The language-specific nature of grammatical development: Evidence from bilingual language learners. *Developmental Science* 7 (2), 212–224.

Mayor, J. and Plunkett, K. (2011) A statistical estimate of infant and toddler vocabulary size from CDI analysis. *Developmental Science* 14 (4), 769–785.

McLaughlin, B. (1984) Early bilingualism: Methodological and theoretical issues. In G. Duncan and J. Brooks-Gunn (eds) *Consequences of Growing Up Poor* (pp. 35–48). New York: Russell Sage Foundation.

Miller, J.F., Sedey, A.L. and Miolo, G. (1995) Validity of parent report measures of vocabulary development for children with Down Syndrome. *Journal of Speech, Language and Hearing Research* 38 (5), 1037–1044.

Nelson, H.D., Nygren, P., Walker, M. and Panoscha, R. (2006) Screening for speech and language delay in preschool children: Systematic evidence review for the US Preventive Services Task Force. *Pediatrics* 117 (2), 298–317.

Norwegian Social Science Data Services (2010) Fieldwork documents: Showcards main questionnaire (card 64) (European Social Survey (ESS) Round 5 Data, Edition 2.0). See http://ess.nsd.uib.no/ess/round5/ (accessed 25 May 2012).

Oller, D.K. and Eilers, R.E. (2002) Balancing interpretations regarding effects of bilingualism: Empirical outcomes and theoretical possibilities. In D.K. Oller and R.E. Eilers (eds) *Language and Literacy in Bilingual Children* (pp. 281–292). Clevedon: Multilingual Matters.

O'Toole, C. and Fletcher, P. (2010) Validity of a parent report instrument for Irish-speaking toddlers. *First Language* 30 (2), 199–217.

O'Toole, C. and Hickey, T. (2013) Diagnosing language impairment in bilinguals: Professional experience and perception. *Child Language Teaching and Therapy* 29 (1), 91–109.

Paradis, J. (2011) Individual differences in child English second language acquisition: Comparing child-internal and child-external factors. *Linguistic Approaches to Bilingualism* 1 (3), 213–237.

Paradis, J., Emmerzael, K. and Sorenson Duncan, T. (2010) Assessment of English language learners: Using parent report on first language development. *Journal of Communication Disorders* 43, 474–497.

Patterson, J.L. (2000) Observed and reported expressive vocabulary and word combinations in bilingual toddlers. *Journal of Speech, Language and Hearing Research* 43 (6), 121–128.

Patterson, J.L. and Pearson, B.Z. (2012) Bilingual lexical development, assessment, and intervention. In B.A. Goldstein (ed.) *Bilingual Language Development and Disorders in Spanish–English Speakers* (pp. 113–129). Baltimore, MD: Brookes.

Paul, R. and Roth, F.P. (2011) Characterizing and predicting outcomes of communication delays in infants and toddlers: Implications for clinical practice. *Language, Speech and Hearing Services in Schools* 42 (3), 331–340.

Pearson, B.Z. (1992) Rationale for English–Spanish CDI Mapping. Technical Paper. University of Miami.

Pearson, B.Z. (2013) Distinguishing the bilingual as a late talker from the late talker who is bilingual. In L.A. Rescorla and P.S. Dale (eds) *Late Talkers: Language Development, Interventions, and Outcomes* (pp. 67–87). Baltimore, MD: Brookes.

Pearson, B.Z., Fernández, S. and Oller, D.K. (1993) Lexical development in bilingual infants and toddlers: Comparison to monolingual norms. *Language Learning* 43 (1), 93–120.

Pearson, B.Z. and Fernández, S. (1994) Patterns of interaction in the lexical growth in two languages of bilingual infants and toddlers. *Language Learning* 44 (4), 617–653.

Pearson, B.Z., Fernández, S. and Oller, D.K. (1995) Cross-language synonyms in the lexicons of bilingual infants: One language or two? *Journal of Child Language* 22 (2), 345–368.

Pearson, B.Z., Fernández, S., Lewedeg, V. and Oller, D.K. (1997) The relation of input factors to lexical learning by bilingual infants. *Applied Psycholinguistics* 18 (1), 41–58.

Poulin-Dubois, D., Bialystok, E., Blaye, A., Polonia, A. and Yott, J. (2012) Lexical access and vocabulary development in very young bilinguals. *International Journal of Bilingualism* 17 (1), 57–70. doi: 10.1177/1367006911431198.

Reese, E. and Read, S. (2000) Predictive validity of the New Zealand MacArthur Communicative Development Inventory: Words and sentences. *Journal of Child Language* 27 (2), 255–266.

Reilly, S., Bavin, E.L., Bretherton, L., Conway, L., Eadie, P., Cini, E., Prior, M., Ukoumunne, O.C. and Wake, M. (2009) The Early Language in Victoria Study (ELVS): A prospective, longitudinal study of communication skills and expressive vocabulary development at 8, 12 and 24 months. *International Journal of Speech-Language Pathology* 11 (5), 344–357.

Rescorla, L. (1989) The Language Development Survey: A screening tool for delayed language in toddlers. *Journal of Speech and Hearing Disorders* 54 (4), 587–599.

Rescorla, L. (2009) Age 17 language and reading outcomes in late-talking toddlers. *Journal of Speech, Language and Hearing Research* 52 (1), 16–30.

Rescorla, L. (2013) Late-talking toddlers: A 15-year follow-up. In L.A. Rescorla and P.S. Dale (eds) *Late Talkers: Language Development, Interventions, and Outcomes* (pp. 219–240). Baltimore, MD: Brookes.

Rescorla, L., Mirak, J. and Singh, L. (2000) Vocabulary growth in late talkers: Lexical development from 2;0 to 3;0. *Journal of Child Language* 27 (2), 293–311.

Roberts, J.E., Burchinal, M. and Durham, M. (1999) Parents' report of vocabulary and grammatical development of African and American preschoolers: Child and environmental associations. *Child Development* 70 (1), 92–106.

Robinson, B. and Mervis, C. (1999) Comparing productive vocabulary measures from the CDI and a systematic diary study. *Journal of Child Language* 26 (1), 177–185.

Rowe, M.L. (2008) Child-directed speech: Relation to socioeconomic status, knowledge of child development and child vocabulary skill. *Journal of Child Language* 35 (1), 185–205.

Rutter, M. (2008) Diagnostic concepts and risk processes. In C.F. Norbury, J.B. Tomblin and D.V.M. Bishop (eds) *Understanding Developmental Language Disorders: From Theory to Practice* (pp. 205–215). Hove: Psychology Press.

Tallal, P., Townsend, J. and Curtiss, S. (1991) Phenotypic profiles of language-impaired children based on genetic/family history. *Brain and Language* 41 (1), 81–95.

Tan, S.H. (2010) Multilingual infant vocabulary development in Singapore. In M. Cruz-Ferreira (ed.) *Multilingual Norms* (pp. 279–322). Frankfurt am Main: Peter Lang.

Taylor, C.L., Zubrick, S.R. and Rice, M.L. (2013) Population and public health perspectives on late language emergence at 24 months as a risk indicator for language impairment at 7 years. In L.A. Rescorla and P.S. Dale (eds) *Late Talkers: Language Development, Interventions, and Outcomes* (pp. 23–40). Baltimore, MD: Brookes.

Tomblin, J.B. (2008) Validating diagnostic standards for specific language impairment using adolescent outcomes. In C.F. Norbury, J.B. Tomblin and D.V.M. Bishop (eds) *Understanding Developmental Language Disorders: From Theory to Practice* (pp. 93–114). Hove: Psychology Press.

Tuller, L. and Messarra, C. (2010) *Beirut-Tours Questionnaire*. See http://www.bi-sli.org/files_members/background-questionnaires/ *Beirut-Tours Questionnaire* (accessed 11 December 2014).

Unsworth, S. (2013) Assessing the role of current and cumulative exposure in simultaneous bilingual acquisition: The case of Dutch gender. *Bilingualism: Language and Cognition* 16 (1), 86–110.

Unsworth, S., Argyri, F., Cornips, L., Hulk, A., Sorace, A. and Tsimpli, I. (2011) On the role of age of onset and input in early child bilingualism in Greek and Dutch. In M. Pirvulescu, M.C. Cuervo, A.T. Pérez-Leroux, J. Steele and N. Strik (eds) *Selected Proceedings of the 4th Conference on Generative Approaches to Language Acquisition North America (GALANA 2010)* (pp. 249–265). Somerville, MA: Cascadilla Proceedings Project.

Zubrick, S., Taylor, C., Rice, M. and Slegers, D. (2007) Late language emergence at 24 months: An epidemiological study of prevalence, predictors and covariates. *Journal of Speech, Language, and Hearing Research* 50 (6), 1562–1592.

Appendix A: Adaptations of the MacArthur–Bates Communicative Development Inventories (CDI)

Acarlar, F., Aksu-Koç, A., Küntay, A.C., Maviş, İ., Sofu, H., Topbaş, S. and Turan, F. (2009) Adapting MB-CDI to Turkish: The first phase. In S. Ay, Ö. Aydın., İ. Ergenç, S. Gökmen, S. İşsever and D. Peçenel (eds) *Essays on Turkish Linguistics: Proceedings of the 14th International Conference on Turkish Linguistics: August 6–8, 2008* (pp. 17–20). Wiesbaden: Harrassowitz Verlag.

Bockmann, A.-K. and Kiese-Himmel, C. (2012) *Eltern Antworten – Revision (ELAN-R)*, German CDI-type adaptation. Göttingen: Beltz.

Gatt, D. (2010) *Kliem li jgħidu tfal żgħar Maltin bejn sena u sentejn u nofs*, Maltese-English adaptation of the vocabulary checklist of the MacArthur Communicative Development Inventories: Words and Sentences. Unpublished material. University of Malta.

Kern, S. and Gayraud, F. (2010) *L'Inventaire Français du Développement Communicatif (IFDC)*. Grenoble: Les Editions de la Cigale.

Lima, R. (forthcoming) *Inventário do desenvolvimento de habilidades comunicativas MacArthur, palavras e frases, 16-30 meses*, Portuguese adaptation of the MacArthur–Bates Communicative Development Inventories: Words and Sentences. Centro de Investigação em Estudos da Criança (CIEC), Universidade do Minho.

Maital, S.L., Dromi, E., Sagi, A. and Bornstein, M.H. (2000) The Hebrew Communicative Development Inventory. Unpublished vocabulary checklist.

Meints, K. and Fletcher, K. (2001) Toddler Communicative Development Inventory, a UK adaptation of the MacArthur–Bates Toddler Communicative Development Inventories. University of Lincoln Babylab. See http://www.lincoln.ac.uk/home/media/universityoflincoln/schoolofpsychology/CDItodler.pdf (accessed 25 January 2011).

O'Toole, C. (2005) *Faradal Forbairt Teanga Gaeilge: Focail agus Abairtí*, Irish-English adaptation of the MacArthur–Bates Communicative Development Inventories: Words and Sentences. Unpublished material. University College Cork, Ireland.

Smoczyńska, M. (1999) *Inwentarz rozwoju mowy i komunikacji: Słowa i zdania*, Polish adaptation of the MacArthur–Bates Communicative Development Inventories: Words and Sentences. Unpublished material. Jagiellonian University, Krakow.

Adaptations of the PABIQ (see Tuller, this volume) and PABIQ-IT

dos Santos, C. (2011) *Questionnaire pour les parents d'enfants bilingues : version pour les enfants de 6 mois à 3 ans*, French adaptation of the *Questionnaire for Parents of Bilingual Children: Infants and Toddlers Version (PaBiQ-IT)*. Université François-Rabelais, Tours.

Gatt, D. (2011) *Kwestjonarju għall-Ġenituri ta' Tfal li Jisimgħu u/jew Jitkellmu Żewġ Lingwi: Verżjoni għal tfal ta' inqas minn tliet snin*, Maltese adaptation of the *Questionnaire for Parents of Bilingual Children: Infants and Toddlers Version (PaBiQ-IT)*. University of Malta.

O'Toole, C. and Hickey, T. (2011) *Ceistneoir do thuismitheoirí páistí dátheangach: Leagan Naíonáin agus Páistí Beaga*, Irish adaptation of the *Questionnaire for Parents of Bilingual Children: Infants and Toddlers Version (PaBiQ-IT)*. University College Cork, Ireland.

Otwinowska-Kasztelanic, A. and Haman, E. (2011) *Kwestionariusz dla rodziców dzieci dwujęzycznych: niemowlęta i dzieci najmłodsze*, Polish adaptation of the *Questionnaire for Parents of Bilingual Children: Infants and Toddlers Version (PaBiQ-IT)*.University of Warsaw.

Rinker, T. and Kaya, M. (2012) *COST-Fragebogen für Eltern bilingualer Kinder. Überarbeitete/reduzierte Version*, German adaptation of the *Questionnaire for Parents of Bilingual Children (PaBiQ)*. Universität Konstanz.

Appendix B: Questionnaire for Parents of Bilingual Children: Infant and Toddler Version (PABIQ-IT)[11]

To be completed by the child's main caregiver i.e. the person who spends most time with the child

Please specify your relationship to the child e.g. mother, father, grandmother etc. _____

Today's date _____

1. General information about the child

1.1 Birth date: _____ 1.2 Place of birth: _____

1.3 If place of birth is not country of residence, date of arrival in country of residence: _____

1.4 Gender: MALE   or   FEMALE (please circle)

1.5 Birth order (please circle): 1st born (oldest) 2nd born 3rd born 4th born 5th born 6th born

1.6 Brothers and/or sisters (if any):

Birth order	Birth date	Sex (Male/Female)
1st born (oldest) brother or sister		
2nd born brother or sister		
3rd born brother or sister		
4th born brother or sister		
5th born brother or sister		

2. Child's developmental history

2.1 Were there any complications during pregnancy/at birth?   YES   or   NO   If YES, please specify. _____

2.2 What was your child's birth weight? _____

2.3 How old was your child when he/she first walked? _____

2.4 How old was your child when he/she spoke his/her first word? _____

2.5 Does your child put words together to make short sentences?

YES   or   NO

[1] Short version of the Beirut-Tours Questionnaire (Tuller & Messarra, 2010), adapted from 'Paradis' (2007) ALEQ and ALDeQ questionnaires

2.6 Do you have any concerns about your child's language? YES or NO

If YES, please describe briefly. _____

_____

2.7 Does your child present with any medical conditions? YES or NO
If YES, please specify. _____

2.8 Has your child experienced:
(a) Frequent colds: YES or NO (b) Hearing loss: YES or NO
(c) Allergies: YES or NO (d) Frequent ear infections: YES or NO
If YES, how many ear infections did your child experience over the
past year? 1 2 3 4 5 6
(e) Grommet insertion: YES or NO
(f) Other (specify): _____

2.9 Is your child exposed to:

	0 Never	1 Rarely	2 Sometimes	3 Usually	4 Always		Score/4
Language X						X	
Language Y						Y	
Other (specify)						Other	
Other (specify)						Other	

2.10 At what age did this exposure begin?

	Age in months
Language X	
Language Y	
Other (specify)	
Other (specify)	

3. Languages used with and by the child

3.1 Main caregiver e.g. mother, father, grandparent. State your relationship
to the child here _____

	Language YOU use with CHILD					Language CHILD uses with YOU				
	0 Never	1 Rarely	2 Some- times	3 Usually	4 Always	0 Never	1 Rarely	2 Some- times	3 Usually	4 Always
Language X										
Language Y										
Other (specify)										
Other (specify)										

3.2 Does another adult regularly take care of your child (e.g. grandparent,
babysitter, day-care staff)?   YES   or   NO
If YES, specify who this person is here _____ and
complete the table below.
Use additional tables if other adults regularly take care of the child.

	Language used by OTHER REGULAR CAREGIVER with CHILD					Language used by CHILD with OTHER REGULAR CAREGIVER				
	0 Never	1 Rarely	2 Some- times	3 Usually	4 Always	0 Never	1 Rarely	2 Some- times	3 Usually	4 Always
Language X										
Language Y										
Other (specify)										
Other (specify)										

3.3 For each child in the family, complete a separate table. *Use additional tables if necessary.*

Language used by BROTHER/SISTER 1[1] with CHILD						Language used by CHILD with BROTHER/SISTER[1]				
	0 Never	1 Rarely	2 Some-times	3 Usually	4 Always	0 Never	1 Rarely	2 Some-times	3 Usually	4 Always
Language X										
Language Y										
Other										
Other										

Language used by BROTHER/SISTER 2[2] with CHILD						Language used by CHILD with BROTHER/SISTER[2]				
	0 Never	1 Rarely	2 Some-times	3 Usually	4 Always	0 Never	1 Rarely	2 Some-times	3 Usually	4 Always
Language X										
Language Y										
Other										
Other										

3.4 Tick the descriptor which best summarises the language exposure pattern typically received by your child.

Language use DIRECTED TO CHILD	√
Language X only	
Mostly Language X with some Language Y words	
Approximately equal proportions of Language X and Language Y	
Mostly Language Y with some Language X words	
Language Y only	
Language X, Language Y and additional language/s	

3.5 Tick the descriptor which best summarises the language pattern typically used in the child's home

Language use AMONG FAMILY MEMBERS	√
Language X only	
Mostly Language X with some Language Y words	
Approximately equal proportions of Language X and Language Y	
Mostly Language Y with some Language X words	
Language Y only	
Language X, Language Y and additional language/s	

4. Information about the child's mother and father
4.1 Information about the mother
4.1.1 In which country and region (if applicable) were you born?

4.1.2 Are you currently working?   YES   or   NO
    If yes, what is your job? Where do you work? _____
4.1.3 Education:

		Number of years	Further information
Primary school	Yes / No		
Secondary school	Yes / No		
University	Yes / No		
Other professional training	Yes / No		

4.2 Information about the father
4.2.1 In which country and region (if applicable) were you born?

4.2.2 Are you currently working?   YES   or   NO
    If yes, what is your job? Where do you work? _____
4.2.3 Education:

		Number of years	Further information
Primary school	Yes / No		
Secondary school	Yes / No		
University	Yes / No		
Other professional training	Yes / No		

5. Difficulties
In each cell, please indicate   YES   or   NO

	Child's siblings (any)	Mother	Father	Father's family	Mother's family
Difficulties at school					
Difficulties mainly with reading and spelling					
Repeated one or more grades in school					
Difficulties understanding others when they speak					
Difficulties expressing one-self orally (pronunciation, forming sentences, finding the right word, etc.)					

Languages used with and by the child
For any other adult taking care of the child regularly, fill in the table and specify their relationship to the child (e.g. grandparents etc.) here:

ADULT 1 = _____ (state relationship to child)
ADULT 2 = _____ (state relationship to child)
ADULT 3 = _____ (state relationship to child)

	Language used by ADULT 1 with CHILD					Language used by CHILD with ADULT 1				
	0 Never	1 Rarely	2 Some-times	3 Usually	4 Always	0 Never	1 Rarely	2 Some-times	3 Usually	4 Always
Language X										
Language Y										
Other										
Other										
	Language used by ADULT 2 with CHILD					Language used by CHILD with ADULT 2				
	0 Never	1 Rarely	2 Some-times	3 Usually	4 Always	0 Never	1 Rarely	2 Some-times	3 Usually	4 Always
Language X										
Language Y										
Other										
Other										

Language used by ADULT 3 with CHILD					Language used by CHILD with ADULT 3				
0 Never	1 Rarely	2 Some- times	3 Usually	4 Always	0 Never	1 Rarely	2 Some- times	3 Usually	4 Always
Language X									
Language Y									
Other									
Other									

For any other child in the family, please fill in the relevant table.

Language used by BROTHER/SISTER 3[3] with CHILD					Language used by CHILD with BROTHER/SISTER[3]				
0 Never	1 Rarely	2 Some- times	3 Usually	4 Always	0 Never	1 Rarely	2 Some- times	3 Usually	4 Always
Language X									
Language Y									
Other									
Other									

Language used by BROTHER/SISTER 4[4] with CHILD					Language used by CHILD with BROTHER/SISTER[4]				
0 Never	1 Rarely	2 Some- times	3 Usually	4 Always	0 Never	1 Rarely	2 Some- times	3 Usually	4 Always
Language X									
Language Y									
Other									
Other									

Language used by BROTHER/SISTER 5[5] with CHILD						Language used by CHILD with BROTHER/SISTER[5]				
	0 Never	1 Rarely	2 Some-times	3 Usually	4 Always	0 Never	1 Rarely	2 Some-times	3 Usually	4 Always
Language X										
Language Y										
Other										
Other										

[1]Brother/sister 1 refers to the 1st born brother/sister in Section 1.6 of the questionnaire.
[2]Brother/sister 2 refers to the 2nd born brother/sister in Section 1.6 of the questionnaire.
[3]Brother/sister 3 refers to the 3rd born brother/sister in Section 1.6 of the questionnaire.
[4]Brother/sister 4 refers to the 4th born brother/sister in Section 1.6 of the questionnaire.
[5]Brother/sister 5 refers to the 5th born brother/sister in Section 1.6 of the questionnaire.

8 Designing Cross-Linguistic Lexical Tasks (CLTs) for Bilingual Preschool Children

Ewa Haman, Magdalena Łuniewska and Barbara Pomiechowska

Overview

This chapter addresses the need for comparable measures of lexical knowledge in both languages of a bilingual child. Typically, tools designed to identify specific language impairment (SLI) do not take into account whether a child is bilingual and how this might affect raw test scores, often leading to misdiagnosis. Both vocabulary size and processing speed can be confounding variables when diagnosticians attempt to disentangle bilingualism from SLI at the lexical level. Lexical abilities can also be used as a baseline assessment of bilingual dominance/proficiency. Hence the need for such tools as we describe here.

Delayed and impaired lexical abilities are among the earliest indicators of SLI (Leonard, 1998). Children with SLI show a delay in lexical development both in terms of the overall number of words and in reaching lexical milestones (i.e. first 50, 100, 200 words; Leonard & Deevy, 2004). They also display relatively weak semantic categories (McGregor *et al.*, 2002). Bilingual children often have smaller lexicons in both of their languages (Bialystok *et al.*, 2010) when compared to monolinguals. However, the number of words in the two languages of a bilingual child added together may not be different from those measured by monolingual norms (Marchman *et al.*, 2009). The processing load in lexical tasks as measured by reaction time is claimed to be higher in bilinguals than in monolinguals (Bialystok *et al.*, 2008; Chen, 1990; Dijkstra, 2003; Kohnert & Bates, 2002). At the same time, children with SLI experience reduced processing capabilities in comparison with typically developing (TD) children (Lahey & Edwards, 1996; Lahey *et al.*, 2001; Montgomery, 2002).

Lexical abilities are potentially an early identification measure of bilingual SLI (Gatt *et al.*, 2008), although they should not be used as the only diagnostic variable for this purpose (Gray et al., 1999; Spaulding et al., 2013). The assessment of processing speed and accuracy in lexical tasks may enhance the identification process (Pérez et al., 2013).

The cross-linguistic lexical tasks (CLTs) designed within COST Action IS0804 were conceived to provide a fully comparable assessment of vocabulary and lexical processing in 34 different languages. We present the innovative method of the CLTs' construction: a multilingual parallel task-construction procedure, which enables an objective test of vocabulary and processing skills in any pair of languages included in the process.

The CLTs target comprehension and production of nouns and verbs. The response accuracy measured in the CLTs indicates the level of receptive and expressive vocabulary size. Measuring reaction time (i.e. comprehension and naming speed) provides insight into the processing demands of passive and active knowledge across the two word classes. Picture choice and picture naming were chosen as being tasks least involving other types of linguistic or conceptual skills.

Currently, the CLTs have been prepared for 21 of the 34 languages and are available for use by researchers. Their use in diagnostics will be warranted as soon as norming studies addressing specific populations of mono- and bilingual children have been completed.

Background

Two main phenomena characterise early word learning: a rapid vocabulary growth and a significant improvement in speed of lexical processing (for vocabulary growth, see Bloom, 2000; Carey, 1978; Goldfield & Reznick, 1990; for lexical processing, see Fernald et al., 2006; Garlock et al., 2001). Thus, lexical development seems to be best described by the following variables: vocabulary size and lexical processing speed. For children younger than 3 years of age, standardised or normed vocabulary tests, such as the MacArthur–Bates Communicative Development Inventories (MB CDIs), are available for a number of languages (Dale & Penfold, 2011). However, for bilingual children, after the age of 3 there are no tools to directly compare the vocabulary size, or the lexical processing speed, in both of their languages.

Bilingual children tested in only one of their languages appear to know fewer words than their age-matched monolinguals peers (Bialystok et al., 2010; Pearson et al., 2006; Umbel et al., 1992), but a single language vocabulary assessment does not fairly represent the full lexical competence in bilingual individuals. The lack of appropriate methods for assessing the performance of bilingual children in both of their languages makes the domain of lexical development especially prone to inappropriate assessment in these children. Most importantly, reduced vocabulary size in one of the languages of a bilingual individual may be confounded with delays in lexical development, such as is found in monolingual children with SLI (Leonard & Deevy, 2004). Lexical knowledge, as measured by normed vocabulary tests, has low predictive value in monolingual SLI diagnosis when used as the only marker of language deficits (Gray *et al.*, 1999; Spaulding *et al.*, 2013). However, it is still a factor accompanying other SLI markers and should be incorporated in the process of full diagnosis (Hewitt *et al.*, 2005; Mainela-Arnold *et al.*, 2010).

The goal of the current chapter is to present the rationale and to give an overview of the multi-language parallel task-construction procedure. This procedure results in the building of CLTs for individual languages. Although the CLTs are not identical in all languages (in terms of target words used), the construction procedure ensures that they are fully comparable across all languages and within any language pair. This method has so far been fully developed for 21 individual languages (see Appendix C) and is under development in additional languages. We expect that the CLTs may reliably demonstrate the differences in lexical knowledge (vocabulary size and lexical processing) between bilingual and monolingual populations, and for bilingual children in both of their languages. We also propose that the CLTs may allow us to establish the extent to which the potential gaps in lexical knowledge between bilinguals and monolinguals can be interpreted as situated within the range of typical development, and when they may indicate the risk for SLI or other developmental delays in a bilingual child. The strength of this particular assessment method is the comparability of results between the child's two languages, assuming the languages are included in our design (for a full list of languages, see Table 8.1; for the current list of CLTs versions, see Appendix C).

We contrast the way in which our multi-language parallel task tools were constructed with the more usual procedure of adapting tools from one language for use in another (as in the case of most Peabody Picture Vocabulary Test [PPVT] adaptations). Although the translation of a measure initially designed for only one language may seem an obvious solution when preparing a similar tool for another language, important arguments against this approach are presented below.

The following sections describe the construction procedure of the multi-language parallel CLTs as developed and elaborated within the COST Action. To the best of our knowledge, this is the first attempt ever to coordinate the parallel construction of vocabulary-assessment tasks for such a wide range of languages. The aim was to design uniform tools for use in bilingual populations of any language pair from all the languages included. The CLTs are available in two versions: the traditional 'paper and pencil' version (which measures response accuracy and classifies error types) and a computerised version (which additionally measures reaction time). These three measures allow for a deeper insight into the nature of

Table 8.1 Languages involved in the procedure aimed at obtaining CLT-candidate nouns and verbs

| | Indo-European | | | | | Semitic | Uralic | | Other |
| | | | | | | | Finnic | Ugric | |
Germanic	Romance	Slavic	Hellenic	Celtic	Baltic				
Afrikaans (3)	Catalan (3)	Croatian (1)	Cypriot Greek (3)	Irish (2)	Lithuanian (1)	Hebrew (3)	Finnish (3)	Hungarian (1)	Basque (1)
Danish (1)	French (3)	Polish (3)	Greek (1)	Welsh (1)		Lebanese (3)			isiXhosa (3)
Dutch (2)	Italian (3)	Russian (3)				Maltese (3)			Turkish (2)
English GB (3)	Portuguese (2)	Serbian (2)							
English SA (3)	Romanian (1)	Slovak (3)							
German (3)	Spanish (1)								
Icelandic (2)									
Luxembourgish (3)									
Norwegian (3)									
Swedish (3)									

Note: Numbers in parentheses indicate how many competent judges accomplished the procedure entirely.

lexical-semantic problems in bilingual children in general, and in bilingual SLI in particular (Pérez et al., 2013).

We start by explaining our motivation for concentrating on bilingual vocabulary assessment at preschool age. We then review measures of vocabulary currently in use with preschoolers and we review the literature on bilingual lexical processing during childhood. Next, we address the main assumptions behind the CLTs' construction. Subsequent sections describe the phases of the CLTs' development and the method of their construction. We conclude that the multi-language parallel task-construction procedure ensures the comparability of the CLTs results across various pairs of languages, which is crucial for the adequate assessment of lexical knowledge in bilingual children. Further studies, including norming studies for individual languages or language pairs, are needed to prove the diagnostic validity of the CLTs.

Target age

In contrast to the chapter by Gatt et al. (this volume), which concentrates on the beginnings of lexical development, the focus of the present chapter is on preschool children and more specifically on the age of 5 years, which in most European countries is just before school entrance age (EURYDICE at NFER, 2010; Huebler, 2010). Children's lexical knowledge at this age might directly influence their school performance. Most educational institutions in Europe are monolingual and use the majority language as the language of instruction. If a bilingual child's vocabulary in the language of schooling is insufficient, this can potentially hinder her/his communication skills, emerging literacy and comprehension of written texts at school. Thus, before children start formal schooling, timely and accurate recognition of potential disadvantages in the domain of lexical knowledge can lead to early intervention, even though there is no simple way to close the gap between children with substantially different vocabulary levels (Becker, 2011; Hart & Risley, 2003; Hoff, 2009).

An accurate diagnosis at this age has a double advantage. First, it can lead to early intervention (i.e. maximising the child's chances for school success). Second, it minimises misdiagnosis. Misdiagnosis may be damaging in two ways. A child whose language impairment goes unrecognised loses the benefits of early intervention. A child who is erroneously labelled as impaired may experience impediments to her/his development (Paradis, 2007). Testing a child in the majority language can only assist in predicting her/his educational success in that language, but cannot be decisive for assessing the risk of language impairment. Language impairment in bilingual populations can be diagnosed only if full language competence, i.e. competence in both languages, is taken into account (Armon-Lotem, 2011; Kohnert, 2010; Paradis, 2007).

Measures for assessing vocabulary size in preschoolers

For children under the age of 3 years, lexical knowledge may be assessed by questionnaire methods (e.g. parental reports, see Gatt *et al.*, this volume). The availability of tests adapted from the MB CDI-I and MB CDI-II (Fenson *et al.*, 1993a, 1993b) for 61 languages (Dale & Penfold, 2011) enables early assessment, even if the clinician does not speak both of the child's languages, because vocabulary checklists are filled in by the caregivers communicating with the child in their respective languages. Although the MB CDI-III for older children is currently being developed in some languages (American and British English, Danish, Dutch, Sasak, Swedish; Dale & Penfold, 2011), this is still a much less common tool than the MB CDI-I and MB CDI-II and it is not available when the child's age exceeds 42 months (depending on the language). Our aim is to bridge this gap by designing a set of tasks, fully comparable across different languages, for children aged between 3 and 5 years.

Bilingual children in preschool and of school age are often assessed on their vocabulary size in only one of their languages and their performance is compared to that of their monolingual peers. This approach is problematic for two reasons. First, monolinguals and bilinguals receive qualitatively different language input. Second, tests designed in a single language for monolingual speakers may in fact involve some interference from other languages (e.g. including cognates or homonyms). This in turn can affect the bilingual child's performance on the test (Gathercole *et al.*, 2008). Therefore, it is essential to construct tasks suitable to assess the child's vocabulary size in both languages in a comparable manner. The tasks presented in the current chapter are an attempt to solve this issue in a systematic way for a wide variety of languages by controlling the difficulty of test items across different language versions of our test materials.

So far, the research on lexical assessment in bilingual preschool children has mainly involved specific language pairs, especially Spanish and English, and a few other language pairs (for Spanish–English, see Allman, 2005; Barnett & Lamy, 2006; Duursma *et al.*, 2007; Fernandez *et al.*, 1992; Gorman, 2012; Hammer *et al.*, 2008; Kohnert *et al.*, 1999; Mancilla-Martinez & Lesaux, 2011; Peña *et al.*, 2013; for Dutch–Arabic or Dutch–Turkish, see Messer, 2010; Scheele, 2010; Van Tuijl *et al.*, 2001; for English–French, see Chiang & Rvachew, 2007; Elin Thordardottir, 2011; for English–Greek, see Loizou & Stuart, 2003; for English–Hmong, see Kan & Kohnert, 2005; for English–Mandarin, see Dixon, 2011). The aim of the present project was to overcome the constraint of single pairs of languages for bilingual assessment. Given the variety of language combinations in bilingual and multilingual populations in Europe, we aimed to construct quasi-universal lexical tasks which could be freely paired from within an extensive list of languages.

Lexical processing in preschool age

Lexical processing constitutes another confounding variable in disentangling bilingualism and SLI. When compared to monolingual speakers, both TD bilingual children and children with SLI exhibit reduced lexical processing capabilities. Their lexical processing seems to be slowed down and lexical access appears to be hindered (for bilingual data, see Bialystok *et al.*, 2008; Chen, 1990; Dijkstra, 2003; Kohnert & Bates, 2002; for SLI data, see Lahey & Edwards, 1996; Lahey *et al.*, 2001; Montgomery, 2002). However, bilingual and SLI individuals differ in the *profile* of their lexical processing limitations. SLI children display a suppression of verb processing which contrasts with an almost intact noun processing (Andreu *et al.*, 2012). Bilinguals are slower to process both nouns and verbs. The specific profile of processing limitations in bilingual SLI children might be a factor potentially differentiating bilingualism and SLI. Therefore, measuring reaction time in addition to traditional accuracy scoring in various language tasks may significantly add to the understanding of the complexity and the nature of the problems related to lexical knowledge, in particular in a bilingual population (see also Pérez *et al.*, 2013). For this reason, the CLTs are prepared not only in traditional paper versions, but also in computerised versions, which allow for measuring the processing speed (reaction time) as well as providing accuracy scores.

Basic Assumptions Underlying the Construction of the CLTs

Word classes: Nouns and verbs

One of the fundamental issues of the CLTs' construction was the choice of word categories to be included in the tasks as targets. To make the CLTs as universal as possible, we used the two most common word categories: nouns and verbs. These two word classes exist in all languages (Vogel & Comrie, 2000; Wierzbicka, 1988) and emerge early in development, although they may not be acquired at the same time and there may be some cross-linguistic differences in the relative timing of their acquisition (Gopnik *et al.*, 1996; Tomasello *et al.*, 1997). The long-standing discussion on the developmental differences between verbs and nouns (e.g. Gentner, 1982; Goldfield, 2000; McDonough *et al.*, 2011; Tomasello *et al.*, 1997), including various cross-linguistic comparisons (Gopnik *et al.*, 1996; Kauschke *et al.*, 2007; Tardif *et al.*, 1997) clearly underlines that word knowledge assessment should not be limited to nouns.

SLI children seem to learn the meanings of verbs with greater effort than the meanings of nouns. Therefore, the differences in the knowledge of nouns vs verbs are greater in SLI children than in the TD population

(Andreu *et al.*, 2012; Black & Chiat, 2003; Windfuhr *et al.*, 2002). However, Skipp *et al.* (2002) compared early word learning in TD and SLI children and suggested that at the age of 3, more differences between the two groups can be found in nouns than in verbs with respect to grammatical knowledge. In any case, both word categories differentiate TD and SLI children, which might also be reflected in bilingual populations. We thus included both nouns and verbs when designing the CLTs.

Type of knowledge assessed: Comprehension and production

The assessment of two language modes, comprehension and production, in bilingual and language-impaired populations is important for several reasons. First, comprehension is viewed as an accurate and representative measure of a child's lexical knowledge because it minimises the impact of potentially interfering variables, such as lexical access and pronunciation, and even temperamental problems (e.g. shyness), on the child's results (Clark, 2009). Second, production typically reveals lower results than comprehension with respect to vocabulary size (Benedict, 1979; Goldfield, 2000; Harris *et al.*, 1995; Reznick & Goldfield, 1992) and in particular is often impaired in SLI (Capone & McGregor, 2005; McGregor *et al.*, 2002; Messer & Dockrell, 2006). Testing both comprehension and production gives one the opportunity to assess receptive and expressive knowledge and to account for the possible difference between the two. Although lexical measures cannot be used as unique predictors in SLI diagnosis (Gray *et al.*, 1999; Spaulding *et al.*, 2013), low performance on these measures is common in SLI (Spaulding *et al.*, 2012).

Type of tasks: Picture choice and picture naming

The most common ways of assessing word knowledge in children are tasks involving picture identification for comprehension and picture naming for production (D'Amico *et al.*, 2001; Gathercole *et al.*, 2008; Jared *et al.*, 2012; Kambanaros *et al.*, 2010; Masterson & Druks, 1998; Masterson *et al.*, 2008). Especially useful for children who cannot read, these tasks are used in most vocabulary tests (for comprehension assessment, see PPVT: Dunn & Dunn, 1997; for production assessment, see Expressive Vocabulary Test [EVT]: Williams, 2006; Expressive One-Word Picture Vocabulary Test [EOWPVT]: Gardner, 1979) and in experimental tasks (Kan & Kohnert, 2005; Kauschke *et al.*, 2007; Kohnert *et al.*, 1998, 1999; Messer, 2010; Scheele, 2010). Another advantage of using picture tasks is that they minimise the interference of other potentially confounding variables in lexical knowledge assessment such as reasoning, verbal fluency and syntactic abilities. Picture identification provides the child with a limited number of possible answers (usually four), which are single referents for words. Picture naming typically involves naming a single item in the absence of any background or interfering material. In this way, basic knowledge of single word meanings can be assessed. The limitation of picture identification and naming tasks is that they do not show whether the child can understand or use the word in various linguistic or social contexts. Children with SLI are claimed to have not only limited vocabulary size (lexical breadth) but also poor lexical-semantic organisation (lexical depth), the two factors being strongly related (Sheng & McGregor, 2010). The lexical-semantic organisation may be approached to some extent in picture naming tasks when both accuracy and error types are scored. We consider picture identification and picture naming to be the best way to gauge the child's access to meanings of single words. This is why we used these tasks to assess lexical comprehension and production in designing the CLTs.

Narrowing the list of potential target words

The utility of new language adaptations of tasks initially designed for one language only (Bates *et al.*, 2003; Kauschke *et al.*, 2007) can be questioned on several grounds. One of the basic problems is the translation of test items. Target word characteristics might change in unpredictable ways from language to language. Such changes include word form complexity, word frequency, typical contexts of occurrence or the age of acquisition (AoA). These factors may potentially affect the results and make them difficult to be compared cross-linguistically.

Kauschke *et al.* (2007) designed comprehension and production lexical tasks for nouns and verbs in German, where the word length, morphological complexity, frequency, AoA[1] and picture naming agreement[2] were controlled. For the comprehension task involving picture identification, semantic distractors were selected. Semantic distance between each distractor and the target word was controlled in a preparatory study with adult native speakers assessing the distance on a Likert-like scale. Afterwards, the authors adapted the tasks into Korean and Turkish by translating the target words from German. In the adapted *naming tasks*, the target words were controlled only for naming agreement. Other variables (i.e. morphological complexity, frequency, AoA) characterising the target words in the German version were ignored in the adapted tasks. The adaptations also resulted in narrowing the list of the equivalent targets in the language of adaptation, from 72 in the German original to 54 for Korean and to 68 for Turkish. The *comprehension task* was adapted only for Korean. The semantic distance between the distractors and the target words was controlled after the translation by adult ratings. This resulted in narrowing down the Korean version by 5 items in comparison to the original German version of 72 items. Unfortunately, narrowing the number of items and using target words with different characteristics affected the general task's characteristics.

The lack of control for target words' features in new adaptations hindered the comparability of results in the three languages. Our design of the CLTs' multi-language parallel task-construction procedure avoids the flaws of such traditional translation-adaptations by promoting a different approach as described below.

The CLTs' design assumes that target words are selected in each language according to the same criteria instead of being translated from a word list created initially for a single language. Therefore, the target words themselves may differ across languages but their characteristics are stable. For practical reasons (i.e. preparing a common set of pictures to be potentially used in the tasks in all languages involved), the CLTs are based on a limited set of potential target words shared across all languages. The target words for each particular language can be selected from this common pool according to the rules established for all languages in the multi-language parallel task-construction procedure.

Developing a list of words that are equivalent in meaning across a wide range of languages was our goal in the CLTs' construction (Phase 1) described below. These words constitute a source of possible targets for the CLTs in each language version and we call them the CLT-candidate words. To ensure the comparability of the targets across all the languages, we controlled for their formal characteristics (Phase 2) and their AoA in each of the languages involved (Phase 3). The process of selecting the target words for individual languages is described in Phase 4. The phases of the CLTs design are meant to ensure the comparability of the results of single language assessments across a wide range of languages and within any given pair of languages in the case of bilingual assessments. Phase 1, involving the picture naming and rating study, was shared among all languages and data for each language contributed to the overall result. The joint result of Phase 1 was the list of potential targets, i.e. CLT-candidate words. Subsequent phases were intended to apply the same procedures for each language, but were carried out for each language independently. This chapter shows the potential of the CLTs' construction for 34 languages, although currently the tasks are available only for a subset of 21 languages (see Appendix C for the list of languages and authors).

CLTs' Construction Phase 1: Are There Words Shared Across 34 Languages?

The main goal of Phase 1 was to select CLT-candidate words shared across all the languages under scrutiny. To this end, we designed a picture naming and rating study for adult native speakers. We reasoned that if there are objects and actions that are easily and unequivocally named across the languages, their labels could be subsequently used for the CLTs' construction. Additionally, based on the picture rating data, we determined which pictorial style was most universal cross-culturally and should be used for the design of the new set of CLTs' pictures.

Method

Stimuli

We created a picture database with different types of pictures for objects and actions. The database contained only pictures that had previously been used in psycholinguistic studies in one or more of 15 different languages. The stimuli were gathered from COST Action IS0804 members' resources (Russian–German, Polish, Greek, Finnish and Lebanese sets) and from open access sources (BOSS, SVLO and IPNP sets, see Table 8.2). Table 8.2 provides detailed information about the sources, the number of pictures used and the characteristics of the pictures within each source.

The database included 1024 pictures with a balanced proportion of objects (507 pictures) and actions (517 pictures). Each source contributed a number of pictures, from 81 (7.9% of the database) up to 275 (26.8% of the database). Three sources (BOSS, IPNP and the Polish set) originally included more pictures than could be considered in the study. Based on the data from previous studies which used these stimuli (i.e. the naming agreement ratings from adults in a single language or a small list of languages), we only included pictures with the highest within-language naming agreement scores, i.e. pictures that were named with the same word by most of the participants in a naming study.

Even though these pictures had already passed the validation procedures for experimental use, they had not previously been used in such a wide range of languages and cultures. Some pictures from different sources depicted the same objects or actions, but all were included in the database. The subsets of pictures differed significantly in style (photos, black and white line drawings, different types of colour drawing). Different pictorial representations of a concept could differ in their clarity and general style, which was to be assessed in the study independently from the naming task. This enabled us to establish the most appropriate style of pictures. All in all, the picture naming and rating study enabled an empirical evaluation of the relative cultural validity of different styles of picture.

Participants

Native-speaker judges (n=93, 81 females, 12 males) representing 34 languages were recruited from the COST Action IS0804 members and their collaborators. All the participants were fluent speakers of English. Twenty-eight (34%) identified themselves as bilingual or multilingual with English close to native, while the remainder spoke English as a foreign language. The vast majority of the judges had extensive experience in fields directly

Table 8.2 Sources of the pictures used in Phase 1

Source	Languages	No. of pictures used (objects: actions)	Picture type	Initial selection	Reference
Provided by COST ISO804 Members					
Russian–German set (provided by Natalia Gagarina)	German, Russian	81 (39:42)	Coloured pictures (pencil drawing)	No selection, all pictures included	Gagarina et al. (2010)
Polish set (provided by Ewa Haman)	Polish	200 (100:100)	Coloured pictures (watercolour)	Selection according to picture naming agreement rates	Haman (2009)
Greek set (provided by Maria Kambanaros)	Cypriot Greek, Greek	84 (42:42)	Colour photos (with background)	No selection, all photos included	Kambanaros (2003)
Finnish set (provided by Sari Kunnari)	Finnish	85 (75:10)	Coloured pictures (homogeneous colours, no shadows)	No selection, all pictures included	Kunnari et al. (2012)
Lebanese set (provided by Camille Messara and Edith Kouba-Hreich)	French, Lebanese	84 (46:48)	Black and white line drawings	No selection, all pictures included	Khomsi (2001)

(Continued)

Table 8.2 (Continued)

Source	Languages	No. of pictures used (objects: actions)	Picture type	Initial selection	Reference
Open Access					
BOSS	English	88 (88:0)	Colour photos (with no background)	Selection according to picture naming agreement rates	Brodeur et al. (2010)
SVLO: Coloured Snodgrass and Vanderwart pictures	French	127 (127:0)	Coloured pictures (homogeneous colours with shadowing)	Selection according to picture naming agreement rates	Rossion and Pourtois (2004)
IPNP	Seven languages (including English)	275 (0:275)	Black and white line drawings	No selection, all pictures for actions included	Szekely et al. (2004, 2005)
Total (all sources)	15 different languages	1024 (507:517)			

related to child language research or practice, including linguistics ($n=47$; 57%), speech and language therapy ($n=22$; 27%) and psychology ($n=8$; 10%), while only 7% identified themselves as from a different professional background ($n=6$). Thirty-one of the judges (40%) declared previous direct experience in designing picture tasks for children. Even if only one informant was available for some languages, the data provided by him/ her could be used in the final analysis. In all but five languages (Basque, Croatian, Lithuanian, Romanian and Spanish), we had two to four judges contributing to the rating. For the final analysis presented here, only the data from the 76 judges who rated the full set of pictures (100%) were used (see Table 8.1 for exact number of judges for each language). Data from judges who rated at least 25% of the items were used in partial analyses not presented here (seven judges rated more than 25% of the items). Data from 10 additional judges were excluded from the analyses due to an insufficient number of items rated (less than 13% of items).

Procedure

An online picture naming and rating procedure was made accessible to the participants through a password-protected website. All instructions and questions were presented in English, which was our lingua franca for establishing the dominant responses in the naming task across all languages. The participants followed the procedure (i.e. they named the pictures) in their native languages and provided the English translation of each word used.

The pictures were grouped into the two word categories, so that informants assessed pictures for nouns and verbs separately. The order of the two categories was randomised across participants. The order of the pictures within each category was randomised for each participant to avoid order effects.

The pictures were presented one by one and each was accompanied by four questions, two relating to its label and two relating to its style. The image was placed in the top left corner of the screen (occupying about a quarter of the screen space). The questions were displayed on the right-hand side of the screen.

Picture naming. First, the participants judged whether the picture easily evoked a word in their native language. They rated the pictures on a 5-point scale ('no, not at all'; 'no, but I have some vague ideas'; 'yes, it evokes several words different in meaning'; 'yes, it evokes several words similar in meaning'; 'yes, it evokes one word'). Then, they named the picture with the first word they could think of. They provided a word in their native language first and then translated it into English. The participants were encouraged to use a dictionary if they were not sure about the best English equivalent.

Picture-style rating. The next two questions were aimed at assessing the style of the picture. The participants were asked whether the picture was an accurate example of the object/action they had just named and whether the general style of the picture (manner of drawing, shapes, colours) would be suitable for children in their country. Results obtained for these two questions were then used to determine the general style of the new pictures to be designed for the CLTs and to give specific instructions to the illustrator who was to draw them (see 'Designing and Sharing Pictures for CLTs' below). For both questions referring to the style, a 4-point scale ('very good'; 'satisfactory'; 'a bit strange'; 'very strange') was used.

Results

We conducted two separate analyses. First, we determined which words evoked uniform answers across most languages. Second, we selected the picture style that was the most suitable across cultures.

Naming

The aim of the first analysis was to identify the words which would be most suitable for the CLTs construction.[3] We wanted to avoid objects/ actions which did not evoke a word in a given language or evoked more than one word of different meanings. We expected that pictures named consistently with just one word or with several words similar in meaning were going to be most suitable for the purposes of vocabulary assessment. First, based on the English-language equivalents provided by the judges, we identified a dominant naming response for each of the 1024 pictures, that is, the name that was provided by the largest number of participants. Then, for each picture, we calculated the following two indices: a Dominant Name Index (DNI) and a Meaning Availability Index (MAI).

DNI. The DNI for each picture was the proportion derived from the number of times the dominant English equivalent was used for the given picture, divided by the total number of responses. For instance, a picture presenting a pharmacy was named *a pharmacy* by 53 out of 76 judges.[4] Thus, the DNI of this picture was 0.70 (53/76).

MAI. The MAI for each picture was the proportion derived from the number of ratings 'evoking one word' or 'several words similar in meaning', divided by the total number of ratings. For example, 50 judges assessed the same picture of a pharmacy as 'evoking one word' and 13 other judges decided that it 'evoked several words similar in meaning'. Thus, the MAI of this picture was 0.83 (63/76). Both the DNI and MAI values for all CLT-candidate words are given in Appendix A. The DNI and MAI indices were in general higher for pictures featuring objects (evoking nouns, DNI: M=0.77, SD=0.22, MAI: 0.92, SD=0.12) than for pictures featuring actions (evoking verbs, DNI: M=0.64, SD=0.22, MAI: M=0.77, SD=0.16). These results are in line with the well-established claim that nouns are much more stable cross-linguistically than verbs (Gentner, 1981, 2006). This shows that in a wide cross-linguistic comparison: (1) the object pictures are named in a more uniform way than the action pictures and (2) the object pictures seem to evoke fewer words of different meanings than the action ones. Thus, when selecting words that evoked the most uniform responses in the picture naming task, we adopted different threshold criteria for nouns and verbs to reflect the specificity of these two word categories. We selected 158 nouns and 142 verbs as CLT-candidate words, from which target words for various language versions of CLTs could be chosen in Phase 4 (see Sections 'Nouns' and 'Verbs' below).

Nouns. The CLT-candidate noun list was comprised of the naming responses for pictures with MAI scores of at least 0.99 (see Appendix A). Out of 507 pictures, 232 representing objects met this criterion. However, the final noun sample consisted of 158 words, because 49 objects were represented at least twice in the set of pictures selected. We also controlled for the DNI of the selected pictures. Out of the total of 158 items, 34 (22%) resulted in DNI=1.00 and 112 pictures (71%) had a DNI higher than 0.90. Only six items had a DNI lower than 0.50. The DNI for the six pictures was so low because they were named with two competing words (close synonyms) of similar frequency (e.g. a picture illustrating a cap was labelled as *cap* by 38% of judges and as *hat* by 33% of them).

Verbs. The CLT-candidate verb list was comprised of all the verbs which met a minimum criterion of MAI ≥0.90. Out of 517 pictures, 269 met this criterion. These 269 pictures corresponded to 142 words, since there were some illustrations depicting the same activity and 66 of the chosen verbs were represented by at least two pictures. The majority (56%) of the selected verb pictures had a DNI higher than 0.80. Only 17 images (12%) resulted in a DNI lower than 0.50 (see Appendix A). Once again, this situation was associated with the occurrence of more than óne dominant synonymic answer for some pictures (e.g. the picture illustration for calling was named *to talk* by 21% of the judges, and *to call, to phone* or *to talk on the phone* by 19%, 19% and 10%, respectively).

The CLT-candidate noun and verb lists were used in Phases 2–4 of the CLTs design. In Phase 2, their phonetic and morphological characteristics were obtained for each language under scrutiny. In Phase 3, we assessed the AoA of the words for each of the languages. Finally, in Phase 4, we selected target words for each language.

Picture-style rating

Below we report the results obtained through two picture-style questions. Participants' answers were analysed across the different source picture sets and word categories. Since not all picture sets contained both objects and actions, we report the results for the two categories separately.

Mean responses for individual pictures between 1 and 2 (corresponding to responses: 'very good' and 'satisfactory') were considered as meeting the criteria of sufficient picture accuracy (first question) and adequate style (second question). Not surprisingly, the ratings for picture accuracy were significantly correlated with the ratings for general style (object pictures: $r=0.86$, $p<0.01$; action pictures: $r=0.74$, $p<0.01$).

For general style, the mean ratings for all sets were below 2, except for one. This indicated that most sets were rated as at least satisfactory in style (1 corresponded to 'very good' and 4 to 'very strange'). Only the black and white drawings from the IPNP set (verbs only) obtained a mean rating of 2.19 (SD=0.29).

For the object pictures, photos without background (the BOSS set, M=1.49; SD=0.37) and coloured pictures without shadowing (Finnish set, M=1.49; SD=0.35) obtained the best mean ratings. Next came the SVLO set (see Table 8.2) (coloured pictures without shadowing, M=1.51; SD=0.29). Other coloured pictures or photo sets (the Polish, Greek and Russian–German sets) were rated from M=1.67 to M=1.71. The lowest rating was obtained for the black and white line drawings (the Lebanese set), with M=1.97 (SD=0.27).

For the action pictures, the highest mean rating was obtained with the Finnish set (M=1.26; SD=0.17) and the second highest were the watercolour pictures (Polish set, M=1.50; SD=0.25). There were differences between the ratings of other sets. The Russian–German set (coloured pictures, some shadowing) was rated at almost the same level as the Lebanese set (M=1.95; SD=0.32), and similarly the photos with background (Greek set, M=1.92; SD=0.024). The black and white line drawings scored lowest (IPNP: M=2.19; SD=0.29; Lebanese set: M=1.94; SD=0.20).

Overall, the coloured pictures without shadows were rated best for both objects and actions. This became our default drawing style for the new picture database. The DNI of individual pictures was used to inform the artist about how accurate they were assessed to be (described in detail in 'Designing and Sharing Pictures for CLTs' below).

CLTs' Construction Phase 2: CLT-Candidate Words – Assessing Their Characteristics Across 34 Languages

Our aim in Phase 2 was to determine how morphologically and phonetically complex the CLT-candidate words were. Below, we summarise the method established by our team to assess word complexity.

First, on the basis of literature reviews and discussions within the COST Action, we established a list of word features that can affect the accuracy and reaction time in picture naming and word comprehension tasks. These word features were then used as input for calculating the Complexity Index (CI) for each CLT-candidate word in each language under scrutiny.

Expert linguists (one person per language) provided information on characteristics of the CLT-candidate words by filling in specially designed questionnaires. We inquired about the phonological and morphological structure of the chosen words. In the phonological domain, we asked about the word length in phonemes (Morrison *et al.*, 1992), the presence of consonant clusters (Brown & Watson, 1987; Santiago *et al.*, 2000) and the initial frication (Barca *et al.*, 2002; Brown & Watson, 1987). In the morphological domain, we collected information about word formation in order to identify items formed by derivation and those formed by compounding (Baayen *et al.*, 2006; Juhasz *et al.*, 2003; Zwitserlood *et al.*, 2000). Additionally, we gathered information on word etymology to establish whether a particular word was a recent loanword. Experts also provided information on children's direct exposure to word referents (e.g. snowmen are non-existent in Israel, hence a child's direct exposure to these entities may be very limited there).

We then used this information to compute the CI for each word in each of the languages. The CI was calculated in the same way for nouns and verbs across all the languages involved in order to enable comparisons between individual words, as well as word classes within and across languages.

The CI was derived from the following formula:

$$CI=L+SLP+B+D+S+P+E+F+I+InitC+InterC$$

where:

L means being *a recent loanword* (1 point if the word is a loanword, 0 if it is not)

SLP means *doubled standardised length in phonemes* in a given language, calculated separately for nouns and verbs[5]

B means *number of roots* (consequently, more than 1 point for the compound words)

D means being *a derived word* (1 point if the word is derived, 0 if it is not)

S, P means *suffixes* and *prefixes* (1 point for each suffix and prefix)

E means *exposure to the referent* (0 point if the object/action is available to children based on direct experience in a given culture, 1 point if it is not)

F means *subjective frequency of exposure* (0.5 or 1 point for rare objects, 0 for common ones)

I means *initial frication* (1 point if the word begins with frication, 0 if it does not)

InitC means *initial consonant clusters* (1 point if the word begins with a consonant cluster)

InterC means *internal consonant clusters* (1 point if the word contains a consonant cluster)

For instance, the CIs of the English words *ball* and *blackboard* equal −0.59 and 7.86, respectively. The word *ball* is relatively short (shorter than most other nouns; SLP=−1.59; as SLP is a standardised measure, its values are *negative* for all words shorter than average and *positive* for all words longer than average) and formed with one root only (so B=1). It is neither a loanword nor a derived word and it does not contain any initial frication, initial or internal consonant clusters, and is a familiar object in the children's environment. The CI of this word is the sum of SLP and B (all other components are 0), which is –1.59+1=–0.59. The word *blackboard* is not a loanword (L=0), it is relatively long (longer than most other nouns; SLP=2.86), consists of two roots: *black* and *board* (B=2), is not derived (D=0), does not begin with an initial frication (I=0) but contains both initial and internal consonant clusters (InitC=1, InterC=1). Blackboards are available for children in the British culture (E=0) but were assessed as rare in their direct experience (F=1). Thus, the CI of the word *blackboard* is 2.86 (SLP)+2(B)+1(InitC)+1(InterC)+1 (F)=7.86.

For the design of CLTs, the CI is used as only one of two indicators of word difficulty which can potentially affect the accuracy and latency of children's responses. The other factor is the AoA (see next section describing Phase 3 of CLTs' construction). We explain how the CI value is included in the CLTs' design in the section in the section 'CLTs' Construction Phase 4: Selecting Targets for Each Language'.

CLTs' Construction Phase 3: Are CLT-Candidate Words Acquired at a Similar Point in All Languages? AoA Study

Another factor which we chose as potentially affecting children's performance in lexical tasks was the AoA of words, i.e. the estimated age at which children acquiring a given language start to comprehend a word (e.g. Stadthagen-Gonzalez & Davis, 2006). Although there are many studies assessing both subjective AoA (estimation of AoA on the basis of adults' reports: answers to questions like 'when did you learn this word?') and objective AoA (the actual measurement of the age at which at least 75% of native speakers recognise a given word in various lexical tasks, mostly in picture naming), the data in these studies were gathered in various designs and for various sets of words, which makes direct comparisons difficult (Perez & Navalon, 2005). Previous studies showed that there is a strong relationship between both measures of AoA (Gilhooly & Gilhooly, 1980; Morrison *et al.*, 1997; Pind *et al.*, 2000). Moreover, the AoA data are not available for all languages involved in the CLTs. Thus, COST IS0804 launched a new study on subjective AoA to obtain fully comparable data for all the languages under scrutiny and for all the CLT-candidate words chosen in Phase 1 (for the results of this procedure, see Łuniewska *et al.*, submitted). Below, we briefly present the method used to obtain the subjective AoA data and we explain how these data were applied in the construction of the CLTs.

Method: Subjective AoA measurement

Given that our study was going to be conducted in multiple languages, we chose the subjective AoA measurement as it had previously proved to be well adapted for multilingual contexts. Our procedure closely resembles the one used in previous studies (e.g. Carroll & White, 1973; Gilhooly & Logie, 1980; Morrison *et al.*, 1997). We introduced one change: we applied a different scale from that commonly used in earlier studies. The majority of AoA studies used either a 9-point scale ranging from 1 (age 2) to 9 (age 13+) proposed by Carroll and White (1973), or a 7-point scale ranging from 1 (age 0–2 years) to 7 (age 13+) introduced by Gilhooly and Logie (1980). These ranges are widely accepted as methods of representing age in the AoA literature. However, the scale introduced by us is more precise in the age intervals relevant for CLTs' construction. It ranges from 1 to 18, with steps representing the exact age in years. This scale was both easier to understand by participants and more accurate for AoA measurement of early words. The results obtained with the new AoA scale can also be easily transformed and so they can be compared with the results of any previous studies, in contrast to data collected with scales which include points representing intervals longer than one year.

Furthermore, most of the previous AoA studies relied on paper-based questionnaires (e.g. Carroll & White, 1973; Gilhooly & Gilhooly, 1980; Morrison *et al.*, 1997). We launched an electronic version of the study. The online procedure enables the fast and efficient recruitment of participants from many different countries and speaking different languages. For each language, a separate version of the AoA assessment was prepared by the members of the COST Action.

Participants

Participants were recruited by the members of COST IS0804. Samples for the individual languages ranged from 20 to 136 adult participants (M=33.62, SD=23.00). There was a strict minimum of 20 participants per language. They were all adult native speakers of the languages selected who volunteered to participate in the study. Their demographics (age, gender, education, number of children) as well as self-reported data about language skills and use (number of known and used languages) were collected.

Procedure

Participants were asked to download a questionnaire in their mother tongue from the project's website (http://words-psych.org/) and then fill it in. The questionnaires included detailed instructions, questions about demographic data and, most importantly, lists of nouns and verbs for the AoA estimation. Subjects were asked to estimate the age at which they learned the word (i.e. started to understand it), by typing a number between 1 (if they thought they had learned the word when they were 1 year old) and 18 (if they thought they had learned the word when they were 18 or older). Each participant was presented with a different random order of words to minimise the risk of latent order effects. Nouns and verbs were presented separately. Each participant was given the full list of all 300 CLT-candidate words. The task duration was about half an hour. This procedure was applied to all languages included in this phase apart from Norwegian. The Norwegian AoA study was conducted with the very same target questions but with a different online procedure (Lind *et al.*, 2013, 2015; Simonsen *et al.*, 2012). However, comparison of the results reveals that the Norwegian data resemble all other data: correlation coefficients between the AoA rates in Norwegian and in other languages included in the study do not differ from those obtained in other pairs of languages tested. For three of the languages (Hebrew, Irish and Luxembourgish) the online procedure failed for practical reasons (problems with recruitment). That is why the questionnaires were printed out and delivered in paper versions in a form exactly matching the questionnaires accessed from the website in these languages.

Results

Preliminary outcomes (Haman *et al.*, 2011; Łuniewska *et al.*, 2012a, 2012b, 2013, 2014; Southwood *et al.*, 2011) suggest that there is a strong relationship between the estimated AoA of the words among all the languages included in the study, and that the majority of the CLT-candidate words are typically assessed to be acquired before the age of 8 years (for detailed results, see Łuniewska *et al.*, submitted). The words acquired earliest in a sample of 20 languages[6] are: *nose* (M=2.24, SD=0.63), *ball* (M=2.24, SD=0.52) and *bed* (M=2.24, SD=0.56), and the words acquired latest are: *computer* (M=8.46, SD=1.95), *to surf* (M=8.12, SD=1.91) and *to hitchhike* (M=7.93, SD=1.43). The overall mean of AoA in these 20 languages differs between nouns (M=3.21, SD=1.01) and verbs (M=4.86, SD=1.48). Overall, the results suggest that the CLT-candidate words are acquired in a similar order and at approximately the same time in all languages studied.

The results for individual languages were employed in the next phase of CLTs' construction. The AoA value, i.e. the mean per item per language, was used together with the CI to determine the difficulty level according to which the target words could be selected for each version of the CLTs. The precise application of these two factors to select the targets is described below.

CLTs' Construction Phase 4: Selecting Targets for Each Language

The CLTs are a series of four sub-tasks for: the comprehension of nouns, the comprehension of verbs, the production of nouns and the production of verbs. The comprehension tasks use the picture identification procedure and the production tasks use picture naming. The number of targets for each task and each word category is limited to 30 items per category. This number ensures that both the comprehension and the production of nouns and verbs can be assessed with satisfactory accuracy and that testing can be accomplished within a reasonable time. Additionally, there are two training items for each task/word category.

Below, we describe detailed criteria for the selection of targets for production and comprehension and also of distractors for word comprehension. We used three distractors for each target. Presenting the child with four pictures (one target plus three distractors) for each item minimises the probability of random choice and at the same time does not overtax the perceptual load. This four-picture solution is used in many standardised word comprehension tests (e.g. PPVT: Dunn & Dunn, 1997; BPVS: Dunn et al., 2009; OTSR: Haman & Fronczyk, 2012). Additionally, target words for production are chosen from distractors in the comprehension task. The targets for comprehension and production are thus matched as closely as possible in accordance with the criteria described below, to guarantee a similar level of difficulty between the two tasks.

During Phases 2 and 3 of the CLTs' construction, a CI (Phase 2) and a value of AoA (Phase 3) was assigned to each CLT-candidate word in each language. According to these values for each particular language, all CLT-candidate words were now assigned to one of *four difficulty levels* in a 2×2 design (CI: low/high; AoA: earlier/later). For each task and word category, the same number of targets for each difficulty level (combined CI and AoA) are to be selected. This will enable subsequent assessment of whether these variables affect the children's results in an ANOVA design. Table 8.3 presents the distribution of targets across tasks, word categories and difficulty levels.

Additionally, to ensure semantic variety, nouns and verbs were assigned to one of three broad semantic categories. Nouns were divided into animate natural kinds (e.g. *butterfly, frog, tiger*), inanimate natural kinds (e.g. *cucumber, cloud, leaf*) and artefacts (e.g. *drum, lamp, snowman*) (Keil, 1989). Verbs were divided into physical actions performed by humans (e.g. *to laugh, to paint, to peel*), actions performed by animals (e.g. *to bark, to hatch, to sting*) and states or unintentional actions (e.g. *to boil, to drip, to rain*). Thus, for each difficulty level, we aimed at including targets from different semantic categories.

Table 8.3 Distribution of target words across CLTs' sub-tasks (comprehension and production), word categories (nouns and verbs) and difficulty levels (based on Complexity Index and Age of Acquisition)

Task	Comprehension					Production				
	Target NOUNS (and distractors)		*Target VERBS (and distractors)*		*Sum*	*Target nouns*		*Target verbs*		*Sum*
Word category										
Practice items	2 (6)		2 (6)		4 (12)	2		2		4
CI	Low	High	Low	High		Low	High	Low	High	
AoA: early	7 (21)	8 (24)	7 (21)	8 (24)	30 (90)	7	8	7	8	30
AoA: later	8 (24)	7 (21)	8 (24)	7 (21)	30 (90)	8	7	8	7	30
Sum	15 (45)	15 (45)	15 (45)	15 (45)	60 (180)	15	15	15	15	60
All (targets+distractors)	128		256		30	60		30		60

Note: Number of distractors for comprehension is given in parentheses

In the process of target words selection, we used the CI and AoA values together with the information on whether the word form is a loanword in a given language and whether and how often the children may have had direct experience with the word's referent (in a given language/cultural context). At first, 32 pairs of target words for production and comprehension for each word class were determined, with exactly 8 pairs in each level of difficulty within each word class. The words in each pair were taken from the same semantic category and matched for their CI and AoA values. Whenever possible, loanwords and words with referents not directly accessible to children were avoided as targets. Then, the additional two distractors were chosen from the set of CLT-candidate words for each of the comprehension targets on the basis of difficulty level and semantic domain. We avoided phonological distractors such as words phonetically similar to the target, e.g. *doll–dog* or *fly–flag* in English, as well as perceptual distractors such as words with pictures similar in shape to the target picture. For example, a picture of a leaf similar in shape to a feather should be excluded as a distractor for the target word *feather*. Phonological distractors were not considered at all since for a wide range of languages involved in the CLTs, it would not be possible to systematically select phonological distractors for each target word from a limited set of CLT-candidate words.

For each language included in our sample, the procedure of selecting targets and distractors is exactly the same. Detailed instructions and all basal data (CI, AoA values, etc.) are available in an MS Excel file that supports the automatic sorting of words, controls for the number of targets/distractors at each of the difficulty levels and monitors the semi-random placement of the target words in the comprehension tasks. For each language, the national teams in the COST Action composed the list of targets. These teams are the authors of each language version of the CLTs. We list the versions already available together with the names of authors in Appendix C.

Administering Cross-Linguistic Lexical Tasks: The Method

In this section, we describe the intended target groups and the procedure for testing children using the CLTs. The paper and pencil version of the CLTs used for assessing accuracy is considered to be the basic one. This is due to expected constraints in testing for diagnostic purposes, such as speech and language therapists' limited access to professional electronic equipment in many countries. The electronic version that can be used for assessing both accuracy and latency is intended mainly for research purposes, but diagnostic use is not excluded. It should be emphasised that the diagnostic use of the CLTs will only be possible if the tasks are normed in relevant languages with the relevant groups targeted. Extended research is needed for each language/language pair before any use in clinical or diagnostic setting is possible.

Expected target groups/participants

The CLTs were designed to assess lexical knowledge before children start formal schooling. It is expected that, for each language, baseline data for monolingual 5-year-old children will be gathered. Our main targeted groups: TD bilingual children, monolingual SLI children and bilingual SLI children, are going to be compared to these baseline groups. Each group should consist of at least 20 children characterised by homogeneous background variables (socio-economic status [SES], exposure to languages, etc.).

Procedure

Items within each of the four tasks are randomly ordered with the two simplest practice items at the beginning of each task. The pictures for the comprehension tasks are also semi-randomly assigned to one of four positions (upper/lower and left/right; see Appendix B for sample picture boards). This is done according to three rules: (1) each of the four positions gets quarter pictures for target words; (2) target pictures cannot be located in the same position in more than three consecutive picture boards; (3) across seven subsequent items, target pictures appear in each position at least once. The instructions as well as the answer sheets were originally prepared in English and were adapted to each of the languages involved (for the list of authors, see Appendix C). Since the comprehension tasks include distractors which are used in the production tasks, a potential influence of task order on the results cannot be ruled out. Thus, for research purposes the order in which the tasks are administered should be balanced across participants. We recommend that the comprehension tasks (for nouns and verbs) be administered consecutively, and that the production tasks be administered one after the other as well. The order of the tasks involving nouns and verbs is balanced across participants. All four tasks can be delivered in a single session or with breaks in between. No break should be allowed within a task. The estimated total time of testing for all four tasks is up to 20 minutes. Children should be tested in a monolingual mode with the experimenter communicating with them in one language. Although spontaneous answers in other languages are not rejected, they should not be encouraged.

Paper and pencil version

For the comprehension tasks, each item is comprised of a four-picture board (each representing one target word and three distractors). Pictures in black frames (7.5×7.5 cm) are symmetrically located on an A4 page and numbered clockwise (horizontal view). For the production tasks, single pictures in black frames (7.5×7.5 cm) are centrally located on an A5 page (horizontal view) (see Appendix B). Each board is accompanied by a question prompt. For the comprehension tasks, the question is 'Where is ... (target noun)?' (e.g. 'Where is the gate?') or 'Who is ... (target verb in relevant form)?' (e.g. 'Who is kissing?').

Before starting the actual testing session, the child is informed that she/he is going to watch a series of pictures and will be asked questions about the pictures. The child is also asked whether she/he agrees to attend the session. Having agreed, the child is instructed to point to the picture which goes best with the word in the prompt question (for comprehension tasks), or to answer the question by naming the picture (for production tasks). For the latter tasks, single word responses are encouraged ('one word is enough'). For the first two practice items, the child is given feedback when her/his answer is not correct. For all the remaining items no feedback is given. For each answer, the experimenter provides only the minimal natural reaction to sustain interaction, with no overt positive or negative feedback to the child's answers ('aha', 'okay', etc.). At the end of all 32 items of the task, the next task is delivered or a break is offered if needed. After all four tasks, the child is congratulated and is thanked for her/his participation. For the comprehension tasks, the experimenter notes the child's response on the answer sheet (the number of picture pointed to); no recording is required. For the production tasks, an audio recording is required. The experimenter notes the child's response on the answer sheet only to the extent that it does not affect natural communication. The recording is then considered to be the basis for transcription and scoring. Notes on the answer sheet can be used to support transcription if needed. During the testing with both types of tasks, the experimenter is asked to make a note of any atypical behaviour from the child.

Computerised version

The pilot electronic version (developed as a desktop application in C# using .NET Framework 4.5; Etenkowski & Łuniewska, 2012) was prepared so that it resembles the paper version as closely as possible. The picture boards are presented on a touchscreen in the same order and layout as in the paper and pencil version. The prompts are pre-recorded and a strict timing schedule is followed. Prompt questions are played before the forthcoming picture board becomes visible (with a 100 ms lag from the offset). For comprehension, children are supposed to touch the screen while pointing to the picture of their choice. The next question is played automatically after a delay of 150 ms from the child's response. The child's picture choices and her/his reaction times (the latency from the moment of the picture board emergence to the moment when the child touches the screen) are stored automatically. For production, children are supposed to watch the pictures on the screen and answer the pre-recorded questions. The next picture board is presented on the screen after the child has finished responding. The child's responses are audio recorded.

Expected outcomes: Preliminary results

The method of CLTs' construction described in this chapter was designed to ensure the effects we list below. At the moment, these are still anticipated results of future research although partial data already available support our predictions (Haman & Łuniewska, 2013). The CLTs are expected to differentiate between groups of monolingual, bilingual, TD and SLI children. The accuracy and reaction times for the comprehension tasks are expected to exceed those for production. It is also expected that the accuracy scores on the noun tasks will exceed the scores on the verb tasks. It is predicted that there should be an interaction of the word category and task type for SLI children. While both noun and verb comprehension tasks should reveal the gap similar to TD children, the difference between the two word categories in production should be significantly wider as verbs are particularly difficult for SLI children. If children younger than 5 years of age (baseline) are tested, the accuracy of the CLTs is expected to increase with the child's age. We also expect the level of difficulty or other effects of complexity and AoA to influence the results. We predict that words with low CI values will be understood and produced earlier and processed quicker. An analogous effect is expected for the AoA factor: the words with a low AoA index are expected to be understood and produced earlier than those with a high AoA index.

So far, the CLTs versions listed in Appendix C have been piloted and administered to some groups of monolinguals and bilinguals, TD children and those diagnosed for SLI (Haman & Łuniewska, 2013). However, results obtained to date have been incomplete (some groups were tested in one language only, for some languages only TD children were tested, etc.). Hence, they cannot be used as conclusive evidence for the general findings we list above. Presentation of the empirical results goes beyond the aims of the current chapter. The actual results for the relevant languages and targeted groups will be published in a series of separate publications.

Designing and Sharing Pictures for CLTs

The results of the picture naming and rating study (described in 'CLTs' Construction Phase 1: Are There Words Shared Across 34 Languages?' above) indicated that the most widely accepted style of pictorial stimuli are homogeneously coloured drawings with no shadowing. Using this observation, a new set of pictures has been designed exclusively for the CLTs. The electronic CLTs' picture database comprises pictures for all 300 words from the CLT-candidate word list (158 nouns and 142 verbs). For some of them, several variants are available. There are 416 distinct .jpg files of uniform parameters in the database, including 361 base pictures and 55 variants.

The artist responsible for the picture design (who is experienced in designing various types of pictures for child language research) was informed in detail about the aims of the project. In addition to the list of CLT-candidate words to be illustrated, she received the relevant pictures rated and named in Phase 1 (see 'CLTs' Construction Phase 1: Are There Words Shared Across 34 Languages?') together with the ratings for their accuracy and style. She was instructed about the preferred style of pictures (coloured line drawing without shadowing) and about the additional criteria listed below.

The additional criteria ensured the cross-cultural fairness of pictures. They were adopted according to the conclusions resulting from discussions in the COST Action meetings:

(1) Balancing the number of male and female characters performing actions (verb pictures).
(2) Avoiding gender stereotypes (i.e. women performing typical household actions and men technical and professional activities) with the reservation that the gender of the character performing a particular action should not be conspicuously incongruous (e.g. a woman shaving her face).
(3) Avoiding racial stereotypes (i.e. avoiding pictures in which only Caucasian characters perform actions) with the reservation that for cultures where ethnic diversity is scarce the final set of pictures should not include many examples of characters from different ethnic groups.

These criteria were fulfilled and a balanced number of male and female characters within the whole database was assured; 32% of pictures showed female characters, 40% male characters and 28% were gender neutral, i.e. with both genders represented in one picture, or no gender information provided, such as when only hands are visible. In order to avoid ethnic stereotypes, variants of some pictures were created to represent distinct ethnic groups (African, Chinese, Asian, Indian). The CLTs picture database includes 34 ethnic variants of action pictures involving human characters (24% of all verbs) and 8 single action pictures with figures from non-Caucasian ethnic groups (6% of all target verbs). Considering that 16 action pictures (11% of all verbs) do not involve any human character (pictures for verbs like *to rain*, *to burn*), it turns out that one third of the action pictures involving human characters is available with non-Caucasian people. We argue that the CLTs' picture database is by and large ethnically appropriate for use in various European contexts.

All the pictures were reviewed by a panel of 15 COST Action members from 9 different countries. Following their suggestions, 41 pictures were modified (14% of all 300 CLT-candidate words). Some of these modifications resulted in adding new pictures to the database. For example, pictures for both red and grey squirrels are available; as well as two differently shaped tree leaves or two types of scales.

The electronic CLTs' picture database was funded by the Ministry of Science and Higher Education (Poland) with the copyright held by the University of Warsaw (Poland). Access to the database for research purposes as described in the present chapter is given to all interested parties on the basis of a free license agreement between the University of Warsaw and relevant institutions where members are involved in constructing the CLTs language versions. The CLTs language versions with full instructions and pictorial material are going to be available for research purposes via the COST Action IS0804 website for the child language research community.

Conclusions

The CLTs were designed as a set of lexical tasks assessing comprehension and production of nouns and verbs in bilingual children and children with SLI. This assessment was required to be fully comparable between the two languages of a bilingual child. To meet this need, the CLTs were designed in separate languages, but they can be paired across a wide range of languages without changing the CLTs' characteristics. The different phases of the CLTs' development were conceived to guarantee the stable characteristics of tasks across all languages included in the sample (see Table 8.1). The results available so far for monolingual, bilingual, mono-SLI and bi-SLI children confirm that the CLTs can differentiate between these groups (Haman & Łuniewska, 2013). For research purposes (e.g. in experimental designs), monolingual children are regarded as the control group, but the CLTs can equally well be used simply for this group if necessary. Norming data for each language still need to be obtained before we can consider the CLTs to be a tool fit for diagnosis. Moreover, during the normative data collection in various languages for the CLTs it will be essential to carefully define the populations for which a given norm is to be valid. It was already shown that the amount of input (Gathercole et al., 2008) or of cumulative exposure (Unsworth et al., 2011) can differentiate groups of bilinguals in terms of language proficiency. Hence, gathering the normative data should be accompanied by careful control of current language input and language history of the child. To this end, the questionnaires designed within COST Action IS0804 can be used: the Parents of Bilingual Children

Questionnaire (PABIQ; Tuller, this volume) or the Parents of Bilingual Children Questionnaire: Infant & Toddler version (PABIQ:IT; Gatt et al., this volume).

It would not have been possible to accomplish the CLTs design without the joint effort of numerous members of COST Action IS0804. In all phases of the CLTs development, national teams worked to provide relevant information (Phases 1 and 2), to adapt and conduct the AoA study in their language (Phase 3), to select the targets and distractors for single language versions of the CLTs, and finally to adapt the instructions and all relevant materials. The members of WG3 also served as experts in reviewing the pictures prepared for the CLTs, which significantly improved the picture database and in particular its cross-cultural adequacy. These teams should thus be regarded as co-authors of particular language versions of the CLTs.

Acknowledgements

The CLTs construction process outlined in this chapter would not have been possible without the enormous collective efforts of members and collaborators of COST Action IS0804 (in particular the Polish team within the Action). We would like to express our immense gratitude to all of them and in particular to Jakub Szewczyk, Shula Chiat, Frenette Southwood, Hanne Gram Simonsen and Sharon Armon-Lotem. Our recognition also goes to all competent judges in Phase 1, all experts in Phase 2, all those who recruited participants for Phase 3 and all participants. Programming and technical support for Phase 3 was provided by Bartłomiej Etenkowski. All pictures were drawn by Justyna Kamykowska, the design artist.

Research presented in this chapter was partly financed by the Ministry of Science and Higher Education of Poland within the project 'Cognitive and language development of Polish bilingual children at school entrance age – risks and opportunities' (Grant No. 809/N-COST/2010/0), awarded to the Faculty of Psychology, University of Warsaw: principal investigators: Ewa Haman (University of Warsaw) and Zofia Wodniecka (Jagiellonian University).

Notes

(1) Age of acquisition of target words was obtained in a separate study with caregivers assessing at what age their children first produced the word (De Bleser & Kauschke, 2003).

(2) Picture naming agreement was obtained in a separate study with adult native speakers of German. The proportion of answers with the target word provided for the picture should be at least 80% to qualify the item as showing an acceptable level of naming agreement.

(3) Detailed comparisons of picture naming differences between nouns and verbs will be presented in a separate publication (Haman et al., in preparation). In this chapter, we present the basic outcome of the study: the process of selection of 158

nouns and 142 verbs which form a list of CLT-candidate words shared across most of the languages involved.
(4)   Some other labels for this picture were *a hospital, a drug store* and *a chemist*.
(5)   The standardised length in phonemes was doubled in order to emphasise the impact of this factor on overall complexity of the word.
(6)   Data included in the analysis comprise Afrikaans, South African English, British English, Catalan, Finnish, German, Hebrew, Italian, Lebanese, Lithuanian, Luxembourgish, Maltese, Norwegian, Polish, Russian, Serbian, Slovak, Swedish and Turkish.

References

Alario, F.X. and Ferrand, L. (1999) A set of 400 pictures standardized for French: Norms for name agreement, image agreement, familiarity, visual complexity, image variability, and age of acquisition. *Behavior Research Methods* 31 (3), 531–552.

Allman, B. (2005) Vocabulary size and accuracy of monolingual and bilingual preschool children. In J. Cohen, K.T. McAlister, K. Rolstad and J. MacSwan (eds) *Proceedings of the 4th International Symposium on Bilingualism* (pp. 58–77). Somerville, MA: Cascadilla Press.

Andreu, L., Sanz-Torrent, M. and Guàrdia-Olmos, J. (2012) Auditory word recognition of nouns and verbs in children with specific language impairment (SLI). *Journal of Communication Disorders* 45 (1), 20–34.

Armon-Lotem, S. (2011) Introduction: Bilingual children with SLI – the nature of the problem. *Bilingualism: Language and Cognition* 15 (1), 1–4.

Baayen, R.H., Feldman, L.B. and Schreuder, R. (2006) Morphological influences on the recognition of monosyllabic monomorphemic words. *Journal of Memory and Language* 55 (2), 290–313.

Barca, L., Burani, C. and Arduino, L.S. (2002) Word naming times and psycholinguistic norms for Italian nouns. *Behavior Research Methods* 34 (3), 424–434.

Barnett, W.S. and Lamy, C. (2006) *Estimated Impacts of Number of Years of Preschool Attendance on Vocabulary, Literacy and Math Skills at Kindergarten Entry*. New Brunswick, NJ: National Institute for Early Education Research.

Barry, C., Hirsh, K.W., Johnston, R.A and Williams, C.L. (2001) Age of acquisition, word frequency, and the locus of repetition priming of picture naming. *Journal of Memory and Language* 44 (3), 350–375.

Bates, E., D'Amico, S., Jacobsen, T., Székely, A., Andonova, E., Devescovi, A. and Tzeng, O. (2003) Timed picture naming in seven languages. *Psychonomic Bulletin & Review* 10 (2), 344–380.

Becker, B. (2011) Social disparities in children's vocabulary in early childhood. Does preschool education help to close the gap? *The British Journal of Sociology* 62 (1), 69–88.

Benedict, H. (1979) Early lexical development: Comprehension and production. *Journal of Child Language* 6 (2), 183–200.

Bialystok, E., Craik, F.I.M. and Luk, G. (2008) Lexical access in bilinguals: Effects of vocabulary size and executive control. *Journal of Neurolinguistics* 21 (6), 522–538.

Bialystok, E., Luk, G., Peets, K.F. and Yang, S. (2010) Receptive vocabulary differences in monolingual and bilingual children. *Bilingualism: Language and Cognition* 13 (4), 525–531.

Black, M. and Chiat, S. (2003) Noun-verb dissociations: A multi-faceted phenomenon. *Journal of Neurolinguistics* 16 (2–3), 231–250.

Bonin, P., Perret, C., Méot, A., Ferrand, L. and Mermillod, M. (2008) Psycholinguistic norms and face naming times for photographs of celebrities in French. *Behavior Research Methods* 40 (1), 137–146.

Brodeur, M.B., Dionne-Dostie, E., Montreuil, T. and Lepage, M. (2010) The Bank of Standardized Stimuli (BOSS), a new set of 480 normative photos of objects to be used as visual stimuli in cognitive research. *PloS ONE* 5 (5), e10773.

Brown, G.D. and Watson, F.L. (1987) First in, first out: Word learning age and spoken word frequency as predictors of word familiarity and word naming latency. *Memory & Cognition* 15 (3), 208–216.

Cameirao, M.L. and Vicente, S.G. (2010) Age-of-acquisition norms for a set of 1,749 Portuguese words. *Behavior Research Methods* 42 (2), 474–480.

Capone, N.C. and McGregor, K.K. (2005) The effect of semantic representation on toddlers' word retrieval. *Journal of Speech, Language, and Hearing Research* 48 (6), 1468–1480.

Carroll, J.B. and White, M.N. (1973) Age-of-acquisition norms for 220 picturable nouns. *Journal of Verbal Learning and Verbal Behavior* 12 (5), 563–576.

Chen, H.C. (1990) Lexical processing in a non-native language: Effects of language proficiency and learning strategy. *Memory & Cognition* 18 (3), 279–288.

Chiang, P.Y. and Rvachew, S. (2007) English-French bilingual children's phonological awareness and vocabulary skills. *Canadian Journal of Applied Linguistics (CJAL)/Revue canadienne de linguistique appliquée (RCLA)* 10 (3), 293–308.

Clark, E.V. (2009) *First Language Acquisition* (2nd edn). Cambridge: Cambridge University Press.

Cortese, M.J. and Khanna, M.M. (2008) Age of acquisition ratings for 3,000 monosyllabic words. *Behavior Research Methods* 40 (3), 791–794.

D'Amico, S., Devescovi, A. and Bates, E. (2001) Picture naming and lexical access in Italian children and adults. *Journal of Cognition and Development* 2 (1), 71–105.

Dale, P.S. and Penfold, M. (2011) *Adaptations of the MacArthur–Bates CDI into Non-U.S. English Languages.* See http://www.sci.sdsu.edu/cdi/documents/AdaptationsSurvey7-5-11Web.pdf (accessed 12 December 2014).

De Bleser, R. and Kauschke, C. (2003) Acquisition and loss of nouns and verbs: Parallel or divergent patterns? *Journal of Neurolinguistics* 16 (2), 213–229.

Dijkstra, T. (2003) Lexical processing in bilinguals and multilinguals: The word selection problem. In J. Cenoz, B. Hufeisen and U. Jessner (eds) *The Multilingual Lexicon* (pp. 11–26). Netherlands: Springer.

Dixon, L.Q. (2011) The role of home and school factors in predicting English vocabulary among bilingual kindergarten children in Singapore. *Applied Psycholinguistics* 32 (1), 141–168.

Dunn, L.M. and Dunn, L.M. (1997) *PPVT-III: Peabody Picture Vocabulary Test.* Circle Pines, MN: American Guidance Service.

Dunn, L.M., Dunn, L.M., Whetton, C. and Burley, J. (2009) *The British Picture Vocabulary Scale* (3nd edn). London: GL Assessment.

Duursma, E., Romero-Contreras, S., Szuber, A., Proctor, P., Snow, C., August, D. and Calderon, M. (2007) The role of home literacy and language environment on bilinguals' English and Spanish vocabulary development. *Applied Psycholinguistics* 28 (1), 171–190.

Elin Thordardottir, E. (2011) The relationship between bilingual exposure and vocabulary development. *International Journal of Bilingualism* 15 (4), 426–445.

Ellis, A.W. and Morrison, C.M. (1998) Real age-of-acquisition effects in lexical retrieval. *Journal of Experimental Psychology: Learning, Memory, and Cognition* 24 (2), 515–523.

Etenkowski, B. and Łuniewska, M. (2012) The Cross-linguistic Lexical Tester (Version 1.0) [Computer software] Bartłomiej Etenkowski – projektowanie i programowanie systemów komputerowych.

EURYDICE at NFER (2010) Compulsory age of starting school in European countries. See http://www.nfer.ac.uk/nfer/index.cfm?9B1C0068-C29E-AD4D-0AEC-8B4F43F54A28 (accessed 1 March 2013).

Fenson, L., Dale, P.S., Reznick, J.S. and Thal, D. (1993a) *The MacArthur–Bates Communicative Development Inventories (CDI I): Words and Gestures*. Baltimore, MD: Paul Brookes Publishing.

Fenson, L., Dale, P.S., Reznick, J.S. and Thal, D. (1993b) *The MacArthur–Bates Communicative Development Inventories (CDI II): Words and Sentences*. Baltimore, MD: Paul Brookes Publishing.

Fernald, A., Perfors, A. and Marchman, V.A. (2006) Picking up speed in understanding: Speech processing efficiency and vocabulary growth across the 2nd year. *Developmental Psychology* 42 (1), 98–116.

Fernandez, M.C., Pearson, B.Z., Umbel, V.M., Oller, D.K. and Molinet-Molina, M. (1992) Bilingual receptive vocabulary in Hispanic preschool children. *Hispanic Journal of Behavioral Sciences* 14 (2), 268–276.

Ferrand, L., Bonin, P., Méot, A., Augustinova, M., New, B., Pallier, C. and Brysbaert, M. (2008) Age-of-acquisition and subjective frequency estimates for all generally known monosyllabic French words and their relation with other psycholinguistic variables. *Behavior Research Methods* 40 (4), 1049–1054.

Gagarina, N., Klassert, A. and Topaj, N. (2010) Sprachstandstest Russisch für mehrsprachige Kinder [Russian language proficiency test for multilingual children]. *ZAS Papers in Linguistics* 54.

Gardner, M.F. (1979) *Expressive One-Word Picture Vocabulary Test*. Novato, CA: Academic Therapy Publications.

Garlock, V.M., Walley, A.C. and Metsala, J.L. (2001) Age-of-acquisition, word frequency, and neighborhood density effects on spoken word recognition by children and adults. *Journal of Memory and Language* 45 (3), 468–492.

Gathercole, V.C., Thomas, E.M. and Hughes, E. (2008) Designing a normed receptive vocabulary test for bilingual populations: A model from Welsh. *International Journal of Bilingual Education and Bilingualism* 11 (6), 678–720.

Gatt, D., Letts, C. and Klee, T. (2008) Lexical mixing in the early productive vocabularies of Maltese children: Implications for intervention. *Clinical Linguistics & Phonetics* 22 (4–5), 267–274.

Gentner, D. (1981) Some interesting differences between verbs and nouns. *Cognition and Brain Theory* 4 (2), 161–178.

Gentner, D. (1982) Why nouns are learned before verbs. Linguistic relativity versus natural partitioning. In S. A. Kuczaj (ed.), *Language development: Vol. 2. Language, thought and culture* (pp. 301–334). Hillsdale, NJ: Erlbaum.

Gentner, D. (2006) Why verbs are hard to learn. In K. Hirsh-Pasek and R. Golinkoff (eds) *Action Meets Word: How Children Learn Verbs* (pp. 544–564). Oxford, UK: Oxford University Press.

Gilhooly, K.J. and Gilhooly, M.L.M. (1980) The validity of age-of-acquisition ratings. *British Journal of Psychology* 71 (1), 105–110.

Gilhooly, K.J. and Logie, R.H. (1980) Age-of-acquisition, imagery, concreteness, familiarity, and ambiguity measures for 1,944 words. *Behavior Research Methods* 12 (4), 395–427.

Goldfield, B.A. (2000) Nouns before verbs in comprehension vs. production: The view from pragmatics. *Journal of Child Language* 27 (3), 501–520.

Gopnik, A., Choi, S. and Baumberger, T. (1996) Cross-linguistic differences in early semantic and cognitive development. *Cognitive Development* 11 (2), 197–227.

Gorman, B.K. (2012) Relationships between vocabulary size, working memory, and phonological awareness in Spanish-speaking English language learners. *American Journal of Speech-Language Pathology* 21 (2), 109–123.

Gray, S., Plante, E., Vance, R. and Henrichsen, M. (1999) The diagnostic accuracy of four vocabulary tests administered to preschool-age children. *Language, Speech, and Hearing Services in Schools* 30 (2), 196–206.

Haman, E. (2009) University of Warsaw Picture Database for Vocabulary Test (Obrazkowy Test Słownikowy - Rozumienie OTSR). Unpublished material. Faculty of Psychology, University of Warsaw.

Haman, E., Łuniewska, M. and Pomiechowska, B. (2011, November). Preparatory study for assessing word difficulty: An update on age of acquisition (AoA study). Paper presented at the 5th General Meeting of COST IS0804, Malta.

Haman, E. and Fronczyk, K. (2012) *Obrazkowy Test Słownikowy – Rozumienie (OTSR)*. Gdańsk: Pracownia Testów Psychologicznych i Pedagogicznych.

Haman, E. and Łuniewska, M. (2013, May) Cross-linguistic lexical tasks (CLTs) assessing word knowledge and lexical processing in bilingual children. Plenary talk presented at Child Language Impairment in Multilingual Contexts (final COST IS0804 conference), Kraków, Poland.

Haman, E., Szewczyk, J., Łuniewska, M., Mieszkowska, K., Pomiechowska, B., Wodniecka, Z., Chiat, S. and Armon-Lotem, S. (in preparation) Naming objects and actions across 34 languages: Can we establish a common set of nouns and verbs?

Hammer, C.S., Lawrence, F.R. and Miccio, A.W. (2008) Exposure to English before and after entry into Head Start 1: Bilingual children's receptive language growth in Spanish and English. *International Journal of Bilingual Education and Bilingualism* 11 (1), 30–56.

Harris, M., Yeeles, C., Chasin, J. and Oakley, Y. (1995) Symmetries and asymmetries in early lexical comprehension and production. *Journal of Child Language* 22 (1), 1–18.

Hart, B. and Risley, T.R. (2003) The early catastrophe: The 30 million word gap by age 3. *American Educator* 27 (1), 4–9.

Hewitt, L.E., Hammer, C.S., Yont, K.M. and Tomblin, J.B. (2005) Language sampling for kindergarten children with and without SLI: Mean length of utterance, IPSYN, and NDW. *Journal of Communication Disorders* 38 (3), 197–213.

Hoff, E. (2009) Do vocabulary differences explain achievement gaps and can vocabulary-targeted interventions close them? Paper presented at the National Research Council Workshop on the Role of Language in Education, 15–16 October.

Huebler, F. (2010) International education statistics: Primary school entrance age and duration. *International Education Statistics*. See http://huebler.blogspot.com/2010/05/age.html (accessed 30 May 2010).

Jared, D., Pei Yun Poh, R. and Paivio, A. (2012) L1 and L2 picture naming in Mandarin–English bilinguals: A test of bilingual dual coding theory. *Bilingualism: Language and Cognition* 16 (2), 383–396.

Juhasz, B.J., Starr, M.S., Inhoff, A.W. and Placke, L. (2003) The effects of morphology on the processing of compound words: Evidence from naming, lexical decisions and eye fixations. *British Journal of Psychology* 94 (2), 223–244.

Kambanaros, M. (2003) *Verb and noun processing in late bilingual individuals with anomic aphasia*. Doctoral dissertation, Flinders University, Adelaide.

Kambanaros, M., Grohmann, K.K. and Theodorou, E. (2010) Action and object naming in mono- and bilingual children with language impairment. In A. Botinis (ed.) *Proceedings of ISCA Tutorial and Research Workshop on Experimental Linguistics 2010* (pp. 25–27).

Kan, P.F. and Kohnert, K.J. (2005) Preschoolers learning Hmong and English: Lexical-semantic skills in L1 and L2. *Journal of Speech, Language and Hearing Research* 48 (2), 372–383.

Kauschke, C., Lee, H.W. and Pae, S. (2007) Similarities and variation in noun and verb acquisition: A crosslinguistic study of children learning German, Korean, and Turkish. *Language and Cognitive Processes* 22 (7), 1045–1072.

Keil, F.C. (1989) *Concepts, Kinds, and Cognitive Development*. Cambridge, MA: The MIT Press.

Khomsi, A. (2001) *Évaluation du Langage Oral*. Paris: ECPA.

Kohnert, K.J. (2010) Bilingual children with primary language impairment: Issues, evidence and implications for clinical actions. *Journal of Communication Disorders* 43 (6), 456–473.

Kohnert, K.J., Hernandez, A. and Bates, E. (1998) Bilingual performance on the Boston naming test: Preliminary norms in Spanish and English. *Brain and Language* 65 (3), 422–440.

Kohnert, K.J., Bates, E. and Hernandez, A.E. (1999) Balancing bilinguals: Lexical-semantic production and cognitive processing in children learning Spanish and English. *Journal of Speech, Language and Hearing Research* 42 (6), 1400–1413.

Kohnert, K.J. and Bates, E. (2002) Balancing bilinguals II: Lexical comprehension and cognitive processing in children learning Spanish and English. *Journal of Speech, Language, and Hearing Research* 45 (2), 347–359.

Kunnari, S., Savinainen-Makkonen, T. and Saaristo-Helin, K. (2012) *Fonologiatesti: Lasten äänteellisen kehityksen arviointi* [*Finnish Test of Phonology: Assessment of Phonological Skills in Children*]. Jyväskylä: Niilo Mäki Instituutti.

Lahey, M. and Edwards, J. (1996) Why do children with specific language impairment name pictures more slowly than their peers? *Journal of Speech and Hearing Research* 39 (5), 1081–1098.

Lahey, M., Edwards, J. and Munson, B. (2001) Is processing speed related to severity of language impairment? *Journal of Speech, Language, and Hearing Research* 44 (6), 1354–1361.

Leonard, L.B. and Deevy, P. (2004) Lexical deficits in specific language impairment. In L. Verhoeven and H. van Balkom (eds) *Classification of Developmental Language Disorders* (pp. 209–233). Mahwah, NJ: Lawrence Erlbaum.

Lind, M., Simonsen, H.G., Hansen, P., Holm, E. and Mevik, B.-H. (2013) "Ordforrådet" – en leksikalsk database over et utvalg norske ord. *Norsk tidsskrift for logopedi* 59 (1), 18–26.

Lind, M., Simonsen, H. G., Hansen, P., Holm, E. and Mevik, B. H. (2015) Norwegian Words: a lexical database for clinicians and researchers. *Clinical Linguistics and Phonetics*. Early online view (accessed 14 January 2015), 1–15.

Loizou, M. and Stuart, M. (2003) Phonological awareness in monolingual and bilingual English and Greek five-year-olds. *Journal of Research in Reading* 26 (1), 3–18.

Łuniewska, M., Pomiechowska, B., Southwood, F., Slančová, D., Kapalková, S., Ege, P., Unal, O. and Haman, E. (2012, May) Measuring the age of acquisition of words for new cross-linguistic lexical tasks: Results of on-line study for Afrikaans, Polish, Slovak and Turkish. Poster presented at the 6th General Meeting of COST IS0804, Berlin, Germany.

Łuniewska, M. et al. (2012, September) Age of acquisition of Bi-Sli WG3 'best words' – An update for 15 languages. Paper presented at the 7th General Meeting of COST IS0804, Padua, Italy.

Łuniewska, M. and Bi-SLI WG3 (2013, February) AoA results for 15 languages: New data & new analyses. Paper presented at the 8th General Meeting of COST IS0804, Lisbon, Portugal.

Łuniewska, M., Anđelković, D., Armon-Lotem, S., Chiat, S., Dabašinskienė, I., Ege, P., ..., Haman, E. (2014, July). *AoA norms for nouns and verbs in 22 languages*. Poster presented at the 13th International Congress for the Study of Child Language, Amsterdam, The Netherlands.

Łuniewska, M., Haman, E., Armon-Lotem, S., Etenkowski, B., Anđelković, D., Blom, E., ..., Ünal-Logacev, Ö. (submitted). Ratings of age of acquisition of 299 words across 25 languages. Is there a cross-linguistic order of words?

Mainela-Arnold, E., Evans, J.L. and Coady, J.A. (2010) Explaining lexical-semantic deficits in specific language impairment: The role of phonological similarity, phonological working memory, and lexical competition. *Journal of Speech, Language, and Hearing Research* 53 (6), 1742–1756.

Mancilla-Martinez, J. and Lesaux, N.K. (2011) Early home language use and later vocabulary development. *Journal of Educational Psychology* 103 (3), 535–546.

Marchman, V.A., Fernald, A. and Hurtado, N. (2009) How vocabulary size in two languages relates to efficiency in spoken word recognition by young Spanish–English bilinguals. *Journal of Child Language* 37 (4), 817–840.

Marques, J.F., Fonseca, F.L., Morais, S. and Pinto, I.A. (2007) Estimated age of acquisition norms for 834 Portuguese nouns and their relation with other psycholinguistic variables. *Behavior Research Methods* 39 (3), 439–444.

Masterson, J. and Druks, J. (1998) Description of a set of 164 nouns and 102 verbs matched for printed word frequency, familiarity and age of acquisition. *Journal of Neurolinguistics* 11 (4), 331–354.

Masterson, J., Druks, J. and Gallienne, D. (2008) Object and action picture naming in three- and five-year-old children. *Journal of Child Language* 35 (2), 373–402.

McDonough, C., Song, L., Hirsh-Pasek, K., Golinkoff, R.M. and Lannon, R. (2011) An image is worth a thousand words: Why nouns tend to dominate verbs in early word learning. *Developmental Science* 14 (2), 181–189.

McGregor, K.K., Newman, R.M., Reilly, R.M. and Capone, N.C. (2002) Semantic representation and naming in children with specific language impairment. *Journal of Speech, Language and Hearing Research* 45 (5), 998–1014.

Messer, D. and Dockrell, J.E. (2006) Children's naming and word-finding difficulties: Descriptions and explanations. *Journal of Speech, Language and Hearing Research* 49 (2), 309–324.

Messer, M.H. (2010) Verbal short-term memory and vocabulary development in monolingual Dutch and bilingual Turkish-Dutch preschoolers. Igitur Archief – Utrecht Publishing and Archiving Service. See Open Educational Resources (OER) portal at http://www.temoa.info/node/351822 (accessed 10 June 2012).

Montgomery, J.W. (2002) Examining the nature of lexical processing in children with specific language impairment: Temporal processing or processing capacity deficit? *Applied Psycholinguistics* 23 (3), 447–470.

Morrison, C.M., Ellis, A.W. and Quinlan, P.T. (1992) Age of acquisition, not word frequency, affects object naming, not object recognition. *Memory & Cognition* 20 (6), 705–714.

Morrison, C.M., Chappell, T.D. and Ellis, A.W. (1997) Age of acquisition norms for a large set of object names and their relations to adult estimates and other variables. *The Quarterly Journal of Experimental Psychology* 50A (3), 528–559.

Paradis, J. (2007) Bilingual children with specific language impairment: Theoretical and applied issues. *Applied Psycholinguistics* 28 (3), 512–564.

Pearson, B.Z., Fernandez, S.C. and Oller, D.K. (2006) Lexical development in bilingual infants and toddlers: Comparison to monolingual norms. *Language Learning* 43 (1), 93–120.

Peña, E.D., Bedore, L.M. and Fiestas, C. (2013) Development of bilingual semantic norms: Can two be one? In V.C.M. Gathercole (ed.) *Solutions for the Assessment of Bilinguals* (pp. 103–124). Bristol: Multilingual Matters.

Pérez, M.A. and Navalón, C. (2005) Objective-AoA norms for 175 names in Spanish: Relationships with other psycholinguistic variables, estimated AoA, and data from other languages. *European Journal of Cognitive Psychology* 17 (2), 179–206.

Pérez, M.Á., Izura, C., Stadthagen-González, H. and Marín, J. (2013) Assessment of bilinguals' performance in lexical tasks using reaction times. In V.C.M. Gathercole (ed.) *Issues in the Assessment of Bilinguals* (pp. 130–160). Bristol: Multilingual Matters.

Pind, J., Jonsdottir, H., Gissurardottir, H. and Jonsson, F. (2000) Icelandic norms for the Snodgrass and Vanderwart (1980) pictures: Name and image agreement, familiarity, and age of acquisition. *Scandinavian Journal of Psychology* 41 (1), 41–48.

Reznick, J.S. and Goldfield, B.A. (1992) Rapid change in lexical development in comprehension and production. *Developmental Psychology* 28 (3), 406–413.

Rossion, B. and Pourtois, G. (2004) Revisiting Snodgrass and Vanderwart's object pictorial set: The role of surface detail in basic-level object recognition. *Perception* 33 (2), 217–236.

Santiago, J., MacKay, D.G., Palma, A. and Rho, C. (2000) Sequential activation processes in producing words and syllables: Evidence from picture naming. *Language and Cognitive Processes* 15 (1), 1–44.

Scheele, A. (2010) Home language and mono- and bilingual children's emergent academic language. A longitudinal study of Dutch, Moroccan-Dutch, and Turkish-Dutch 3- to 6-olds. Unpublished doctoral dissertation, University of Amsterdam.

Sheng, L. and McGregor, K.K. (2010) Lexical-semantic organization in children with specific language impairment. *Journal of Speech, Language, and Hearing Research* 53 (1), 146–159.

Simonsen, H.G., Lind, M. and Hansen, P. (2012, May) Collecting AoA data for Norwegian: An alternative method. Paper presented at the 6th General Meeting of COST IS0804, Berlin, Germany.

Skipp, A., Windfuhr, K.L. and Conti-Ramsden, G. (2002) Children's grammatical categories of verb and noun: A comparative look at children with specific language impairment (SLI) and normal language (NL). *International Journal of Language & Communication Disorders* 37 (3), 253–271.

Southwood, F., Łuniewska, M., Pomiechowska, B. and Haman, E. (2011, November). Lexical tasks construction: Subjective age of acquisition of words (AoA). Data for Afrikaans and Polish. Poster presented at the 5th General Meeting of COST IS0804, Malta.

Spaulding, T.J., Swartwout Szulga, M. and Figueroa, C. (2012) Using norm-referenced tests to determine severity of language impairment in children: Disconnect between US policy makers and test developers. *Language, Speech, and Hearing Services in Schools* 43 (2), 176–190.

Spaulding, T.J., Hosmer, S. and Schechtman, C. (2013) Investigating the interchangeability and diagnostic utility of the PPVT-III and PPVT-IV for children with and without SLI. *International Journal of Speech-Language Pathology* 15 (5), 1–10.

Stadthagen-Gonzalez, H. and Davis, C.J. (2006) The Bristol norms for age of acquisition, imageability, and familiarity. *Behavior Research Methods* 38 (4), 598–605.

Szekely, A., Jacobsen, T., D'Amico, S., Devescovi, A., Andonova, E., Herron, D. and Wicha, N. (2004) A new on-line resource for psycholinguistic studies. *Journal of Memory and Language* 51 (2), 247–250.

Szekely, A., D'Amico, S., Devescovi, A., Federmeier, K., Herron, D., Iyer, G., Jacobsen, T., Arévalo, A.L., Vargha, A. and Bates, E. (2005) Timed action and object naming. *Cortex* 41 (1), 7–26.

Tomasello, M., Akhtar, N., Dodson, K. and Rekau, L. (1997) Differential productivity in young children's use of nouns and verbs. *Journal of Child Language* 24 (2), 373–387.

Umbel, V.M., Pearson, B.Z., Fernández, M.C. and Oller, D.K. (1992) Measuring bilingual children's receptive vocabularies. *Child Development* 63 (4), 1012–1020.

Unsworth, S., Argyri, F., Cornips, L., Hulk, A., Sorace, A. and Tsimpli, I. (2011) On the role of age of onset and input in early child bilingualism in Greek and Dutch. *Applied Psycholinguistics* 35 (4), 1–41.

Van Tuijl, C., Leseman, P.P.M. and Rispens, J. (2001) Efficacy of an intensive home-based educational intervention programme for 4-to 6-year-old ethnic minority children in the Netherlands. *International Journal of Behavioral Development* 25 (2), 148–159.

Vogel, P.M. and Comrie, B. (2000) *Approaches to the Typology of Word Classes.* Berlin: Walter de Gruyter.

Wierzbicka, A. (1988) *The Semantics of Grammar.* Amsterdam: John Benjamins Publishing Company.

Windfuhr, K.L., Faragher, B. and Conti-Ramsden, G. (2002) Lexical learning skills in young children with specific language impairment (SLI). *International Journal of Language & Communication Disorders* 37 (4), 415–432.

Zwitserlood, P., Bölte, J. and Dohmes, P. (2000) Morphological effects on speech production: Evidence from picture naming. *Language and Cognitive Processes* 15 (4–5), 563–591.

Appendix A: The List of CLT-Candidate Words (English Equivalents of 158 Nouns and 142 Verbs) Selected in Phase 1 with Values of DNI and MAI Used for Selection

Nouns			Verbs		
Word	MAI	DNI	Word	MAI	DNI
airplane	1.00	0.53	bark	0.99	0.99
ant	1.00	0.96	bath	0.91	0.69
apple	1.00	1.00	beg	0.94	0.87
axe	1.00	0.70	bite	0.99	0.96
ball	1.00	0.92	blow	0.99	0.99
balloon	0.99	0.87	boil	0.92	0.79
banana	1.00	1.00	box	0.94	0.46
barrel	1.00	0.88	break	0.90	0.72
basket	0.99	0.95	brush	0.97	0.48
battery	0.99	0.96	build	0.90	0.60
bear	1.00	1.00	burn	0.99	0.88
bed	1.00	1.00	burst	0.93	0.33
bell	1.00	0.97	carry	0.92	0.92
belt	1.00	0.99	carve	0.95	0.45
bicycle	1.00	0.67	clap	0.93	0.64
bird	1.00	0.96	clean	0.90	0.56
blackboard	1.00	0.76	climb	0.93	0.93
bone	1.00	1.00	comb	1.00	0.92
boot	1.00	0.82	conduct	0.90	0.77
bottle	1.00	0.99	cook	0.92	0.97
broom	1.00	0.93	crawl	0.93	0.91
brush	1.00	0.46	cry	1.00	1.00
bus	1.00	0.96	cut	1.00	0.99
butterfly	1.00	1.00	dance	0.99	0.99
button	1.00	0.99	dig	0.92	0.77
candle	1.00	0.99	dive	0.96	0.59
cap	0.99	0.38	draw	0.99	1.00
car	0.99	0.97	drill	0.99	0.85

(Continued)

Nouns			Verbs		
Word	MAI	DNI	Word	MAI	DNI
carrot	1.00	0.96	drink	1.00	1.00
cat	1.00	0.99	drip	0.97	0.80
chain	0.99	0.99	drive	1.00	0.98
chair	1.00	1.00	drown	0.95	0.79
cheese	1.00	0.97	dry	0.99	0.67
cigarette	0.99	0.96	eat	1.00	1.00
clock	1.00	0.88	erupt	0.92	0.63
cloud	1.00	0.96	extinguish	0.96	0.47
comb	1.00	0.96	fall	0.93	0.97
computer	1.00	0.98	feed	0.97	0.97
cow	1.00	1.00	fight	0.90	0.77
crocodile	1.00	0.93	file	0.90	0.75
cucumber	1.00	1.00	fish	0.98	0.98
desk	0.99	0.79	fly	1.00	0.96
dog	1.00	1.00	glue	0.90	0.58
doll	1.00	0.96	grate	1.00	0.74
door	1.00	0.99	grill	0.94	0.33
dress	0.99	0.97	hammer	0.96	0.42
drum	1.00	0.93	hatch	0.92	0.71
duck	1.00	0.97	hitchhike	0.90	0.62
ear	1.00	1.00	hug	0.90	0.75
elephant	1.00	0.98	hunt	0.92	0.95
envelope	1.00	0.91	iron	1.00	1.00
eye	1.00	1.00	jump	0.96	0.92
feather	1.00	0.95	kick	0.91	0.77
fish	1.00	1.00	kiss	0.99	0.99
flag	1.00	0.98	knit	1.00	0.84
flower	1.00	1.00	knock	0.93	0.89
fly	0.99	0.99	laugh	0.99	0.95
fork	1.00	1.00	lick	0.99	1.00
frog	1.00	0.96	light	0.90	0.90
frying pan	1.00	0.51	listen	0.93	0.88
gate	1.00	0.84	marry	0.91	0.93
giraffe	1.00	0.97	massage	0.96	0.96

Nouns			Verbs		
Word	MAI	DNI	Word	MAI	DNI
glass	1.00	0.91	measure	0.99	0.97
glasses	1.00	0.83	melt	0.90	0.96
goat	1.00	0.91	milk	0.99	0.97
guitar	1.00	0.96	mix	0.96	0.50
gun	1.00	0.59	mop	0.95	0.46
hat	1.00	1.00	open	0.92	0.93
heart	1.00	1.00	operate	0.93	0.85
helicopter	1.00	0.93	paint	1.00	0.98
hen	1.00	0.58	pee	0.96	0.61
horse	1.00	0.96	peel	0.98	0.87
house	1.00	0.99	photograph	0.96	0.34
iron	1.00	0.91	pick	0.96	0.68
kangaroo	1.00	0.95	pinch	0.94	0.91
key	1.00	1.00	plant	0.93	0.92
knife	1.00	1.00	play	1.00	0.50
ladder	1.00	0.89	play golf	0.90	0.43
lamp	1.00	0.88	plow	0.90	0.70
leaf	1.00	1.00	post	0.91	0.43
leg	1.00	0.91	pour	0.96	0.92
lemon	1.00	1.00	pull	0.93	0.82
lighter	1.00	0.98	push	1.00	0.96
lion	1.00	1.00	rain	1.00	0.99
lipstick	1.00	0.98	rake	0.92	0.61
match	1.00	0.91	read	0.99	0.97
monkey	1.00	0.95	ride	0.97	0.81
moon	1.00	0.98	ring	0.95	0.58
motorbike	0.99	0.45	roast	0.91	0.52
mouse	1.00	0.95	row	0.96	0.84
mushroom	1.00	0.83	run	0.99	0.99
needle	1.00	0.87	sail	0.90	0.92
nest	0.99	0.89	saw	0.99	0.74
newspaper	0.99	0.87	search	0.90	0.53
nose	1.00	1.00	sew	0.99	0.89

(Continued)

Nouns			Verbs		
Word	MAI	DNI	Word	MAI	DNI
onion	1.00	1.00	sharpen	0.97	0.83
orange	1.00	0.99	shave	0.98	0.96
owl	1.00	0.99	shear	1.00	0.48
paintbrush	1.00	0.59	shower	0.93	0.70
pear	1.00	1.00	sing	1.00	0.96
pen	1.00	0.76	sink	0.97	0.91
pencil	1.00	0.97	sit	0.96	0.96
penguin	1.00	0.96	skate	0.97	0.46
pineapple	0.99	0.99	ski	0.96	0.91
pizza	1.00	1.00	sleep	1.00	1.00
postman	1.00	0.76	slide	0.93	0.63
rabbit	0.99	0.79	slip	0.97	0.80
racket	1.00	0.68	smell	0.97	0.93
rainbow	0.99	0.97	smoke	0.99	0.97
roof	1.00	0.99	snow	0.91	0.90
ruler	1.00	1.00	spill	0.91	0.75
sandwich	1.00	0.96	spin	0.93	0.63
saw	1.00	0.95	squeeze	0.94	0.83
scale	0.99	0.42	steal	0.94	0.90
scarf	0.99	0.97	sting	0.92	0.65
scissors	1.00	0.99	stir	0.90	0.74
sewing machine	1.00	0.95	stroke	0.96	0.31
shirt	0.99	0.93	sunbath	0.97	0.50
shoe	1.00	1.00	sunbathe	0.96	0.61
slide	1.00	0.91	surf	0.90	0.92
snail	1.00	1.00	sweat	0.92	0.90
snake	0.99	0.93	sweep	1.00	0.92
snowman	1.00	1.00	swim	1.00	0.93
sock	1.00	0.89	swing	0.98	0.90
socks	1.00	0.83	take a photo	0.94	0.37
sofa	1.00	0.67	talk	0.97	0.21
spoon	1.00	0.91	tear	0.99	0.73
squirrel	1.00	0.98	throw	0.92	0.88
stairs	0.99	0.71	tie	0.94	0.71

Nouns			Verbs		
Word	MAI	DNI	Word	MAI	DNI
star	1.00	0.99	type	0.94	0.76
stool	0.99	0.80	vacuum	0.94	0.65
strawberry	1.00	1.00	wake up	0.90	0.86
sun	1.00	0.97	walk	0.96	0.88
sunglasses	0.99	0.86	wash	0.99	0.89
sweater	0.99	0.41	watch	0.97	0.57
swing	1.00	0.96	water	1.00	0.96
tail	1.00	0.99	wave	0.90	0.46
tank	1.00	0.88	weigh	1.00	0.93
telephone	1.00	0.76	whisper	0.90	0.84
television	1.00	0.55	whistle	0.99	0.57
tennis ball	1.00	0.75	wink	0.93	0.76
thermometer	1.00	0.98	write	1.00	1.00
tie	1.00	0.89			
tiger	1.00	0.95			
tomato	1.00	0.97			
toothbrush	1.00	0.96			
tractor	1.00	1.00			
tree	0.99	1.00			
trousers	1.00	0.64			
truck	1.00	0.70			
turtle	1.00	0.68			
umbrella	1.00	0.99			
vest	1.00	0.51			
wardrobe	1.00	0.42			
watch	1.00	0.93			
watermelon	0.99	0.72			
wave	1.00	0.98			
whistle	1.00	0.92			
zebra	1.00	1.00			

Note: Some words are repeated with different values of DNI and MAI (sock / socks, photograph / take a photo, sunbath / sunbathe). In the database for Phase 1, there were two pictures for each of these words, which got different dominant names in the naming study. In the final list of CLT-candidate words each word was used just once.

Appendix B: Sample Picture Board for Comprehension (A4 Format). Sample Picture Board for Production (A5 Format).

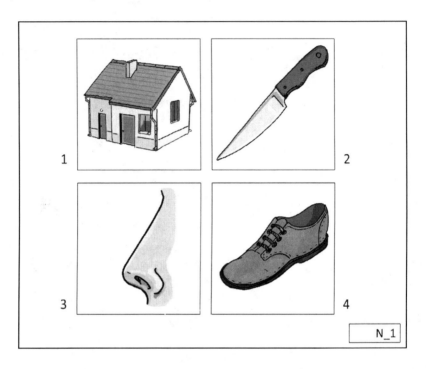

Note: In the original version CLTs pictures are colorful.

Appendix C: CLTs Language Versions Currently Available and Their Authors

	Language	Authors			
1	Afrikaans	Frenette Southwood			
2	Catalan	Anna Gavarró	Laia Montes		
3	English/UK	Ewa Haman	Magdalena Łuniewska	Kamila Polišenská	Karolina Mieszkowska	Shula Chiat
4	English/SA	Frenette Southwood			
5	Finnish	Sari Kunnari			
6	German	Tanja Rinker	Natalia Gagarina		
7	Hebrew	Sharon Armon-Lotem	Efrat Harel		
8	Hungarian	Inger-Anne Ehret			
9	Italian	Maja Roch	Chiara Levorato	Roberta Tedeschi	
10	isiXhosa	Frenette Southwood	Anneke Potgieter		
11	Lebanese	Camille Messara	Edith Kouba-Hreich	Ewa Haman	Magdalena Łuniewska
12	Lithuanian	Agnė Blažienė	Ineta Dabašinskienė	Magdalena Łuniewska	
13	Luxembourgish	Pascale Engel de Abreu	Peter Gilles	Magdalena Łuniewska	Ewa Haman

(Continued)

	Language	Authors				
14	Maltese	Daniela Gatt	Magdalena Łuniewska			
15	Norwegian	Hanne Gram Simonsen	Pernille Hansen	Magdalena Łuniewska		
16	Polish	Ewa Haman	Magdalena Łuniewska	Barbara Pomiechowska	Jakub Szewczyk	Zofia Wodniecka
17	Russian	Olga Nenonen				
18	Serbian	Jasmina Vuksanović	Jovana Bjekić			
19	Slovak	Svetlana Kapalková	Daniela Slančová	Magdalena Łuniewska	Ewa Haman	
20	Spanish	Myriam Cantú Sánchez				
21	Swedish	Natalia Ringblom	Gisela Håkansson	Josefin Lindgren		
22	Turkish	Özlem Ünal-Logacev	Aylin Müge Tuncer	Pinar Ege		

Part 3
Beyond Modality

9 Assessment of Narrative Abilities in Bilingual Children

Natalia Gagarina, Daleen Klop,
Sari Kunnari, Koula Tantele,
Taina Välimaa, Ingrida Balčiūnienė,
Ute Bohnacker and Joel Walters

Introduction and Overview

The Multilingual Assessment Instrument for Narratives (MAIN; Gagarina et al., 2012) was developed to assess the narrative production and comprehension abilities of bilingual children from 3 to 10 years (later referred to as the Language Impairment Testing in Multilingual Settings: Multilingual Assessment Instrument for Narratives – LITMUS-MAIN).

Different types of narratives offer a platform for examining a wide range of linguistic abilities in context (cf. Hughes et al., 1997). These abilities concern story structure, discourse features (e.g. coherence and cohesion), morphosyntax, complex syntax, lexis and uniquely bilingual phenomena such as code-switching and cross-linguistic interference. Children's narratives also provide an index of their cognitive, semantic and social abilities (Liles, 1993). Narrative analysis is considered by researchers and clinicians to be an ecologically valid way to investigate communicative competence (Botting, 2002) and to be less biased against bilingual children than norm-referenced assessment tools (Paradis et al., 2011). Oral narratives provide a rich source of data about a child's language use in a relatively natural context. Finally, narrative analysis allows clinicians to assess multiple linguistic features in context – including macrostructure, e.g. story grammar categories such as goals, attempts and outcomes; microstructure features, e.g. lexical diversity, relational and referential devices – using relatively short language samples (Heilmann et al., 2010a, 2010b).

Narrative skills are important for later success in school, e.g. in literacy and for comprehension of the language of mathematics (Bishop & Edmundson, 1987; Bliss et al., 1998; McCabe, 1996; McCabe & Rollins, 1994; Walach, 2008; Westby, 1991). They form a bridge between oral language and literacy by providing exposure to and experience in using extended, contextualised, cohesive discourse units and abstract texts that children will encounter in written texts (Hadley, 1998; Westby, 2005). According to Kaderavek and Sulzby (2000) and Oakhill and Cain (2007), reading comprehension has its roots in the comprehension of narrative discourse that develops simultaneously with other early language skills prior to formal reading instruction. The ability to tell a story links oral language skills to literacy, since it requires children to plan and produce contextualised and cohesive discourse. Intervention studies have shown that directly teaching narrative skills improves comprehension and production of oral narratives as well as reading comprehension (Hayward & Schneider, 2000; Swanson et al., 2005). Moreover, narrative abilities at the macrostructure level, i.e. composition of cohesive event sequences, reflect capacities which go beyond the specifics of one language. Thus, the assessment of narratives can be seen as especially appropriate for bilingual children: 'language tasks that require a cognitive component might also be less biased against dual language children, because the cognitive component could be tapping into language-general capacities' (Paradis et al., 2011: 221).

History and overview. Our initial goal was to examine and evaluate different tasks used to elicit narratives and to identify specifically bilingual features in narrative discourse. The review of existing tasks and tests showed that while elicitation procedures and scoring were usually sound, they did not provide sufficiently parallel stimuli for elicitation and assessment of narrative abilities in both of the languages of a bilingual child. Existing pictorial stimuli were not grounded in the present theoretical story grammar framework, nor did they take into account internal state terms (ISTs). The use of ISTs provides important information about the narrator's awareness of characters' mental states, motivations, intentions and goals (Nippold et al., 2005). In addition, the protagonists and the lexical items denoting them were often not controlled for, e.g. for frequency of use and perceptual complexity.

This led to the development of new pictorial stimuli, involving more than 200 revisions of pictures and story scripts piloted prior to the design presented here. This design and its accompanying research programme comprises the elicitation of narratives in two modes, (i) story telling (story generation) and (ii) story retelling, as well as the assessment of comprehension of macrostructure components and ISTs. The design allows for another possible elicitation mode, storytelling after listening to a model story that is similar in structure yet different in content from the story to be told. The model story is thus a variant of the retelling procedure. In addition, a set of background questions (based on Gagarina et al., 2010) forms part of the assessment procedure to evaluate the quality and quantity of the input to the child in both of her/his languages.

Stimulus pictures and scripts for retelling include a combination of macrostructure, microstructure and internal state features of narrative discourse in order to investigate each child's performance cross-linguistically in a within-subject design. The materials were developed in multiple languages in order to make it possible to screen and identify children at risk for specific language impairment (SLI) in both their languages. The present version of the tool (see http://www.zas.gwz-berlin.de/zaspil56.html; Gagarina *et al.*, 2012) has been piloted in 17 languages and 14 language pairs with more than 500 monolingual and bilingual children.

Following this general introduction, the remainder of the chapter is organised as follows: The first section provides the conceptual framework and a literature overview, emphasising the distinction between macrostructure and microstructure and providing information about internal state language and bilingual aspects of narrative abilities. The next section gives a detailed presentation of the telling and retelling elicitation tasks, stimulus pictures, stimulus scripts, the narrative comprehension task and how the instrument is administered. The third section deals with transcription, coding and scoring of the data. The following section gives some preliminary findings from the studies which have been conducted thus far, and the final section concludes the chapter.

Conceptual Framework and Literature

Methods for collecting and analysing narrative speech samples are highly varied. There are different sampling procedures (e.g. spontaneous or elicited), different types of narratives (e.g. scripted, personal and fictional stories) and different elicitation methods (e.g. story generation/telling and story retelling). One characteristic feature of narratives is that they contain information at two levels: macrostructure and microstructure. Macrostructure analysis focuses on higher-order hierarchical organisation, including episodic structure and story grammar components (Heilmann *et al.*, 2010a) and can be said to be language independent (Pearson, 2002). Microstructure focuses on the linguistic structures used in the construction of coherent discourse, *inter alia*, number, length and complexity of utterances or communication units, lexical diversity, use of referential noun phrases, connectives, tense, etc. Macrostructure and microstructure abilities represent two distinct but interrelated areas underlying narrative discourse competence (Liles *et al.*, 1995). These abilities are not often examined in a single framework. Rather, most narrative tests focus on language-specific capacities and microstructure features such as vocabulary and/or grammar. LITMUS-MAIN examines narrative production of microstructure and macrostructure elements, in combination with the comprehension of macrostructure features. It also includes ISTs, thereby providing information about skills at the cognitive–linguistic interface.

Various theoretical approaches (e.g. Bruner, 1986; Labov & Waletzky, 1967; Mandler & Johnson, 1977; Stein & Glenn, 1979; Westby, 2005) and elicitation options were examined prior to pilot testing different measures. Narrative assessment calls for a wide-scoped, integrative framework, which includes macrostructure and microstructure as well as production and comprehension. The breadth as well as the particular emphasis on internal states and bilingual features makes LITMUS-MAIN unique in scope as well as focus. The components of the instrument can be found in the third section.

Macrostructure

The story grammar model (see e.g. Mandler & Johnson, 1977; Stein & Glenn, 1979), according to which all stories have a setting and episode structure claimed to capture a universal organisational pattern for story knowledge (Trabasso & Nickels, 1992), served as our initial theoretical framework. Story grammar research has been conducted with a wide variety of data collection procedures and a wide variety of populations, including bilingual children (Fiestas & Peña, 2004; Gutiérrez-Clellen et al., 2008; Pearson, 2001, 2002; Pearson & de Villiers, 2005; Uccelli & Paéz, 2007) as well as bilingual children with language impairment (e.g. Cleave et al., 2010; Gutiérrez-Clellen et al., 2009; Iluz-Cohen & Walters, 2012; Simon-Cereijido & Gutiérrez-Clellen, 2009).

In the instrument described below, a slight adaptation of the story grammar model is used. The stories begin with a setting statement, which specifies time and place and introduces the protagonist. This component is followed by three episodes. Each episode consists of (i) a goal (G) statement for the protagonist, (ii) an attempt (A) by the protagonist to reach the goal, (iii) an outcome (O) of the attempt in terms of the goal and (iv) internal states which initiate the goal and express reactions. The scripts for the retelling version of each story (see Table 9.1, Section 2) are coded to indicate goals, attempts and outcomes as well as ISTs.

Structural complexity

Analysis of structural complexity provides information about the child's level of narrative development and allows comparison across languages. The approach taken here is grounded in clinical assessment and based on Westby's binary decision tree (Westby, 2005), illustrated in Figure 9.1, where episodes within the stories are classified into one of three levels of structural complexity: (i) sequences, where no goal statement has been generated; (ii) incomplete episodes, which include a goal statement, but lack a complete GAO (goal-attempt-outcome) structure due to omission of an attempt or outcome; and (iii) complete episodes, which include all three GAO components. The ability to produce well-formed episodes in narratives

Table 9.1 English stimulus scripts for the Cat and Dog stories

Cat	*Dog*
Pictures 1/2:	Pictures 1/2:
One day there was a *playful* cat who *saw* a yellow butterfly sitting on a bush. He *leaped forward* because he *wanted to catch it*. Meanwhile, a *cheerful* boy was coming back from fishing with a bucket and a ball in his hands. He *looked* at the cat chasing the butterfly.	One day there was a *playful* dog who *saw* a grey mouse sitting near a tree. He *leaped forward* because he *wanted to catch it*. Meanwhile, a *cheerful* boy was coming back from shopping with a bag and a balloon in his hands. He *looked* at the dog chasing the mouse.
Pictures 3/4:	Pictures 3/4:
The *butterfly flew away* quickly and the *cat fell into a bush*. He *hurt* himself and was very *angry*. The boy was so *startled* that the ball fell out of his hand. When he *saw* his ball rolling into the water, he *cried*: 'Oh no, there goes my ball'. He was *sad* and *wanted to get his ball back*. Meanwhile, the cat *noticed* the boy's bucket and *thought*: 'I *want to grab a fish*'.	The *mouse ran away* quickly and the *dog bumped into the tree*. He *hurt* himself and was very *angry*. The boy was so *startled* that the balloon slipped out of his hand. When he *saw* his balloon flying into the tree, he *cried*: 'Oh no, there goes my balloon'. He was *sad* and *wanted to get his balloon back*. Meanwhile, the dog *noticed* the boy's bag and *thought*: 'I *want to grab a sausage*'.
Pictures 5/6:	Pictures 5/6:
At the same time, the boy began *pulling his ball out of the water* with his fishing rod. He did not *notice* that the *cat was grabbing a fish*. In the end, the cat was very *pleased* to *eat such a tasty fish* and the boy was *happy* to have *his ball back*.	At the same time, the boy began *pulling his balloon out of the tree*. He did not *notice* that *the dog was grabbing a sausage*. In the end, the dog was very *pleased* to *eat such a tasty sausage* and the boy was *happy* to *have his balloon back*.

Note: Coded for *goal*, *attempt*, *outcome* and *internal state terms*.

indicates understanding of narrative schemata, causality, perspective taking, meta-awareness of the ability to plan and the need to justify plans and actions (Trabasso & Nickels, 1992; Trabasso & Rodkin, 1994). Additionally, the number of isolated goals is noted in order to provide a more fine-tuned differentiation between the various populations involved.

Internal state terms usage

Cohesive and coherent narratives presuppose awareness of others' states of mind on different levels. Story understanding involves interpreting emotions, goals and intentions of protagonists. In addition, storytellers must provide such information for the listener so that she/

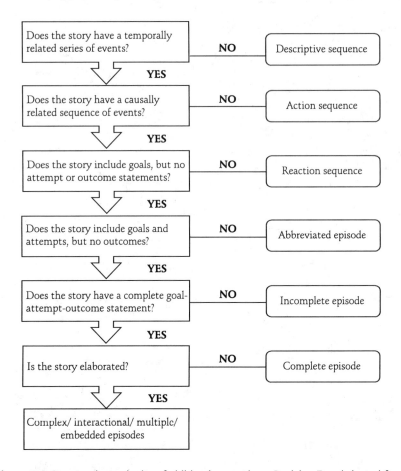

Figure 9.1 Structural complexity of children's narratives: Decision Tree (adapted from Westby, 2005)

he can follow and understand a narrative. Mental and internal states attributed to the self and others have been studied in the context of theory of mind (ToM) skills, such as intention reading, perspective taking and repair strategies in instances of communicative breakdown (Berman & Slobin, 1994; Lorusso *et al.*, 2007; Tomasello, 2003).

Analysis of internal state language in children's narratives can provide information about their metalinguistic and metacognitive knowledge as well as ToM abilities. The use of metalinguistic verbs (referring to acts of speaking, such as *shout, say*), metacognitive verbs (referring to acts of thinking, such as *think, wonder*) and words expressing emotion (e.g. *sad, angry*) can be taken as evidence of awareness of others' states of mind and as indications of cognitive processes required to interpret intentionality and of the ability to make inferences about aspects of stories (Nippold *et al.*, 2005; Westby, 2005). The use of internal state language in narratives is associated with a literate style that forms a crucial aspect of school-based discourse (Curenton & Justice, 2004; Grazzani & Ornaghi, 2012) and the development of complex syntax (Heilmann *et al.*, 2010a; Nippold *et al.*, 2005).

Taxonomies for investigating ISTs focus primarily on mental state verbs, including motivational verbs (e.g. *want, need*), experiential expressions (e.g. *see, surprised, thirsty*), belief verbs (e.g. *think, know*), verbs of saying and telling (e.g. *say, call, shout*) and emotion terms (e.g. *sad, happy, angry*) (Grazzani & Ornaghi, 2012; Greenhalgh & Strong, 2001; Westby 2005). Internal state language is assessed by LITMUS-MAIN at the macrostructure level in production as well as in comprehension, and it is interpreted as a marker of children's understanding and awareness of intentionality and goal-directed behaviour of protagonists. Since parallel lexical items were selected for all languages, ISTs should be comparable across languages. All instances of ISTs (perceptual state terms: *see, hear*; physiological state terms: *thirsty, hungry*; consciousness terms: *alive, awake*; emotion terms: *sad, happy, angry, worried, disappointed*; mental verbs: *want, think, know, forget, decide*; verbs of saying and telling [linguistic verbs]: *say, call, shout*; etc.) are calculated in the production section of the scoring form (illustrated in Appendix C) and further analysed in the comprehension section (also illustrated in Appendix C) in response to inference questions, e.g. *How do you think the cat feels?*

Comprehension

Assessing the comprehension of the main components of story structure is an important complement to storytelling and/or retelling, because some typically developing (TD) bilingual children and bilingual children with SLI might show similar profiles in production, while differing in story comprehension. Comprehension is elicited by means of questions which are asked after the production part of the assessment procedure. Ten questions were developed: three of them target the three goals (with the goal being the main macrostructure component), six target the ISTs as goals, initiating events and reactions. The tenth question (*Who does the mother goat like best ... and why?*) as well as some of the earlier questions (e.g. *Why do you think he is feeling ...?*) tap ToM, as they require the child to draw inferences from the pictures, and describe how she/he has come to a certain conclusion.

Microstructure

Microstructure elements cover a wide range of linguistic aspects including general measures of length and lexis, aspects of morphosyntax and discourse domain, and bilingual phenomena. Microstructure elements are language specific, and it is inevitable that some will differ across languages. In order to select the most relevant characteristics which might be diagnostic for (bilingual) children with SLI, we reviewed recent studies which made use of narratives elicited with picture stimuli.

It is well known that the narratives of monolingual children with SLI differ from those with typical language development in the area of morphosyntax (e.g. Reilly *et al.*, 2004), verbosity/story length (Schneider *et al.*, 2006; Strong & Shaver, 1991), topic maintenance, event sequencing, informativeness (Biddle *et al.*, 1996; Lucas, 1980; Olley, 1989; Roth & Spekman, 1986) and referencing of events and individuals. Syntactic complexity is another vulnerable area in SLI as suggested by various studies (Kit-Sum To *et al.*, 2010; Liles *et al.*, 1995). Narratives of children with and without SLI have also been found to differ concerning several productivity and complexity measures (Gillam & Johnston, 1992; Newman & McGregor, 2006). These include story length as measured in words, mean length of communication unit (c-unit, where each independent clause with its modifiers forms one c-unit [Loban, 1976]) and number of minimal terminable units (t-units, where each main clause and all the subordinate clauses attached to it form one t-unit [Hunt, 1965]), percentage of complex t-units per narrative, frequency of grammatically well-formed t-units and frequency of subordinate clauses (Gillam & Johnston, 1992).

Studies of microstructure features in the narratives of TD and SLI bilingual children which examine data in both of a child's developing languages are still relatively scant, as usually only the child's second language (L2) is studied. There are difficulties in generalising microstructural markers of SLI across languages. Morphosyntactic symptoms of SLI are discussed in other chapters of this volume, and while they can be investigated on the basis of narrative data elicited with LITMUS-MAIN, they will not be focused on in the present chapter, given their inherently language-specific nature. Therefore, a basic set of microstructure features to be analysed in LITMUS-MAIN (including productivity, variety and fluency) has been developed (see 'Transcription, Coding and Scoring' below) giving the researchers the possibility to include analyses essential for specific research interests.

LITMUS-MAIN Tasks and Stimulus Materials

Elicitation tasks: Telling (story generation) and retelling

Two narrative elicitation tasks, telling and retelling, are used to assess children's narrative abilities along a continuum of complexity. The 'telling' format is presumed to be more difficult, since the child is required to generate his/her own story without the benefit of a prior script.

Nevertheless, telling may offer the child more freedom to use his/her imagination and thus may better reflect the child's lexis. Telling formats may therefore provide more information about children's independent narrative formulation abilities than retelling (Schneider *et al.*, 2006). Telling also avoids a potential confound with retelling, as retelling performance is intertwined with story recall, verbal memory and attention (Boudreau, 2007; Dodwell & Bavin, 2008; Graybeal, 1981; Gutiérrez-Clellen, 2002).

Previous studies (Hayward *et al.*, 2007; Liles, 1993; Schneider & Dubé, 2005) have found that children with and without language impairment often provide longer, more detailed and grammatically more accurate language samples during retelling. This was, however, not confirmed by our preliminary findings, since retelling on LITMUS-MAIN did not result in more detailed or complex narratives than telling. Retelling involves reconstruction and reinterpretation of the story, and is more than just a repetition of the stimulus narrative. Retelling thus provides information about how children modify and assimilate a story's vocabulary and grammatical structures, as well as the content of the story (Gillam & Carlisle, 1997). In addition, retelling offers the researcher control over certain aspects of the narrative, e.g. length, complexity and content, and allows for error analyses and assessment of comprehension by providing a model story (Hadley, 1998; Liles, 1993). However, similar control can also be achieved for telling formats with the help of carefully constructed stimulus materials, e.g. when stories based on parallel picture sequences are elicited and their comprehension is assessed, as the content of the target narrative is then known to the researcher beforehand.

LITMUS-MAIN includes both telling and retelling in two languages, which generates four narratives for each child and allows within-subject, cross-language comparisons. However, several pilot studies (e.g. Klop *et al.*, 2011, 2012) showed carry-over effects from one task to another when children performed both telling and retelling tasks in both languages. In an attempt to minimise carry-over, a third elicitation option, a model story, was introduced. The model story option provides more contextual support than the telling task and a base for asking comprehension questions.

Development of stimulus pictures

Initially, major narrative assessment instruments which employ picture stimuli were reviewed. These included the *Renfrew Bus Story* (Glasgow & Cowley, 1994), the Test of Narrative Language (TNL; Gillam & Pearson, 2004), the Edmonton Narrative Norms Instrument (ENNI; Schneider & Hayward, 2005) and the Hamburger Verfahren zur Analyse des Sprachstands Fünfjähriger (Hamburg Procedure for the Analysis of Language Proficiency in Five-year-olds, HAVAS 5; Reich & Roth, 2004) and also the frequently used picture book *Frog Where Are You?* (Mayer,

1969). The pictorial content of these tools may not be appropriate for children from diverse cultural, linguistic and socio-economic backgrounds. Further, none of the aforementioned tools provides enough parallel pictorial stimuli to assess both languages of a bilingual child.

To overcome these shortcomings of existing assessment instruments, four six-picture sequences (see Figures 9.2 to 9.5) were developed based on 3- to 9-year-old children's linguistic and cognitive (working memory, attention) abilities. Four separate sequences were needed due to the bilingual and task requirements of the instrument, which implemented a 2×2 factorial design involving Language (L1/L2) and Task (Telling: Baby Birds story and Baby Goats story/Retelling or Model story: Cat story and Dog story).

The pictorial sequences were designed to portray clearly depicted actions. Working closely with a professional illustrator, each episode was

Episode 1: Bird Goal – to feed the baby birds
Episode 1: Bird Attempt – flies away to get food
Episode 2: Cat Goal – to get the baby bird(s)

Episode 1: Bird Outcome – returns with food
Episode 2: Cat Attempt – climbs the tree to catch a baby bird
Episode 2: Cat Outcome – catches the baby bird
Episode 3: Dog Goal – to save the baby bird(s)

Episode 3: Dog Attempt – bites, pulls the cat's tail
Episode 3: Dog Outcome – chases the cat away / the cat runs off

Figure 9.2 Baby Birds stimulus pictures (based on Hickmann, 2003)

Figure 9.3 Baby Goats stimulus pictures (based on Gülzow & Gagarina, 2007)

Figure 9.4 Cat stimulus pictures (story retelling/model story)

scripted, and careful attention was paid to the protagonists' intentions, emotions and actions, to their relative size and to the characters' facial expressions. In order to achieve comparability across narratives, we aimed for congruence across the set of scripts as well as between scripts and pictorial content by creating parallel storylines for the different sets of pictures. Details attended to included: (a) protagonists: the number of protagonists, the timing of the introduction of new protagonists, their relative position in the pictures and interaction, their size in relation to other objects and the angle from which they were looking at the other

Figure 9.5 Dog stimulus pictures (story retelling/model story)

protagonists; (b) background and foreground: these had to be contrasted and closely connected to and motivated by the actions of the main protagonists, with similar cognitive complexity and visual representation density across pictures and stories; (c) content: comparable onset, development and conclusion of the storyline. In general, the aim was to achieve parallelism across all four stories.

Content development was based on the components of story grammar, namely initiating events, character's goals, attempts to reach the goal, outcomes of the attempts and reactions following the outcomes. Instructions to the illustrator ensured that these components were explicitly portrayed in the pictures. For example, to portray the goal of the cat in the Baby Birds story, the cat's facial expression, gaze direction and movements towards the birds convey its intention to jump, while the baby birds' facial expression and gaze and the mother's protective stance portray anxiety (see Figure 9.2). The distance between the characters was designed to imply time for the protagonist's reactions. Special emphasis was put on clearly depicting the emotions of the protagonists in order to justify the use of ISTs, e.g. the baby birds' beaks are opened and their gaze is directed towards the mother to show that they are hungry.

The content of each picture sequence was designed to portray three short episodes. The rationale for portraying three episodes in each picture sequence was to provide more than one opportunity for a child to produce each story structure element targeted for macrostructure analysis. In terms of story grammar (e.g. Stein & Glenn, 1979), this affords the child three opportunities to produce initiating events, goals, attempts, outcomes and reactions.

The four picture sequences – Baby Birds and Baby Goats; Cat and Dog – are all matched for the number of main protagonists and GAO sequences; additionally, each pair of picture sequences (Baby Birds/Baby Goats and Cat/Dog) is parallel in the structure of the plot, ISTs and general actions performed by the main protagonists (see Figures 9.2 to 9.5).

In short, this story design has advantages over longer and more elaborate narrative elicitation methods in that it is carefully structured, allowing identification of the category that has been generated or retold by the child. It also has advantages over shorter narratives where only a single episode is presented.

Cultural and age appropriateness

The findings of pilot studies from 20 countries attest to the cultural robustness of the materials for eliciting veridical narrative data. These studies informed the process of continual revision over a period of two years to arrive at the final stimulus pictures in Figures 9.2 to 9.5. As the instrument targets children from 3 to 10 years, protagonists were selected that would be familiar to children from different ages across a wide variety of cultures. Birds, goats, cats and dogs are frequent in children's and child-directed speech and in fairy tales, and pretesting showed them to be easily identifiable by a wide range of children.

The number of protagonists per picture and the timing/sequence of their appearance in each story were also controlled for. For example, in the first picture in each of the four stories, only the main protagonist is presented (in Baby Birds/Baby Goats the two babies are presented additionally); in all stories, the second protagonist appears only in the second picture, where he/she/it is seen only partially in order to convey a process of 'entering' or first appearance. Furthermore, plurality was controlled across the set of stories, e.g. in the Baby Birds and Baby Goats stories, there are two baby birds and two baby goats. Finally, background details were kept to a minimum in order not to distract the child from the primary content and structure. (A detailed description of the materials development and the rationale behind can be found in Gagarina et al., 2012: Chapter 2.) In summary, the pictorial content was controlled for macrostructure, characters and their actions and feelings as well as cultural appropriateness and robustness.

In order to implement the 2×2 (language by task) design, two additional sets of pictures, e.g. Cat and Dog (see Figures 9.4. and 9.5) were generated. These also maintain the three-episode (goal-attempt-outcome) and internal state macrostructure of the Baby Birds and Baby Goats stories, but differ slightly in complexity (recall scripts for Cat and Dog story in Table 9.1).

Stimulus scripts for retelling task and comparability across languages

The stimulus scripts were designed to be comparable in terms of both macrostructure and microstructure information. Table 9.1 displays the English stimulus scripts for the two stories (Cat/Dog) designed for retelling or serving as a model story, coded for goals, attempts, outcomes and ISTs. Cross-linguistic syntactic and lexicalisation differences made it impossible to maintain all the microstructure features across languages.

Macrostructure and ISTs are identical across languages in LITMUS-MAIN, as all languages use the same stimulus pictures and score story structure components in production and comprehension in the same way (see the third section). The number and sequence of goals, attempts, outcomes and ISTs (as initiating events and as reactions) per protagonist are identical across the parallel versions of the stimulus scripts. This was done for all the languages that LITMUS-MAIN has been piloted in, so that bilingual children can be assessed in both of their languages in an identical and reliable fashion. When developing the different language versions, the microstructure in the story scripts was also designed to be as similar as possible across stories. Lists were kept of grammatical/lexical difficulties which occurred during adaptation and of important variations due to language-specific requirements. For example, for the sentence 'She flew away because she wanted to find food for them', the Russian equivalent uses the perfective verb 'fly out of the nest' and no subordinate conjunction 'because': Ona vyletela iz gnezda, čtoby najti dlja nich korm (lit.: She flew out of the nest-GEN, in order to find for them food-ACC) and the German sentence exhibits the typical word order with the final position of the verb in an infinitival clause introduced by the complementizer um 'in order to': Sie flog weg, um Futter für die Kleinen zu finden (She flew away to food-ACC for small-children-ACC find-INF).

The logical sequence of clauses/utterances was kept the same across languages and stories, as were many other linguistic features. For the full set of guidelines for adapting the story scripts to other languages, see Gagarina et al. (2012).

Narrative comprehension

The comprehension section in LITMUS-MAIN provides additional opportunities for the child to demonstrate understanding of macrostructure. Children with limited proficiency in one language may score low on the production measures but, when probed with focused questions, may demonstrate an understanding of the macrostructure elements.

Ten questions are asked for each story. Three questions elicit goal statements, e.g. *Why does the mother bird fly away?* Another six questions elicit ISTs connected either to the initiating event or to reactions, e.g. *How does the fox feel?* If the child does not provide an explanation or rationale for his/her answer, an additional question is asked, e.g. *Why do you think that the fox is feeling...?* These questions assess inference, i.e. the child's ability to interpret physical and emotional cause–effect relationships and recognise characters' goals, the reasons for these goals and reactions following attempts to reach the goals (Hedberg & Westby, 1993). Finally, the aim of the last question is to see if the child can infer meaning about the story as a whole, e.g. *Who does the mother goat like best, the fox or the bird? Why?*

Procedures

Presentation modes

The stimulus pictures are presented in fold-out fashion. Fold-out presentation was motivated in part by the results of previous studies on narratives with both TD preschoolers and preschoolers with language impairment (Gazella & Stockman, 2003; Liles, 1993). The pictures are dense in pictorial content, and the intent was to facilitate production of the three episodes in each story by presenting the pictures two at a time during both the telling and retelling tasks. Eye movement studies of children listening to stories presented orally also show evidence that children with language impairment attend to less semantically relevant information when all the pictures are presented in one go (Andreu *et al.*, 2011). Thus, it was decided to present the pictures in fold-out fashion, initially showing the whole story with all six pictures. When the child is ready to tell the story, the pictures are unfolded in pairs of two (pictures 1 and 2 unfolded; pictures 1–4 unfolded; pictures 1–6 unfolded).

To control for effects of shared knowledge and joint attention, the child chooses a story from one of three envelopes and is instructed not to let the examiner see which story is selected (Serratrice, 2007; Van der Lely, 1996). In addition, during initial viewing and telling/retelling of the story, the pictures are unfolded in such a way that only the child sees them.

An alternative mode involves presentation of the story on a computer screen with audio input via headphones, using the same procedure as described above for the paper version. On the screen, the child first sees three coloured envelopes and is asked to choose one. The child 'clicks' on his/her choice and then sees a PowerPoint presentation, with identical timing for exposure duration and transitions for all languages. The child first sees the entire set of six pictures in the middle of the screen. Then each pair of pictures is presented just like in the paper version, the only difference being that the child pushes a key on the keyboard in order to proceed to the next pair of pictures.

One unresolved difference across research groups is the size of the screen used with the computer version. The 9×9 cm size used for each picture in the paper version is difficult to maintain for the computer version due to limits in screen sizes.

Administering the telling and retelling/model story tasks

Instructions for administering the LITMUS-MAIN are provided in Appendix A for the Baby Goats story. A detailed manual with guidelines and the full set of instructions is available at http://www.zas.gwz-berlin.de/zaspil56.html.

Bilingual considerations in the procedures include the following: (i) native-speaker examiners for each language (in order to promote a monolingual context (Grosjean, 1998)), (ii) 4- to 7-day test intervals between sessions in each language in order to minimise cross-language influence as well as training and carry-over effects, and (iii) implementation of the 2×2 design with the Baby Birds/Baby Goats stories for telling and the Cat/Dog stories for retelling/model story to allow counterbalancing of language and task.

Transcription, Coding and Scoring

Transcription and scoring of macrostructure

After a session with a child has ended, his/her narrative(s) are transcribed, and production and comprehension are scored on the scoring sheets. Several transcription systems were initially considered, and CHILDES/CHAT (MacWhinney, 2000) was selected. The full set of macrostructure features assessed is given in Table 9.2. Coding is carried out manually.

The LITMUS-MAIN protocol begins with a brief set of background information concerning the child's birthdate, date of testing, age at the time of testing, gender, the name of the data collector, the language tested, length of exposure to L2, age at the time of enrolment in preschool and the

Table 9.2 Macrostructure features coded and assessed

I. Production
(A) Story structure components: goals, attempts, outcomes, goal-related and outcome-related internal state terms (initiating events and reactions)
(B) Structural complexity
(C) Internal state terms
II. Comprehension
(D) Goals, internal state terms, inferencing, theory of mind

name of the preschool (see Appendix A). This is followed by the instructions for administering the task. The scoring form is divided into two sections with the following subsections: Section I: Production (A. Story Structure; B. Structural Complexity; C. Internal State Terms [ISTs]) and Section II: Comprehension (10 questions). These are illustrated in Appendices B and C with data from a 5-year, 6-month-old English–Hebrew bilingual child doing the 'telling' task for the Baby Goats picture stimuli in his/her first language (L1; which was English). The full transcript in CHILDES format is given in Appendix B. The scoring forms for the production and comprehension of Baby Goats are provided in Appendix C. They have been filled in to illustrate how the English–Hebrew child scores on the telling task and the comprehension task.

The protocols and scoring sheets for the four parallel stories of MAIN spell out which kind of prompting to use in order to elicit natural data and avoid echoic narration.

The scoring system for the story structure components (Setting, Goals, Attempts, Outcomes, ISTs) is designed to accommodate different languages and different formulations for the same macrostructure components. The potential range of scores for story structure components is large enough so as to avoid ceiling effects, with a maximum of 17 points for story structure components in production and a maximum of 10 points in comprehension (Gagarina et al., 2012: 109–134). No weighting system is imposed for structural complexity; rather, the scoring includes a measure of how often a child produces partial event sequences (AO, single G), incomplete (GA/GO) and complete episodes (GAO).

Unexpected responses which appeared in pilot data led to revisions in scoring for story production and comprehension questions. One major goal was to make the scoring system and data evaluation user-friendly. Additional scoring and evaluation guidelines are provided in the manual (http://www.zas.gwz-berlin.de/zaspil56.html; Chapter 3). See Appendices B and C for detailed examples of the coding and scoring of macrostructure categories and ISTs.

Nothing precludes the possibility for researchers to analyse narratives elicited by LITMUS-MAIN from other microstructure perspectives, e.g. lexical richness, literary language style, tense marking, percentage of error-free clauses, percentage of content words vis-à-vis function words, use of different types of noun phrases (i.e. lexical, pronominal, clitic, null) for referent introduction and maintenance, etc.

Transcription and coding of microstructure

Based on the literature overview, the 10 features shown in Table 9.3 were chosen to serve as the initial basis for the microstructure analysis of narratives in LITMUS-MAIN.

Table 9.3 Microstructure features coded and assessed (as an initial basis recommended to be assessed for all languages)

(A) Narrative length and lexis

- Total number of word tokens with mazes (TNTm), where only those words related to the pictorial content of the story are included (extraneous material is excluded). Linguistic disfluencies (Sieff & Hooyman, 2006), also called mazes (Loban, 1976) of all four categories – hesitations, fillers, repetitions and revisions (Fiestas *et al.*, 2005) are considered in this analysis.
- Total number of word tokens without mazes (TNT). It may be informative to compare narrative length once all mazes have been detracted.
- Number of different words (NDW), where words are viewed as equivalent to lemmas or root forms.
- Number of communication units (c-units, also CU). For microstructure of oral language samples, recorded speech must be segmented into one base unit. Options included: utterances (MacWhinney, 2000), t-units (=minimally terminable units; Hunt, 1965) and c-units (=communication units [CUs]; Loban 1976). The c-unit was chosen as the base unit to allow for straightforward comparison of results between research groups.

(B) Syntactic complexity and discourse cohesion

- Mean length of c-units (calculated as the number of CUs divided by TNT).
- Mean length of the three longest c-units (calculated as the three longest CUs divided by TNT).
- Proportion of verb-based clauses (calculated as percentage of the total number of verb-based clauses out of CUs).
- Proportion of subordinating constructions (calculated as percentage of subordinate constructions out of CUs).
- Proportion of coordinating constructions, excluding the conjunction *and* (calculated as percentage of coordinating constructions out of CUs), if *and* is used as an (repeated) additive cohesion marker (like in Appendix B, lines 4, 5, 7, etc.: *And then somebody came ... And then he wanted to eat him ... And then the mom was want to drink ...*). This type of use should not be confused with *and* as a coordinating conjunction (e.g. *The mother bird flew away and came back with a worm*).

(C) Bilingualism

- Number and percentage of word tokens *not* in the target language of a session (code-switching).

Background questions

In addition to the narrative assessment tool, a set of background questions was developed (based on Gagarina *et al.*, 2010) in order to evaluate the acquisition conditions and the quality and quantity of the input to the child in both of her/his languages. The background questions can be used as a questionnaire to be filled in by the parents and/or the preschool/schoolteacher, on their own or with the help of an experimenter, if desired. They can also serve as a base for a (telephone) interview with parents and/or day-care staff.

Preliminary Findings

During the COST Action IS0804, different research groups conducted pilot studies based on the picture sequences and procedures described above, investigating macrostructure in the narratives of monolingual and bilingual children with and without language impairment. This was done for different languages and age groups. Members reported the results of their pilot studies at COST meetings and workshops and in online discussions. This information was used to inform the development and refinement of the LITMUS-MAIN materials.

During 2011–2012, narratives were collected from 267 monolingual and 302 bilingual children aged 43–109 months (i.e. 3;6–9;1 years). These included 185 monolingual TD and 82 monolingual SLI children, 285 bilingual TD and 17 bilingual SLI children. Seventeen languages were represented (Afrikaans, Albanian, Croatian, Cypriot Greek, Dutch, English, Finnish, French, German, Greek, Hebrew, Italian, Lithuanian, Russian, Polish, Swedish, Turkish). For the bilingual children, who told the stories in their two languages, 14 different language pairs were represented, as illustrated in Table 9.4. Slightly over half the children performed both telling and retelling tasks; the rest did telling only, and a few children did the 'model story' and telling.

Four categories of macrostructure data were assessed: Story structure (including setting, goal, attempt, outcome, ISTs as initiating events and as reactions), structural complexity, ISTs and story comprehension. Only preliminary trends from these pilot studies are reported here.

First, in the narratives of both monolingual TD and bilingual TD children, story structure components in production increase as a function of age, e.g. from scores of 4–5 points (out of 17) at 65 months to 9–10 points at 109 months.

Second, for monolinguals with SLI, children from four out of six groups show substantially lower story structure scores than their TD peers. Story complexity (i.e. production of full GAO episodes) proved to be generally low for most children, but still lower for children with SLI as compared to TD children. This measure did in fact differentiate TD and SLI children for some languages (cf. Skerra et al., 2013 for German). ISTs in the narratives of SLI children were less frequent than for their TD peers.

Third, bilingual children score similarly to monolingual peers, and TD bilingual children score equally high on story structure in both their languages even when parents report one of the child's languages to be weaker than the other. This preliminary finding is particularly important,

Table 9.4(a) Monolingual children: Languages, number of children (in order of increasing mean age)

Language	No. of children	Mean age in months
Monolingual TD children		
Afrikaans	28	65
Lithuanian	12	65
Turkish	15	65
Finnish	21	66.8
Russian	15	68
German	10	68.1
Greek	5	73
Albanian	10	78.3
Croatian	20	78.6
Albanian	14	78.8
Cypriot Greek	6	79.8
Swedish	9	80.9
French	12	81.9
French	8	82
Monolingual SLI children[1]		
German	18	61.5
Lithuanian	8	65
Russian	9	68
Croatian	20	77.8
Greek	18	100.6
Afrikaans	9	106
Total	Number 267	Mean age 75.5

[1]Exclusionary criteria: History of hearing, neurological or developmental problems.

since it may show that the instrument is less biased against bilingual children than norm-referenced language assessment tools. Similar story structure scores in both languages also provide support for the view that abilities at the macrostructure level, i.e. composition of cohesive event sequences, reflect capacities which go beyond the specifics of one language (Berman & Slobin, 1994; Fiestas & Peña, 2004; Pearson, 2002; see introductory section of this chapter). The analysis of the narratives' microstructure, which is highly language specific, will be the next step in the development of the instrument and should be performed initially on a single language level before cross-linguistic comparisons are carried out.

Fourth, the TD bilingual children in these pilot studies score similarly on story comprehension to monolinguals, with a range from 2.5 points

Table 9.4(b) Bilingual children: Language pairs, number of children (in order of increasing mean age)

L2	L1	No. of children	Mean age in months
Bilingual typically developing children			
German	Turkish	6	43.6
Swedish	Russian	10	64
Finnish	Swedish	10	65
German	Turkish	15	65
Lithuanian	Russian	6	65.3
Italian	English	13	66
German	Russian	10	66.9
English	Hebrew	9	67.3
Finnish	Russian	10	68.2
Hebrew	English	21	70.1
Swedish	English	20	77
Afrikaans	English	10	78
German	Turkish	7	78
Greek	Albanian	6	78
Italian	English	25	78
English	Polish	12	78.5
Afrikaans	English	20	79
Swedish	English	16	81
Swedish	French	21	82
Dutch	Turkish	6	94.3
Afrikaans	English	19	103
German	Russian	22	109
Bilingual SLI children[1]			
Swedish	Russian	5	66
Greek	Albanian/German/ Bulgarian/French/Romanian	12	111.3
Total		Number 302	Mean age 76.4

[1]Exclusionary criteria: History of hearing, neurological or developmental problems.

for the very young (at 43.6 months) to 8–9 points (out of 10) for older children. TD bilingual children who produce few macrostructure components often still show evidence of good story comprehension.

And finally, bilingual children score very similarly on story comprehension in both their languages, even when one language is reported by parents to be weaker than the other. For 10 out of the 14 bilingual groups in the data, story comprehension scores differed at most 1 point between L1 and L2. If upheld more generally, this may suggest that story comprehension as well as some components of story macrostructure are probably not language specific, but rather language universal.

Summary and Conclusion

LITMUS-MAIN was developed within COST Action IS0804 as a tool for the evaluation of narrative abilities of bilingual children across languages. The story grammar model served as a theoretical framework to create materials for the assessment of narratives in both languages of bilingual children across cultures. These materials can also be used for screening and identification of bilingual children at risk for SLI. Two sets of parallel picture sequences and accompanying story scripts that are controlled for macro- and microstructural features were developed, as well as guidelines for implementation and protocols for administering and scoring. Materials development was informed by the experience gathered while pilot versions of the assessment tool were tested in more than 20 countries, with children speaking 17 different languages and 14 different language pairs. LITMUS-MAIN is currently available in 26 languages (http://www.zas.gwz-berlin.de/zaspil56.html).

The design of LITMUS-MAIN allows for the elicitation of narratives in three modes: (i) telling (story generation), (ii) retelling and (iii) telling after listening to a model story. A set of comprehension questions which focus on macrostructure components and ISTs also forms part of the assessment procedure.

The instrument can be used to collect data from bilingual children with and without language impairment for a variety of languages and language combinations. This allows for cross-linguistic comparisons and the development of theoretical perspectives. LITMUS-MAIN also provides clinicians with a diagnostic tool to guide and inform intervention in children with language impairment.

Acknowledgement

This work was supported in part by Bundesministerium für Bildung und Forschung (BMBF) (Grant No. 01UG0711), COST Action IS0804, Israel Science Foundation and the Academy of Finland. The authors are grateful to Katrin Reichenbach for assistance in the technical preparation of this chapter.

References

Andreu, L., Sanz-Torrent, M., Guàrdia Olmos, J. and MacWhinney, B. (2011) Narrative comprehension and production in children with SLI: An eye movement study. *Clinical Linguistics and Phonetics* 25 (9), 767–783.

Berman, R.A. and Slobin, D.I. (1994) Narrative structure. In R.A. Berman and D.I. Slobin (eds) *Relating Events in Narrative: A Cross-Linguistic Developmental Study* (pp. 39–84). New York/London: Psychology Press.

Biddle, K.A., McCabe, A. and Bliss, L. (1996) Narrative skills following traumatic brain injury in children and adults. *Journal of Communication Disorders* 29 (6), 447–469.

Bishop, D.V.M. and Edmundson, A. (1987) Language impaired 4-year olds: Transient from persistent impairment. *Journal of Speech and Hearing Disorders* 52 (2), 156–173.

Bliss, L., McCabe, A. and Miranda, E. (1998) Narrative assessment profile: Discourse analysis for school-age children. *Journal of Communication Disorders* 31 (4), 347–363.

Botting, N. (2002) Narrative as a tool for the assessment of linguistic and pragmatic impairments. *Child Language Teaching and Therapy* 18 (1), 1–21.

Boudreau, D.M. (2007) Narrative abilities in children with language impairments. In R. Paul (ed.) *Language Disorders From a Developmental Perspective: Essays in Honour of Robin S. Chapman* (pp. 331–356). Mahwah, NJ: Lawrence Erlbaum Associates.

Bruner, J. (1986) *Actual Minds, Possible Worlds*. Cambridge, MA: Harvard University Press.

Cleave, P.L., Girolametto, L.E., Chen, X. and Johnson, C.J. (2010) Narrative abilities in monolingual and dual language learning children with specific language impairment. *Journal of Communication Disorders* 43 (6), 511–522.

Curenton, S.M. and Justice, L.M. (2004) Use of literate language features in low-income preschoolers' narratives. Paper presented at the Head Start 7th National Research Conference, Washington, DC.

Dodwell, K. and Bavin, E.L. (2008) Children with specific language impairment: An investigation of their narratives and memory. *International Journal of Language and Communication Disorders* 43 (2), 201–218.

Fiestas, C.E. and Peña, E.D. (2004) Narrative discourse in bilingual children: Language and task effects. *Language, Speech, and Hearing Services in Schools* 35 (2), 155–168.

Fiestas, Ch.E., Bedore, L.M., Peña, E.D. and Nagy, V.J. (2005) Use of mazes in the narrative language samples of bilingual and monolingual 4- to 7-year old children. In J. Cohen, K.T. McAlister, K. Rolstad and J. MacSwan (eds) *Proceedings of the 4th International Symposium on Bilingualism* (pp. 730–740). Somerville, MA: Cascadilla Press.

Gagarina, N., Klassert, A. and Topaj, N. (2010) Russian language proficiency test for multilingual children. *ZAS Papers in Linguistics* 54 - special issue. Berlin: ZAS.

Gagarina, N., Klop, D., Kunnari, S., Tantele, K., Välimaa, T., Balčiūnienė, I., Bohnacker, U. and Walters, J. (2012) MAIN: Multilingual assessment instrument for narratives. *ZAS Papers in Linguistics* 56 (includes manual and MAIN materials for assessment). See http://www.zas.gwz-berlin.de/zaspil56.html

Gazella, J. and Stockman, I.J. (2003) Children's story retelling under different modality and task conditions: Implications for standardizing language sampling procedures. *American Journal of Speech-Language Pathology* 12 (1), 61–72.

Gillam, R.B. and Johnston, J.R. (1992) Spoken and written language relationships in language/learning-impaired and normally achieving school-age children. *Journal of Speech and Hearing Research* 35 (6), 1303–1315.

Gillam, R.B. and Carlisle, R. (1997) Oral reading and story retelling of students with specific language impairment. *Language, Speech, and Hearing Services in Schools* 28 (1), 30–42.

Gillam, R.B. and Pearson, N.A. (2004) *Test of Narrative Language (TNL)*. Austin, TX: PRO-ED.

Glasgow, C. and Cowley, J. (1994) *Renfrew Bus Story – North American Edition (RBS-NA)*. Centerville, DE: Centerville School.

Graybeal, C.M. (1981) Memory for stories in language-impaired children. *Applied Psycholinguistics* 2 (3), 269–283.

Grazzani, I. and Ornaghi, V. (2012) How do use and comprehension of mental-state language relate to theory of mind in middle childhood? *Cognitive Development* 27, 99–11.

Greenhalgh, K.S. and Strong, C.J. (2001) Literate language features in spoken narratives of children with typical language and children with language impairments. *Language, Speech, and Hearing Services in Schools* 32, 114–125.

Grosjean, F. (1998) Transfer and language mode. *Bilingualism: Language and Cognition* 1 (3), 175–176.

Gülzow, I. and Gagarina, N. (2007) Noun phrases, pronouns and anaphoric reference in young children narratives. *ZAS Papers in Linguistics* 48, 203–223.

Gutiérrez-Clellen, V.F. (2002) Narratives in two languages: Assessing performance of bilingual children. *Linguistics and Education* 13 (2), 175–197.

Gutiérrez-Clellen, V., Simon-Cereijido, G. and Wagner, C. (2008) Bilingual children with language impairment: A comparison with monolinguals and second language learners. *Applied Psycholinguistics* 29 (1), 3–20.

Gutiérrez-Clellen, V.F., Simon-Cereijido, G. and Erickson Leone, A. (2009) Code-switching in bilingual children with specific language impairment. *International Journal of Bilingualism* 13 (1), 91–109.

Hadley, P.A. (1998) Language sampling protocols for eliciting text-level discourse. *Language, Speech, and Hearing Services in Schools* 29, 132–147.

Hayward, D. and Schneider, P. (2000) Effectiveness of teaching story grammar knowledge to preschool children with language impairment. An exploratory study. *Child Language Teaching and Therapy* 16 (3), 255–284.

Hayward, D.V., Gillam, R.B. and Lien, P. (2007) Retelling a script-based story: Do children with and without language impairments focus on script and story elements? *American Journal of Speech-Language Pathology* 16 (3), 235–245.

Hedberg, N.L. and Westby, C.E. (1993) *Analyzing Storytelling Skills. Theory to Practice*. Tucson, AZ: Communication Skill Builders.

Heilmann, J., Miller, J.F. and Nockerts, A. (2010a) Sensitivity of narrative organization measures using narrative retells produced by young school-age children. *Language Testing* 27 (4), 603–626.

Heilmann, J., Miller, J.F., Nockerts, A. and Dunaway, C. (2010b) Properties of the narrative scoring scheme using narrative retells in young school-age children. *American Journal of Speech-Language Pathology* 19 (2), 154–166.

Hickmann, M. (2003) *Children's Discourse: Person, Space and Time Across Languages*. Cambridge: Cambridge University Press.

Hughes, D., McGillvray, L. and Schmidek, M. (1997) *Guide to Narrative Language: Procedures for Assessments*. Eau Claire, WI: Thinking Publications.

Hunt, K. (1965) *Grammatical Structures Written at Three Grade Levels*. NCTE Research report No. 3. Champaign, IL: National Council of Teachers of English.

Iluz-Cohen, P. and Walters, J. (2012) Telling stories in two languages: Narratives of bilingual preschool children with typical and impaired language. *Bilingualism: Language and Cognition* 15 (1), 58–74.

Kaderavek, J.N. and Sulzby, E. (2000) Narrative production by children with and without specific language impairment: Oral narratives and emergent readings. *Journal of Speech, Language, and Hearing Research* 43 (1), 34–49.

Kit-Sum To, C., Stokes, S.F., Cheung, H. and T'sou, B. (2010) Narrative assessment for Cantonese-speaking children. *Journal of Speech, Language and Hearing Research* 52 (3), 648–669.

Klop, D., Visser, M. and Oosthuizen, H. (2011) Narratives in bilingual South African children. Paper presented at 4th Meeting of COST Action IS0804, Eskişehir, Turkey.

Klop, D., Visser, M. and Oosthuizen, H. (2012) Narrative profiles of 20 bilingual normally developing 6–7 year old South African children. Paper presented at 6th Meeting of COST Action IS0804, Berlin, Germany.

Labov, W. and Waletzky, J. (1967) Narrative analysis. In J. Helm (ed.) *Essays on the Verbal and Visual Arts* (pp. 12–44). Seattle, WA: University of Washington Press.

Liles, B.Z. (1993) Narrative discourse in children with language disorders and children with normal language: A critical review of the literature. *Journal of Speech and Hearing Research* 36 (5), 868–882.

Liles, B.Z., Duffy, R.J., Merritt, D.D. and Purcell, S.L. (1995) Measurement of narrative discourse ability in children with language disorders. *Journal of Speech and Hearing Research* 38, 415–425.

Loban, W. (1976) *Language Development: Kindergarten Through Grade Twelve*. Urbana, IL: National Council of Teachers of English.

Lorusso, M.L., Galli, R., Libera, L., Gagliardi, C., Borgatti, R. and Hollebrandse, B. (2007) Indicators of theory of mind in narrative production: A comparison between individuals with genetic syndromes and typically developing children. *Clinical Linguistics and Phonetics* 21 (1), 37–53.

Lucas, E.V. (1980) *Semantic and Pragmatic Language Disorders*. Rockville, MD: Aspen.

MacWhinney, B. (2000) *The CHILDES Project: Tools for Analyzing Talk* (3rd edn). Mahwah, NJ: Lawrence Erlbaum Associates.

Mandler, G. and Johnson, N. (1977) Remembrance of things parsed: Story structure and recall. *Cognitive Psychology* 9 (1), 111–151.

Mayer, M. (1969) *Frog, Where Are You?* New York: Dial Books.

McCabe, A. (1996) Evaluating narrative discourse skills. In K. Cole, P. Dale and D. Thal (eds) *Assessment of Communication and Language* (pp. 121–142). Baltimore, MD: Paul H. Brookes.

McCabe, A. and Rollins, P.R. (1994) Assessment of preschool narrative skills. *American Journal of Speech-Language Pathology* 3, 45–56.

Newman, R.M. and McGregor, K.K. (2006) Teachers and laypersons discern quality differences between narratives produced by children with and without SLI. *Journal of Speech Language and Hearing Research* 49 (5), 1022–1036.

Nippold, M.A., Ward-Lonergan, J.M. and Fanning, J.L. (2005) Persuasive writing in children, adolescents, and adults: A study of syntactic, semantic, and pragmatic development. *Language, Speech, and Hearing Services in Schools* 36 (2), 125–138.

Oakhill, J. and Cain, K. (2007) Issues of causality in children's reading comprehension. In D. McNamara (ed.) *Reading Comprehension Strategies: Theories, Interventions, and Technologies* (pp. 47–72). New York: Erlbaum.

Olley, L. (1989) Oral narrative performance of normal and language impaired school aged children. *Australian Journal of Human Communication Disorders* 17 (1), 43–65.

Paradis, J., Genesee, F. and Crago, M. (2011) *Dual Language Development and Disorders: A Handbook on Bilingualism and Second Language Learning* (2nd edn). Baltimore, MD: Paul H. Brookes.

Pearson, B.Z. (2001) Language and mind in the stories of bilingual children. In L. Verhoeven and S. Strömqvist (eds) *Narrative Development in Multilingual Contexts* (pp. 373–398). Amsterdam: John Benjamins.

Pearson, B.Z. (2002) Bilingual infants: What we know, what we need to know. In M. Suarez-Orozco and M. Paéz (eds) *Latinos: Remarking America* (pp. 306–320). Berkeley, CA: University of California Press.

Pearson, B.Z. and de Villiers, P.A. (eds) (2005) *Encyclopedia of Language and Linguistics* (2nd edn). Oxford: Elsevier.

Reich, H.H. and Roth, H.-J. (2004) *Hamburger Verfahren zur Analyse des Sprachstands Fünfjähriger – HAVAS 5.* Landesinstitut für Lehrerbildung und Schulentwicklung Hamburg.

Reilly, J., Losh, M., Bellugi, U. and Wulfeck, B. (2004) "Frog, where are you?" Narratives in children with specific language impairment, early focal brain injury, and Williams syndrome. *Brain and Language* 88 (2), 229–247.

Roth, F.P. and Spekman, N.J. (1986) Narrative discourse: Spontaneously generated stories of learning-disabled and normally achieving students. *Journal of Speech and Hearing Disorders* 51 (1), 8–23.

Schneider, P. and Dubé, R.V. (2005) Story presentation effects on children's retell content. *American Journal of Speech-Language Pathology* 14 (1), 52–60.

Schneider, P., Dubé, R.V. and Hayward, D. (2005) The Edmonton Narrative Norms Instrument. See http://www.rehabresearch.ualberta.ca/enni. (accessed 12 December 2014)

Schneider, P., Hayward, D. and Dubé, R.V. (2006) Storytelling from pictures using the Edmonton Narrative Norms Instrument. *Journal of Speech Pathology and Audiology* 30 (4), 224–238.

Serratrice, L. (2007) Referential cohesion in the narratives of bilingual English–Italian children and monolingual peers. *Journal of Pragmatics* 39 (6), 1058–1087.

Sieff, S. and Hooyman, B. (2006) Language-based disfluency: A child case study. Hearing Association Annual Convention, Miami, FL.

Simon-Cereijido, G. and Gutiérrez-Clellen, V. (2009) A cross-linguistic and bilingual evaluation of the interdependence between lexical and grammatical domains. *Applied Psycholinguistics* 30 (2), 315–337.

Skerra, A., Adani, F. and Gagarina, N. (2013) Diskurskohäsive Mittel in Erzählungen als diagnostischer Marker für Sprachentwicklungsstörungen. In T. Fritzsche, C.B. Meyer, A. Adelt and J. Roß (eds) *Spektrum Patholinguistik 6* (pp. 123–154). Potsdam: Universitätsverlag Potsdam.

Stein, N.L. and Glenn, C.G. (1979) An analysis of story comprehension in elementary school children. In R. Freedle (ed.) *Discourse Processing: Multidisciplinary Perspectives* (pp. 53–120). Norwood, NJ: Ablex.

Strong, C.J. and Shaver, J.P. (1991) Stability of cohesion in the spoken narratives of language-impaired and normally developing school-aged children. *Journal of Speech and Hearing Research* 34 (1), 95–111.

Swanson, L., Fey, M., Mills, C. and Hood, L. (2005) Use of narrative-based language intervention with children who have specific language impairment. *American Journal of Speech-Language Pathology* 14 (2), 131–143.

Tomasello, M. (2003) *Constructing a Language: A Usage-Based Theory of Language Acquisition.* Cambridge, MA: Harvard University Press.

Trabasso, T. and Nickels, M. (1992) The development of goal plans of action in the narration of a picture story. *Discourse Processes* 15 (3), 249–275.

Trabasso, T. and Rodkin, P.C. (1994) Knowledge of goals/plans: A conceptual basis for narrating "Frog where are you?". In R.A. Berman and D.I. Slobin (eds) *Relating Events in Narrative: A Cross-Linguistic Developmental Study* (pp. 85–106). Mahwah, NJ: Lawrence Erlbaum Associates.

Uccelli, P. and Paéz, M. (2007) Narrative and vocabulary development of bilingual children from kindergarten to first grade: Developmental changes and associations among English and Spanish skills. *Language, Speech, and Hearing Services in Schools* 38 (3), 225–236.

Van der Lely, H.K.J. (1996) Grammatical specific language impaired children: Evidence for modularity. In C. Koster and F. Wijnen (eds) *The Groningen Assembly on Language Acquisition* (pp. 273–282). Groningen: University of Groningen Press.

Walach, G.P. (2008) *Language Intervention for School-Age Students: Setting Goals for Academic Success*. St. Louis, MO: Mosby.

Westby, C.E. (1991) Assessing and remediating text comprehension problems. In A. Kamhi and H. Catts (eds) *Reading Disabilities: A Developmental Language Perspective* (pp. 199–260). Boston, MA: Allyn & Bacon.

Westby, C.E. (2005) Assessing and facilitating text comprehension problems. In H. Catts and A. Kamhi (eds) *Language and Reading Disabilities* (pp. 199–259). Boston, MA: Allyn & Bacon.

Appendix A: Instructions for Administering Main, Baby Goats Story (Telling)

(For detailed guidelines and instructions, see Gagarina *et al.*, 2012)

Protocol for Baby Goats (Telling)

Name of child: _____

Date of birth: _____

Date of testing: _____

Age of testing (in months): _____

Gender: _____

Name of examiner: _____

Exposure to L2 (in months): _____

Kindergarten entry date: _____

Name of kindergarten: _____

Be sure that all the envelopes are on the table before testing begins.

Prepare the audio recorder in order to record the session. Begin recording before warming up.

Warming-up

Ask for example: Who is your best friend? What do you like to watch on TV? Do you like telling stories? Do you like listening to stories?

Instructions:

Sit opposite the child. Say to the child: Look, here are three envelopes. There is a different story in each envelope. Choose one and then you can tell me a story. *Unfold the pictures so that the whole sequence is visible to the child only.* First look at the whole story. Are you ready?

Unfold the first two pictures. Say to the child: Now I want you to tell the story. Look at the pictures and try to tell the best story you can. *Allowable prompt if the child is reluctant to begin:* 'Tell me a story about this picture' *(point to picture). When the child has finished telling the first two pictures, unfold the next (so that all pictures from 1 to 4 are visible). Repeat the process until the end of the story. Allowable prompts if the child is silent in the middle of the story:* 'Anything else?', 'Continue', 'Tell me more', 'Let's see what else is in the story'. *If the child stops talking without indicating that he/she has finished, say:* 'Tell me when you are finished'.

When the child has finished, praise the child and then ask the comprehension questions.

Appendix B: An Example of a Transcript of the Baby Goats Story Told by an English–Hebrew Bilingual Child Age 5 Years 6 Months

(1)   *CHI: The mom wants to get the baby.

(2)   *CHI: And (be)cause he fell inside the water.

(3)   *CHI: He wanted to drink.

(4)   *CHI: And then somebody came.

(5)   *CHI: And then he wanted to eat him.

(6)   *CHI: Then he got his foot.

(7)   *CHI: And then the mom was want to drink.

(8)   *CHI: And then saw the baby was drinking.

(9)   *CHI: And the bird he &he said that.

(10) *CHI: The bird bited his tail.

(11) *CHI: And then and they saw it.

(12) *CHI: And then they saw the bird and biting his tail.

(13) *CHI: And then saw the mom.

(14) *CHI: And then saw the baby.

Appendix C: Scoring Protocol For Baby Goats Story

The narrative provided in Appendix B is scored here to provide an example of how the scoring is done.

Section I: Production

A. Story Structure; B. Structural complexity; C. Internal State Terms (IST)

A. Story Structure			
	Examples of correct responses[1]	Score	Comments[2]
A1. Setting	Time and/or place reference, e.g. once upon a time/one day/long ago... In a forest/in a meadow/at the lake/at the pond...	0 1 2[3]	
Episode 1: Mother/Goat (episode characters: baby goat and mother/goat)			
A2. IST as initiating event	**Baby goat** was scared/in danger/ drowning/needed help/cried/called the mother **<Mother/Goat etc.>** saw that baby goat was scared/in danger/drowning/ couldn't swim/was worried about the baby goat in the water	0 1	
A3. Goal	**Mother goat** wanted to help the baby/ to save/rescue the baby/to push the baby out of the water	0 1	*1 point 'wants to get the baby'*
A4. Attempt	**Mother goat** ran/went into the water/ is pushing	0 1	
A5. Outcome	**Mother goat** pushed the baby out of the water/saved/rescued the baby **Baby goat** was saved/out of the water	0 1	
A6. IST as reaction	**Mother goat** was happy/relieved **Baby goat** was relieved/satisfied/ happy/glad/not scared any more	0 1	
Episode 2: Fox (episode characters: fox and baby goat)			
A7. IST as initiating event	**Fox** saw mother looking away/saw that the baby was alone/saw that there was food/fox was hungry	0 1	
A8. Goal	**Fox** wanted to eat/catch/kill the baby goat	0 1	*1 point 'wanted to eat him'*
A9. Attempt	**Fox** jumped towards/jumped up/ jumped out/tried to reach/grab/catch the baby goat	0 1	

A10.	Outcome	**Fox** got/grabbed/caught the baby goat	0	1	*1 point 'got his foot'*
A11.	IST as reaction	**Fox** was happy **Baby** goat was scared	0	1	

Episode 3: Bird (episode characters: bird, fox and baby goat)

A12.	IST as initiating event	**Bird** saw that the goat was in danger **Baby goat** was in danger	0	1	
A13.	Goal	**Bird** decided/wanted to stop the fox / help/protect/save the baby goat	0	1	
A14.	Attempt	**Bird** bit/dragged the fox's tail/ attacked/chased the fox	0	1	*1 point 'bited his tail'*
A15.	Outcome	**Bird** chased the fox away **Fox** let go of the baby goat/ran away **Baby goat** was saved / rescued	0	1	
A16.	IST as reaction	**Bird** was relieved/happy/proud to have saved / rescued the baby goat/ **Fox** was angry/disappointed **Baby goat/goats** was/were relieved/ happy/safe	0	1	
A17.		**Total score out of 17:**			*4 out of 17*

[1] If in doubt or the response of the child is not on this scoring sheet consult the manual.
[2] Write down responses here or indicate No response.
[3] Zero points for wrong or no response, 1 point for one correct response, 2 points for reference to both *time* and *place*.

B. Structural complexity

(Note that this results from subsection A.)

Number of AO sequences	Number of single G (without A or O)	Number of GA/GO sequences	Number of GAO sequences
B1.	B2.	B3.	B4.
(0)	(1)	(1)	(0)

C. Internal State Terms (IST)

C1.	Total number of IST in **tokens**. IST include:	10
	Perceptual state terms, e.g. *see, hear, feel, smell*;	*(want, wanted,*
	Physiological state terms, e.g. *thirsty, hungry, tired, sore*;	*wanted, want,*
	Consciousness terms, e.g. *alive, awake, asleep*;	*saw, said, saw,*
	Emotion terms, e.g. *sad, happy, angry, worried, disappointed*;	*saw, saw, saw)*
	Mental verbs, e.g. *want, think, know, forget, decide, believe, wonder, have/make a plan*;	
	Linguistic verbs/verbs of saying/telling, e.g. *say, call, shout, warn, ask*	

Section II: Comprehension

The right-hand column shows how the child from Appendices B and C responded to the comprehension questions and how these were scored. (Question D10 was not asked.)

	Examples of correct responses	Examples of wrong responses	Score	Comments
0	Did you like the story?	Warm-up question, not scored		
D1.	Why was the mother goat in the water? (point to pictures 1–2) (Episode 1: Goal/IST as initiating event)	Wants to save/to help/rescue/ worried about the baby/the baby goat is in danger/ drowning/scared/ the baby was crying for help	Is swimming/ playing/ wants to take a bath/to wash herself/to wash the baby goat	0 1	To get the baby (1 point)
D2.	How does the baby goat feel? (point to baby goat in the water, picture 1) (IST as initiating event)	Bad/scared/in danger/horrified	Good/fine/ happy/ playing/freezing/ cold/hungry/thirsty/dirty/ clean/stupid/refreshed	0 1	Sad (1 point)
D3.	(only ask D3 if the child gives a correct response without explanation/rationale in D2. If a correct explanation is provided in D2, then give a point in D3 and proceed to D4) Why do you think that the baby goat is feeling bad/scared/in danger etc.?[74]	Because he has fallen into the water/is not able to get out of the water/is drowning/ cannot swim	Because he is hungry/ swimming/ playing in the water/ wasn't allowed to stand there	0 1	(Be)cause he's stuck inside the water (1 point)

D4.	Why does the fox leap forward? (point to picture 3) (Episode 2: Goal)	Wants/to get/to kill/to eat the baby goat/couldn't resist to eat the baby goat/ takes the opportunity when mother is not looking/is far away	To play with the baby goat	0 1	(Be)cause he wants to eat him (1 point)
D5.	How does the fox feel? (point to picture 5-6) (IST as reaction)	Bad/sad/angry/ mad/scared/still hungry/hurt/ stupid/disappointed	Good/fine/happy/ playful	0 1	Hungry (1 point)
D6.	(only ask D6 if the child gives a correct response without explanation/ rationale in D5. If a correct explanation is provided in D5, then give a point in D6 and proceed to D7) Why do you think that the fox is feeling bad/scared/hungry/ disappointed etc.?[5]	Because he did not get the baby goat/he was still hungry/ afraid/scared of the bird/the bird was biting/ chasing him	Because the bird saw that the goat was in danger/ the fox is running away/I don't know	0 1	
D7.	Why does the bird bite the fox's tail? (point to picture 5) (Episode 3: Goal)	Wants/decided to save/rescue the baby goat/wants to stop the fox/to make the fox let the goat go/saw that the goat was in danger	Wants to eat the fox/eat the goat/ play with the fox	0 1	(Be)cause he didn't want the fox to eat the baby (1 point)
D8.	Imagine that the bird sees the goats. How does the bird feel? (point to picture 6)	Good/fine/happy/ relieved/ satisfied/ proud/like a hero	Bad/sad/angry/mad/ sorry/stupid/"I have to get the fox"	0 1	Hm, sad (0 points)

(Continued)

	Examples of correct responses	Examples of wrong responses	Score	Comments
D9.	Because he stopped the fox/got the fox out of there/ saved/rescued the goat/sees that the goats are happy/ unharmed/now the fox won't come back	Because he is smiling/ angry at the fox/wants to eat the baby goat himself	0 1	(Be)cause he wanted to; (be)cause he took his foot (0 points)
(only ask D9 if the child gives a correct response without explanation/rationale in D8. If a correct explanation is provided in D8, then give a point in D9 and proceed to D10)				
Why do you think that the bird is feeling good/fine/happy etc.?[76]				
D10.	The bird – give at least one reason (he saved/helped the baby goat/ chased the fox away)	The fox/I don't know / other irrelevant answer	0 1	This question was not asked
Who does the mother goat like best, the fox or the bird? Why?				
D11.	**Total score out of 10:**			6 out of 10

[4]Use the same IST provided by the child in response to D2.
[5]Use the same IST provided by the child in response to D5.
[6]Use the same IST provided by the child in response to D8.

10 Executive Functions in the Assessment of Bilingual Children with Language Impairment

Kristine Jensen de Lopéz and
Anne E. Baker

Introduction

Why might executive functions (EFs) be important tools for the assessment of bilingual children with specific language impairment (SLI), that is children whose main impairment is in language? Until recently, children with SLI have been described primarily in terms of their linguistic profile. Relatively few studies have also addressed the relationship between the children's language profile and their cognitive profile other than looking at non-verbal IQ. In the discussion on the cause of SLI there is currently debate as to whether the impairment should exclusively or primarily be attributed to maturation deficits, to limited processing capacities or more recently to limited executive functioning. When integrating the notion of executive functioning as a potential predictor of SLI, it is important to also take into account the increasing literature showing that bilinguals are enhanced in certain areas of their executive functioning compared to monolinguals (Bialystok, 2011). From a theoretical perspective, Peets and Bialystok (2010) suggest that for bilingual children with SLI these executive functioning advantages might compensate for some of the challenges the children experience because they learn two language systems and lexicons in parallel. Executive functioning is necessary in order to coordinate, plan, monitor and execute cognitive activities such as language and in many ways it relies on experience. This perspective makes it important to consider the development of EFs in considering SLI.

A comparison of the executive functioning of bilingual children with SLI with monolingual children with SLI and in turn with monolingual and bilingual typically developing (TD) children should shed light upon the influence of (1) bilingualism and (2) SLI on the developmental trajectories of these groups of children. We expect any variance seen in the executive functioning of bilingual and monolingual children with SLI to mirror itself in the severity of their language impairment (LI), while differences might present themselves across the two language groups with bilingual children being equally or less impaired than the monolingual children. With such information it might also be possible to identify a particular relationship between SLI and executive functioning independent of bilingualism. This relationship might then support the development of more stringent methods for diagnosing bilingual children with SLI as a separate group. Results from executive functioning could then function as a screening tool that could be used complementarily to the linguistic profiles that are addressed in other chapters in this volume.

Executive functioning in development

EFs are diversely defined as the set of higher-order cognitive skills responsible for conscious and effortful control of thought and behaviour (Oh & Lewis, 2008) and are also described as processes that regulate thought and action (Freidman et al., 2006; in Henry et al., 2012). Executive skills are also described as a constellation of abilities required to deal with unfamiliar situations or novelty (Henry, 2012: 114).

Executive functioning covers a wide range of abilities (Miyake et al., 2000). Following Pennington and Ozonoff (1996) and Henry (2012) the five main components of EFs are:

- switching;
- fluency;
- planning;
- inhibition;
- working memory/updating.

There is still considerable debate about these components and the relationship between them but it is beyond the scope of this chapter to discuss this further. We will return to the main components in more detail in the following section.

When investigating the impact of EFs in SLI children, it is important to consider at what age children have an adult-like command of EFs. Specific core functions can take a considerable time to unfold with development continuing into puberty (Epsy et al., 2001; Huizinga et al., 2006). It is certainly not the case that young TD children perform at ceiling level on all executive functioning components or tasks, and thus we should also not expect young children with SLI to have fully developed EF skills. It is also important to point out that different EF tasks can capture several aspects of different EF skills at the same time and to a different degree (Huizinga et al., 2006). This is often referred to as the *problem of impurity* within the individual measures of each executive skill. For example, it is difficult to imagine that no planning at all is taking place during a switching task. In research on the development of EFs, some studies have been able to identify the same components in children as those seen in adults, while others have found evidence for additional components such as speed in responding and fluency (see Henry [2012] for a recent overview).

At this point in time, we know little about the cognitive profile of bilingual children with SLI. There is, however, accumulating evidence from monolingual children with SLI that can serve as a starting point. Monolingual children with SLI are known to perform more poorly than TD children on general measures of cognitive processing such as non-verbal memory (Windsor et al., 2008), visual-spatial skills (Hick et al., 2005; Windsor et al., 2008) and mental rotation (Johnston & Weismer, 1983). More recently, a few studies have also investigated specific EFs of children with SLI, again primarily in monolingual children. Montgomery et al. (2010) provide an overview of this research with results showing that working memory and inhibition are indeed challenging for children with SLI. A more recent study by Henry et al. (2012) administered a large battery of verbal and non-verbal EF tasks to a large group of older monolingual children with SLI and showed significant problems in working memory, inhibition, planning and fluency. In the following section, we will discuss the five core components as set out earlier and evaluate the results to date.

Brief overview of the five core executive functions

As mentioned in the previous section, executive functioning is defined here as a set of five cognitive skills: switching/shifting, fluency, planning, inhibition and working memory/updating. These will be briefly discussed and, where available, a short review of relevant research that has investigated how children with SLI and bilingual children perform on the specific executive skill will be presented.

Switching or set shifting involves the ability to navigate fluently between different sets of instructions, mental states or tasks, which also involves moving attention from one thing to another (Best & Miller, 2010; Henry, 2012; Miyake et al., 2000). Switching tasks also require minimum ability to inhibit previously activated mental sets in order to perform (switch to) a new operation.

Most studies have shown that children with SLI perform at the same level as TD children on non-verbal switching tasks (Henry et al., 2012; Im-Bolter et al., 2006; Kiernan et al., 1997; Laloi et al., 2012; Lukács

& Kemeny, 2011; Parriger, 2012; Weyandt & Willis, 1994). However, one study showed that 6-year-old children with SLI performed below the level of their age-matched TD peers (Marton, 2008). In summary, the evidence is inconclusive as to whether children with SLI differ from TD children on switching or shifting tasks. It is worth pointing out here that some tasks depend heavily on language skills such as counting, which is for example part of the shifting task employed in the study by Im-Bolter *et al.* (2006). This point will be returned to later.

Fluency requires that the child generates items around a particular theme or based on a set or arbitrary rules. The task measures the extent to which children can come up with different alternatives on their own (Henry, 2012). Fluency tasks are often associated with verbal tasks such as rapid naming and semantic fluency, where the child is asked to generate words from a specific conceptual category, such as animals. Children with SLI perform below the level of TD children on verbal fluency tasks (Lukács & Kemeny, 2011; Jensen de López & Søndergaard Knudsen, 2013). Non-verbal fluency has also been tested to some degree with children with SLI. A standardised measure of non-verbal fluency is 'design' fluency, which is a task where the child must draw as many different 'four-line' figures or boxes by connecting dots. In one study there was no difference between monolingual SLI children and their TD age-matched peers on non-verbal fluency (Weyandt & Willis, 1994), but in the larger study of Henry *et al.* (2012) a significant difference was found between the two groups. Results are therefore also somewhat inconclusive regarding non-verbal fluency in this area.

Planning is the organisation of thought and action to accomplish a specific goal. It also involves the ability to look forward before starting a task. Planning can involve concrete problem solving and refers to the ability to generate solutions to overcome difficulties in achieving goals and organise how these solutions might be carried out (Henry, 2012). It requires high-level functioning and also includes, to a certain extent, the ability to monitor and update one's working memory representations (Miyake *et al.*, 2000). In everyday tasks, planning requires children to coordinate with other cognitive abilities. Four studies have shown that children with LI perform at a lower level than TD children (Henry *et al.*, 2012; Lukács & Kemeny, 2011; Marton, 2008; Weyandt & Willis, 1994), but in one study no difference was found (Laloi *et al.*, 2012). The majority of studies suggest that planning might be a challenging ability for children with LI.

Inhibition involves the ability to delay a certain behaviour which is often a previously learned response. Inhibition is not a unitary concept and a distinction is commonly drawn between response inhibition and interference inhibition (Chung *et al.*, 2013). Response inhibition is the ability to actively suppress a learned response and replace it with a new but less-automatised reaction. For example, such a task involves first learning to imitate a hand shape but subsequently under a different condition having to suppress that reaction or make a different hand shape. Interference inhibition or control is the ability to resolve a perceptual conflict by discarding misleading stimuli and therefore only attending to relevant information (Chung *et al.*, 2013; Martin-Rhee & Bialystok, 2008).

When testing non-verbal inhibition, a bilingual advantage has been found in interference inhibition (Bialystok & Viswanathan, 2009; Engel de Abreu *et al.*, 2012), but not in response inhibition (Carlson & Meltzoff, 2008; Martin-Rhee & Bialystok, 2008). If they have equal accuracy rates, bilingual children resolve visual conflicts faster than their monolingual peers (Bialystok & Viswanathan, 2009). This speed advantage is usually observed on tasks involving a high degree of interference only (Martin-Rhee & Bialystok, 2008). This is often explained by the constant need of bilingual children in daily life to monitor two competing languages and to inhibit the interfering language. Regular practice involving language interference is, however, needed to develop this cognitive benefit: studies with children enrolled in a second language (L2) immersion programme did not show the same effect as found in simultaneous bilinguals (Carlson & Meltzoff, 2008; Nicolay & Poncelet, 2013). High proficiency in both languages also seems to be necessary (Iluz-Cohen & Armon-Lotem, 2013). A recent study controlling for children's socio-economic status showed a bilingual advantage for the children's reaction time, but not for their ability to respond correctly on a computer-based inhibition task (Engel de Abreu *et al.*, 2012). Hence, the bilingual effect is not an effect of high socio-economic status. The absence of a bilingual advantage in response inhibition can be explained by the fact that bilinguals do not have any extra practice opportunity in this area: they do not need to resist the motor impulse to speak (Martin-Rhee & Bialystok, 2008).

To date, research on non-verbal inhibition in SLI children has often treated inhibition as one single construct, but the focus has in fact mainly been on response inhibition. The majority of studies on monolingual SLI children have reported a deficit in this domain (Bishop & Norbury, 2005; Henry *et al.*, 2012; Im-Bolter *et al.*, 2006; Lukacz & Kemeny, 2011). However, one study that specifically screened monolingual SLI children for attention deficit hyperactivity disorder (ADHD) did not find any effect (Parigger, 2012). The few studies that have assessed performance on interference inhibition in monolingual SLI children have reported mixed results: some studies find group differences (Iluz-Cohen & Armon-Lotem, 2013; Spaulding, 2010), while others do not (Noterdaeme *et al.*, 2001). There is little research available so far on non-verbal inhibition in bilingual SLI children. The results from one study suggest that bilingual SLI children outperform their monolingual peers in interference inhibition, pointing to a compensatory effect of bilingualism on SLI in this domain (Iluz-Cohen

& Armon-Lotem, 2013). This interpretation should, however, be taken with caution as the sample of children was small. Response inhibition appears not to show this compensation and so may be more useful in examining bilingual children with SLI.

Working memory refers to the mental processes that allow limited information to be held in a temporary accessible state during cognitive processing and involves concurrent information processing and storage (Cowan *et al.*, 2005; in Montgomery *et al.*, 2010). Most work on the development of working memory in children has been conducted within Baddeley's tripartite framework that distinguishes between the central executive, short-term memory and the episodic buffer (Baddeley & Hitch, 1974). As working memory consists of several mechanisms there are also several ways to measure working memory. For a review of working memory and SLI, see Montgomery *et al.* (2010).

The Backwards Digit Span task, which involves naming numbers in reverse order, is considered a verbal phonological short-term memory task. Unlike the Forward Digit Span task, it has been shown to discriminate between monolingual children with and without SLI. However, some researchers have argued that Digit Span tasks may be confounded by the verbal modality (e.g. Montgomery *et al.*, 2010).

Non-verbal working memory studies have found children with SLI to perform poorly as reviewed in Montgomery *et al.* (2010) and as found in the large study of older children by Henry *et al.* (2012). When using the same task as in the Henry *et al.* study across different language groups, some studies have found group differences at some ages for monolingual children's non-verbal working memory, but not at other ages (Lukács & Kemeny, 2011; Parigger, 2012; Rispens & Baker, 2013; Sundahl Olsen & Jensen de López, 2010). Research with bilingual children shows that they do not develop advanced abilities in working memory when compared to monolingual children (Engel de Abreu, 2011). For these reasons, we find the working memory to be an adequate executive functioning task.

Behaviour-based rating scales of executive functions

Before proceeding to the discussion of specific EF tasks that could be appropriate tools for investigating the EF profile of bilingual children with SLI, it is worth mentioning two standardised questionnaires that capture components of executive functioning and that are potentially useful assessment tools. These questionnaires rely on adults' observations of the children's behaviour. Executive dysfunctioning can also be captured through questionnaires, which may be seen as complementary to experimental and performance-based EF tasks.

The Behaviour Rating Inventory of Executive Functions (BRIEF; Gioi *et al.*, 2000) is quite commonly used. It has been developed in three forms: a parent questionnaire, a teacher questionnaire and a self-report questionnaire for older schoolchildren. It is appropriate for children aged between 5 and 18 years. A pre-school version has also been developed (2–5 years). It consists of two scales: *behavioural regulation*, covering inhibition, shifting and emotional control, and *metacognition*, including initiating, working memory, planning, organisation and monitoring. In a study by Hughes *et al.* (2009), adolescents with SLI as well as their parents rated their EFs as poor on the BRIEF self-report questionnaire. BRIEF has been translated from English into several languages, for example Dutch and Danish. There may also be cultural differences in the perception of behaviour, so that the test needs to be standardised for a specific culture. A second challenge to using the BRIEF is that it is necessary for a psychologist to interpret it.

Another instrument is the Strengths and Difficulties questionnaire (Goodman, 1997). This questionnaire contains five different scales:

- emotional symptoms;
- conduct problems;
- hyperactivity/inattention;
- peer relationship problems;
- prosocial behaviour.

The Strengths and Difficulties questionnaire is freely available and has been adapted for more than 30 languages. Some countries have also provided norms for the questionnaire, for example for Swedish children (Smedje *et al.*, 1999).

Both questionnaires are useful and to be recommended but await validation and standardisation in different languages. It is important to be aware that recent research has pointed out that measures from reported executive functioning abilities do not necessarily assess the same constructs as performance-based executive functioning abilities do (Toplak *et al.*, 2013). This means that results from rating scales should always be supported by results from performance-based measures and vice versa.

Our aim in this chapter is to identify and develop EF tasks that are appropriate for young children at different ages, across difference cultures, and also to pilot these tasks with monolingual and bilingual children with and without SLI. We will present considerations for the selection of EF components and present the specific tasks that were recommended.

General approach

On the basis of the findings of research on non-verbal EF in children with SLI, four non-verbal domains of EFs emerge as the best candidates for assessing children with SLI (Table 10.1). As mentioned in the introduction, the aim is to help identify SLI in multilingual children using information about the child's executive functioning. In order to do this, children with SLI should display a problem in an EF component whether or not they are bilingual. The value of EF is also supported by an intervention study: a study by Ebert and Kohnert (2009) has shown that training general cognitive processing can actually enhance language abilities in bilingual children with SLI.

The four domains selected as the main focus were fluency, planning, inhibition and working memory. The component shifting/switching is not as clearly associated with SLI but it will, nevertheless, be discussed.

In order to disentangle the relationship between EFs and LI in bilingual and multilingual children, the results from four language groups need to be compared with one another. The specific effect of SLI emerges by comparing TD monolingual children to monolingual SLI children and TD bilingual children to bilingual SLI children (see Figure 10.1).

It is premature to make clear predictions as to the effect of SLI on the one hand and the effect of bilingualism on the other hand based on the specific EF profile of bilingual children with SLI. If SLI correlates with poor EF, we should expect bilingual children with SLI to perform poorly in these areas, just like monolingual children with SLI. However, if bilingual children have an advantage in certain EF components as a result of their bilingualism, these areas may be less affected in bilingual children with SLI compared to monolingual children with SLI. When aiming to identify SLI in multilingual children, it is necessary to find EF components and tasks that show the effect of SLI in bilingual children with SLI, yet minimise the bilingual effect on EF. In other words, we wish to identify tasks that discriminate children with SLI from children without SLI independent of whether the child is monolingual or bilingual.

Table 10.1 Summary of findings as to whether non-verbal EF tasks differentiate children with and without LI

Executive function component	Difference between children with and without SLI*
switching	inconclusive
fluency	inconclusive
planning	yes
inhibition	yes
working memory	yes

*The conclusion as to whether a specific component differentiates between children with and without SLI was based not only on the number of studies pointing in the same direction, but also on whether evidence was available from bilingual children specifically in terms of avoiding a bilingual effect.

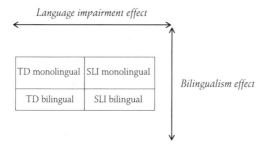

Figure 10.1 Comparing the four population groups

Selection Criteria for Recommended EF Tests

In order for EF tasks to be suitable for use with children with SLI and bilingual children and to be appropriate for basic research and diagnosis, they need ideally to conform to certain criteria. We will discuss these criteria briefly in the sections below.

Reduction of language component as a confounder

The amount of exposure to the L2 is an important factor when considering bilingual children. Consequentially, any EF task that manipulates verbal stimuli will have a verbal confound. For this same reason, it is also important to minimise the demand on language in administering a specific EF task. The search is for tasks that tap into primarily non-verbal EFs. Many studies showing that cognitive tasks are challenging for children with SLI have used explicitly verbal tasks such as the Competing Language Processing Task (CLPT) (Gaulin & Campbell, 1994). Several of the studies referred to in the introductory section of this chapter, that distinguish SLI and TD children, used tasks with a language component. For example, Digit Span tasks used to measure working memory involve the naming of the numbers in a language form (see Chen & Stevenson, 1988). Such tasks are not considered ideal for the purpose here. Other tasks involve a considerable amount of language in terms of the instruction needed. For example, the dot-joining task from the Delis–Kaplan Executive Function System (D-KEFS battery; Delis *et al.*, 2001), used to measure non-verbal fluency, requires the child to draw as many designs as possible by joining up dots using four straight lines, but with no line in isolation, in one minute, and these rules need to be explained using language.

However, in the study reported in Henry *et al.* (2012), verbal and non-verbal tests were matched in terms of the EF component studied. The authors report a low to moderate degree of association between the within-group results on each component, concluding that the non-verbal tasks used in that study made low demands on linguistic abilities.

Level appropriate to age

It is important that an early diagnosis of SLI can be made. Many tests for EF are, however, not suitable for use with children under the age of 5 years. The EF test battery, the Cambridge Neuropsychological Test Automated Battery (CANTAB, 2006), for example, is recommended only for use with children above the age of 6 years.

As mentioned earlier, EF abilities develop well into puberty. It is therefore essential to find tests that will discriminate impaired children from non-impaired children at different ages. The CANTAB, for example, provides norms from 6 years into adulthood, the D-KEFS battery for children aged 8 years into adulthood. There are, however, relatively few tests that provide norms for younger children (but see the NEPSY test; Epsy *et al.* 2001).

In general, the majority of studies have investigated groups older than 7 years so that there is little information about tasks suitable for use with younger children. The study of English and Hebrew children with and without SLI reported in Iluz-Cohen and Armon-Lotem (2013) investigated children between the ages of 4;1 and 7;1. Certain adaptations were made for use with younger children. For the sorting task, they adapted the procedures for children who were unable to complete the task in the first instance. The ability to answer independently was included as a minus in the scoring.

In sum, there is a dearth of tests that can be used with younger children and of normed tests – and normed tests are needed for clinical practice.

Ease of use and availability

As mentioned above, the aim is to develop guidelines for assessment techniques for early identification of bilingual SLI that can easily be used by practitioners. Tasks are required that are easy to administer and clinically friendly. Also, pencil and paper tasks are preferable to computer tasks since in many countries computer equipment is scarce and computer test batteries are expensive.

The avoidance of computer-based tests imposes restrictions, however, on the measures that can be used. The CANTAB (2006), for example, contains only computer-based tasks that often include measures of reaction time as well as accuracy. Although reaction times seem to decrease during childhood for TD children, less is known about changes in reaction time over time for children with SLI. Comparing non-linguistic visual tasks performed by SLI and TD monolingual and bilingual children, task accuracy has been shown not to distinguish SLI and TD children, whereas reaction time did distinguish the groups (Windsor *et al.*, 2008). Reaction time does therefore seem to be important, while on the other hand using online computer-based tasks presents a problem for clinical practice in many countries. For all tasks described below, it is possible to consider using time measurement via a handheld stopwatch as in most standardised IQ tests, e.g. the Wechsler Adult Intelligence Scale (WAIS) and the Wechsler Intelligence Scale for Children (WISC), but norms need to be created using this method.

Non-Verbal EF Tasks

In this section, we will describe a small selection of tasks that can be considered for use in research and clinical practice assessing bilingual children with SLI. The tasks have been selected on the basis of the selection criteria mentioned in the previous section.

Switching

For older children, the classic task for switching/shifting, named the Wisconsin Card Sorting Task, developed many decades ago (Berg, 1948) is appropriate for testing switching abilities. This task involves shifting between different sorting principles. The child is presented with four key cards numbered 1–4. The task requires the child to match a series of response cards with any of the four key cards. Response cards could be matched on colour, shape or number. Once the child has made 10 consecutive correct sorts, the sorting principle is changed. The order of the sorting principles is randomised. The variables that are of interest are the number of shifts achieved and the proportion of perseverative errors (this error occurring when the child is required to switch to another sorting principle, but persists in responding to the previously correct sorting principle). The classical version is appropriate for adults and young adults from age 7, but is too complicated for younger children (Huizinga & van de Molen, 2007). The ability to switch mental sets within a task (e.g. sorting cards) was shown to be present in TD children by the age of 5 years (Brooks et al., 2003), but in that study a much simpler task was used. A computer version of the classic task is included in the CANTAB (2006).

A similar task that captures the ability to shift between response sets and that is suitable for young children is the Classification Task (Iluz-Cohen & Armon-Lotem, 2013). This task is adapted from earlier work (Ben-Zeev, 1997; Jacobs et al., 2001; Smidts et al., 2004; in Illuz-Cohen & Armon-Lotem, 2013). Similarly to previous tasks, the child's ability to sort or classify cards based on shapes, colours and quantity is tested as well as his/her ability to shift sorting strategy. The child is presented with 18 cards representing three different shapes (circle, triangle, square) and three different patterns (no colour, partially coloured, fully coloured) (Figure 10.2). Nine of the cards show three examples of each

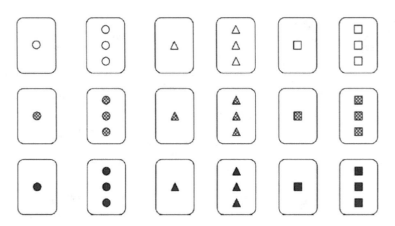

Figure 10.2 The cards used in the classification task (Iluz-Cohen & Armon-Lotem, 2013)

item (indicating three), while the other nine cards show one example of each item (indicating one). After a practice trial, the child is asked to sort the cards into groups. The experimenter then reorganises the cards in exactly the same order presented in the first round and asks the child to reclassify the cards now in a *different* order, in other words to shift his/her strategy. This procedure is run a third time in order for the child to have the opportunity to sort in the three possible ways based on colour, shape or quantity. If the child does not succeed in shifting to a new sorting strategy, i.e. persists with the same classification, the experimenter provides up to three verbal prompts to help the child switch category. Assisted shifts are also coded.

The task is coded using two different coding procedures. Firstly, all trials are coded as (1) successful independent of assistance, (2) unsuccessful or (3) trials needing assistance from the experimenter to complete. Secondly, on each trial the child's performance is given a score from 0 to 3. A score of zero is registered if the child is not able to perform the sorting after receiving three prompts from the experimenter, a score of 1 is registered if the child is able to perform the sorting after receiving just two prompts, a score of 2 is registered if the child is able to perform the sorting after receiving just one prompt, and finally a score of 3 is registered if the child is able to perform the sorting on his/her own with no prompt needed from the experimenter.

Two measures are included in the scoring procedure. The first is the mean of all three classifications, and the second measure considers each classification separately.

This task does not require a computer implementation and can be used with children as young as 4 years of age. It has shown to distinguish between TD and SLI in monolingual and bilingual children (Iluz-Cohen & Armon-Lotem, 2013).

Non-verbal fluency

The dot-joining task is a non-verbal fluency task that is part of the standardised D-KEFS (Delis *et al.*, 2001), which tests executive functioning. The test was developed for children from the age of 8 years. As described earlier, the child is presented with a piece of paper and a pencil and is asked to make as many different four-line designs as possible by connecting the empty dots with straight lines (Figure 10.3). The task consists of three conditions, which become increasingly difficult. The child only has one minute to complete each condition. A score is then calculated based on the total amount of different four-line designs the child is able to correctly complete. The test was used by Henry *et al.* (2012) and was able to significantly predict a large amount of the variance in the SLI children's language performance (see also the NEPSY-II; Korkman *et al.*, 2007a, 2007b). Since the differences are seen in the conditions with increased difficulty, this effect cannot be attributed to children with SLI having difficulties understanding the verbal instructions.

A second non-verbal fluency task, the Hungry Frog task, is currently under development (Jensen de Lopéz, 2013). Like the D-KEFS task, this new task consists of three different conditions and the child is given one minute to complete as many different designs within each condition. However, in this task, the materials are more ecologically valid than in the dot pattern task and the task is also freely available. In the Hungry Frog task, children are shown a picture of a hungry frog and are told that they need to help the frog capture flies for his dinner. They are then presented with six different pictures of a fly in different contours (dotted, striped, etc.) and are asked to lay the flies in a vertical line to create a pattern (Figure 10.4). After completing the first line, the child is then given a new set of six pictures and is asked to arrange the flies in a new combination. One minute per condition is allowed. The task consists of three conditions, which become increasingly difficult, e.g. in the second trial only two black pictures of flies may be placed beside each other. The total score is the

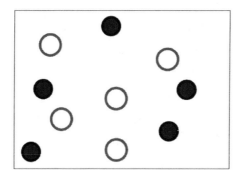

Figure 10.3 Example of dot pattern in the non-verbal fluency task (Delis *et al.*, 2001)

Figure 10.4 Example of the Hungry Frog and one pattern of flies (Jensen de López, 2013)

number of different patterns (vertical lines) constructed by the child. The task can be carried out using the paper version. It is currently being developed into an app that will make it possible to administer on an iPad and offers the possibility of measuring reaction time. It will be piloted with children younger than 8 years of age.

The traditional tasks developed to measure planning consist of Tower of Hanoi (TOH; Welsh *et al.*, 1991) or Tower of London (TOL; Shallice, 1982; in Huizinga *et al.*, 2006; Phillips *et al.*, 2001). Both tasks are a measure of problem solving and planning. In the TOH task, the child is asked to move three discs across pegs to achieve the model configuration in successively more difficult problems (see Figure 10.5). In the TOL task, the

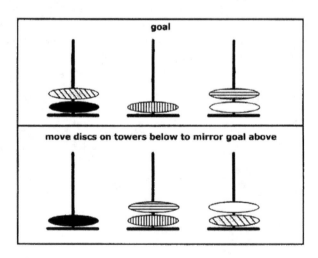

Figure 10.5 Example of the Tower of London task from Philips *et al.* (1999: 210)

child is required to move differently coloured rings across three different-sized pegs, but needs to follow a set of rules, e.g. only move one ring at a time. The dependent measure is the total number of problems solved in the minimal prescribed number of moves. This task is suitable for children from age 5.

The task can be performed with simple apparatus but there are also computer versions as in the CANTAB (2006) where it is called the Stockings of Cambridge task. In this version, accuracy and reaction time are the dependent measures.

Non-verbal inhibition

Two tasks were considered for non-verbal inhibition since both have been shown in some work to discriminate TD and SLI children and can be used with younger children in a face-to-face procedure. However, as discussed in the introduction, the tasks measure different constructs of inhibition.

The first task, a motor response inhibition task, was developed and used by Henry *et al.* (2012). It has similarities to the 'Simon Says' task that has been used in other studies. In this task, the experimenter makes a hand gesture such as a flat hand or fist, which the child has to copy. In the second block, the child must provide the opposite gesture, so when the experimenter makes a fist, the child must inhibit copying and provide a flat hand. This is then followed by another copying block and another inhibit block. Each block consists of 20 trials. Henry *et al.* (2012) repeated the four blocks with different stimuli, so that in total 80 trials in each part could be scored for accuracy. It is important in this task that the speed is kept constant and quite fast. If the hand shapes are presented too slowly, the task becomes too easy. The task requires that a second experimenter notes the child's responses or that the responses are video recorded.

The second task, for testing information inhibition, was developed by Iluz-Cohen and Armon-Lotem (2013) on the basis of previous embedded figures tasks (De Avila & Duncan, 1980; Pascual-Leone, 1989; Piaget & Inhelder, 1967). The child is shown a series of pictures in a picture book and is asked to find a mouse embedded in a picture as quickly as possible. The 10 pictures used increase in difficulty in terms of the amount of information contained in the picture (compare Figure 10.6a and b). The child gains a score per correct identification of the mouse. This task was used successfully with children as young as 4 years of age.

Non-verbal working memory

There are many tasks testing non-verbal working memory but the one that best meets the criteria discussed in the first section is the Odd

(a)

(b)

Figure 10.6 Two pictures from the embedded figures task (a) being less complex than (b) (Kor, 1992)

One Out task developed by Henry (2001) and used in the study by Henry *et al.* (2012).

The task tests visual-spatial working memory by asking the child to remember the position of a shape, which is the *odd one out* of three items as in Figure 10.7, and then identify its position on a picture of 'empty' boxes. The task starts with a list with just one item to be identified at a time and then continues with longer lists of up to six items. At list Level 2 for example the child first sees three shapes as in Figure 10.7a, and identifies the odd one out. Then, the second set of three shapes is presented to the child as in Figure 10.7b. Finally, two pictures of empty boxes are presented to the child and the child is asked to recall the position of the two odd-one-out figures identified previously (see Figure 10.7c). The test has a cut-off point after the child has responded incorrectly on several trials.

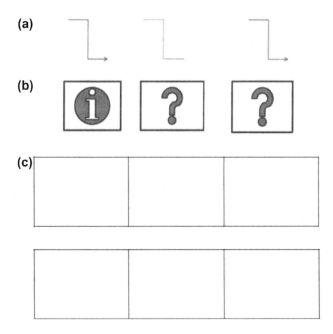

Figure 10.7 Example of an item at Level 2 on the Odd One Out task (Henry 2001)

This test can be administered using cards presented on paper or in PowerPoint on a computer. An E-prime version has also recently been developed (Duinmeijer & Jansen, 2013) and has the advantage of automatically registering accuracy and speed through the touchscreen.

Conclusions and Future Directions

The set of non-verbal EF tasks presented in this chapter can be seen as the starting point for an EF profile battery suited for young children with SLI. Currently, it is theoretically challenging to hypothesise links between specific language abilities and specific EF components. For example, it is plausible that there is a link between the child's non-verbal planning and narrative abilities and/or between the child's non-verbal working memory and sentence repetition abilities. The language abilities of the child have to be studied in detail and the child's exposure to more than one language has to be well described. Future work has considerable scope to explore these aspects.

As stated at the beginning of this chapter, a main goal is to suggest non-verbal executive tasks that will help assess SLI in bilingual children. This is an empirical question and whether this is possible will become obvious on the basis of results from further research derived from the four language groups described in Figure 10.1. We consider the battery of selected tasks described in the previous section to be a good basis for conducting this empirical research. However, in order to capture task-specific developmental trajectories, it is necessary to employ several tasks at different age points. Lastly, we should not assume that all non-linguistic EF tasks are equally sensitive to the SLI profile of bilingual children. It is therefore crucial to identify more precisely which underlying cognitive mechanisms are associated with which different aspects of SLI and at which specific age. It is also important to investigate the relationship between the degree of a child's executive functioning deficit and the degree of his/her SLI. It is our hope that these EF tasks may serve as a starting point for the systematic investigation of how to adequately capture the cognitive profile of bilingual children with SLI on the road to assessment (see also Kohnert (2010) for challenges in assessing bilingual children with SLI).

References

Baddeley, A.D. and Hitch, G.J. (1974) Working memory. In G.A. Bower (ed.) *The Psychology of Learning and Motivation* (Vol. 8; pp. 47–89). New York: Academic Press.

Berg, E.A. (1948) A simple objective technique for measuring flexibility in thinking. *Journal of General Psychology* 39 (1), 15–22.

Best, J.R. and Miller, P.H. (2010) A developmental perspective on executive function. *Child Development* 81 (6), 1641–1660.

Bialystok, E. (2011) Reshaping the mind: The benefits of bilingualism. *Canadian Journal of Experimental Psychology* 65 (4), 229–235.

Bialystok, E. and Martin, M. (2004) Attention and inhibition in bilingual children: Evidence from the dimensional change card sort task. *Developmental Science* 7 (3), 325–339.

Bialystok, E. and Viswanathan, M. (2009) Components of executive control with advantages for bilingual children in two cultures. *Cognition* 112 (3), 494–500.

Bishop, D. and Frazer-Norbury, C. (2005) Executive functions in children with communication impairments, in relation to autistic symptomatology I: Generativity. *Autism* 9 (1), 7–27.

Blom, E., Küntay, A.C., Messer, M., Verhagen, J., and Leseman, P. (2014) The benefits of being bilingual: working memory in bilingual Turkish-Dutch children. *Journal of Experimental Child Psychology* 128, 105–119.

Brooks, P.J., Hanauere, J.B., Padowska, B. and Rosman, H. (2003) The role of selective attention in preschooler's rule us in a novel dimensional card sort. *Cognitive Development* 18, 195–215.

CANTAB (2006) *Cambridge Neuropsychological Test Automated Battery (CANTAB)*. Cambridge: Cambridge Cognition Ltd.

Carlson, S.M. and Meltzoff, A.M. (2008) Bilingual experience and executive functioning in young children. *Developmental Science* 11 (2), 282–298.

Chen, C. and Stevenson, H.W. (1988) Cross-linguistic differences in digit span of preschool children. *Journal of Experimental Child Psychology* 46 (1), 150–158.

Chung, H.J., Weynandt, L.L. and Swentovsky, A. (2013) The physiology of executive functioning. In S. Goldstein and J.A. Naglieri (eds) *Handbook of Executive Functioning* (pp. 13–27). Frankfurt: Springer.

De Avila, E.A. and Duncan, S.E. (1980) The language minority child. A psychological, linguistic, and social analysis. In J. Atlatis (ed.) *Current Issues in Bilingual Education* (pp 104–137). Washington, DC: Georgetown University Press.

Delis, D.C., Kaplan, E. and Kramer, J.H. (2001) *Delis–Kaplan Executive Function System (D-KEFS)*. London: The Psychological Corporation Ltd.

Duinmeijer, I. and Jansen, B. (2013) An E-prime version of Henry's Odd One Out task. University of Amsterdam.

Ebert, K. and Kohnert, K. (2009) Nonlinguistic cognitive treatment for primary language impairment. *Clinical Linguistics and Phonetics* 23 (9), 647–664.

Engel de Abreu, P. (2011) Working memory in multilingual children: Is there a bilingual effect? *Memory* 19 (5), 529–537.

Engel de Abreu, P., Puglisi, M., Cruz-Santos, A., Befi-Lopes, D.M. and Bialystok, E. (2012) Bilingualism enriches the poor: Enhanced cognitive control in low-income minority children. *Psychological Science* 23 (11), 1364–1371.

Epsy, K.A., Kaufmann, P.M., Glisky, M.L. and McDiarmid, M.D. (2001) New procedures to assess executive functions in preschool children. *The Clinical Neuropsychologist* 15 (1), 46–58.

Gaulin, C. and Campbell, T. (1994) Procedure for assessing verbal working memory in normal school-age children: Some preliminary data. *Perceptual and Motor Skills* 79, 55–64.

Gioia, G.A., Isquith, P.K., Guy, S.C. and Kenworthy, L. (2000) *Behavior Rating Inventory of Executive Function (BRIEF)*. Lutz, FL: Psychological Assessment Resources.

Goodman, R. (1997) The Strengths and Difficulties Questionnaire: A research note. *Journal of Child Psychology and Psychiatry* 38 (5), 581–586.

Henry, L.A. (2012) *The Development of Working Memory in Children*. London: Sage Publications.

Henry, L.A., Messer, D. and Nash, G. (2012) Executive functioning in children and young people with specific language impairment. *Journal of Child Psychiatry and Psychology* 50 (1), 37–45.

Hick, R., Botting, N. and Conti-Ramsden, G. (2005) Cognitive abilities in children with specific language impairment: Consideration of visuo-spatial skills. *International Journal of Communication Disorders* 40 (2), 137–149.

Hughes, D.M., Turkstra, L.S. and Wulfeck, B.B. (2009) Parent and self-ratings of executive function in adolescents with specific language impairment. *International Journal of Language and Communication Disorders* 44 (6), 901–916.

Huizinga, M., Dolan, C.V. and van der Molen, M.W. (2006) Age-related change in executive function: Developmental trends and a latent variable analysis. *Neuropsychologia* 44 (11), 2017–2036.

Huizinga, M. and van der Molen, M. (2007) Age-group differences in set-switching and set-maintenance on the Wisconsin Card Sorting Task. *Developmental Neuropsychology* 31 (2), 193–215.

Iluz-Cohen, P. and Armon-Lotem, S. (2013) Language proficiency and executive control in bilingual children. *Bilingualism: Language and Cognition* 16 (4), 884–899.

Im-Bolter, N., Johnson, J. and Pascual-Leone, J. (2006) Processing limitations in children with specific language impairment: The role of executive function. *Child Development* 77 (6), 1822–1841.

Jensen de Lopéz, K. (2013) *The Hungry Frog Task – A Non-Verbal Fluency Task*. Denmark: Aalborg University.

Jensen de López, K. and Knudsen Søndergaard, H. (2013) Developmental profiles of Danish SLI children's verbally loaded and non-verbally loaded working memory. Poster presented to EUCLDIS Workshop 'The development of language and cognition in children with linguistic and cognitive challenges', NIAS, Wassenaar, The Netherlands, 26–28 June.

Johnston, J. and Ellis Weismer, S. (1983) Mental rotation abilities in language disordered children. *Journal of Speech and Hearing Research* 26 (3), 397–403.

Kiernan, B., Snow, D., Swisher, L. and Vance, R. (1997) Another look at nonverbal rule induction in children with SLI: Testing a flexible reconceptualisation hypothesis. *Journal of Speech, Language and Hearing Research* 40 (1), 75–82.

Kohnert, K. (2010) Bilingual children with primary language impairment: Issues, evidence and implications for clinical practice. *Journal of Communication Disorders* 43 (6), 456–473.

Kor, P. (1992) *Where is the Mouse?* Tel Aviv: Zmora Bitan (in Hebrew).

Korkman, M., Kirk, U. and Kemp, S.L. (2007a) *NEPSY II. Administrative Manual.* San Antonio, TX: Psychological Corporation.

Korkman, M., Kirk, U. and Kemp, S.L. (2007b) *NEPSY II. Clinical and Interpretative Manual.* San Antonio, TX: Psychological Corporation.

Laloi, A., Baker, A.E. and de Jong, J. (2012) Monolingual SLI children's performances on four executive functioning tasks. Paper to the Anela conference, Lunteren.

Lukács, Á. and Kemeny, F. (2011) Results from LI children in Hungarian on EF and language tasks. Paper to COST IS0804 meeting, Malta, November 2011.

Martin-Rhee, M.M. and Bialystok, E. (2008) The development of two types of inhibitory control in monolingual and bilingual children. *Bilingualism: Language and Cognition* 11 (1), 81–93.

Marton, K. (2008) Visuo-spatial processing and executive functions in children with specific language impairment. *International Journal of Language and Communication Disorders* 43 (2), 181–200.

Miyake A., Friedman, N.P., Emerson, M.J., Witzki, A.H., Howerter, A. and Wager, T.D. (2000) The unity and diversity of executive functions and their contributions to complex 'frontal lobe' tasks: A latent variable analysis. *Cognitive Psychology* 41 (1), 49–100.

Montgomery, J.W., Magimairaj, B.M. and Finney, M.C. (2010) Working memory and specific language impairment: An update on the relation and perspectives on assessment and treatment. *American Journal of Speech-Language Pathology* 19 (1), 78–94.

Nicolay, A. and Poncelet, M. (2013) Cognitive advantage in children enrolled in a second-language immersion elementary school program for three years. *Bilingualism, Language and Cognition* 16 (3), 597–607.

Noterdaeme, M., Amorosa, H., Mildenberger, K., Sitter, S. and Minow, F. (2001) Evaluation of attention problems in children with autism and in children with specific language disorder. *European Child and Adolescent Psychiatry* 10 (1), 58–66.

Oh, S. and Lewis, C. (2008) Korean preschooler's advanced inhibitory control and its relation to other executive skills and mental state understanding. *Child Development* 79 (1), 80–99.

Pacual-Leone, J. (1989) An organismic process model of Witkin's field-dependence-independence. In T. Globerson and T. Zelniker (eds) *Cognitive Style and Cognitive Development* (pp. 36–70). Norwood, NJ: Ablex.

Parriger, E.M. (2012) *Language and executive functioning in children with ADHD.* PhD thesis, University of Amsterdam. See http://dare.uva.nl/record/431858 (accessed 11 December 2014).

Peets, K.F. and Bialystok, E. (2010) An integrated approach to the study of specific language impairment and bilingualism. Commentary. *Applied Psycholinguistics* 31 (2), 315–319.

Pennington, B.F. and Ozonoff, S. (1996) Executive functions and developmental psychopathology. *Journal of Child Psychology and Psychiatry* 37 (1), 51–87.

Phillips, L.H., Wynn, V.E., McPherson, S. and Gilhooly, K.J. (2001) Mental planning and the Tower of London task. *Quarterly Journal of Experimental Psychology – Section A: Human Experimental Psychology* 54 (2), 579–597.

Piaget, J. and Inhelder, B. (1967) *The Child's Conception of Space.* New York: Norton.

Rispens, J. and Baker, A.E. (2013) Non-word repetition: The relative contributions of phonological short-term memory and phonological representations in children with language and reading impairment. *Journal of Speech and Hearing Disorders* 55 (3), 683–694.

Smedje, H., Borman, J.E., Hetta, J. and von Knorring, A.L. (1999) Psychometric properties of a Swedish version of the 'Strengths and Difficulties Questionnaire'. *European Child and Adolescent Psychiatry* 8 (2), 63–70.

Spaulding T.J. (2010) Investigating mechanisms of suppression in preschool children with specific language impairment. *Journal of Speech, Language and Hearing Research* 53 (3), 725–738.

Sundahl Olsen, K. and Jensen de López, K. (2010) SLI er mere end blot forsinket udvikling af sproglige færdigheder. (SLI is more than just delayed language competence.) *Psyke and Logos* 2, 485–504.

Toplak, M.E., West, R.F. and Stanovish, K.E. (2013) Practitioner review: Do performance-based measures and ratings of executive function assess the same construct? *Journal of Child Psychology and Psychiatry* 54 (2), 131–143.

Welsh, M.C., Pennington, B.F. and Groisser, D.B. (1991) A normative-developmental study of executive function: A window on prefrontal function in children. *Developmental Neuropsychology* 7 (2), 131–149.

Weyandt, L.L. and Willis, W.G. (1994) Executive functions in school-aged children: Potential efficacy of tasks in discriminating clinical groups. *Developmental Neuropsychology* 10 (1), 27–38.

Windsor, J., Kohnert, K., Loxtercamp, A.L. and Kan, P-F. (2008) Performance on nonlinguistic visual tasks by children with language impairment. *Applied Psycholinguistics* 29 (2), 237–268.

Part 4
From Theory to Practice

11 Clinical Use of Parental Questionnaires in Multilingual Contexts

Laurice Tuller

Introduction

This chapter focuses on questionnaires designed for use with parents of children growing up in multilingual contexts, to collect information which could help determine whether a child experiencing language difficulties might have specific language impairment (SLI). It will be argued that there is now growing support for the conclusion that parental questionnaires can be of considerable use as a tool with which to tackle the 'Bi-SLI problem', summarised as in (1).

(1)   How can it be ascertained whether low language performance in a bilingual child is due to SLI?

We propose, in the first section, a review of results from the literature on parental report on questions related to typical language development in their children (late language emergence, current language skills, family history for language impairment) and to their children's early and current language input and use. The second section presents the design, content and guidelines for use of a parental questionnaire developed specifically for use with parents of children growing up in multilingual contexts, which was piloted in a number of countries across Europe and beyond.

Why Use a Parental Questionnaire?

The major goal of using parental questionnaires to tackle the Bi-SLI problem is to provide a way of gathering information enabling the clinician to interpret language performance in the child's second language (L2). This is indeed the typical situation facing clinicians in many countries. It may not be feasible for clinicians to test the child's first language (L1), due to lack of knowledge of this language, lack of (appropriate) standardised tests for assessing this language and/or simply lack of time for assessment of both the L1 and the L2 (because time for language screening and assessment may be limited, for example, by the country's health system). Furthermore, even in cases where both the L1 and the L2 can be easily assessed by the clinician, low performance in each of the languages is not automatically indicative of SLI, since it is possible for a child to have not yet reached age-level performance in the L2 and yet to be manifesting, at the same time, L1 attrition/incomplete acquisition (on the latter, see Montrul, 2008). Low performance both in cases where only the L2 is tested and in cases where each of the child's languages has been tested can benefit from consideration of data which can be gathered from parents. In both of these situations, the goal is to find out if low performance is because there is reason to suspect SLI or because there is reason to suspect insufficient exposure and/or use (in quantity and/or quality).

What constitutes reasonable suspicion of SLI or of under-exposure? SLI, apart from exclusionary criteria, is based on language performance that is significantly below age expectations. If a child has SLI, language impairment will be apparent in each of his/her languages. Knowing that a child has normal L1 performance is thus of utmost importance to understanding low L2 performance. Apart from impaired language itself, children with SLI are also characterised by late emergence of language and, for many of them, a family history of language difficulties. Knowing about both of these for children in multilingual settings thus may provide a way of helping confirm or disconfirm SLI. On the other hand, it is known that children growing up with more than one language may be experiencing difficulties in one of their languages due to insufficient exposure and/or use, quantitatively and/or qualitatively. Knowledge about a bilingual child's early and current use of his/her different language could provide information about L1 maintenance and adequate opportunities for L2 acquisition.

In sum, parental questionnaires are a potential source for knowing about all of these factors: Were the child's early language milestones on time or delayed? Is the child performing typically in the L1 (in the case where this language cannot be tested, or where only monolingual norms are available)? Does the child have a family history of language difficulties? Studies based on parental report have studied these factors and there is general consensus that it is indeed possible to obtain reliable information on them from parents.

Late language emergence

Late emergence of language is an integral part of the symptomatology of SLI. The *Diagnostic and Statistical Manual of Mental Disorders*–5th edition (DSM-5; American Psychiatric Association, 2013) description for SLI includes the following: 'The child's first words are likely to be *delayed*, early grammatical and morphosyntactic forms may be *late to appear*, vocabulary size can be *smaller* and less varied than expected, awareness of the phonemic and morphemic structures of words can be *delayed* well into the school-age years, [...]' [emphasis mine, LT]. The DSM-5 description of SLI ends with the explicit requirement that 'Symptoms must be present in early childhood (but may not become fully manifest until language demands exceed limited capacities)'. This description mirrors what can be found in research articles on SLI: 'Late onset of language is a hallmark characteristic of children with language impairments. In the case of children with SLI, late talking can be the first diagnostic symptom' (Rice, 2007). While children with SLI, by definition, all seem to have been late talkers, all late talkers are not necessarily later diagnosed for SLI. There are two questions here: How frequent is late language emergence? And, what proportion of children with a history of late language emergence ends up with a clinical diagnosis for SLI?

The frequency of late language emergence depends, of course, on how this is defined. Late talkers are commonly taken to be children whose language is delayed in terms of vocabulary or syntax onset and/or vocabulary size.

(2)   Definitions of late language emergence
      Late onset of first word stage (>18 months)
      Late onset of word combinations (>24 months)
      Expressive vocabulary <50 words at age 24 months
      Vocabulary score on CDI ≤10th, 15th percentile, etc. (depending on age)

Children who had an expressive vocabulary of fewer than 50 words or who did not have any word combinations made up 10% of the sample of 24-month-old children studied by Fenson (1993), via use of the MacArthur Child Developmental Inventory (CDI), and 9.7% of the sample of 422 24- to 26-month-old children studied by Rescorla and Alley (2001), via the Language Development Survey. Zubrick *et al.* (2007), in a much larger sample of 1766 24-month-old Australian children, used both the Language Development Survey and The Ages and Stages Questionnaire (a six-item parent report scale about comprehension and production milestones); 13.4% of these children performed below –1 SD and 19.1% were at this level for the single criterion of 'no or only occasional word combinations'. In a study of 174 children aged 4–12, Preston *et al.* (2010) asked parents whether they thought their child spoke two- to three-word sentences early, on time or late, and also to give an age estimate.

The late-talker group so defined consisted of 20.6% of this sample, and none of these children were reported to have produced their first sentences before age 24 months. Despite different methodologies, these studies, which also took place in different countries, arrive at remarkably similar results.

The question of what proportion of these late-talking children continue to be behind age expectations has been studied for some time, though only recently have results of large epidemiological studies of ascertained populations become available. Reviewing earlier studies, Rice (2007) concludes that the range of SLI diagnosis at age 6 in children with a late-talker history seems to be between 17% and 25%. Rice *et al.* (2008) reported on a follow-up study at age 7 of the 24-month-old children of the Zubrick *et al.* (2007) study. Defining the late-talker cohort as those children who at age 24 months had a vocabulary size below 70 words or who had no word combinations, it was found that, at age 7, 20% of them were below –1 SD on a measure of general language ability, compared to 11% in a control cohort, 18% were below –1 SD on the syntax score (vs 8% of controls) and 9%–23% (depending on the particular measure) were below –1 SD on different morphosyntactic measures (vs 2%–14% of controls). The children in the late-talker group were thus much more likely to have low scores than children in the control group. In this study, as in smaller studies (see, for example, Preston *et al.*, 2010), most children with late language emergence made up for their late language onset since most of them later performed within norms.

The results on late language emergence rely very heavily on parental report, often retrospective. Numerous studies have been undertaken to ascertain the validity of this method of gathering information about late-talker status. It might be imagined that in the case of a multilingual setting, parents might have more difficulty reporting on early language milestones. This has not so far been found to be the case. Paradis *et al.* (2010) indeed found parental report of early milestones to be the strongest discriminator between a group of typically developing (TD) bilingual children (*n*=139) aged 4;10–5;6 and a group of bilingual children aged 4;10–9;1, recruited from caseloads of speech-language pathologists (SLPs) or who were attending special kindergarten programmes for children with language delays (*n*=29). Interestingly, Paradis *et al.* note that the ages provided by parents for the early language milestones (mean first word onset of 13.0 for the TD group and 22.0 for the language-impaired group, mean first sentence onset of 20.8 for TD and 34.1 for language impaired) were entirely consonant with what is found for monolingual American children. In other words, parents are able, even in a multilingual setting, to recall the timing of basic language milestones as reliably as parents in monolingual settings.

Current language skills

How well are parents able to evaluate their child's current language skills? Several studies have compared parental report and standardised tests of children's language performance. Many of these are based on use of the MacArthur CDI (see Gatt et al., this volume, for review and discussion), in which parents fill out checklists about vocabulary and sentence comprehension and production.

Studies using other types of parental reports have found similar results. A large French study reported in Callu et al. (2003) sought to examine how well parental reports predict language performance by testing a group of 670 children in the second year of nursery school (mean age 4;7) and 799 children in the final year of nursery school (mean age 5;11). The four items from parental questionnaires which were most predictive of language scores for the younger children (out of a 16-item questionnaire) and for the older children (out of a 10-item questionnaire) are given in (3). Children were divided between those with no parental report of a language problem (0 or 1 positive response to the four items in (3)) and those with parental report of a language problem (all others). Seventeen percent of the younger children and 9% of the older children were in the language-problem groups. Next, children who performed in the lowest 10% on the standardised language tests were separated from all other children, yielding, once again, two groups. The groups identified by parental report and by standardised measures of language production were found to be highly correlated. It was, moreover, found that this correlation did not significantly differ according to parental education level.

(3) Four most predictive items from parental questionnaires
     (Callu et al., 2003)

Parents of younger children	Parents of older children
Pronounces words well	Child pronounces words correctly
Is easily understood by other people	Child is easily understood by people who don't know him/her
Frequently uses the wrong word	Child has difficulty putting words together to make sentences
Distorts words	We are worried about the way our child talks

Although the correlation between parental report and language scores was highly significant, it was not perfect. The diagnostic fit of a tool is typically measured in terms of its sensitivity, its ability to identify positive results (here, what percentage of children with language impairment, as independently measured by standardised measures of the children's language production, were identified by parental report), its specificity and its ability to identify negative results (here, what percentage of children without language impairment were reported by parents to have no language difficulties). For the group of younger children in the lowest tenth percentile, parental report had a sensitivity of 79% (79% of these children were identified by their parents as having language difficulties) and the specificity of parental report was 83% (meaning that 17% of the children without difficulties were incorrectly identified by their parents as having difficulties). In the group of older children, sensitivity of parental report was 55% and specificity was 81%.[1]

Summarising, there is considerable evidence in support of the validity of parental report of children's language skills, at different ages. This validity has also been shown to hold for parental reporting of children in multilingual contexts. Restrepo (1998) found that parental report of their child's speech and language skills was one of the four measures (together with parental report of family history of speech and language problems and two spontaneous language measures) which best discriminated a group of bilingual Spanish–English children with SLI from a group of TD Spanish–English bilingual children. Similarly, Paradis et al. (2010), in a study taking place in a Canadian multilingual setting, with a variety of home languages, found that, despite evidence for L1 loss in both the group of TD bilingual children and the group of bilingual children with SLI, parental report of current L1 abilities was the second strongest discriminator between the two groups (after early language milestones). These studies show that parents, even in multilingual settings, are able to evaluate their child's current L1 skills.

Family history of language difficulties

Rates for the incidence of language impairment in family members (both nuclear and extended) of children with SLI vary widely in published family aggregation studies, and depend in part on whether reading problems are included or just difficulties with oral language (see Flax et al., 2009, for review): Stromswold's (1998) review of 18 family aggregation studies showed rates of impaired language varying from 24% to 78% (mean 46%, median 35%), whereas in control families it ranged from 3% to 46% (mean 18%, median 11%). To illustrate this type of study and results, consider Rice et al.'s (1998) study, summarised in (4). The families of a group of 31 4- and 5-year-old children with SLI were investigated and compared to 67 control families, on the basis of telephone (or personal) interviews in which, for each family member (mother, father, siblings, mother's parents, siblings, nieces and nephews, father's parents, siblings, nieces and nephews), a list of symptoms was examined, for each of which the parent responded yes or no. As (4) shows, a positive family history for language impairment was considerably more frequent in the SLI families than in the control families, a now familiar result.

(4) Positive family history for language impairment (Rice *et al.*, 1998)

	Speech-language disorders (%)	Reading/spelling/learning disorders (%)	Overall affectedness (composite) (%)
31 SLI proband families	58.1	35.5	64.5
67 control families	19.4	22.4	37.3

The robust conclusion stemming from such studies is that a familial history of language impairment places children in a 'high-risk' category. Studies which have concentrated on these at-risk children have indeed found substantial proportions of children with early language delay and persistent low language scores. Spitz *et al.* (1997) found that 50% of 16- to 24-month-old children with a positive family history (5/10 children) performed below 1.5 SD on expressive and receptive language tests, compared to 0% of children with no family history (0/10 children). Choudhury and Benasich (2003) found that 28% of a cohort of 32 at-risk 3-year-olds performed below 1 SD, compared to 7% of a cohort of 60 3-year-olds with no family history. Flax *et al.* (2008) reported significant differences in language outcomes at ages 2, 3, 5 and 7 for a group of 40 children with a positive family history for language learning impairment (both oral and written language), compared to a control group with no family history. Setting 'low language' at below −1 SD, in the positive family history group, this rate was 49% at age 2, 28% at age 3, 31% at age 5 and 19%–37% (depending on language domain) at age 7 (though different tests were used at different ages).

As illustrated above, studies of family history of language difficulties have relied heavily on parental report of language difficulties, generally in the form of questionnaires administered in an interview with one of the parents. Examples of such questions are given in (5) and (6).

(5) Family report on symptoms of speech and language impairment (Rice *et al.*, 1998)
"Does anyone in your family have a history of...
being slow in learning to talk?
using awkward sentence structure?
having a hard time carrying on a conversation?
having difficulty thinking of words (s)he wants to say when talking?
having a poorer vocabulary than other family members?
being hard to follow when (s)he tells you something?
having difficulty explaining things?
being less talkative?
stuttering?
mispronouncing long words?

being a poor speller?
not reading well?
not liking to read?

(6) Language History Questions from Choudhury and Benasich (2003)
Is there a history of delayed language (e.g. late talking) or reading/learning impairment in your immediate family (please include both parents, siblings, grandparents, aunts and uncles)? YES/NO
If yes, please identify family member(s), specify type of impairment and also state whether the impairment(s) has been diagnosed by a physician or specialist, and if so, when.
Did she/he receive any type of intervention (speech therapy, special education)? YES/NO
If yes, please specify the type of support, when support was given and the frequency and duration for which it was received.

The results obtained through the use of these types of questionnaires to study family history for language impairment have provided extremely useful information, which is in concord with the results of twin studies, adoption studies and genetic linkage studies, providing evidence that language heritability plays a substantial role in the variation in linguistic abilities in individuals with (and without) language disorders (Stromwold, 2001). Conti-Ramsden *et al.* (2006) directly addressed the validity of using parental questionnaires to find out about family language impairment. Results from parental interviews were compared to direct language and literacy assessments of immediate family members, and it was shown that the two methods yielded equivalent prevalence rates for language and literacy disorders: 34.5% based on parental report and 35% based on direct assessment. This result is similar to what has been found in previous studies addressing questionnaire methodology, such as that conducted by Gilger (1992), who compared, on the one hand, retrospective self-report on past academic achievement in dyslexic proband and control family members to archival longitudinal academic data, and, on the other hand, parental report of their child's academic achievement and current academic test scores. It was found that self-reports and parental reports about academic achievement, both of which were filled in at home and returned by mail, were both moderately correlated with actual tests scores; these results were taken to indicate that self-report and parental report are valid methods with which to gather information about family history (and current achievement).

Summarising, there is considerable evidence that children born to families with a history of language impairment are themselves at high risk for language delay and for SLI. Knowing that a child has a positive family history for language difficulties can thus provide valuable information to the clinician faced with a bilingual child who is experiencing language difficulties. It is important to bear in mind that a risk factor is precisely that – existence of a positive family history for language difficulties increases (considerably) the chances that a child will have language difficulties and absence of this risk factor decreases (considerably) the chance that a child will have language impairment. It does not mean that every child with a positive family history will have language impairment, and that no child without a positive family history for language impairment will have language impairment, as was shown here. In other words, this information in and of itself is not sufficient to determine a child's language status.

Language input and use, L1 and L2

The literature on 'external factors' in child bilingual acquisition is growing, though the relative influence of the variables in question is far from being fully understood, and this is particularly so in the case of bilingual children who also have language impairment. Yet, it is obvious that having a clear idea about the quantity and the quality of input and use for each language should help clinicians in interpreting language scores in the L2, as well as the L1 (when such scores are available). Proposed factors behind input quantity and quality include total length of exposure (LoE), frequency of exposure in various contexts (home, school, elsewhere), language used in different types of activities (reading, playing games, multimedia) and more widely studied acquisition variables such as socio-economic status (SES; as measured by parental education levels, parental profession/income level). Paradis (2011) provides an extensive review of studies exploring these factors. In spite of some differing results concerning the relative importance of these different factors in determining L2 (and L1) development in children, effects of variation in LoE and richness of L2 exposure have found consistent support (Bohman *et al.*, 2010; Paradis, 2011; Scheele *et al.*, 2010, among others). Furthermore, there is support for the conclusion that, alongside input, the child's output, the quality and quantity of language use by the child, is a factor of (perhaps even greater) importance (Bohman *et al.*, 2010; Paradis, 2011).

It is noteworthy that the variables which have been found to be related to language input and use are likely to affect different aspects of language differently. For example, Chondrogianni and Marinis (2011) studied a group of 43 TD successive bilingual Turkish–English children aged 6–9 with an age of L2 onset (AoO) of between 2;6 and 5;0. They not only found that vocabulary and complex syntax grow along with LoE, but also that children with a later AoO had higher vocabulary scores, and that children whose mothers had a low self-rated L2 (and SES status) had lower vocabulary and complex syntax scores. However, these same variables had no influence on the accuracy of tense marking morphology. Scheele *et al.* (2010) reported that home language learning activities for TD bilingual children have an influence especially on children's vocabulary skills. More results of this type will help clinicians know which language scores are likely to be explained by which variables concerning language input and richness.

Summary

It emerges from the preceding reviews that studies on parental reports used in multilingual contexts are limited, and those that target children with language impairment in these contexts are even fewer. Some of the conclusions about the validity of parental reports come from studies limited to monolingual families. For example, Callu et al. (2003) found that the correlation between parental report and child language scores was not dependent on parents' level of education, but this study looked only at monolingual TD children. Moreover, the studies including bilingual children with SLI were conducted exclusively in North America, either in the US in the particular situation of Spanish–English bilingualism or in Canada, a country in which multilingualism is extremely frequent, reaching 18%–26% of children under age 10 in large urban centres such as Edmonton and Toronto, where the Canadian study took place (Paradis et al., 2010). It thus seems probable that for a non-English/non-French-speaking family in Canada or a Spanish-speaking family in the US, it would not feel so unusual to be in this situation. Do parents with children growing up multilingually in other countries feel comfortable talking about their child's and their own use of language? There are, for example, countries in which language choice and use is a sensitive issue, having political (and religious) overtones. In both the Restrepo and the Paradis et al. studies, administration of parental questionnaires relied on bilingual interviewers familiar with the culture of the parents to administer parental questionnaires. In many communities, either such persons are not available or they are not accessible to clinicians. Is it feasible to use parental questionnaires in such contexts?

The COST Action IS0804 Parental Questionnaires

Rationale for design

Within COST Action IS0804, members sought to develop a single questionnaire incorporating questions about both possible developmental risk factors and about quantity and quality of language exposure and use for each of the child's languages. We thus naturally turned to the two questionnaires developed and used in Canada specifically for parents of bilingual children. The Alberta Language and Development Questionnaire (ALDeQ; Paradis et al., 2010), summarised in (7), gathers information about early development and language use. Section A, B, C and D each give rise to a sub-score, and together they constitute a total score.

(7)   Alberta Language and Development Questionnaire (ALDeQ; J.
        Paradis)

A. Early milestones	Age of onset of walking, first word, first sentence; how different was child's early language from age peers?
B. Current abilities in the first language	Expression, pronunciation, conversational ability, sentences, general satisfaction with child's language, comparison with children in home country, reason for lack of satisfaction
C. Behaviour patterns and activity preferences	Reading and writing in mother tongue compared with age peers, language/cognitive/physical/ other games or activities, speed in learning new things, behaviour pattern in performing activities, frustration when unable to communicate ideas
D. Family history	Education/profession of relatives, difficulties learning to read and write or in speaking and pronunciation, slow to learn to talk, repeating one or more grades at school – siblings, father, mother, father's relatives, mother's relatives

The Alberta Language Environment Questionnaire (ALEQ),
summarised in (8), questions parents about current language input and use
(Paradis, 2011). It is designed to produce a Language Use in the Home score
(with a high score indicating English use and a low score indicating mother
tongue use), an English richness score and a mother tongue richness score,
as well as to allow for calculation of AoE and months of exposure measures.

(8)   Alberta Language Environment Questionnaire (ALEQ; Paradis, 2011)

A. Questions to target child's mother	N yrs. lived in Canada, date of child's arrival in Canada, self-rating in English, language (lg.) spoken with child and lg. child speaks to this person.
B. Questions to target child's father	Lg. most often spoken by this person in home, Lg. of workplace. Yrs. of education.
C. Questions about other family members in the home	Is person primary caregiver (lg. spoken to child and lg. child speaks to this person). Other adults interacting regularly with child (lg. spoken to child and lg. child speaks to this person), brothers and sisters (lg. each one uses with child and lg. child uses with each one), birth order.

| D. Questions to parents about the target child | School attended/day care/babysitter, English exposure each day (hrs/week). Age of onset of consistent and significant exposure to English, weekly literacy and other lg. activities (reading, computer, TV/movies, storytelling, singing songs). Weekly literacy and other lg. activities in the mother tongue, extra-curricular activities (frequency and lg.), lgs. spoken between child and regular playmates. |

The idea was to unify these two questionnaires into one questionnaire which would enable clinicians to find answers to questions such as the following:

(9) (a) Is language performance, as measured by tests in the L2 or the L1, or as evaluated by the parent, related to a possible risk for language impairment?

(b) Is L2 performance affected by a lack of sufficient, sustained, quality exposure to the L2?

(c) Are L1 skills, as evaluated by parent or as measured by tests in the L1, affected by a lack of sufficient, sustained, quality exposure to the L1?

(d) Could any other factors be affecting the child's language profile? Hearing loss? Exposure to L2 primarily from parents who have limited skills in this language?

The goal in developing a parental questionnaire was for Action members to have a basis from which to adapt and pilot a specific questionnaire destined for clinical use in their countries. As reviewed above, very few studies have tested the use of parental questionnaires in multilingual contexts with the explicit goal of determining whether a child might have SLI. Furthermore, most studies of parental questionnaire use in multilingual contexts have been carried out in the North American context. Thus, not only were more studies needed, overall, but also a wider array of studies was needed, in order to broaden the national/cultural contexts to determine whether widespread use of this tool could be recommended. At the same time, the Action questionnaire was to be used to gather information needed to analyse results from the lexical, phonological, (morpho)syntactic, narrative and executive function tasks developed within the Action to address the Bi-SLI question (1), and presented in the other chapters of this volume.

Long and short versions

A first series of pilot studies was carried out using a long questionnaire incorporating many questions from the ALDeQ and the ALEQ questionnaires, a version of which was circulated as the 'Beirut-Tours questionnaire'. Country members were encouraged to use these basic questions, and to add supplementary questions deemed important in the particular country context. The basic long version included the sections and items listed in (8).

(10) The long version of the COST IS0804 Questionnaire: Beirut-Tours questionnaire

Sections	Items
1. General info. about the child	Birth date, country of birth, order of birth, list of siblings (age), languages currently spoken, Language most at home with.
2. Child's early history	Age walked, first word, first sentence, early lg. concerns, hearing problems, lg. exposition <age 4 (frequency –never/rarely/sometimes/usually/ always, age of onset, contexts)
3. Current skills	Nine items eliciting parental assessment of child's language. One question on L1 attrition.
4. Languages used at home	With whom and how often (parents, other adult, siblings), specifying lg. spoken to child and lg. child speaks to person. Lg. used between parents. Lg.-related activities.
5. Languages spoken outside the home	Name of school, lg. of schooling (hrs/week for each lg.), extra-curricular activities in each lg, lg. with playmates, lg. with family friends, lg. with visitors from other countries, travel to other countries where L2 is spoken.
6. Information about the mother and the father	Country of birth, current job, lg. at workplace, self-assessment of each lg.; years of education.
7. Difficulties	At school, with reading and spelling, understanding, expressing oneself; repeating a grade at school (siblings, mother, father, mother's family, father's family)

Pilot study design was basically the following: for a group of bilingual children who apparently were TD (no speech-language therapy, regular educational setting) and a group of bilingual children identified by current means as having SLI (seeing an SLP, in a special language programme), language performance on standardised tests in L1, where possible, and in L2 was compared with parental report to determine in what ways parental responses are predictive of child language performance. The objective of this first round of pilot studies was to select the questions which proved to be the most useful and the easiest to use and to arrive in this way at a short version of a unified parental questionnaire. Indeed, the parental interviews for the long version took between 20 minutes and 1 hour, making it not feasible for typical clinical use.

Studies in several countries led to a reduction of this questionnaire via elimination of the following questions: (1) questions that did not correlate well with children's L1 skills, where these could be independently tested; (2) questions that were redundant with other questions in terms of how well they correlated with children's L1 skills; and (3) questions which interviewers agreed made parents extremely uncomfortable, and which also did not have very strong predictive power. The number of questions was considerably reduced, and a common short version, the Parents of Bilingual children Questionnaire (PABIQ) emerged, and served as the basis for further piloting, with most studies reporting an interview time of a maximum of 15 minutes.

(11) The short version of COST Action IS0804 Questionnaire: PABIQ (COST Action IS0804, 2011)

Sections	Items
1. General info. about the child	Birth date, country of birth, languages currently spoken, Language most at home with.
2. Child's early history	First word, first sentence, early lg. concerns, hearing problems, lg. exposition <age 4 (frequency −never/rarely/sometimes/usually/always, age of onset, contexts)
3. Current skills	Five items: How child expresses himself/herself compared to children of the same age. Whether child speaks like a monolingual child of the same age. Difficulties making correct sentences. Satisfaction with child's ability to express himself/herself. Whether child feels frustrated when unable to communicate.
4. Languages used at home	Lg. used between child and parents/other adult/ siblings, lg.-related activities.
5. Languages richness	Weekly extra-curricular activities in each lg, lg. with playmates, lg. with family friends.
6. Information about the mother and the father	Country of birth, lg. at workplace, years of education, self-assessment of each lg.
7. Difficulties	With reading and spelling, understanding, expressing oneself (siblings, mother, father).

Overview of questionnaire pilot studies within COST Action IS0804

Pilot studies of questionnaires have been undertaken by 15 research labs in 12 different countries: Cyprus, Denmark, France, Germany, Greece, Iceland, Israel, Lebanon, Luxembourg, Malta, Poland and the UK. Studies in additional countries are currently underway. These studies have included groups of both TD bilingual children and bilingual children with SLI, with a very wide variety of L1–L2 combinations: some studies focused on specific combinations (Russian/Greek, English/Greek, Arabic/French, English/Arabic, Reunion Creole/French, Russian/German, Turkish/German, Lebanese/English, Lebanese/French, Maltese/English, Polish/English, English/Polish), while other studies had groups of children whose L1 varied and L2 was the country language (for example, L1 Polish, Hindi, Bengali, Gujardi or Nepalese and L2 English; L1 English, Arabic, Spanish, Bosnian, Vietnamese, Turkish, Kurdish, Moroccan, Urdu and L2 Danish). While some of these studies were based on already existing 'in-house' questionnaires designed for use with parents of bilingual children, most have used some form of the COST Action IS0804 Questionnaire, the PABIQ (or the BIPAQ; Abutbul-Oz *et al.*, 2012), which, as described in the previous section, is an outgrowth of Johanne Paradis' ALDeQ and ALEQ questionnaires (Paradis, 2011; Paradis *et al.*, 2010). Given the wide variety of national contexts, and language/cultural combinations, the results of these different pilot studies are extremely encouraging, providing reliable information that accurately distinguishes bilingual children with language impairment from TD bilingual children, and suggesting that clinical use of this tool is something to be universally recommended.

The above-mentioned pilot studies, however, like the Paradis *et al.* (2010) study, reported on the use of parental questionnaires with parents of bilingual children, with and without language impairment. The parents of the Bi-SLI children in these studies knew that their child was seeing a speech-language pathologist (and/or was attending a special language programme) when they completed the questionnaire. As Restrepo (1998) and Paradis *et al.* (2010) point out, being aware of a diagnosis for SLI might make parents rate their child accordingly on questions about current skills. And, even if prior knowledge of diagnosis might have less effect on how parents remember ages for early milestones, we cannot be certain of this. More generally, testing diagnostic usefulness based on studies of already diagnosed children is clearly not sufficient. The alternative, of course, is to conduct studies on children before clinical diagnosis has taken place. Such studies mimic the actual clinical situation of a bilingual child who comes for language assessment. Within COST Action IS0804, two prospective studies of this type have so far been carried out with parental questionnaires. Abutbul-Oz and Armon-Lotem (2013) have used a one-page questionnaire based on the BIPAQ (Abutbul-Oz *et al.*, 2012) for parents to fill-in in a clinical setting in Israel, and Kouba Hreich and Messarra (2013) have used the PABIQ in a clinical setting in Lebanon. The Lebanese study examined 30 bilingual Lebanese children aged 3–8 who came to a university language clinic for screening, after referral from their school. The Israeli study examined 41 bilingual children aged 2;6–6;6 who had been referred to an SLP and 12 children who had not been referred. Preliminary results of these studies are quite promising, suggesting that information obtained from parental questionnaires of children later diagnosed as having language impairment was reliably different from that obtained from parents of children who did not receive such a diagnosis. In other words, parents were able to accurately assess their child's early milestones and current language skills (of the child's L1) without prior knowledge of clinical diagnosis.

A complementary way of looking at parental report in Bi-SLI contexts, which is not entirely tied to previous parental knowledge of language impairment, is to explicitly look at whether children with the Bi-SLI label are truly SLI and whether children without this label are truly TD. This type of study requires large numbers of participants and some independent way of ascertaining language impairment, such as the availability of bilingual language norms. In Germany, where a standardised language battery with separate bilingual norms is available, Grimm and Schulz (2014) recruited and tested monolingual and bilingual 4- to 6-year-old children, both with and without a clinical diagnosis of language impairment. On the basis of language scores, children were assigned to either an SLI group or a TD group, and then these groups were compared for misdiagnosis and for risk factors for SLI determined via a parental questionnaire (age of first word, age of first multiword utterances, existence of family members with oral or written language impairment). Cases of over-diagnosis and under-diagnosis were found in the monolingual and in the bilingual children; however, there was much more over-diagnosis in the latter, though overall, under-diagnosis was more common than over-diagnosis in both groups. As for the prevalence of SLI risk factors, onset of multiword stage after age 24 months and family history of oral language impairment were nearly twice as frequent in each of the monolingual and the bilingual SLI groups compared to the corresponding TD groups. In other words, parents of bilingual children did not differ from parents of monolingual children in their ability to report on these particular risk factors for SLI. As Grimm and Schulz (2014) are careful to emphasise, reliance solely on such information would not have been sufficient to allow for diagnosis: Only about half of the children assigned to the SLI group on the basis of standardised language scores (with appropriate norms) had one or more risk factors for SLI.

Guidelines for administration, scoring and interpretation

Who fills out the questionnaire? The PABIQ was designed to be administered in person by a trained interviewer. The pilot studies described above generally used student interviewers, often students with SLP training, but some research groups have conducted phone interviews. Other groups have had parents fill in the questionnaire by themselves, and one group has even set up an online form. To our knowledge, no data are available so far that would allow comparison of the reliability/efficacy of these different methods for the Bi-SLI research question.

What language is the questionnaire administered in? Who 'translates'? Obviously, the questionnaire must be presented in a language which the parents have sufficient knowledge of. It is sometimes not obvious what 'sufficient knowledge' really means, and, in many cases it will be necessary to be able to administer the questionnaire, or at least part of it, in the home language. This is fine for clinicians who have access to bilingual personnel, who are linguistically and culturally able to administer the questionnaire to bilingual parents who do not know the country language (well enough). Another option is to use a specialised interpreter or a 'multicultural broker' (Paradis *et al.*, 2010). Many clinicians do not have access to either, or not for (all of) the languages for which this would be needed. In the pilot studies described above, other means have been used, such as relying for translation on an older sibling, an adult relative or friend; these practices are probably not optimal, but may be better than nothing. Although, as far as we know, no specific data are available regarding the comparative reliability of these practices, use of these varying practices in the various pilot studies does not seem to have invalidated the results, which points to the usefulness of the same questions that were proven to be useful in previous studies where a specialised translator or multicultural broker was available. For example, the predictive value of early language milestone ages was very high in the Paradis (2010) study, and it also was in the pilot studies carried out within COST Action IS0804, including those where unconventional means were used to communicate with the parent.

What about 'false' answers? Some answers given by parents clearly cannot be true: for example, first word at age 6 months or first sentence at age 10 months. In our experience these 'ridiculously' early milestone answers are given only by parents of TD children. In other words, they merely indicate how satisfied the parents were with their child's early language development. Such answers thus are in fact useful for this reason. Interestingly, we have not observed parents of TD children giving ridiculously late milestone answers. It goes without saying that the interviewer should be instructed not to comment on such parental responses, and not to try to coax the parent into supplying an alternative answer.

Another false answer we have encountered requires much greater skill on the part of the interviewer. We have encountered parents claiming to speak only the school language at home, contrary to fact (for example, in contradiction with the fact that the parents' native language is quite obviously the child's dominant language). Based on what other parents have told us, and on knowledge of the local and national language environments, we believe that parents make these claims because they have been explicitly instructed to use the language of the school by school personnel or because they have heard about national language decrees which warn against using any other language at home. Such parents may even have the impression that the purpose of the questionnaire is to check up on whether they are following such guidelines. Such reactions, obviously, have to be taken into account when evaluating the information gathered from these particular parents for these questions. Patiently explaining to parents how natural and beneficial it is to maintain communication in the parental native language and what the purpose of the questionnaire is can bring parents to 'admit' that they do in fact use their language with their child.

What about disagreement between parents? When both parents are present at the interview, there can sometimes be (subtle) disagreement between them regarding significant points. For example, we saw a case where the father assured the interviewer that his child had developed language 'on schedule' and that he and his spouse had never been concerned about the child's language, while the mother, who was standing just behind her husband, made faces and shook her head. Again, interviewers should be instructed not to comment on such contradictions, but to carefully note them. We decided to code such mixed reactions as 'yes' for parental concern, since at least one of the parents was concerned. When parents gave two different ages for first word and/or first sentence, we coded the mean between the two, and indicated each of the parents' estimates in an accompanying commentary.

Identifying minority languages/multilingualism. Minority languages in many countries are sometimes not considered to be languages even by the people who speak them. Many parents thus will not spontaneously provide the name of the language spoken in the home. In addition, there may be cultural/political impetus to claim to use the country's majority language in the home. For example, many speakers of Berber languages (such as Tamazight, Riff and Shilha in Morocco, and Kabyle and Shawiya in Algeria) claim to speak Arabic at home, when in fact no Arabic is used at all, and the children growing up in these families may thus not have any knowledge of Arabic. It is therefore important that interviewers know the names of the minority languages in the country so that they can directly ask, 'Do you speak Kabyle with your child? With your spouse?', 'I think/ I've heard that some people from your country speak Kabyle or some other language at home. Do you ever speak Kabyle or some other language?' Since some parents might be convinced that their language is 'merely a dialect', it would probably even be useful to ask if 'any other language *or dialect* is spoken at home'. It is very important for interviewers to always ask if any other language is spoken in the home or known by the child. This is especially so if assessment tools are available for assessing some home languages, and therefore a child might run the risk of being evaluated in a language he/she does not know at all, or which is in fact a (little known) third language. The 'other language' column in the PABIQ, even in cases which are assumed to be straightforward cases of *bi*lingualism, should not be neglected, as many children in fact speak three or more languages.

Scoring. Paradis' ALDeQ and ALEQ questionnaires make use of a scoring scheme in which individual questions have points, which can be grouped together for section scores, and finally for a general score for the entire questionnaire. The ALDeQ yields a score from 0 to 1.0, where 1 corresponds to typical language development and 0 is meant to be 'indicative of children with language delay/impairment'. The ALEQ yields two scores from 0 to 1.0, for each of the child's languages: Language use in the home and Richness. Such scores are designed for clinicians to be able to easily compare input and use in the child's languages.

The PABIQ currently yields several different sub-scores. Different teams within COST Action IS0804 are currently testing different ways of collapsing sub-scores into indices, along the lines of the ALEQ and ALDeQ schemes. Indices including those summarised in (10) have yielded promising results in distinguishing Bi-SLI and Bi-TD children in very different multilingual contexts, in France and in Lebanon (Tuller *et al.*, in press), when used in combination with language assessment tools developed specifically to be used with bilingual children (see Chiat, this volume; Marinis and Armon-Lotem, this volume; Schulz, this volume).

(12) A Scoring Scheme for the PABIQ

(a) Positive Early Development: ___ /14

Age of first word	≤15 months: 6 points; 16–24 months: 4 points; ≥15 months: 0 points
Age of first sentence	≤24 months: 6 points; 25–30 months: 4 points; ≥31 months: 0 points
Early parental concerns	No: 2 points; Yes: 0 points

(b) Positive Family History: ___ /9

No=1 point; yes=0 points	Siblings	Mother	Father
Difficulties mainly with reading and spelling no/yes			
Difficulties understanding others when they speak no/yes			
Difficulties expressing oneself orally (pronunciation, forming sentences, finding the right word, etc.) no/yes			

(c) No Risk Index: ___ /23

Positive Early Development	/14
Positive Family History	/9

(d) L1 Use and Richness ___ (0–1.0)   (e) L2 Use and Richness ___ (0–1.0)

Early exposure L1	Current richness L1		Early exposure L2	Current richness L2	
Use and contexts <age 4	Use at home	Activities, playmates, family friends	Use and contexts <age 4	Use at home	Activities, playmates, family friends

The interpretation of the current skills sub-score, not surprisingly, is particularly delicate, leading researchers to avoid collapsing this score with other scores. For one thing, it is not at all clear that all parents are able to estimate their child's skills in the L2, especially if they themselves do not master that language. Another potential problem is the question of L1 maintenance/attrition/incomplete acquisition. As Paradis (2011) notes, parental report on a child's current L1 skills can be expected to vary according to the particular bilingual situation: Is the country language becoming the child's dominant language to the detriment of the original home language? Even though it therefore might be prudent to interpret this score separately, we would like to emphasise that the available results of the studies undertaken so far have shown that parents are apparently able to take such different contexts into account: indeed, parental reports of current skills have proven to be accurate, supporting the conclusions of the previous studies of Bi-SLI and Bi-TD populations.

Summary and Next Steps

Summarising, we can recommend the clinical use of a parental questionnaire such as the PABIQ in order to gather information about potential risk for SLI (early developmental history) and information about early and current exposure and use of languages. Such questionnaires can be easily and successfully used in very different clinical settings, need not be time consuming and provide valuable information which can be used to better understand the reasons behind a bilingual child's low language scores, and thus contribute to clinical diagnosis for SLI.

Currently, the PABIQ is being further refined and adapted to the needs of particular multilingual contexts in various countries. Our objective, from the outset, has not been to create an identical tool to be simply translated into different country languages, but rather to propose a basic version for researchers and clinicians to adapt, in collaboration, for optimal clinical efficiency in particular national and linguistic contexts. Interested researchers and clinicians are encouraged to contact COST Action IS0804 members from their country, listed on http://www.bi-sli.org, to enquire about use of the PABIQ or a similar questionnaire.

Acknowledgements

Thanks to Hadar Abutbul-Oz, Angela Grimm, Edith Kouba Hreich, Camille Moitel Messarra, Philippe Prévost and an anonymous reviewer for helpful input on this chapter.

Note

(1)   Sensitivity of parental report in the older group is low. It is not clear whether this might not have been a function of the particular language tests used (which were not the same as those used with the younger children).

References

Abutbul-Oz, H., Armon-Lotem, S. and Walters, J. (2012) *Bilingual Parents Questionnaire (BIPAQ)*. Ramat-Gan: Bar Ilan University.
Abutbul-Oz, H. and Armon-Lotem, S. (2013) The use of the Bilingual Parents Questionnaire (BIPAQ) in a clinical setting. Ms. Bar Ilan-University.
American Psychiatric Association (2013) *Diagnostic and Statistical Manual of Mental Disorders, Fifth Edition (DSM-5™)*. Arlington, VA: American Psychiatric Publishing.
Bohman, T., Bedore, L., Peña, L., Mendez-Perez, A. and Gillam, R. (2010) What you hear and what you say: Language performance in Spanish-English bilinguals. *International Journal of Bilingual Education and Bilingualism* 13 (3), 325–344.
Callu, D., Jacquier-Roux, M., Cusin, F., Giannopulu, I. and Dellatolas, G. (2003) Pertinence du repérage par les parents des retards de langage chez l'enfant entre quatre et six ans. *Archives de pédiatrie* 10, 1061–1067.
Chondrogianni, V. and Marinis, T. (2011) Differential effects of internal and external factors on the development of vocabulary, tense morphology and morpho-syntax in successive bilingual children. *Linguistic Approaches to Bilingualism* 1 (3), 318–345.
Choudhury, N. and Benasich, A.A. (2003) A family aggregation study: The influence of family history and other risk factors on language development. *Journal of Speech, Language, and Hearing Research* 46 (2), 261–272.
Conti-Ramsden, G., Simkin, Z. and Pickles, A. (2006) Estimating familial loading in SLI: A comparison of direct assessment versus parental interview. *Journal of Speech, Language, and Hearing Research* 49 (1), 88–101.
COST Action IS0804 (2010) Beirut-Tours questionnaire. See http://www.bi-sli.org/files_members/background-questionnaires/Beirut-Tours-Questionnaire_French.pdf (accessed 11 December 2014).
COST Action IS0804 (2011) Questionnaire for Parents of Bilingual Children (PABIQ). See http://www.bi-sli.org/files_members/background-questionnaires/COST_Questionnaire_Short_English.pdf (accessed 11 December 2014).
Flax, J.F., Realpe-Bonilla, T., Roesler, C., Choudhury, N. and Benasich, A. (2008) Using early standardized language measures to predict later language and early reading outcomes in children at high risk for language-learning impairments. *Journal of Learning Disabilities* 42 (1), 61–75.

Gilger, J.W. (1992) Genetics in disorders of language. *Clinics in Communication Disorders* 2, 35–47.

Grimm, A. and Schulz, P. (2014) Specific Language Impairment and early second language acquisition: The risk of over- and underestimation. *Child Indicators Research*, 7, 821–841. Published online DOI 10.1007/s12187-013-9230-6.

Kouba Hreich, E. and Messarra, C. (2013) Assessment of L2 children in the Lebanese multilingual context: Using Questionnaire for Parents of Bilingual Children (PABIQ) scores as diagnostic indicators for language impairment. Ms., Saint Joseph University, Beirut.

Montrul, S. (2008) *Incomplete Acquisition in Bilingualism: Re-examining the Age Factor.* Amsterdam: John Benjamins Publishing Company.

Paradis, J. (2011) Individual differences in child English second language acquisition: Comparing child-internal and child-external factors. *Linguistic Approaches to Bilingualism* 1 (3), 213–237.

Paradis, J., Emmerzael, K. and Sorenson Duncan, T. (2010) Assessment of English language learners: Using parent report on first language development. *Journal of Communication Disorders* 43 (6), 474–497.

Preston, J.L., Frost, S.J., Mencl, W.E., Rulbright, R.K., Landi, N., Grigorendko, E., Jacobsen, L. and Pugh, K. (2010) Early and late talkers: School-age language, literacy and neuro-linguistic differences. *Brain* 133 (Pt.8), 2185–2195.

Rescorla, L. and Alley, A. (2001) Validation of the Language Development Survey (LDS). *Journal of Speech, Language, and Hearing Research* 44 (2), 434–445.

Restrepo, M.A. (1998) Identifiers of predominantly Spanish-speaking children with language impairment. *Journal of Speech, Language, and Hearing Research*, 41 (6), 1398–1411.

Rice, M.L. (2007) Children with specific language impairment: Bridging the genetic and developmental perspectives. In E. Hoff and M. Shatz (eds) *Handbook of Language Development* (pp. 411–431). Oxford: Blackwell Publishers.

Rice, M.L., Haney, K.R. and Wexler, K. (1998) Family histories of children with SLI who show extended optional infinitive. *Journal of Speech, Language, and Hearing Research*, 41 (2), 419–432.

Rice, M.L., Taylor, C.L. and Zubrick, S.R. (2008) Language outcomes of 7-year-old children with or without a history of late language emergence at 24 months. *Journal of Speech, Language, and Hearing Research* 51 (2), 394–407.

Scheele, A.F., Leseman, P.P.M. and Mayo, A.Y. (2010) The home language environment of monolingual and bilingual children and their language proficiency. *Applied Psycholinguistics* 31 (1), 117–140.

Spitz, R.V., Tallal, P., Flax, J. and Benasich, A.A. (1997) Look who's talking: A prospective study of familial transmission of language impairments. *Journal of Speech and Hearing Research* 40 (1), 990–1001.

Stromswold, K. (1998) The genetics of spoken language disorders. *Human Biology* 70 (2), 297–324.

Stromswold, K. (2001) The heritability of language: A review and meta-analysis of twin, adoption, and linkage studies. *Language* 77 (4), 647–723.

Tuller, L., Abboud, L., Ferré, S., Fleckstein, A., Prévost, P., dos Santos, C., Scheidnes, M., Zebib, R. (in press) Specific language impairment and bilingualism: Assembling the pieces. In Cornelia Hamann & Esther Ruigendijk (eds) *Language Acquisition and Development: Proceedings of GALA 2013.* Newcastle: Cambridge Scholars Publishing.

Tuller, L., Messarra, C., Prévost, P. and Zebib, R. (2011) Questionnaire pour parents d'enfants bilingues, French version of the PaBiQ (COST Action IS0804, 2011). Ms., Université François Rabelais, Tours.

Zubrick, S.R., Taylor, C.L., Rice, M.L. and Siegers, D.W. (2007) Late language emergence at 24 months: An epidemiological study of prevalence, predictors, and covariates. *Journal of Speech, Language, and Hearing Research* 50 (6), 1562–1592.

Appendix A: COST Action IS0804 Questionnaire for Parents of Bilingual Children (PABIQ Questionnaire)

Child Code: .... Date of interview: .... Parent interviewed: Mother ☐ Father ☐

****

COST Action IS0804 *Questionnaire for Parents of Bilingual Children* (**PABIQ Questionnaire**)[1]

1. **General Information about the Child**
   1.1   Birth Date: _____
   1.2   If place of birth is not country of residence, date of arrival in country of residence: _____
   1.3   What languages does your child speak now?

Home language (specify)	Country language	Other (specify)

   1.4   Which language do you think your child feels the most at home with? _____

2. **Child's early history: Language, etc.**
   2.1   How old was your child when he/she spoke his/her first word? _____
   2.2   How old was your child when he/she first put words together to make short sentences? _____
   Example: *more water; more milk;* etc.
   2.3   Before your child was 3 or 4 years old, were you ever concerned about his/her language?   NO   or   YES
   _____

   2.4   Has your child ever had any hearing problems or frequent ear infections?   NO   or   YES _____
   2.5   At what age was your child first in contact with each of his/her languages?

	Age (months if possible)		Age (months if possible)
Home language		Other (specify)	
Country language		Other (specify)	

2.6   In general, before your child was 4 years old, was he/she exposed to:

	0 Never	1 Rarely	2 Sometimes	3 Usually	4 Very often/ always
Home language (specify)					
Country language					
Other (specify)					

2.7   In what context and at what age did this exposure (before age 4) begin (put age in all appropriate cells)?

	Home language (specify)	Country language	Other
a. Mother			
b. Father			
c. Grandparents			
d. Babysitter/childminder			
e. Other adults (specify)			
f. Siblings			
g. Nursery school/day care centre			
h. Kindergarten			
Total *(1 point per cell)*			
Total by language	/8	/8	/8

3.   Current Skills

	Home language (specify)	Country language	Other
3.1 Compared to other children the same age, how do you think your child expresses himself/herself in ...? *0=not very well/not as well as them; 1=a little less well/a few differences; 2=(generally) the same; 3=very well, better*	0 1 2 3	0 1 2 3	0 1 2 3

3.2 Compared to other children the same age, do you think your child has difficulties making correct sentences? *0=yes, many difficulties; 1=some difficulties; 2=(generally) the same; 3=no difficulties, better than other children*	0	1	2	3	0	1	2	3	0	1	2	3
3.3 Are you satisfied with your child's ability to express himself/herself in ...? Always? *0=not at all satisfied; 1=not very satisfied; 2=pretty satisfied/ generally satisfied; 3=very/totally satisfied*	0	1	2	3	0	1	2	3	0	1	2	3
3.4 Does your child feel frustrated when he/she can't communicate in ...? *0=very frustrated/almost always frustrated/very often frustrated; 1=often frustrated/yes; 2=sometimes frustrated, but not often; 3=(almost) never frustrated/no*	0	1	2	3	0	1	2	3	0	1	2	3
3.5 Do you think that your child speaks like a child the same age who only speaks .....? *0=not very well/not as well as them; 1=a little less well/a few differences; 2=(generally) the same; 3=very well, better*	0	1	2	3	0	1	2	3	0	1	2	3
Total by language	/15				/15				/15			

4. Comparison between languages used at home[2]

4.1 With parents

Mother ↔ Child

	0 Never	1 Rarely	2 Sometimes	3 Usually	4 Very often/always
Home language (specify)					
Country language					
Other					

Father ↔ Child

	0 Never	1 Rarely	2 Sometimes	3 Usually	4 Very often/always
Home language (specify)					
Country language					
Other					

4.2 Is there another adult who regularly takes care of your child? (grandparent, babysitter, etc.)   YES   or   NO

Other Adult ↔ Child

	0 Never	1 Rarely	2 Sometimes	3 Usually	4 Very often/always
Home language (specify)					
Country language					
Other					

4.3 With siblings (brothers and sisters):

Siblings ↔ Child

	0 Never	1 Rarely	2 Sometimes	3 Usually	4 Very often/always
Home language (specify)					
Country language					
Other					

5. Languages spoken in other contexts

5.1 What language activities does your child do each week and in what language(s)?

Activities	Home language (specify)			Country language			Other		
	0 Never or almost never	1 At least once a week	2 Every day	0 Never or almost never	1 At least once a week	2 Every day	0 Never or almost never	1 At least once a week	2 Every day
a. Reading (books, magazines, comic books, newspapers)									
b. Television/movies/cinema									
c. Storytelling									
Total									
Total by language			/6			/6			/6

5.2 What language is spoken between your child and the friends he/she plays with regularly?

Child ↔ Friends

	0 Never	1 Rarely	2 Sometimes	3 Usually	4 Very often/always
Home language (specify)					
Country language					
Other (specify) _____					

5.3 What language is spoken with family friends with whom you are in regular contact?

Family Friends	0 Never 0%	1 Rarely 25%	2 Sometimes 50%	3 Usually 75%	4 Always 100%
Home language (specify)					
Country language					
Other (specify) _____					

6. Information about the mother and the father

6.1 Information about the mother

6.1.1 In which country were you born? _____

6.1.2 If you are currently working, what is the language you use at your workplace? _____

6.1.3 Education:

	Number of years	Further information
Primary school	Yes / No	
Secondary school	Yes / No	
University	Yes / No	
Other professional training	Yes / No	

6.1.4 In your opinion, how well do you speak the following languages?

	0 Only a few words	1 Gets along, but with difficulty	2 Basic abilities (gets along)	3 Well	4 Very well
Home language (specify)					
Country language					
Other					

6.2   Information about the father

6.2.1   In which country were you born? _____

6.2.2   If you are currently working, what is the language you use at your workplace? _____

6.2.3   Education:

		Number of years	Further information
Primary school	Yes / No		
Secondary school	Yes / No		
University	Yes / No		
Other professional training	Yes / No		

6.1.4   In your opinion, how well do you speak the following languages?

	0 Only a few words	1 Gets along, but with difficulty	2 Basic abilities (gets along)	3 Well	4 Very well
Home language (specify)					
Country language					
Other					

7. Difficulties

In each cell, please   YES   or   NO:

	Brother/sister	Mother	Father	Father's family	Mother's family
Difficulties mainly with reading and spelling					
Difficulties understanding others when they speak					
Difficulties expressing oneself orally (pronunciation, forming sentences, finding the right word, etc.)					
Total					

[1] This questionnaire is the short version of a longer questionnaire piloted by research groups in several countries within COST Action IS0804, which was in part based on the ALEQ (Paradis, 2011) and the ALDeQ (Paradis et al., 2010). It should be cited as "COST Action IS0804 (2011 Questionnaire for Parents of Bilingual Children (PABIQ). See http://www.bi-sli.org/files_members/background-questionnaires/COST_Questionnaire_Short_English.pdf (accessed 11 December 2014)"

[2] If the parent asks how to interpret words such as 'rarely' etc., the following explanation can be used: 'Considering the total time in exchanges between you/the father/family friends and your child, how much time is in language X and how much time is in language Y? If this were put over 4 points (with 0 for never and 4 for very often or always) would you say 4 for language X and 0 for language Y, 3 for language X and 1 for language Y, 2 for language X and 2 for language Y, 1 for language X and 3 for language Y, or 0 for language X and 4 for language Y.'

12 Proposed Diagnostic Procedures for Use in Bilingual and Cross-Linguistic Contexts

Elin Thordardottir

COST Action IS0804 brought together researchers and clinicians from various countries in Europe and several neighbouring countries (24 in total) with the common purpose of conducting research on specific language impairment (SLI) in monolingual and bilingual children (termed 'Bi-SLI' in this project) from various language backgrounds. An important focus of this action was the development of research and clinical tools that would be comparable across languages, to facilitate the identification of SLI in monolingual children speaking different languages, in bilingual children speaking different language combinations, and also to enable cross-linguistic comparisons and the examination of language-specific versus universal factors underlying language development and language impairment. The development of various types of assessment tools by researchers affiliated with the COST Action is detailed in other chapters of this volume. However, in order to be able to compare the manifestation of SLI across languages in a meaningful and conclusive manner, it is of paramount importance that the children participating in the research studies be identified in comparable ways as having or not having SLI. European countries and language areas vary greatly in their clinical traditions in speech-language pathology. In some language areas, normative data and standardised tests are readily available; in other areas, test materials are limited to informal procedures, while in yet other areas, SLI is not known at all or not recognised as a condition warranting identification or intervention. European countries also vary in terms of who is in charge of clinical language assessments – in some countries, speech-language pathologists (SLPs; or speech-language therapists, or logopedes) are well established, while in other countries, few people have completed training in this profession. The purpose of this chapter is to outline general principles and specific procedures of clinical language assessment, applicable to monolingual and bilingual children.

Procedures are described that can be used to assess languages in which few or no language tests and little previous research exist – which was the reality faced by many of the Action's researchers who conducted pioneering research on SLI in monolingual and bilingual children speaking various European languages.

At the outset, the assessment committee (AC)[1] of the COST Action had as its role to promote the clinical applicability of the findings and the dissemination of results to clinical communities. Early on in the Action, however, the AC undertook prospective efforts to encourage the use of consistent diagnostic procedures in studies undertaken across language areas – to the extent possible. As a first step, in spring 2011, the AC circulated a survey to all members asking about diagnostic procedures in clinical use in their respective countries. Among the questions asked were (1) whether specific diagnostic criteria are in effect for the identification of language impairment in monolingual and bilingual children, (2) what measures are part of a typical assessment protocol and (3) what referral method the research team in the given language envisioned using in their COST Action related studies. Detailed responses were obtained from 14 countries. As the summary of responses provided in Table 12.1 reveals, some countries set official criteria in terms of specific scores on standardised tests, including Finland, Ireland (for English speakers), Israel, Iceland and France. The specific cut-off points vary, however, including the fifth and tenth percentiles, and –1.5 and – 2 standard deviations (SD) below the mean. The specific tests used for identification purposes vary as well. In their more detailed descriptions, some survey responders reported that some tests had been constructed specifically for their language; however, it was more common for standardised tests to be renormed translations and/or adaptations of previously existing tests, or simple translations without renorming. In contrast to these countries that use standardised tests, the criteria reported for Russia involved specific qualitative findings, including simplified syntax, many grammatical mistakes, highly reduced receptive vocabulary and abnormal phonology. In Poland, it was reported that SLI is not currently recognised nor is it identified clinically. Some of the countries reported variability in criteria across clinics and some reported also that different criteria are used for clinical work and for research (for example Israel; it should be noted that this is not uncommon in published research studies, for example on English). In addition to those assessments that are designated as the official criterion for identification, other procedures reported to be used included formal tests, informal assessments, spontaneous and elicited language samples, informal observations, descriptive data and parent questionnaires. None of the countries from which responses were obtained reported on official criteria being in effect for the identification of SLI in bilingual children.

Table 12.1 Responses to a questionnaire surveying clinical practices in European countries (language refers to monolingual speakers – bilingual speakers within each country speak various language combinations)

Country/ language	Official clinical and research diagnostic criteria in effect for monolingual children?	Typical assessment protocols and measures	Specific official diagnostic criteria in effect for bilingual children	Method of referral for research studies
Finland/ Finnish	ICD-10 Language: Clinic: –2 SD Research: less strict criterion Cognition: IQ of 70 or higher	Several standardised tests, multidisciplinary teams	No official criteria	Clinical referral
Ireland/ English, Irish	Language: –2 SD Non-verbal IQ 70 or higher Hearing 40 dB HL	No standardised tests available for Irish	No official criteria Same procedures as for monolinguals	No studies yet
Israel/Hebrew	Language: Clinic: 1 year delay; family history Research: –1.5 SD	Several standardised tests; observation of morphosyntactic mistakes	No official criteria Parental questionnaires	Clinical referral School referral
Iceland/ Icelandic	ICD-10 10th percentile (–1.3 SD)	Several standardised tests; spontaneous language	No official criteria	Clinical referral School referral
Russia/ Russian	Specific qualitative findings	No standardised tests. Well-established protocol: elicited and spontaneous samples, specific error patterns	No official criteria	Clinical referral

(Continued)

Table 12.1 (Continued)

Country/ language	Official clinical and research diagnostic criteria in effect for monolingual children?	Typical assessment protocols and measures	Specific official diagnostic criteria in effect for bilingual children	Method of referral for research studies
Italian/Italian	DSM IV or ICD-10 Discrepancy between verbal and performance IQ	Several standardised tests	No official criteria	Clinical referral
Croatia/ Croatian	No specific criteria	A few standardised tests. Procedure depends on age and institution	No official criteria	Clinical referral School referral
Malta/Maltese, English	No specific criteria	Informal assessment; potential risk markers	No official criteria Informal procedures as for monolinguals	Clinical referral
UK/English	No specific criteria Identification based on level of handicap rather than specific test results	Well-established protocols, but which differ between clinics	No official criteria	Clinical referral
Norway/ Norwegian	No specific criteria reported	Standardised tests, structured longitudinal observation	No official criteria Testing in both languages Tests translated by interpreters Normed tests for bilinguals available 6–16 years	Clinical referral

Country/ language	Official clinical and research diagnostic criteria in effect for monolingual children?	Typical assessment protocols and measures	Specific official diagnostic criteria in effect for bilingual children	Method of referral for research studies
Cyprus/Cypriot Greek	No specific criteria reported	Several assessment tools, spontaneous language, informal observation	No official criteria	Clinical referral School referral
Poland/Polish	SLI not diagnosed in Poland	Descriptive procedures Assessment tools available for dyslexia and articulation	No official criteria	No studies yet
Netherlands/ Dutch	−1.5 SD on comprehension and production tests	Standardised tests	No official criteria Parental questionnaires	Clinical referral School referral
France/French	Diagnosis of 'dysphasie' made by neuropediatrician (and interdisciplinary team) DSM IV, 5th percentile or −2 SD	Standardised tests, normative data, observational data, informal assessments, specific error patterns	No official criteria	Clinical referral School referral Screening Parent referral

This review of clinical procedures shows on one hand that, across countries, language assessment measures and protocols are actively being developed and that, within each language region, attempts are being made to follow a standard set of procedures and criteria. On the other hand, the review documents great variability in the clinical identification of children with SLI between language regions. It is common in cross-linguistic research to rely on clinical referral for participant recruitment, and the survey in fact confirmed that researchers in the 14 countries overwhelmingly reported using or planning to use such a procedure. Clearly, cross-linguistic studies cannot presume to have recruited comparable groups of children simply on the basis of having used clinical referral. On the contrary, differences should be expected. For example, a hypothetical study comparing Finnish and Icelandic runs the risk of the Finnish children having more severe language impairments given that a stricter cut-off score of –2 SD is in effect in Finland, compared to –1.3 SD in Iceland. A study comparing the grammatical development of children from the Netherlands and Russia with SLI might find a higher frequency of such errors in the Russian-speaking children given that qualitative observations of many grammatical mistakes are part of the diagnostic criteria used in Russia, but not in the Netherlands. Importantly, however, the extent and type of the differences resulting from different tests and cut-off criteria are generally hard to predict, making their impact on study findings unknown. To the extent that the diagnostic accuracy of particular tests has been documented, it has become clear that they vary in how accurately they rule in or out the presence of language impairment, what cut-off score results in the most accurate decisions and the age range in which a particular measure is most accurate (Conti-Ramsden, 2003; Conti-Ramsden et al., 2001; Elin Thordardottir et al., 2011; Plante & Vance, 1994). Furthermore, a test that is adapted and renormed cannot be assumed to retain the same diagnostic accuracy in the language into which it is translated, given differences in the surface manifestation of SLI across languages (e.g. Elin Thordardottir, 2008; Paradis & Crago, 2001), including in the two languages of a bilingual child with SLI (Stavrakaki et al., 2011).

Proposed Diagnostic Guidelines for Cost Action Studies

In light of these vast cross-linguistic differences, a set of guidelines was proposed in spring 2012 to promote consistency in the procedures used for the identification of children with SLI in studies conducted within the Action. At the present time, it is not possible to develop diagnostic guidelines that lead to a uniform and fully comparable way of identifying

SLI across languages. In fact, a main purpose of the COST Action was to help develop such procedures. For now, the strategy proposed was to adopt a common conceptual definition of SLI, to make the most of the resources available for assessment in each language and, most importantly, to *document* in as detailed a way as possible given the available tools, the language level of the children that are recruited for studies. While this procedure cannot standardise the recruitment process across languages, it will greatly aid in the interpretation of findings and in assessing whether findings from different languages can be compared meaningfully. The guidelines were proposed as a practical guide or tutorial, given that in many of the countries involved, there is very little precedent for clinical identification of language impairment and much uncertainty as to how to proceed.

General considerations

Clinical referral, parental referral, screening?
How children are identified for studies can influence the sampling and subsequent results. For example, Ellis Weismer *et al.* (2000) reported on the non-word repetition accuracy of two groups of children with SLI: a group identified based on second-grade diagnostic status and a group identified based on current intervention status, with somewhat different results. Clinical referral may involve children referred from one or several local clinics (e.g. Elin Thordardottir *et al.*, 2011), or in some cases, children enrolled in special classes for children with language impairment based on previous diagnosis (e.g. Conti-Ramsden, 2003; Paradis & Crago, 2001). Clinical referral has the clear advantage that children have already been identified professionally. To have reached this point, the children are likely to have had significant persistent problems which led to clinical testing. However, a limitation is that test procedures may vary widely, not least in language communities where tests and procedures are not well established. Even if children are referred with a previous diagnosis, the researcher should verify that the children have a language impairment by gathering additional background information and conducting language testing as part of the intake protocol for the study. Reasons why discrepancies may be found between the clinical criteria by which the referred children were identified and the inclusionary criteria of a particular research study may include, for example, that different clinicians or clinics may use different operational definitions of severity levels or cut-off criteria. In addition, the criteria may vary in terms of which domains of language contribute most to the identification (for example, some children may have been identified based on a speech disorder rather than a primary language disorder, but may still receive the same official diagnostic label as children identified based on a language disorder).

Another recruitment method is to identify children by screening large groups of children not otherwise considered at particular risk for language impairment, for example as a routine part of school activities or health-care check-ups. An example of a study using large-scale screening is that of Tomblin *et al.* (1996). Other studies have used screenings of smaller groups of children (e.g. Perozzi & Sanchez, 1992). The screening method requires the availability of well-developed screening measures whose accuracy has been demonstrated previously. Two additional things to keep in mind are that failure on a screening test indicates that there is increased likelihood of the presence of the disorder, but does not provide conclusive evidence beyond indicating the need for further testing. Secondly, the course of developmental language impairment includes a history of early significant delays in language development (ICD-10, WHO, 1992, 2004). Such a history will be part of the clinical findings that led to the identification of SLI in children who are referred clinically, but is not necessarily true of children who fail a screening test. For these reasons, whether children are initially identified based on developmental concerns or low test scores on a screening, the presence of SLI needs to be further confirmed by a more thorough evaluation and the screening result should not be the only evidence of the presence of language impairment.

Yet another method of recruitment relies on parental concern. Parents are generally good judges of their children's language development, as shown, for example, by the high validity of parent report measures such as the MacArthur-Bates CDI (Fenson *et al.*, 1993) across many languages. Further, it has been shown that severe parental concerns about children's language development, in particular when part of a detailed interview, indicate a heightened likelihood of language impairment (Restrepo, 1998) and thus constitute a positive screening result in and of themselves. However, parent report has limitations as well, including the sampling bias inherent in self-referral and the tendency of some parents to over- or underestimate their children's progress for various reasons.

To conclude, while there is little evidence to suggest that one referral method is clearly better than other methods, there is evidence that different methods yield different results to some extent. Therefore, it is important to report which method was used. Regardless of the referral method, researchers should test the children referred to them with their own consistent protocol designed to reflect the intake criteria of the study, which should be stated in clear terms. This helps make sure that study participants meet the study criteria (as having or not having SLI) and provides detailed documentation of the children's language level (in each language to the extent possible, if the children are bilingual). Where research criteria differ from clinical criteria, this should be reported and explained. For example, in a study of SLI in French-speaking children in Quebec (Elin Thordardottir *et al.*, 2011), intake criteria included children with *dysphasie* (the French term for primary language and speech impairments), however excluding children whose *dysphasie* identification was primarily based on apraxia, dyspraxia or semantic-pragmatic disorder. At the same time, children with the milder label *hypothèse de trouble* (suspected language impairment), who do not quite qualify for the clinical label of *dysphasie* were included, all this with the goal of identifying children who correspond closely to the definition of SLI employed in published research studies on English. This inclusionary criterion results in a somewhat different sample than would result from the inclusion of children with a clinical diagnosis of *dysphasie*. Care should be taken to ascertain that test results match with case history information (e.g. children who fail a screening test on a given day, but have not had a history of persistent language-related difficulty in all likelihood do not have SLI). Children in control groups of matched children with typical development (TD) also need to be tested with the same methods. In many cross-linguistic studies of SLI, no language testing is reported for the TD control group or groups. Such documentation, however, is essential both to prove that these children's language level is within the normal range, and to show how much it differs from that of the children with SLI. This helps estimate the level of severity of impairment in the SLI group, in particular where the use of norm-referenced tests is not possible.

Who should conduct the assessment?

Diagnostic assessment of language disorders is a specialty area of SLPs or therapists. In some countries, there are no or few SLPs and diagnostic assessment may be performed by other professionals such as psychologists, physicians, special educators, multidisciplinary teams, or by para-professional assistants who may not be the ones who subsequently interpret the results. In many countries, diagnostic assessment is carried out by SLPs who provide a 'recommendation', but the formal 'diagnosis' needs to be signed by a physician (who may not have been involved in the assessment in any way). In any case, researchers should ensure that language assessment for the purpose of identifying language impairment is carried out by professionals who have the specific training and experience required to collect language history information, select and administer the appropriate test measures, conduct necessary observations and integrate the relevant information to determine the presence of a language disorder. Whenever possible, intake assessment should be conducted or, at the very least, overseen by a qualified SLP.

Objective data or clinical judgement?

When conducting a diagnostic evaluation, a qualified professional puts together information of various kinds to arrive at a decision. Clinical judgement without objective criteria is likely to involve significant inter-judge variability and be subject to higher rates of misdiagnosis. Assessment based on test results alone, without clinical interpretation of other factors such as history information and information on the level and type of handicap experienced in various real-life situations, is similarly subject to erroneous conclusions and is, therefore, less believable and negatively affects the ability of the study findings to be interpreted and published.

Proposed Assessment Protocol

A common conceptual definition

The identification of SLI involves both inclusionary and exclusionary criteria (Leonard, 1998; Stark & Tallal, 1981). The inclusionary criteria focus on establishing that a language impairment is indeed present. They may involve test scores falling below a preset cut-off point or the presence of particular clinical markers which may involve particular error patterns or error frequencies. The exclusionary criteria focus on showing that significant impairments are not found in other developmental domains (notably sensory deficits in hearing and vision, emotional disorders and frank neurologic signs need to be ruled out [Leonard, 1998]) – and therefore, that the impairment is principally found in the area of language. In particular the exclusionary criteria have been the subject of considerable debate involving discussion over the extent to which SLI is specific to language. This debate notwithstanding, researchers continue to find it important to study language in children whose cognition falls within normal limits. Many view this as a way to control the cognitive variable without the presumption that cognitive factors have no impact on the language impairment in SLI. There are inconsistencies in how specific speech and language impairments are defined in official diagnostic systems. For example, the ICD-10 (WHO, 2004), which is widely used in Europe, specifies that cognitive scores within normal limits place a child within the disorders labelled in the F80–F89 range (specific disorders) rather than those in the F70–F79 range (disorders entailing mental retardation). However, it is also possible, according to the ICD-10, to label a disorder as within the F80 range *in addition* to the F70 range if a significant *discrepancy* exists between language and cognitive scores (ICD-10, WHO, 2004: 235). The co-occurrence of non-specific language impairment and SLI, while theoretically plausible and permitted in the ICD-10, is inconsistent, however, with the definition of SLI employed in most research studies, in which cognitive scores are required to fall above the range considered to indicate mental retardation (above −2 SD, or a standard score of 70). Figure 12.1 represents the conceptual definition

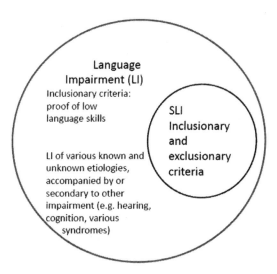

Figure 12.1 Conceptual definition of SLI

of SLI as adopted by the present guidelines. Membership in the larger circle is determined by the inclusionary criteria (the determination of the presence of language impairment). This can entail language impairment of various origins, known or unknown etiologies, including those that are accompanied by or are secondary to other impairments, such as cognitive, hearing or other. Membership in the smaller circle is determined, in addition to the inclusionary criteria, also by the exclusionary criteria. Children falling within this smaller circle have a clinically identifiable language impairment, but no other developmental impairment sufficiently severe to warrant its own diagnosis. The impairment of children within the smaller circle manifests *primarily* (though not necessarily exclusively) in the area of language.

The criterion that is used to rule out cognitive impairment in SLI varies across published studies. Early on, a criterion of a standard score of 85 was most often used (–1 SD) following Stark and Tallal (1981). More recently, many researchers use a criterion of a standard score of 70 (–2 SD). Reasons include, first, that the demarcation between 'normal' cognition and frank mental retardation is at –2 SD. Using a criterion of –1 SD leaves the children who score between –1 and –2 SD in no group, resulting in selection bias. Second, many studies have shown that the language impairment of children with cognitive scores above 85 versus between 85 and 70 is not qualitatively different, making it unnecessary to exclude children whose scores are between 85 and 70 (see e.g. Bishop, 2004; Plante, 1998; Tomblin & Zhang, 1999). Individual studies should clearly document which criterion is adopted.

Although the research attention given to the exclusionary criteria for SLI may have seemed to overshadow the inclusionary criteria over the years, setting the inclusionary criteria accurately is at least as important. The presence of a language impairment generally involves a finding of significant impairment in language, but how exactly *significant* is defined is highly variable. Clinical criteria in effect in different countries vary quite importantly, as seen in Table 12.1, and variability is often seen between clinics within the same country. In some cases, this is due to different philosophies, and in some cases to the choice of assessment tools. It is important to understand that clinical criteria set for official clinical purposes (and which determine who has access to funded intervention) are based partly on research and partly on political grounds (the particular criteria in effect strongly influence the number of children identified – thus those in charge of resource allocation tend to favour stricter criteria). It is not uncommon for criteria used in clinical settings and those used in research to vary somewhat, reflecting different purposes. For example, research may have as its goal to examine language functioning in children who do not have a cognitive deficit as measured by clinical IQ tests in order to control this latter variable, even though the resulting group may not correspond to a distinct clinical group in the area in which the study takes place, but may instead provide opportunity for comparison with other research findings. Generally, criteria used in research tend to be more lax (require less severe assessment results) – some examples of this are seen in Table 12.1. Specific criteria are proposed in a later section of this chapter.

What test materials should be used to identify a significant language impairment?

A comprehensive language evaluation includes a case history and assessment of comprehension and production modalities across domains of language using both formal tests and spontaneous measures (e.g. Paul & Norbury, 2011; Tomblin *et al.*, 1996). To the extent possible, formal tests that have been developed and normed for the population to be tested should be used. Where such tests are not available, informal measures must be used. The following guidelines propose different test protocols for different scenarios, depending on the types of measures available in the language(s) to be evaluated. In addition, it is proposed that certain measures be conducted across all studies and languages. The use of such common measures increases the ability of researchers to ascertain to what extent children recruited across different language areas represent comparable clinical groups in terms of type and severity of language impairment. The different scenarios are depicted in the different columns of Table 12.2, designed to help researchers and clinicians select practical steps that fit their situation.

Table 12.2 Proposed diagnostic procedures and criteria depending on the available tools.

Child referred from a clinic, a school, identified by screening?
Document the procedure you are using
Case history and background information collected (interview and/or questionnaire)
Assessment of level and type of handicap

SELECT FROM THE OPTIONS BELOW THE ONE THAT APPLIES TO YOUR SITUATION:

1. FORMAL TESTS AVAILABLE in *dominant* or weaker lang.	2. TRANSLATED TESTS with no norms for target language	3. NO FORMAL TESTS, but diagnostic tradition in place	4. NO DIAGNOSTIC TRADITION
Cut-off criteria[1]: Monol.: -1.25 SD Dom. Lang.: -1.5 to -1.75 SD Balanced: -1.75 to -2 SD Weaker lang: -2.25 to -2.5 SD In two areas of language	Treat the test as informal assessment and use for descriptive purposes only. Do not refer to norms for the original language of the test. Go to Option 3.	Use the diagnostic decision of experienced professionals. Document the basis for the decision.	Use the concept of significant difficulty in language with no other formal diagnosis or significant difficulty.
Collect and report detailed descriptive information on language level and case history information		Collect and report detailed descriptive information on language level and case history information	Collect and report detailed descriptive information on language level and case history information
Collect language sample (in both languages if applicable)		Collect language sample (in both languages if applicable)	Collect language sample (in both languages if applicable)
Administer NWR (in both languages if applicable)		Administer NWR in both languages (in both languages if applicable)	Administer NWR (in both languages if applicable)
Hearing screening		Hearing screening	Hearing screening
Non-verbal cognition		Non-verbal cognition	Non-verbal cognition

[1]The specific criteria proposed for bilingual children are based on research on simultaneously bilingual children up to age 5 years and are not meant for sequentially bilingual children. A *range* of cut-off scores is suggested, reflecting that the extent to which the scores of bilingual children differ from those of monolingual children vary across measures, being generally larger for formal expressive than receptive tests (thus, the stricter cut-off point is suggested to be more appropriate for expressive tasks).
Note: NWR=non-word repetition.

Measures that should be used across all studies

The measures that are recommended for inclusion in the diagnostic protocol across all languages include a detailed case history, hearing screening, test of non-verbal cognition, spontaneous language sampling and non-word repetition.

Case history: A thorough case history should be collected focusing on general development, early communicative development and situations that are relatively easier or harder for the child, family history and reasons a language impairment was suspected. A developmental language impairment does not appear one day out of the blue. Children with developmental impairments typically have a history of delayed milestones (first words, first word combinations, little talk overall, etc.) even though the impairment may in many cases not become severe enough to be diagnosed until school age. In bilingual children, significant developmental delays may have been overlooked and erroneously attributed to bilingualism or, conversely, normal differences in acquisition rates between bilingual and monolingual children may have been over-interpreted and caused unnecessary concern. This contributes to the high rates of misdiagnosis of SLI in bilingual children (see e.g. Bedore & Peña, 2008). The case history should also include collection of information on relevant background variables such as socio-economic status, birth order and, very importantly for bilingual children, previous language experiences. A questionnaire that can help collect case history information in a systematic and consistent manner was developed within the Cost Action (Tuller, this volume).

Hearing screening: To document that hearing sensitivity is within normal limits on the day of assessment, it is not sufficient to rely on parent or teacher report as hearing impairments, even severe ones, can easily go unnoticed by parents and teachers. Also, ear infections, which can affect hearing quite considerably, are often asymptomatic in other ways and are easily missed. For those who have access to testing by an audiologist, this is the ideal procedure. Reliable audiometric testing can be conducted even with very young children, using a variety of methods including visual reinforcement audiometry, conditioned play audiometry as well as procedures that do not require the active participation of the child, such as auditory brainstem audiometry and oto-acoustic emissions. A full assessment of hearing function includes not only pure tone testing, but also procedures such as speech audiometry and tympanometry to assess middle ear function (ASHA, 2004). For those researchers who do not have access to audiological testing, at the very minimum, pure tone hearing screening should be conducted using a properly calibrated portable audiometer in a quiet place (Harrell, 2002). Some researchers who do not have access to audiological testing have reported using computer-generated pure tones instead of an audiometer. This procedure is discouraged since it must take into account that, because the human ear is not equally sensitive across frequencies, the decibel sound pressure level (dB SPL) that corresponds to 0 dB hearing level (dB HL) (or the intensity that is just audible to normally hearing young adults) is not the same across frequencies – therefore, the intensity of computer-generated tones would need to be appropriately adjusted. For language studies, audiological screening typically involves 500, 1000, 2000 and 4000 Hz at 10 dB HL. Testing normally starts in the right ear and at 1000 Hz because it is the frequency that we hear the best. Presentation of pure tones follows a bracketing procedure, starting with the presentation of a tone at an easily audible level, such as 70 dB HL (do not go higher than that as it may be uncomfortable for the child). The child is asked to indicate when he/she hears the tone, and no longer hears it (such as by raising and lowering his/her hand or by any other method that the child understands and by which he/she can show reliably which tones are heard). After familiarising the child with the procedure by using a clearly audible tone, the examiner then presents progressively less intense tones, going down in 10 dB steps until the child indicates not hearing the tone. The intensity is then increased in 5 dB steps until the child indicates hearing the tone once again. The auditory threshold, or the lowest level the child responds to consistently, can be identified in this way at each frequency that is tested. For screening purposes, it is ascertained that the child responds to tones presented at 10 dB HL and tones below that intensity are not tested in the interest of saving time and because ambient noise may not permit it. However, in a soundproof booth most children can hear 0 dB HL or even –5 or –10 dB HL. Be aware that responses may not be obtained below about 30 dB HL at 500 Hz due to ambient noise if the testing is not conducted in a soundproof booth. Normally, testing starts with the better ear, which is usually the right ear, with the full procedure then repeated in the left ear. When earphones are placed on the child, they must fit over the ear such that the loudspeaker is right over the opening of the ear canal. If no responses or poor responses are obtained, the pressure from the headphones may have caused ear canal collapse and better results may be obtained after the headphones have been repositioned. Alternatively, insert earphones are a good option to prevent ear canal collapse and may be more easily tolerated by children (Harrell, 2002). For some children, pulsed tones are a better signal to use than steady tones, as they are easier to separate out from the background. During the testing, the child should sit with his/her back to the examiner so that she/he doesn't get a visual cue as to when a signal is being presented. The examiner must be careful not to present the tones in a consistent rhythm on which the children can base their responses.

Non-verbal cognition: Depending on the setting, non-verbal cognitive scores may be available from clinical testing conducted by a psychologist or other members of a multidisciplinary team. Alternatively, a number of tests are available that may be used by SLPs (test manuals of individual tests specify the required qualifications of those who administer the test). Most tests of non-verbal cognition have been normed on children whose first language is English. Even when test items and instructions are designed to be language free, results can be influenced by language knowledge and cultural factors. Researchers should avoid the use of tests on which TD children of their language group score significantly differently than the original norms.

Spontaneous language sampling: For consistency, it is recommended that studies of the COST Action that employ common tasks designed to be used across languages include spontaneous language samples as documentation of the participants' language level. Because language sampling requires no previous documentation of the language being tested, it is a logical first step to begin to document the course of language development and establish normative data. In addition, although spontaneous language measures are not directly comparable across languages in terms of absolute numbers (such as actual mean length of utterance [MLU] values or vocabulary diversity; see e.g. Elin Thordardottir, 2005), the availability of spontaneous speech samples collected using a consistent procedure across languages is an invaluable source of information which can also help evaluate the comparability of the identification procedures (for example, it may reveal that criteria used in one country tend to identify children with a more severe disorder than children identified in another country). Spontaneous language gives a different type of information than formal tests (see Leadholm & Miller, 1992). It does not target particular vocabulary or grammatical structures in as focused a way as do formal tests, but has greater ecological validity, that is, it gives a better reflection than do formal tests of children's ability to express themselves in a real-life context. Importantly, spontaneous language also preserves a true communicative intent – speakers are generally more likely to find a way to communicate their own thoughts than to produce particular structures on demand.

Collection of spontaneous language samples: For data to be comparable across children within a study and across studies, *a consistent procedure needs to be followed*. Spontaneous language samples are often contrasted with formal assessment tests and classified as informal, non-standardised assessment. Language sampling can certainly be done in an informal way. However, it can also be done using highly standardised procedures, by an examiner who uses a standard set of materials (such as toys or other props) and behaves in a consistent manner in terms of his/her interaction style. In that case, spontaneous language sampling can be seen as a *standardised assessment of spontaneous language*. Norms are available for language sample measures in several languages. The basis for the collection and use of norms is consistency.

It is recommended here that all studies focusing on preschool children use conversational samples and that studies focusing on school-age children use narrative samples. General considerations and consistent procedures of elicitation of both conversational and narrative language samples are described in Leadholm and Miller (1992). Further, detailed procedures for narrative elicitation and analysis focusing on discourse structure and grammatical development were developed within the COST Action (Gagarina *et al.*, this volume). Narrative samples elicit more complex language and are thus more likely to showcase the complexity of the language of school-age children as well as to bring out the weaknesses in the language of children with SLI. The MLU is consistently longer in a narrative sample than a conversational sample within the same child (Elin Thordardottir, 2008; Leadholm & Miller, 1992). Whereas some early studies proposed that MLU is a useful index only up to age 4 years or up to an MLU of 4 or so (see e.g. discussion in Leonard, 1998), more recent studies and normative data have shown that MLU continues to increase systematically well beyond this point, in particular if narrative samples are used (Leadholm & Miller, 1992) and in many languages, for conversational samples as well. This is even more true in highly inflected languages in which the normal development of grammatical morphology proceeds well into the school years as is the case for example for French and Icelandic (Elin Thordardottir, in press; Ragnarsdottir *et al.*, 1999).

Important aspects to observe in the collection of language samples (see details in Leadholm & Miller, 1992) include how much to talk, the kinds of questions to ask (open ended rather than yes/no) and the complexity of language to use. The most common mistake novice examiners make is to talk too much and ask too many questions. Examiners should keep in mind that no language production is truly completely spontaneous, but is always elicited to some degree by the behaviours of the interlocutor. This is also why the elicitation context often changes markedly when parents participate in the collection of the sample as they tend to start trying to make the child say specific things. For consistency, the context used across children needs to be the same. Where normative reference bases are used, the procedure must be the same as that used to collect the norms. For publication purposes, the exact context needs to be described in detail.

Scoring of language samples: Measures that can easily be applied in any language include MLU in words and lexical measures including number of words and number of different words (type token ratio [TTR] is to be avoided as it can be misleading, see Richards & Malvern [1997]). MLU in words is already a measure commonly found in cross-linguistic studies of SLI. However, the fact that these measures can be computed in all languages does not mean that they are directly comparable across languages in terms of their value. The Action will provide the opportunity to assess to what extent they are comparable by providing language samples collected across many languages using a consistent procedure. Other measures that could be considered include MLU in morphemes, for which procedures have been developed in several languages including English, Spanish, French and Icelandic (Elin Thordardottir, 2005; Elin Thordardottir & Ellis Weismer, 1998; Miller *et al.*, 2011), measures of syntactic complexity, measures of verbal dysfluencies and many more. Some language sample analysis methods relating in particular to bilingual children are described in Gutiérrez-Clellen and Simon-Cereijido (2009) and Elin Thordardottir (2014).

Non-word repetition: Non-word repetition tests are among the measures being developed across languages within the COST Action (Chiat, this volume) and are thus likely to be available in the majority of studies conducted within the Action. It is recommended that a non-word repetition test be administered to all children and in both languages to bilingual children, given the large and growing body of evidence that non-word repetition performance is significantly poorer in children with SLI than in TD comparison groups across various languages (e.g. de Bree *et al.*, 2007; Dollaghan & Campbell, 1998; Elin Thordardottir, 2008; Elin Thordardottir *et al.*, 2011; Girbau & Schwartz, 2007). Furthermore, many studies have documented high diagnostic accuracy for non-word repetition in monolingual children with SLI (Bortolini *et al.*, 2006; Conti-Ramsden, 2003; Elin Thordardottir *et al.*, 2011; Ellis Weismer *et al.*, 2000). For bilingual children, the available evidence is more mixed. Some studies have reported that the diagnostic accuracy of non-word repetition is not as consistent for bilingual children as it is for monolingual children and that the non-word repetition scores of bilingual children vary depending on the test language and on proficiency in that language (Gutiérrez-Clellen & Simon-Cereijido, 2010; Kohnert *et al.*, 2006). However, other studies have reported high diagnostic accuracy of non-word repetition tests in the identification of SLI in bilingual children (Elin Thordardottir & Brandeker, 2013; Girbau & Schwartz, 2008). Elin Thordardottir and Brandeker reported that non-word repetition scores were relatively independent of the amount of previous exposure to the language of the non-words in simultaneously bilingual preschoolers. Similar results were reported for school-age learners of Icelandic as a second language (L2) who performed uniformly high on Icelandic non-word repetition in spite of varying widely in scores on a standardised test of Icelandic (Elin Thordardottir & Anna Gudrun Juliusdottir, 2013). Further research is required to better understand the source of these discrepancies.

Additional procedures to choose from depending on available measures

Scenario 1: Normed tests are available

Recommendations for this scenario are presented in the first column of Table 12.2. The selection of test materials and tools should take into account their validity for the language (or languages) and the population to be tested and their reliability. Assuming appropriate tests are available, cut-off scores should ideally be based on data-driven demonstrations of the diagnostic properties of the particular tests used (i.e. their sensitivity and specificity). However, for most of the numerous English tests available, this information is not available and cut-off scores are set somewhat arbitrarily in terms of standard scores or percentiles, which specify how far below the normative mean a child must score to be considered for a diagnostic label. Similarly, few studies on diagnostic accuracy have been conducted in other languages (a number of studies are available, however, that focus on English, and some on other languages, including measures used in French and Italian: e.g. Bortolini *et al.*, 2006; Conti-Ramsden *et al.*, 2001; Elin Thordardottir & Brandeker, 2013; Elin Thordardottir *et al.*, 2011; Girbau & Schwartz, 2008; Tomblin *et al.*, 1996). Appropriate cut-off scores should not be expected to be identical across language tests (Plante & Vance, 1994). Therefore, cut-off scores determined for a particular measure cannot be applied directly to another measure, nor to measures in another language. Also, it is known that comparison with monolingual norms is generally not an appropriate procedure for identifying language impairment in bilingual children because their language knowledge is distributed over two languages such that full assessment must take both languages into account. For this reason, it is strongly recommended that bilingual children be assessed in both of their languages (e.g. Fredman, 2006). A language impairment, if present, will manifest in *both* languages of a bilingual child, although the types of vulnerabilities observed may differ across the two languages (see e.g. Stavrakaki *et al.*, 2011). Studies focusing on various language combinations are expected to shed further light on the cross-linguistic and bilingual manifestation of SLI.

Much more work is needed on establishing cut-off scores that yield maximal diagnostic accuracy even for monolingual children. However, we must proceed using the data that are available to us at the present time and revise our methods as more evidence becomes available. The ICD-10 (WHO, 2004) does not provide clear guidelines on cut-off levels beyond indicating that scores below −2 SD are a definite indication of impairment in monolingual children. Existing studies of monolingual children in English and some other languages indicate that an appropriate cut-off score for clinical purposes is generally around −1.25 SD (Conti-Ramsden,

2003; Tomblin *et al.*, 1996, for English; Elin Thordardottir *et al.*, 2011, for French). For research purposes, a criterion of –1 SD is often employed in studies focusing on English. For the time being, these criteria seem to offer a reasonable approximation for monolingual children. Although testing both languages of a bilingual child and the awareness that each language represents only part of the child's whole language knowledge is a good start towards more accurate diagnoses, it is still far from clear how to interpret the language assessment scores of bilingual children (see discussion in Elin Thordardottir *et al.*, 2006). Bilingual children can be expected to score lower than the monolingual norm (although many of them ultimately score in the same range in each language as monolingual speakers of these languages, depending on their exposure history, see e.g. Elin Thordardottir, 2011). This means that the cut-off score needs to be set lower for bilingual children when they are tested in each language separately and compared to a monolingual norm. It is typically difficult, however, to decide clinically, by how much bilingual children should be expected to differ from monolinguals. Some preliminary guidelines are suggested here for simultaneous bilingual children, based on recent research.

Elin Thordardottir (2011) provided data that help document the extent to which the performance on widely used receptive and expressive vocabulary standardised tests is affected by bilingual exposure. The study included simultaneously bilingual children with varying degrees of carefully documented bilingual exposure, directly relating previous amount of exposure to typical test scores. Results indicated that at age 5 years, children with a 50/50 exposure pattern (over their entire lifetime) score, on average, about 0.5–1 SD below the monolingual mean (and as a group, do not differ significantly from monolinguals in either language), that those with 75% exposure score, on average, about 0.25–0.5 SD below the monolingual mean, and those with 25% exposure score about 1–1.5 SD below the mean (and differ significantly, as a group, from monolingual speakers). The gap between monolingual and bilingual children was in general somewhat larger for expressive vocabulary than receptive vocabulary measures. Subsequent studies on the same group of children as well as a group of 3-year-old children reported on grammatical performance, non-word repetition and sentence imitation in relation to amount of exposure to each language. The results of these studies are summarised in a review chapter (Elin Thordardottir, 2014), revealing that vocabulary and grammatical development are strongly and similarly affected by amount of exposure to each language, as is sentence imitation; however, non-word repetition was much less affected by language exposure in the young simultaneous learners. The summary also includes a study of monolingual and bilingual children with and without SLI, showing that in vocabulary and sentence imitation, bilingual children with SLI scored the lowest of all groups (Elin Thordardottir & Brandeker, 2013).

At the present time, these data can be used to formulate approximate diagnostic criteria (or rough rules of thumb) for young *simultaneously* bilingual children. This is a novel approach to bilingual assessment that proposes to use different cut-off criteria depending on the previous language history of the child. Based on this, it is recommended here as a reasonable way to proceed, that as long as young simultaneously bilingual children are tested in a language in which they are clearly dominant, they need to score –1.5 to –1.75 SD in two areas of language (as opposed to –1.25 SD in two areas recommended by Tomblin *et al.*, 1996) to be viewed as having language impairment. Children who have a more balanced performance in both languages need to obtain a score of –1.75 to –2 SD in two areas in order to be identified as having language impairment. It is always recommended that testing focus on both languages or the child's stronger language (Fredman, 2006). However, in the event that tests are available only in the child's weaker language (to which the child has received only 25% exposure), the proposed cut-off score is –2.25 to –2.5 SD. It is readily acknowledged that these guidelines can be viewed as crude estimations at best. They are based on the use of monolingual assessment tools applied to bilingual children, however taking into account the amount of previous exposure to each language, which is arguably the single strongest factor influencing the rate of bilingual development (Elin Thordardottir, 2011, 2014; Pearson, 2007). These guidelines, which are based on a careful study of a fairly large group of bilingual children, may offer some help in interpreting the scores of bilingual children and setting some realistic expectations as to the typical performance of bilingual children based on their previous learning opportunities. It is important to stress that these data pertain to young simultaneous learners (up to age 5 years) and that the children reported on were learning French and English – two languages with majority status. The performance of children speaking a minority language may be somewhat lower (Gathercole & Thomas, 2009). This is also why a *range* of scores is proposed in each scenario (the other reason being that expressive scores tend to be farther from bilingual norms than receptive scores, particularly for vocabulary). These criteria are presented as a first step in order to promote consistency and comparability in procedures which will help us in the development of more refined procedures.

Rules of thumb are harder to advance for *sequential* bilingual learners, not the least because they vary very widely not only in the amount and type of exposure they have had to each language, but also in the age at which their bilingual exposure started, among other factors. The rate of bilingual development is influenced in a complex way by a multitude of factors, including the relative status of the languages as minority or majority languages and the age of first bilingual exposure, with research showing that greater amounts of exposure are required to learn languages that have a minority status in the particular country, or on a global scale (Elin Thordardottir & Anna Gudrun Juliusdottir, 2013; Gathercole & Thomas, 2009; Jia et al., 2002). Early studies of sequential learners who are exposed to their L2 primarily in school contexts indicated that high levels of performance are reached in 1–3 years for conversational performance, and in as much as 4–7 years for mastery of the complex language of school (Collier, 1989). These estimates reflect a very large degree of variability. More recent studies continue to indicate persistent gaps between groups of L2 and monolingual speakers. In Hispanic children in the US, important gaps are reported primarily in vocabulary with lesser gaps between L2 and monolingual speakers in grammar (Oller et al., 2007). In this way, school-age L2 speakers may differ from bilingual preschool children (Elin Thordardottir, 2014). However, other factors clearly also contribute to variability in findings. In a study of school-age L2 learners of Icelandic, the majority of participants scored significantly below monolinguals in both vocabulary and grammatical tests (Elin Thordardottir & Anna Gudrun Juliusdottir, 2013), in particular those with shorter lengths of residence in the country. Nevertheless, studies also show that some subgroup of L2 speakers performs comparably to monolingual children, at least in some aspects of language, and in particular when tested in their better language, which may be the L1 or their L2 (Elin Thordardottir & Anna Gudrun Juliusdottir, 2013; Gutiérrez-Clellen et al., 2008). More research will contribute to a better understanding of the typical course of L2 learning and will help make better sense of the heterogeneity found within this group. More guidance on the identification of SLI in bilingual children is found in Kohnert (2013) and Paradis et al. (2010).

Scenario 2: Appropriate normed tests are not available

Where normed tests have not yet been constructed for the population to be tested, there are several possible scenarios, represented by columns 2–4 of Table 12.2. In many test sites, translations of tests are available that have not been renormed or revalidated. These may range from informal translations to more elaborate adaptations. In many areas where such translations are the only available tests, there is a tendency to interpret results with reference to the original norms. This practice is very strongly discouraged as typical outcomes in the new language may vary greatly from those of the original version, and in either direction. Translated tests have the same limitations as their original version, and in addition, the limitation of not having been developed expressly for the new language (Bouchard et al., 2009). Translated tests that have not been renormed should be treated as informal assessment measures and used as such, without reference to norms.

Scenario 3: No tests, but a clinical tradition

In addition to or in lieu of translated tests, in many test sites, there may be a tradition of making decisions based on particular criteria that do not rely on standardised testing (column 3 in Table 12.2). Criteria in use may involve particular error patterns (which may be supported by clinical experience alone or by some research), or particular communicative behaviours or particular areas of difficulty. Traditions such as these can be expected to yield highly variable results (low inter-judge reliability) because they are often based on experience alone rather than controlled documentation and because they tend to be stated in vague terms, for example, a 'high frequency' of a certain error type, not clearly indicating *how high* the frequency should be, in what type of context it should be observed and how the error relates to other language skills. Children's failure to use certain structures may, upon careful study, not result from avoidance of the structure, but from the context not providing opportunities for such use, or from the child's overall language level not yet supporting its use. The validity of use of particular error patterns for diagnostic purposes is very limited if not supported by systematic research. However, in some countries, untested procedures are the only method available at the present time. Not least for this reason, it is extremely important to collect descriptive data, such as spontaneous language samples, to document the children's language level as accurately and in as much detail as possible in order to increase the ability of the study to be interpreted meaningfully and compared to other studies.

Scenario 4: No clinical tradition exists

A final possibility is that no diagnostic tradition exists (last column of Table 12.2). In that case, identification is necessarily the most tentative and needs to be based on informal observations focusing on language behaviours and difficulty compared to same-age children with comparable language experiences. In general, SLI manifests differently across languages in terms of the kinds of errors that are most salient, as demonstrated by a number of cross-linguistic studies which have shown that morphological errors tend to be much less salient in more highly inflected languages (e.g. Elin Thordardottir, 2008; Rom & Leonard, 1990). Within a given language, children with SLI have been shown to use comparable language structures as younger children who speak the same language, including structures used correctly and types of errors made (see e.g. Elin Thordardottir & Namazi, 2007). When forming expectations of error patterns in children with SLI, the error patterns and general language behaviours of *younger children with TD* speaking *the same language* should be used as a guide to what to expect. A case study of a child with SLI speaking French and Greek showed different errors in each language, in each language resembling the error types of monolingual speakers of that language (Stavrakaki *et al.*,

2011). In sequential L2 speakers, error types have been found to resemble those of monolingual children with SLI, causing difficulty in using such errors as clinical markers in L2 speakers (e.g. Grüter, 2005; Paradis, 2005).

As indicated in Table 12.2, clinicians and researchers may need to be creative when working in languages in which few tools are available. In so doing, they should keep in mind the purpose of the assessment, which entails finding ways to demonstrate whether the language abilities of the child are significantly poorer than those of same-age children who speak the same language (or in the case of bilingual children – of children who have had similar opportunities to learn the language being tested). A long-standing focus on error patterns in grammatical morphology in the research literature (see Leonard, 1998) has created the expectation that this is the main area in which problems will be manifest if a child has SLI. However, it is important to keep in mind that while such errors may certainly be found, they are not characteristic of SLI in all languages or at all ages even in languages in which errors are common in some age ranges (Elin Thordardottir, 2008; Elin Thordardottir & Namazi, 2007; Rice et al., 2004). In some languages, and in general in older children, weak grammatical development may manifest not as overt grammatical errors, but rather as lack of comprehension of complex grammatical structures and the use of correct but less sophisticated grammatical structures than expected based on age (e.g. Elin Thordardottir & Ellis Weismer, 2002). Error patterns aside, a consistent finding in SLI across monolingual and bilingual children is a significant delay in language development, typically affecting more than one domain of language (c.g. Elin Thordardottir, 2008; Elin Thordardottir & Namazi, 2007). Many studies also point to language processing limitations as a common finding in SLI across language groups (e.g. de Bree et al., 2007; Dollaghan & Campbell, 1998; Elin Thordardottir, 2008; Elin Thordardottir et al., 2011; Girbau & Schwartz, 2007). The results of several completed and other forthcoming COST Action studies will shed further light on many aspects of the manifestation of SLI in monolingual children speaking a variety of different languages as well as of bilingual children speaking a variety of language combinations.

Conclusions

Even though cross-linguistic research on SLI has been accumulating over past years and decades, the overwhelming majority of studies still target English and the cross-linguistic literature has spanned relatively few languages. Research on SLI in bilingual children is in its infancy. The Bi-SLI COST Action undertook the momentous task of documenting the characteristics of SLI in monolingual and bilingual children across a variety of languages, many of which have received little or no previous research attention in terms of SLI or TD. However, in order to study SLI in these languages, SLI must first be reliably identified. This is no easy task, given the lack of established and proven language tests, and even the lack of normative data on language development in many of the languages. And yet, the success of the COST Action project – its ability to produce findings on various language groups that can ultimately be compared in a meaningful way to arrive at more general conclusions about SLI; its ability to construct versions of the same language tasks in many languages – rests to a very significant degree on how well the participating children are selected to begin with. This chapter has argued that the key to success at this stage is consistency and documentation. There is no question that where established tests and clinical traditions are lacking, examiners need to be creative, but they need to be creative in a controlled and calculated way, and above all, they need to detail clearly the procedures they followed and the characteristics of the children they test in their studies. The procedures presented in this chapter were prepared as a way to promote consistency and comparability between studies carried out in different languages, taking into account that language communities differ sharply in the test measures available to them, and to encourage careful attention to methodological aspects involving the recruitment and selection of participants and the documentation of their characteristics. The particular criteria recommended are based on current knowledge of monolingual and bilingual acquisition and manifestation of SLI across languages and in bilingual children, and as such, are not meant to be final, but rather a reasonable approximation that can help ensure the strength of research work that is undertaken at this point in time and that will contribute to setting more firm identification criteria across languages in the future.

Acknowledgements

The author wishes to thank the members of the assessment committee and the Cost Action members who returned the questionnaire on diagnostic practices across Cost Action countries.

Note

(1) Members of the assessment committee were: Elin Thordardottir, Chair (Iceland), Seyhun Topbaş (Turkey), Helen Grech (Malta), Maria Kambanaros (Cyprus) and Carolyn Letts (UK).

References

ASHA (American Speech, Language and Hearing Organization) (2004) Permanent Childhood Hearing Loss in ASHA's Practice Portal. See http://www.asha.org/policy/GL2004-00002.htm (accessed 12 December 2014)

Bedore, L. and Peña, E. (2008) Assessment of bilingual children for identification of language impairment: Current findings and implications for practice. *International Journal of Bilingual Education and Bilingualism* 11 (1), 1–29.

Bishop, D. (2004) Specific language impairment: Diagnostic dilemmas. In L. Verhoeven and H. van Balkom (eds) *Classification of Developmental Language Disorders: Theoretical Issues and Clinical Implications* (pp. 309–326). Mahwah, NJ: Erlbaum.

Bortolini, U., Arfé, B., Caselli, C., Degasperi, L., Deevy, P. and Leonard, L. (2006) Clinical markers for specific language impairment in Italian: The contribution of clitics and nonword repetition. *International Journal of Language and Communication Disorders* 41 (6), 695–712.

Bouchard, M.-E., Fitzpatrick, E. and Olds, J. (2009) Psychometric analysis of assessment tools using with francophone children. *Canadian Journal of Speech-Language Pathology and Audiology* 33, 129–138.

Collier, V. (1989) How long? A synthesis of research on academic achievement in second language. *TESOL Quarterly* 23 (3), 509–531.

Conti-Ramsden, G. (2003) Processing and linguistic markers in young children with specific language impairment. *Journal of Speech, Language and Hearing Research* 46 (5), 1029–1037.

Conti-Ramsden, G., Botting, N. and Faragher, B. (2001) Psycholinguistic markers for specific language impairment (SLI). *Journal of Speech, Language, and Hearing Research* 42 (6), 1029–1037.

De Bree, E., Rispens, J. and Gerrits, E. (2007) Nonword repetition in Dutch children with (a risk) of dyslexia and SLI. *Clinical Linguistics and Phonetics* 21 (11–12), 935–944.

Dollaghan, C. and Campbell, T. (1998) Nonword repetition and children language impairment. *Journal of Speech, Language and Hearing Research* 41 (5), 1136–1146.

Elin Thordardottir, E. (2005) Early lexical and syntactic development in Quebec French and English: Implications for cross-linguistic and bilingual assessment. *International Journal of Language and Communication Disorders* 40 (3), 243–278.

Elin Thordardottir, E. (2008) Language specific effects of task demands on the manifestation of specific language impairment: A comparison of English and Icelandic. *Journal of Speech, Language, and Hearing Research* 51 (4), 922–937.

Elin Thordardottir, E. (2011) The relationship between bilingual exposure and vocabulary development. *International Journal of Bilingualism* 14 (5), 426–445.

Elin Thordardottir, E. (in press) Typical language development and primary language impairment in French-speaking children. In J. Patterson and B. Rodriguez (eds) *Multilingual Perspectives on Child Language Disorders*. Bristol: Multilingual Matters.

Elin Thordardottir, E. (2014) Effects of exposure on vocabulary, morphosyntax and language processing in typical and impaired language development. In J. Paradis and T. Grüter (eds) *Input and Experience in Bilingual Development*. John Benjamins: TiLAR Series.

Elin Thordardottir, E. and Ellis Weismer, S. (1998) Mean length of utterance and other language sample measures in early Icelandic. *First Language* 18, 1–32.

Elin Thordardottir, E. and Ellis Weismer, S. (2002) Verb argument structure weakness in specific language impairment in relation to age and utterance length. *Clinical Linguistics and Phonetics* 16 (4), 233–250.

Elin Thordardottir, E., Rothenberg, A., Rivard, M.-E. and Naves. R. (2006) Bilingual assessment: Can overall proficiency be estimated from separate measurement of two languages? *Journal of Multilingual Communication Disorders* 4 (1), 1–21.

Elin Thordardottir, E. and Namazi, M. (2007) Specific language impairment in French-speaking children: Beyond grammatical morphology. *Journal of Speech, Language, and Hearing Research* 50 (3), 698–715.

Elin Thordardottir, E., Kehayia, E., Mazer, B., Lessard, N., Majnemer, A., Sutton, A., Trudeau, N. and Chilingaryan, G. (2011) Sensitivity and specificity of French language and processing measures for the identification of primary language impairment at age 5. *Journal of Speech, Language, and Hearing Research* 54 (2), 580–597.

Elin Thordardottir, E. and Anna Gudrun Juliusdottir, A. (2013) Icelandic as a second language: A longitudinal study of language knowledge and processing by school-age children. *International Journal of Bilingual Education and Bilingualism* 16 (4), 411–435.

Elin Thordardottir, E. and Brandeker, M. (2013) The effect of bilingual exposure versus language impairment on nonword repetition and sentence imitation scores. *Journal of Communication Disorders* 46 (1), 1–16.

Ellis Weismer, S., Tomblin, B., Zhang, X., Buckwalter, P., Chynoweth, J. and Jones, M. (2000) Nonword repetition performance in school-age children with and without language impairment. *Journal of Speech, Language, and Hearing Research* 43 (4), 865–878.

Fenson, L., Dale, P., Reznick, S., Thal, D., Bates, E., Hartung, J., Pethick, S. and Reilly, J. (1993) *Technical Manual for the MacArthur Communicative Development Inventories.* San Diego, CA: San Diego State University.

Fredman, M. (2006) Recommendations for working with bilingual children – Prepared by the Multilingual Affairs Committee of IALP. *Folia Phoniatrica et Logopaedica* 58, 458–464.

Gathercole, V. and Thomas, E. (2009) Bilingual first language development: Dominant-language take-over, threatened minority language take-up. *Bilingualism, Language and Cognition* 12 (2), 213–237.

Girbau, D. and Schwartz, R. (2007) Nonword repetition in Spanish-speaking children with specific language impairment. *International Journal of Language and Communication Disorders* 42 (1), 59–75.

Girbau, D. and Schwartz, R. (2008) Phonological working memory in Spanish-English children with and without specific language impairment. *Journal of Communication Disorders* 41 (2), 124–145.

Grüter, T. (2005) Comprehension and production of French object clitics by child second language learners and children with specific language impairment. *Applied Psycholinguistics* 26, 363–291.

Gutiérrez-Clellen, V., Simon-Cereijido, G. and Wagner, C. (2008) Bilingual children with language impairment: A comparison with monolinguals and second language learners. *Applied Psycholinguistics* 29 (1), 3–19.

Gutiérrez-Clellen, V. and Simon-Cereijido, G. (2009) Using language sampling in clinical assessments with bilingual children – Challenges and future directions. *Seminars in Speech and Language* 30 (4), 234–245.

Gutiérrez-Clellen, V. and Simon-Cereijido, G. (2010) Using nonword repetition tasks for the identification of language impairment in Spanish-English-speaking children: Does the language of assessment matter? *Learning Disabilities Research and Practice* 25 (1), 48–58.

Harrell, R. (2002) Pure tone evaluation. In J. Katz (ed) *Handbook of Clinical Audiology* (pp. 71–87). Philadelphia, PA: Lippincott Williams and Wilkins.

Jia, G., Aaronson, D. and Wu, Y. (2002) Long term language attainment of bilingual immigrants: Predictive variables and language group differences. *Applied Psycholinguistics* 23 (4), 599–621.

Kohnert, K. (2013) *Language Disorders in Bilingual Children and Adults* (2nd edn). San Diego, CA: Plural Publishing.

Kohnert, K., Windsor, J. and Yim, D. (2006) Do language-based processing tasks separate children with language impairment from typical bilinguals? *Learning Disabilities Research and Practice* 21 (1), 19–29.

Leadholm, B. and Miller, J. (1992) *Language Sample Analysis: The Wisconsin Guide.* Madison, WI: Wisconsin Department of Public Instruction.

Leonard, L. (1998) *Children with Specific Language Impairment.* Cambridge, MA: MIT Press.

Miller, J., Andriacchi, K. and Nockerts, A. (2011) *Assessing Language Production Using SALT Software.* Middleton, WI: SALT Software LLC.

Muircheartaigh, J. and Hickey, T. (2008) Academic outcome, anxiety and attitudes in early and late immersion in Ireland. *International Journal of Bilingualism and Bilingual Education* 11 (5), 558–576.

Oller, K., Pearson, B. and Cobo-Lewis, A. (2007) Profile effects in early bilingual language and literacy. *Applied Psycholinguistics* 28 (2), 191–230.

Paradis, J. (2005) Grammatical morhology in children learning English as a second language: Implications of similarities with specific language impairment. *Language, Speech and Hearing Services in Schools* 36 (3), 172–187.

Paradis, J. and Crago, M. (2001) The morphosyntax of specific language impairment in French: An extended optional default account. *Language Acquisition* 9 (4), 269–300.

Paradis, J., Genesee, F. and Crago, M. (2010) *Dual Language Development and Disorders: A Handbook on Bilingualism and Second Language Learning.* Baltimore, MD: Paul Brookes Publishing.

Paul, R. and Norbury, C. (2011) *Language Disorders From Infancy Through Adolescence: Assessment and Intervention.* St. Louis, MO: Mosby.

Pearson, B. (2007) Social factors in childhood bilingualism in the United States. *Applied Psycholinguistics* 28 (3), 399–410.

Perozzi, J. and Sanchez, M. (1992) The effect of instruction in L1 on receptive acquisition of L2 for bilingual children with language delay. *Language, Speech and Hearing Services in Schools* 23, 348–352.

Plante, E. (1998) Criteria for SLI: The Stark and Tallal legacy and beyond. *Journal of Speech, Language and Hearing Research* 41, 951–957.

Plante, E. and Vance, R. (1994) Diagnostic accuracy of two tests of preschool language. *American Journal of Speech-Language Pathology* 4, 70–76.

Ragnarsdottir, H., Simonsen, H.G. and Plunkett, M. (1999) The acquisition of past tense morphology in Icelandic and Norwegian children: An experimental study. *Journal of Child Language* 26 (3), 577–618.

Restrepo, M.A. (1998) Identifiers of predominantly Spanish-speaking children with language impairment. *Journal of Speech, Language and Hearing Research* 41 (6), 1398–1411.

Rice, M., Tomblin, B., Hoffman, L., Richman, W.A. and Marquis, J. (2004) Grammatical tense deficits in children with SLI and non-specific language impairment: Longitudinal considerations. *Journal of Speech, Language, and Hearing Research* 47 (4), 816–834.

Richards, B. and Malvern, D. (1997) *Quantifying Lexical Diversity in the Study of Language Development.* Reading: The University of Reading; The New Bulmershe Papers.

Rom, A. and Leonard, L. (1990) Interpreting deficits in grammatical morphology in specifically language-impaired children: Preliminary evidence from Hebrew. *Clinical Linguistics and Phonetics* 4 (2), 93–105.

Stark, R. and Tallal, P. (1981) Selection of children with specific language deficits. *Journal of Speech and Hearing Research* 46, 114–122.

Stavrakaki, S., Chrysomallis, M.-A. and Petraki, E. (2011) Subject-verb agreement, object clitics and wh-questions in bilingual French-Greek SLI: The case study of a French-Greek speaking child with SLI. *Clinical Linguistics and Phonetics* 25 (5), 339–367.

Tomblin, J.B., Records, N. and Zhang, X. (1996) A system for the diagnosis of specific language impairment in kindergarten children. *Journal of Speech and Hearing Research* 39 (6), 1284–1294.

Tomblin, J.B. and Zhang, X. (1999) Language patterns and etiology in children with specific language impairment. In H. Tager-Flusberg (ed.) *Neurodevelopmental Disorders* (pp. 361–382). Cambridge, MA: MIT Press.

World Health Organization (1992). The ICD 10 classification of mental and behavioural.

WHO: World Health Organization (2004) *The ICD-10 Classification of Mental and Behavioural Disorders: Clinical Descriptions and Diagnostic Guidelines.* Geneva: WHO.

Language Index

Subject Index